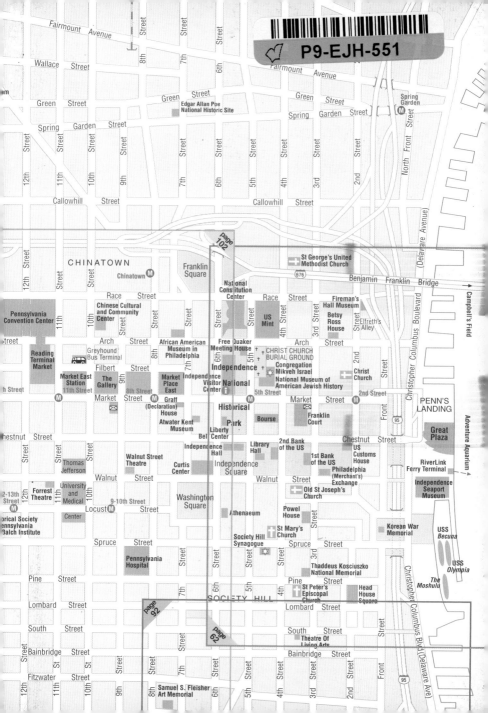

# INSIGHT CITY GUIDE
# PHILADELPHIA

Discovery CHANNEL

APA PUBLICATIONS

Part of the Langenscheidt Publishing Group

# PHILADELPHIA

*Editor*
**John Gattuso**
*Principal photographer*
**Bob Krist**
*Cartography Editor*
**Zoë Goodwin**
*Production*
**Kenneth Chan**
*Editorial Director*
**Brian Bell**

## Distribution

*United States*
**Langenscheidt Publishers, Inc.**
36–36 33rd Street 4th Floor
Long Island City, NY 11106
Fax: (1) 718 784-0640

*UK & Ireland*
**GeoCenter International Ltd**
Meridian House, Churchill Way,
West Basingstoke, Hants RG21 6YR
Fax: (44) 1256-817988

*Australia*
**Universal Publishers**
1 Waterloo Road
Macquarie Park, NSW 2113
Fax: (61) 2 9888 9074

*New Zealand*
**Hema Maps New Zealand Ltd (HNZ)**
Unit D, 24 Ra ORA Drive
East Tamaki, Auckland
Fax: (64) 9 273 6479

*Worldwide*
**Apa Publications GmbH & Co.**
**Verlag KG (Singapore branch)**
38 Joo Koon Road, Singapore 628990
Tel: (65) 6865-1600. Fax: (65) 6861-6438

## Printing

**Insight Print Services (Pte) Ltd**
38 Joo Koon Road, Singapore 628990
Tel: (65) 6865-1600. Fax: (65) 6861-6438

©2007 Apa Publications GmbH & Co.
Verlag KG (Singapore branch)
*All Rights Reserved*

*First Edition 1991*
*Fourth Edition 2007*

# ABOUT THIS BOOK

The first Insight Guide pioneered the use of creative full-color photography in travel guides in 1970. Since then, we have expanded our range to cater to our readers' need not only for reliable information about their chosen destination but also for a real understanding of the culture and workings of that destination. Now, when the internet can supply inexhaustible (but not always reliable) facts, our books marry text and pictures to provide those much more elusive qualities: knowledge and discernment. To achieve this, they rely heavily on the authority of locally based writers and photographers.

## How to use this book

The book is carefully structured both to convey an understanding of the city and its culture and to guide readers through its sights and activities:

◆ To understand Philadelphia today, you need to know something of its past. The first section covers the city's history and culture in lively, authoritative essays.

◆ The main Places section provides a full run-down of all the attractions worth seeing. The main places of interest are coordinated by number with full-color maps.

◆ The Travel Tips listings section provides a point of reference for information on travel, hotels, shops and festivals. Information may be located quickly by using the index printed on the back cover flap – and the flaps are designed to serve as bookmarks.

◆ Photographs are chosen not only to illustrate geography and buildings but also to convey the moods of the city and the life of its people.

**LEFT:** a workman takes a break in Old City's gallery district..

dining scene by **Kirsten Henri**, a Philadelphia-based food writer whose work appears frequently in *Philadelphia Weekly* and other area publications. Henri also wrote about the city's dynamic arts scene, added a new chapter about the attractions of the Main Line, and spruced up much of the neighborhood coverage in the Places section.

Covering sports was Philadelphia sportswriter **Daniel McQuade**, who reviewed not only the checkered history of Philadelphia's professional sports teams but the less-than-forgiving attitude of their fans. McQuade writes about sports for *Philadelphia Weekly.*

Raised in Pennsylvania's Amish heartland, travel writer **Carol Turkington** revised the chapter on Pennsylvania Dutch Country and wrote about the Brandywine Valley. She is the author of more than 30 books and numerous travel articles.

Contributors to previous editions whose work survives in this version include **Susan Lewis**, **Karin Brookes**, **Donald Kraybill**, **Lou Harry** and **Dave Nelson**. **Edward A. Jardim** wrote several sidebars and proofread the text.

The principal photographer of the book was **Bob Krist**, with additional photos by **Richard Nowitz**, **Joseph Nettis** and others. The book was indexed by **Elizabeth Cook**. Thanks are due to **Donna Schorr** of the Greater Philadelphia Tourism Marketing Corporation for helping out with travel arrangements.

## The contributors

This new edition was edited by **John Gattuso** of Stone Creek Publications in New Jersey. A former resident of Philadelphia, he is a veteran of more than a dozen Insight Guides (including the original edition of this book) and editor of Discovery Travel Adventures, a guidebook series for travelers with special interests such as bird-watching, outdoor adventure and scuba diving. For this book, Gattuso wrote about Philadelphia history and several neighborhoods, including Old City, Society Hill, Washington Square and South Philly.

New to this edition are more than 200 restaurant and bar reviews and a feature about Philly's burgeoning

## CONTACTING THE EDITORS

We would appreciate it if readers would alert us to errors or outdated information by writing to:

**Insight Guides, P.O. Box 7910, London SE1 1WE, England. Fax: (44) 20 7403-0290. email: insight@apaguide.co.uk**

# CONTENTS

## Introduction

The Best of Philadelphia ............**6**
The Philadelphia Story .............**15**

## History

The Making of Philadelphia ......**17**
Decisive Dates ........................**30**

## Features

Art and Culture ........................**35**
Philly Eats ..............................**43**
A Passion for Sports ...............**49**

## Places

Introduction ...........................**57**
Old City ..................................**61**
Society Hill and
    Penn's Landing ...................**79**
South Street and
    Queen Village .....................**91**
Washington Square ...............**101**
City Hall, Avenue of the Arts
    and Convention Center ........**111**
Rittenhouse ..........................**125**
Museum District and
    Fairmount Park ...................**137**
University City ........................**151**
South Philly ..........................**159**
Urban Villages ......................**167**
North of Vine .........................**175**
The Main Line ........................**183**
Pennsylvania Dutch Country ....**189**
Bucks County .........................**201**
Brandywine Valley .................**211**

## Photo Features

Architecture: History
    Under Construction ...............**40**
Celluloid City: Philadelphia
    on Film ...............................**88**
Franklin Institute ...................**148**
Down the Shore .....................**198**

## Information Panels

The Wisest American ...............**75**
Colonial Landlord ...................**121**
The Cheesesteak War.............**163**
Valley Forge ..........................**185**
This Hallowed Ground.............**194**

## Maps

Map Legend   **255**
Street Atlas   **256–263**
Philadelphia   **front flap**
   and **58–59**
Center City Historic
   District **62–63**
South Street and
   Queen Village **92**
Center City West **102**
Rittenhouse **126**
Museum District **138**
Fairmount Park **143**
University City **152**
Greater Philadelphia **160**
Pennsylvania Dutch
   Country **190–191**
Bucks County **202**
Brandywine Valley **212**
Philadelphia Subway **273**
Around Philadelphia **back flap**

## Travel Tips

**TRANSPORTATION**
Getting There **218**
Parking **219**
Getting Around **220**
Handicapped Travelers **220**

**ACCOMMODATIONS**
Choosing a Hotel **221**
Bed and Breakfast **221**
Old City **222**
Society Hill **223**
Rittenhouse **223**
Downtown **224**
Museum District **226**
University City **226**
South Philadelphia/Airport **227**
The Main Line/Valley Forge **228**
Brandywine Valley **228**
Bucks County **229**
Pennsylvania Dutch Country **230**

**ACTIVITIES**
Events **231**
Theater **234**
Film **235**
Classical Music **235**
Jazz **236**
Folk **236**
Venues **237**
Dance **237**
Nightclubs **237**
Gay scene **238**
Shopping **239**
Tours **244**
Sports **245**

**A–Z of PRACTICAL INFORMATION**
Accidents **247**
Budgeting for a Visit **247**
Business Hours **247**
Car Rentals **247**
Clothing **248**
Consulates **248**
Discounts **248**
Electricity **248**
Emergency Numbers **248**
Entry Regulations **248**
Government **248**
Handicapped Access **248**
Health and Medical Care **248**
Internet Access **249**
Liquor Laws **249**
Maps **249**
Media **249**
Parking **250**
Postal Services **250**
Religious Services **250**
Reservations **251**
Security & Crime **251**
Telephone Codes **252**
Time Zones **252**
Tipping **252**
Tourist Information **252**
Weather **252**
Websites **252**
Weights and Measures **252**
What To Read **253**

# THE BEST OF PHILADELPHIA

Setting priorities, saving money, unique attractions...
here, at a glance, are our recommendations, plus some
tips and tricks even the locals won't always know

## BEST OF HISTORIC PHILADELPHIA

- **Liberty Bell and Independence Hall.** A new glass pavilion houses the celebrated bell just across the way from the stately Georgian statehouse where the Declaration

of Independence and Constitution were debated and signed. *Page 64.*
- **Christ Church and Burial Ground.** The nation's first Anglican church where many of the Founding Fathers worshiped and were buried, including Benjamin Franklin. Toss a penny on his grave for good luck. *Page 72.*
- **Franklin Court.** A steel "ghost house" stands in place of Ben Franklin's home. Below is an underground museum. A post office on Market Street

hand-cancels mail with Franklin's signature. *Page 67.*
- **Once Upon a Nation.** Offers creative "adventure tours" of colonial Philadelphia, from a Tippler's Tour to a Hunt for Democracy, plus "storytelling benches" where reenactors weave historic tales. *Page 69.*
- **Valley Forge National Historic Park.** The site of General George Washington's pivotal winter encampment during the American Revolution. Take a ranger-guided tour or hear costumed interpreters tell tales of a fateful chapter in American history. There's a museum and miles of hiking and biking trails. *Page 185.*

## PHILADELPHIA FOR FAMILIES

These attractions are popular with children, though not all will suit every age group.

- **Please Touch Museum.** Kids can drive a real bus, feed chickens in a barnyard or play with Maurice Sendak characters. For ages 1–7. *Page 140.*
- **Franklin Institute.** Take a walk through a giant human heart, explore the universe at a planetarium show, or catch a giant-screen film in the Imax theater. *Page 139.*
- **Academy of Natural**

Sciences. See the gargantuan bones of a giganotosaurus, the largest meat-eating dinosaur on earth, or check out a living, breathing exotic iguana in the live animal center. *Page 140.*
- **Philadelphia Zoo.** Visit endangered cats at the new Big Cat Falls, take a "soaring safari" flight in a hot air balloon, and ride the miniature Victorian train at America's oldest zoo. *Page 146.*
- **The Franklin Fountain.** This is an old-fashioned, period-perfect ice cream shop with antique fixtures, bow-tied soda jerks, and a delectable menu of creams, fizzes, sundaes and splits created from historic recipes. *Page 77.*

**RIGHT:** climbing the walls at the Franklin Institute.

## BEST VIEWS OF THE CITY

- **City Hall Clock Tower.** You'll need timed tickets to get into the tower, open weekdays, but the view from the top is worth the trip. *Page 112.*
- **Fairmount Water Works.** The graceful neoclassical buildings just behind the Art Museum are now home to an interpretive center and restaurant, with lovely vistas of the Schuylkill River and Boathouse Row. *Page 143.*
- **Lemon Hill.** The grounds of this historic mansion in Fairmount Park offer a fine view of center city. The house is open for tours Wed–Sun, Apr–Dec. *Page 144.*

## BEST MUSEUMS

- **National Constitution Center.** A new museum devoted to the Constitution features interactive exhibits and opportunities to exercise your First Amendment rights. Get sworn in as President or try a Supreme Court justice robe on for size. *Page 63.*

- **Philadelphia Museum of Art.** World-class art, neoclassical architecture and a host of blockbuster exhibitions, from Cézanne to Dalí. Stop by Friday evening for Art After 5, when visitors stroll the galleries, sip cocktails, nibble on appetizers, and enjoy live jazz in the Great Stair Hall. *Page 142.*
- **Mütter Museum.** Devoted to medical oddities, the grisly collection includes a specimen of a giant colon and a plaster cast of famed conjoined twins Chang and Eng. *Page 133.*
- **Barnes Foundation.** Unparalleled collection of Postimpressionist art, arranged according to the eccentric founder's wishes in a specially constructed manse in Merion. Visit the collection at its original location before a planned move to the Benjamin Franklin Parkway. *Page 186.*
- **Pennsylvania Academy of the Fine Arts.** One of the world's finest collections of American art is housed in an elaborate Frank Furness structure. *Page 113.*

**ABOVE:** visitors peruse a display of human skulls at the Mütter Museum, a collection of medical anomalies.

## FREE PHILADELPHIA

- **Independence National Historic Park.** America's "most historic square mile" encompasses Independence Hall, the Liberty Bell, Carpenters' Hall, Franklin Court, Christ Church and much more. Start at the Independence Visitor Center for maps, schedules and free timed tickets for Independence Hall. *Page 61.*
- **First Friday.** Art lovers crowd Old City galleries on the first Friday evening of the month for receptions, exhibition openings and other special events. *Page 74.*
- **Penn's Landing.** The Delaware waterfront is host to a variety of concerts, ethnic celebrations and food festivals, most of them free to the public. *Page 85.*
- **Curtis Institute.** Aficionados of classical music enjoy free recitals and master classes at this exclusive music conservatory near Rittenhouse Square. *Page 128.*

**BELOW:** a tyrannosaurus fossil greets museum-goers at the Academy of Natural Sciences.

**ABOVE:** the Sunoco Welcome America festival features live concerts, street vendors and a parade.

## BEST FESTIVALS AND EVENTS

- **Philadelphia Fringe Festival.** All manner of performances, from avant-garde to just plain weird, share the billing during a two-week celebration of the performing arts. *Page 236.*
- **Mummers Parade.** The Mummers strut down Broad Street on New Year's Day.

River. *Page 233.*
- **Sunoco Welcome America.** A weeklong celebration of America's birth with live music, parades and piles of food. The festival climaxes on July 4th with fireworks and a headliner concert on the Ben Franklin Parkway. *Page 234.*

## BEST PARKS AND GARDENS

String bands, "fancies," "comics" and other groups decked out in flamboyant costumes delight onlookers and compete for honors. *Page 232.*
- **Dad Vail Regatta.** The largest collegiate rowing competition in the U.S. is held in May on the picturesque Schuylkill

- **Kelly and Martin Luther King Drive.** Bicyclists, joggers and hikers swarm these winding, leafy thoroughfares on either side of the Schuylkill River. The collegiate rowing teams of Boathouse Row line Kelly Drive. MLK Drive is closed to traffic on summer weekends for recreational use. *Page 144.*
- **Japanese House and Garden.** Set in Fairmount Park – the largest city park in the

nation – this replica of a Japanese scholar's home and garden, complete with koi pond, is truly transporting. *Page 146.*
- **Morris Arboretum.** The University of Pennsylvania maintains this serene landscape of flowers, plants and ancient trees in tony Chestnut Hill. *Page 171.*
- **Longwood Gardens.** A former du Pont estate transformed into a glorious horticultural showcase,

complete with Villa d'Este-like fountains. *Page 213.*
- **Rittenhouse Square.** A haven of manicured greenery in the city's swanky heart where the people are as interesting to look at as the plants. *Page 125.*
- **Forbidden Drive.** This shaded gravel trail leads through Fairmount Park along scenic, wooded Wissahickon Creek and is popular with bikers, runners and outdoor enthusiasts. *Page 142.*

**BELOW:** Mummers strut their stuff on Broad Street.

## MOST ROMANTIC PLACES

- **Rodin Museum.** This jewel box on the Ben Franklin Parkway is an ideal spot for a romantic rendezvous. Have a look at *The Kiss,* then do what comes naturally. *Page 141.*
- **Magnolia Garden.** It's worth stealing a few moments – or kisses – at this leafy courtyard within Philly's busy historic district. *Page 79.*

- **Bartram's Garden.** Learn about the birds and bees at this botanical garden on the Schuylkill River where, in spring, the sap rises and love is in full bloom. *Page 156.*
- **New Hope.** Escape to this Bucks County village for candlelight dinners, walks along the Delaware River, and a night or two at a historic inn. *Page 206.*

## FOOD FAVORITES

- **Amada.** Jose Garces' to-die-for Spanish tapas restaurant is nationally acclaimed and locally worshiped. *Page 76.*
- **Continental.** This diner-cum-retro lounge was a catalyst for the Old City revival and is still going

strong a decade later. Beloved for its extensive list of clever cocktails and "global" tapas. *Page 76.*
- **DiBruno Bros.** A new location near Rittenhouse Square is packed with gourmet goodies, including hundreds of cheeses aged in an on-site cave, but nothing quite compares to the character and aroma of the original Italian Market shop. *Page 128.*
- **Le Bec-Fin.** Georges Perrier's temple of French cuisine remains the standard-bearer of fine dining. *Page 134.*
- **Matyson.** One of the city's best BYOBs serves a changing, creative menu of new American cuisine. *Page 134.*
- **Monk's.** This funky

bar is perpetually crowded for a good reason – 300 beers and addictive *frites. Page 134.*
- **Rouge.** Overlooking Rittenhouse Square, this upscale bistro can't be beat for burgers and people-watching. *Page 135.*
- **Walnut Room.** The current darling of the swank Rittenhouse set has cool DJs, a quirky personality and a lively mix of night-crawlers. *Page 135.*
- **Vetri.** A coveted reservation, this 35-seat restaurant serves exquisite Italian fare, served up since 1998 by Marc Vetri. *Page 109.*

**LEFT:** lunch at Rouge.
**BELOW:** costumed "colonials" outside Christ Church.

**ABOVE:** children dig into cheesesteaks outside Geno's Steaks in the Italian Market.

## ONLY IN PHILADELPHIA

- **In the Footsteps of the Founding Fathers.** Where else can you walk the same streets as Jefferson, Washington, Franklin, Adams and the other founders who brought forth a new nation? *Page 61.*
- **The Rocky statue.** Although it's no longer located at the top of the Art Museum steps (after much debate, the

statue has been moved discreetly to a side lawn), Sylvester Stallone fans can still run up the stairs singing the *Rocky* theme. *Page 142.*
- **Mural Arts tours.** Take a trolley tour of Philly's famous public artworks, which adorn buildings and other structures in neighborhoods throughout the city. *Page 246.*
- **Cheesesteaks.** Pat's, Geno's, Jim's – whoever you decide is your favorite, you'll agree that you just can't get a real one anywhere else. "Wiz wit" is the way to go (translation: cheese whiz with onions on top). *Page 165.*

## BEST SOURCES FOR INFORMATION AND DEALS

Either of the city's free weekly newspapers, *Philadelphia Weekly* (published Wednesdays) or *Philadelphia City Paper* (published Thursdays), can provide up-to-date information on both mainstream and quirky art, music, film and food. The *Philadelphia Inquirer* is still the paper of record, but occasionally lags behind the cutting edge in its coverage of what's hot and what's not. The city's official tourism website, www.gophila.com, is packed with information and excellent for trip planning; check the site for special hotel rates or giveaways. The website www.phillyfunguide.com showcases art and culture events around town, has a searchable calendar, and offers discounted tickets.

# THE PHILADELPHIA STORY

**Long celebrated as the birthplace of the nation, Philadelphia is reinventing itself once again – this time as a hip urban center with deep historical roots and a vibrant contemporary culture**

From the very beginning, Philadelphia was a city of ideas. William Penn envisioned a City of Brotherly Love, a place where people of all faiths could worship freely under a tolerant government. Less than a century later, Thomas Jefferson penned the words that severed the colonies from Britain, declaring famously that "all men are created equal." Eleven years later, the Founding Fathers assembled at Independence Hall to draft a new Constitution designed to "secure the Blessing of Liberty to ourselves and our Posterity," a piece of work that John Adams called the "greatest single effort of national deliberation that the world has ever seen." The Declaration of Independence, the Liberty Bell, the Founding Fathers – these are more than historic figures, they are national icons.

Philadelphia is also a city of firsts – site of the country's first capital, as well as the first fire company, hospital, subscription library, insurance company, stock exchange, public bank, motion picture show, daily newspaper and paper mill. Less earthshaking but no less beloved inventions include the cheesesteak, soft pretzels with mustard, and the soulful Philly sound.

With such an inventive spirit, it's no wonder that Philadelphia was the center of young America or that, in recent years, it has redefined itself as a hip urban center with deep historical roots and a forward-looking attitude. It's not unusual to hear newcomers rave about the city – its 18th-century homes and churches, colorful neighborhoods, lively arts scene, fabulous restaurants and scenic countryside.

Recent decades have seen dramatic additions to the skyline as well as a new professional sports complex, convention center and the spectacular Kimmel Center for the Performing Arts. In the historic district, a trio of new facilities – the Constitution Center, Liberty Bell Center and Independence Visitor Center – has revitalized America's "most historic square mile." People are taking note. In 2005 *National Geographic Traveler* magazine named Philadelphia America's "next great city," and tourism is booming.    ❏

**PRECEDING PAGES:** the Philadelphia Museum of Art overlooks the Fairmount Water Works on the Schuylkill River; Rittenhouse Square at night.
**LEFT:** an actor playing Ben Franklin welcomes visitors to the city's historic district.

# THE MAKING OF PHILADELPHIA

William Penn's "holy experiment" served as the
capital of a young nation before it developed
into an industrial powerhouse

It was a hell of a piece of real estate. And William Penn got it for a song. Charles II named it Pennsylvania in honor of Penn's father, Admiral Sir William Penn, a naval commander and loyal courtier. "Penn's Woods" was an enormous tract of land, a vast empire of rich river valleys, rolling mountains and trackless forests stretching from Chesapeake Bay to Lake Erie, and spreading west of the Delaware River as far as the setting sun.

Penn was granted the charter in 1681 in payment of a debt of £16,000 owed by Charles II to his father. An aristocrat by birth and Quaker by conversion, Penn saw the colony as a "holy experiment," an opportunity to replant and reshape English society – and turn a profit in the bargain. Quakers were having a rough go in England. More than 10,000 were thrown into jail for nonconformity. Penn himself had been locked up in the Tower of London for his espousal of radical theology.

## Quaker acres

The New World seemed the Quakers' only hope, and Charles II, struggling to hold onto the crown, was glad to see them go. With a stroke of the royal quill, William Penn – a 39-year-old Quaker, author of theological manifestos, colonial administrator and visionary – became the sole proprietor of a virgin territory rivaling the size of England itself.

**LEFT:** reenactors commemorate Washington's crossing of the Delaware.
**RIGHT:** Ben Franklin organized the first fire company in America.

Penn immediately began planning his capital city. He named it Philadelphia, the City of Brotherly Love, imagining a "greene countrie towne" of homes, gardens and orchards that, unlike the crowded cities of England, "will never be burnt and will always be wholesome." The street plan he designed for the city remains essentially unchanged: a two-mile-long gridiron stretching between the Schuylkill and Delaware Rivers, a large central park (now City Hall Plaza), and four town squares equidistant from the center.

It was to be a city of refuge, a great New World sanctuary where the persecuted masses of Europe – Quakers, Mennonites, Amish and

Pietists – and all "men of universal spirit" could worship freely and live under a rational and benevolent system of government. "Ye shall be governed by laws of your own making," Penn told his colonists, "and live a free, and if you will, a sober and industrious people."

## Prior to Penn

People had been enjoying the fruits of this land long before Penn arrived. There were the Indians, of course, a branch of the Algonquin family known as the Lenni-Lenape who hunted, fished and farmed along the Delaware River and its many tributaries. Compared to his countrymen in Virginia and New England, Penn

dealt fairly with the Indians, requiring that they be well-paid for land occupied by white settlers. Artists have romanticized Penn's supposed meeting with Lenape chief Tammany at Shackamaxon Creek, but whether such a meeting actually occurred is uncertain. In any case, Philadelphia was the only colonial town without a fortress or barricade, partly because Penn expected to live peaceably with the Lenape.

The site Penn chose for Philadelphia saw early European settlers, too. Both the Dutch and British made several attempts to set down roots in the Delaware Valley ever since Henry Hudson sailed into the waterway in 1609. While the British and Dutch bickered over who

### TROUBLE IN PARADISE

Like all utopias, the City of Brotherly Love fell somewhat short of the vision that inspired it. William Penn's Holy Experiment quickly ran up against the harsh realities of establishing a city at the edge of a vast wilderness.

Rather than filling the street grid from river to river, for example, the town tended to hug the wharves, sprawling north and south along the Delaware. In place of a "greene countrie towne," speculators built shoulder-to-shoulder row houses, leaving little if any room for gardens and orchards.

At times, brotherly love was in short supply as well. Political rivalries set Quakers against Anglicans, Quakers against Presbyterians, and Quakers against Quakers.

Smugglers found Philadelphia a convenient refuge from England's hated Navigation Act, and riots of various sorts erupted with some regularity, culminating in the "Bloody Election" of 1742.

Nor was Penn's town the haven of virtue and wholesomeness he envisioned. Town folk persisted in using the streets as a garbage dump. Hogs, dogs and livestock ran wild in the streets. Pickpockets and other petty criminals gave Philadelphia a reputation for lawlessness. The prospect of governing the town seemed so daunting that elected officials often chose to pay a fine rather than serve in city government.

owned the valley, a small colony of Swedes set up house near present-day Wilmington and spread north along the river to the future site of Philadelphia, where the Swedes' Gloria Dei Church, built in 1700, still stands. Under the benign rule of a lusty 300-pound governor known (affectionately, it is presumed) as Printz the Tub, the Swedes carved out a life of rude comforts and relative prosperity. Numbering only about 2,000 souls, the Swedes were no match for the well-armed Dutch, who, in 1655, informed the Swedes that they were guests in New Holland and were expected to pay for the privilege. The Dutch got their comeuppance about nine years later when the British took

The population stood at about 2,000, representing a polyglot mix of English, Welsh, Irish, Germans, Swedes, Finns, Dutch, African slaves, and the occasional group of Indians visiting town to trade. The countryside was also being settled. In 1683, Daniel Pastorius founded Germantown with a group of 13 Mennonite families, and villages in Bucks and Chester counties sprang up just as quickly as land could be cleared. Ironically, Pennsylvania's reputation for tolerance attracted so many sects – among them Mennonites, Pietists and Presbyterians – that by 1700 the Quakers constituted a minority of about 40 percent, although they were still dominant politically.

over New Amsterdam, renamed it New York, and claimed the entire Atlantic Coast from the Carolinas to New England.

The early years were rough going for Penn's first batch of settlers, many of whom lived in caves hollowed out of the riverbank. Penn stayed only two years during his first visit to the colony, but when he made his final visit in 1699 Philadelphia was already a thriving town of merchants and craftsmen. There were three churches, fine brick homes, more than 20 taverns, and a traffic of some 800 ships per year.

**ABOVE:** ships and merchants crowd the banks of the Delaware River, shown here around 1730.

## The wisest American

No single person left a greater stamp on the fledgling city than a young printer from Boston who arrived in 1723. If William Penn was the city's architect, Benjamin Franklin was her carpenter, hammering together ideas and institutions that would serve Philadelphia for generations. Franklin left his mark on almost every aspect of the growing town. He established America's first hospital, first fire insurance company, first circulating library and first fire company. He vastly expanded the colonial postal service, whipped the city's defenses into shape, helped found the College of Philadelphia (forerunner of the University of Pennsylvania) and the American Philosophical Society. He composed, edited and published the enormously influential *Pennsylvania Gazette* and *Poor Richard's Almanac*, turning homespun aphorisms into a national creed. By the late 1750s, he was a celebrated figure in Europe, where he represented colonial interests and delighted high society in London. A man of insatiable curiosity and probing intellect, Franklin's achievements as an inventor include the Franklin stove, bifocals and the lightning rod. His experiments with electricity – culminating in the famous kite-flying episode – won international acclaim and deepened Philadelphia's reputation as a citadel of knowledge.

Franklin's renown in Europe was a reflection of Philadelphia's rising status. By the mid-1700s, William Penn's Quaker village was fast becoming one of the largest cities in the British empire. It was home to many of America's most illustrious families, a leader in commerce and trade, a center of culture and the undeclared capital of the American colonies. Penn's holy experiment evolved in unimagined ways, yielding neither the spiritual nor material riches he expected. Frustrated with English politics and mired in debt, he grew disillusioned. "O Pennsylvania, what hast thou cost me!" he wrote in a letter to James Logan.

And yet, Penn laid the groundwork for the

### LET FREEDOM RING

In 1750, in celebration of the 50th anniversary of Pennsylvania's Charter of Privileges, a bell was ordered from England. It was hung in the Pennsylvania State House (now Independence Hall), the majestic Georgian structure built to house colonial government. The bell cracked the first time it was rung; it was recast once, and then again, before cracking a final time. No one, not even Ben Franklin, a man whose gaze was habitually fixed on the future, could have suspected the full significance of this "liberty bell." Nor could he imagine the revolutionary implications of the inscription on its crown: "Proclaim Liberty thro' all the Land to all the Inhabitants thereof."

greatest political movement of the century. He advanced ideas that would help give birth to a nation and set the stage for a new era in the history of government.

### Birth of a nation

The colonies never really panned out for Britain. There was an empire to administer, wars to fight, domestic unrest to subdue. It was a period of benign neglect for America, a time of discovery and growth. While the royals were looking the other way, America came of age.

By the early 1760s, George III decided that it was time to put an end to all that. With the French contained in North America and the

Seven Years War winding down in Europe, he turned his attention to his increasingly restless subjects in America. And, as always, the job at hand was to squeeze as much money out of them as possible.

George III launched the effort in 1763 with a battery of laws that prohibited colonial currency, cracked down on trade between the northern colonies and the West Indies, and imposed stiff taxes on imported items such as paper and tea. To outraged Americans, the new restrictions were worse than the old Navigation Acts and smacked of the same arbitrary use of power. Newspapers decried the Stamp Act and angry mobs took to the streets, terrorizing tax collectors and attacking the homes of government officials. Philadelphians joined other colonists in a boycott of English goods. Writing anonymously, the influential lawyer John Dickinson issued his widely read *Letters from a Farmer in Pennsylvania*, calling for unity among the colonies, and positing the subversive notion that taxation without representation constituted a form of tyranny.

When the king lashed out with the Coercive Acts, which closed down the port of Boston and dissolved the Massachusetts Assembly, patriots in Philadelphia called for a colonial conference, and in September 1774 the First Continental Congress convened at Carpenters' Hall. The delegates defined their cause in a "Declaration of Rights" and drew up a broad nonimportation agreement against British goods. But more importantly, the First Continental Congress unified the colonies in a common cause. As Virginia delegate Patrick Henry declared: "The distinction between Virginians, Pennsylvanians, New Yorkers, and New Englanders is no more. I am not a Virginian, but an American."

## Independence

The situation worsened almost immediately after the delegates left Philadelphia. In Boston, a tense standoff between redcoats and patriots turned bloody. On April 19, 1775, the "shot heard 'round the world" was fired at Concord. The die was cast; the Revolution was set in motion.

The Second Continental Congress con-

vened at the Pennsylvania State House and chose George Washington as commander of "all continental forces," such as they were. On May 15, 1776, John Adams introduced a resolution urging the colonies to organize themselves as states. On June 7, Richard Henry Lee called for a resolution on independence. A committee including Thomas Jefferson, Benjamin Franklin and John Adams was appointed to draft the document, but it was Jefferson who wrote the first draft, with Franklin and Adams making only a few changes (including the deletion of Jefferson's condemnation of slavery).

Inspired by Enlightenment thought, Jefferson

invoked the natural rights of all men to justify American independence. "We hold these truths to be self-evident, that all Men are created equal, that they are endowed by their Creator with certain unalienable Rights, that among these are Life, Liberty, and the Pursuit of Happiness… " With these words, the young Virginian transformed what had been, in essence, a tax revolt into a manifesto of human rights that would influence people and governments around the world. Unanimously adopted on July 4, 1776, the Declaration of Independence severed America from the mother country in a single, decisive stroke. It was, the delegates knew, an act of treason punishable by death.

**LEFT:** the signing of the Declaration of Independence. **RIGHT:** George Washington was named commander of the Continental Army.

The Continental Army was a ragtag affair and, despite a few bold thrusts – notably at Trenton and Princeton in New Jersey – it suffered punishing defeats at the hands of the British. In 1777, after more than a year of fighting, the redcoats marched into Philadelphia unopposed, greeted by a mob of cheering loyalists. Washington tried to dislodge the British at Germantown, but his complicated battle plan backfired and the Continental forces were forced to retreat. While the British enjoyed the comforts of Philadelphia's finest homes and taverns, Washington's "ragged, lousy, naked regiments" froze at an encampment in Valley Forge.

Oddly, the British never followed up on their victory in Philadelphia, preferring instead to indulge themselves in the pleasures of the city. The British pulled out of Philadelphia the following spring and returned to New York, affording Washington the time to train his men and Congress the opportunity to solicit much-needed foreign aid. The bloodshed continued for another four years after the occupation, raging from Saratoga to Savannah, before Cornwallis got bottled up by a French fleet and finally capitulated at Yorktown. The war was over and independence won, but Philadelphia, and the nation, faced an uncertain future.

## A more perfect union

By 1787, it was clear that the decentralized system of government established under the Articles of Confederation lacked the authority to hold the sprawling nation together. According to George Washington, the fledgling United States was "fast verging to anarchy and confusion."

Congress called for a national conference to amend the Articles of Confederation. The delegates to the Constitutional Convention, as it later came to be known, convened in May 1787 at the Pennsylvania State House, where many had signed the Declaration of Independence only 11 years earlier. Among their first official acts were the election of George Washington as president of the conference and a vow to conduct their affairs in strict secrecy. It was immediately evident that the 55 Constitutional framers would do more than amend the Articles. They would completely restructure the federal government.

The men assembled in Philadelphia couldn't have been more qualified for the job. "An assembly of demi-gods," said Thomas Jefferson, whose diplomatic responsibilities held him in Paris. In addition to Washington, a few of the most notable were James Madison, the brilliant young Virginian who was most responsible for drafting the document; Alexander Hamilton, the radical New Yorker whose proposals for the new government included a lifetime executive and senate; and Benjamin Franklin, who managed to attend every session despite his advanced age and failing health. Although none of the delegates were completely satisfied with the document, Franklin voiced the prevailing opinion: "I consent to this Constitution because I expect no better, and because I am not sure that it is not the best."

Considering the range of opinion, the document was crafted with amazing efficiency. A final draft of the Constitution was completed in a scant four months and adopted by the Convention only two days later. And although ratification faced bitter opposition from various quarters, the states ultimately confirmed the Framers' work. During the signing, Ben Franklin commented on the carving of a sun that adorned Washington's chair. Did it represent dawn or dusk for the American experiment? Franklin's conclusion: "it is a rising and not a setting sun."

For 10 years Philadelphia served as the nation's capital. Robert Morris, the nation's wealthiest man, gave his elegant Walnut Street home to President Washington as an official residence. Congress occupied the Philadelphia County Court House (now Congress Hall), and the Supreme Court convened at Old City Hall. Philadelphia, birthplace of the nation, was poised to plunge into the new century as America's most powerful city.

## Workshop of the world

The years following the Constitutional Convention were a golden age in Philadelphia. Although the federal government shifted its

it was a major player in national commerce.

The early 1800s were also a period of profound transformation. With the development of efficient steam engines in the late 1700s and the discovery of anthracite coal in Pennsylvania in the early 1800s, Philadelphia was poised on the brink of the Industrial Revolution. Factories, mills and foundries sprang up on the outskirts of Old City, spouting thick black smoke over Southwark, Manayunk, Kensington and Nicetown, where a flood of new immigrants provided cheap and plentiful labor. Manufactured goods poured from the city, and coal and other raw materials were taken in. Business boomed, the population

base of operations to the District of Columbia in 1800, Philadelphia remained the wealthiest, most sophisticated and powerful city in the nation. With more than 65,000 residents, it was not only the largest urban center in America, it was the largest English-speaking city outside Great Britain. As headquarters for the Bank of the United States (1791), the Mint (1792) and the Second Bank of the United States (1816), it was the nerve center of American finance. And as one of the busiest ports on the Atlantic Coast,

soared, and industrialists like William Cramp and Matthias Baldwin amassed fortunes manufacturing everything from textiles and toilets to ships and locomotives.

But while the captains of industry were raking in profits, the people who actually did the work – most of them immigrants from Ireland and Germany – were struggling to stay alive. Starting in the 1820s, they poured into Philadelphia by the thousands, many of them poor, hungry, illiterate and desperate for work. By 1850, the population of Philadelphia County shot up to 408,000, a third of them foreign-born. Immigrants crowded into cramped apartments, ramshackle shanties and tiny

---

**LEFT:** a colonial "soldier" reflects on the hardships of life in Washington's ragtag army.

**ABOVE:** Independence Hall in the 19th century.

broken-down "Father, Son and Holy Ghost" (or Trinity) houses with one room, and one family, per floor. Neighborhoods like South-wark and Moyamensing, as well as the hidden alleyways of Old City, were particularly ran-cid, with frequent outbreaks of cholera and yel-low fever, and gangs like the Moyamensing Killers and Blood Tubs marauding the streets.

As if living conditions weren't bad enough, immigrants also had to face nativist agitators like the Know-Nothings, who focused their bigotry on Irish Catholics and other foreigners, whom they linked with a trumped-up papist conspiracy. At the height of nativist activity in the early 1840s, a Know-Nothing gang burned

down two Catholic churches and several homes in Kensington. When a pitched battle broke out a few months later between nativists and Catholics at St Philip de Neri Catholic Church in Southwark, it took the militia four days to stop the fighting, although not before 15 people had been killed and 50 wounded.

Violence was also directed against the black community and anyone, black or white, who was associated with the small but intense anti-slavery movement. Although never widely accepted, the abolition movement had deep roots in Philadelphia, partly because of the traditional Quaker condemnation of slav-ery. The American Anti-Slavery Society was founded in Philadelphia in 1833, and Phila-delphia was a major way station in the Under-ground Railroad before the Civil War.

But in the minds of nativists (and, ironi-cally, many immigrants), abolition was asso-ciated with miscegenation, racial conflict and national disunity. More important yet, it threatened Philadelphia businessmen with the loss of lucrative Southern markets. During the worst of the violence, attacks on African Americans were almost a daily occurrence. Churches were burned, houses looted, blacks assaulted and killed in the streets.

## A house divided

The riots in Philadelphia reflected a broader conflict being played out in cities and villages throughout America. Slavery was tearing the nation apart, and by the late 1850s the issue was rapidly approaching the flash point. In Novem-ber 1860, Abraham Lincoln was elected presi-dent without a single Southern electoral vote. He visited Philadelphia en route to his inaugu-ration, informing the crowd that "there is no need of bloodshed and war… The government will not use force unless force is used upon it." Several weeks later, Fort Sumter was bom-barded by Confederate artillery. At the First Unitarian Church in Philadelphia, abolitionist minister William Henry Furness declared that "The long agony is over!" But the agony of America's bloodiest war had only just begun.

As the birthplace of the nation, Philadelphia immediately joined the effort to keep the nation whole. Philadelphians were among the first volunteers to respond to Lincoln's call for 75,000 men, and its burgeoning industrial

### PARTY TOWN

With the aftershock of civil war fading and the heart-beat of industry pounding in its veins, Philadelphia pre-pared to celebrate the nation's centennial with the biggest, boldest, most extravagant party the country had ever seen. The Centennial Exhibition of 1876 attracted exhibitors from hundreds of countries and more than 10 million visitors. Powered by the towering 700-ton steam engine known as the Corliss Machine, the Exhibition put Philadelphia's industrial might on a world stage. It was a glorious moment, marking the final emergence of Philadelphia as a world-class city of enormous wealth and energy.

might was channeled into war production. But as the war dragged on for month after month and the hope of speedy victory seemed increasingly remote, Philadelphia's enthusiasm turned to discontent. When Robert E. Lee marched Confederate troops into Pennsylvania in the summer of 1863, Philadelphians could hardly be stirred to defend their city. "Many men are pleased with the prospect of invasion," a Philadelphian wrote in his diary. "Nothing would rejoice them more than to see our whole government laid in ashes."

General Lee's army collided with Union forces (under the command of Philadelphia's own General George G. Meade) outside the

along the Delaware River, spilled across the Schuylkill River, and reached out to once isolated warrens like Germantown and Manayunk.

Immigrants continued to pour into the wretched precincts of Southwark and Moyamensing, although by the late 1880s there tended to be as many Italians, Poles and East European Jews as Irishmen and Germans. Southern blacks moved into the city as well, many occupying the slum areas between Lombard and South streets or crossing the Schuylkill into West Philadelphia. By the turn of the century, Philadelphia had the largest African-American population of any northern city. The population of the now-consolidated

town of Gettysburg. The battle that ensued over the following three days in July was the bloodiest in American history. In all, the Confederates suffered more than 28,000 casualties, the Federals more than 25,000. Although Lee retreated to Virginia, it was a costly Union victory.

## Postwar expansion

In the post-Civil War years, Philadelphia continued to grow in leaps and bounds. Penn's "greene countrie towne" spread 7 miles (11 km)

**LEFT:** a Baldwin locomotive manufactured during the height of Philadelphia's industrial expansion.
**ABOVE:** anti-Catholic rioters clash with police in 1844.

city (encompassing the whole of Philadelphia County) topped 1.2 million; nearly 25 percent were foreign-born.

Philadelphia's well-to-do were on the move, too. From the best neighborhoods of Old City, they moved west into sumptuous Victorian mansions around Rittenhouse Square. Later, in the 1880s, the wealthiest of the lot migrated again, this time to suburban estates along Pennsylvania Railroad's exclusive Main Line. City Hall moved west, too, from cramped quarters at Independence Square to a Second Empire behemoth (the largest building of its day) at Broad and Market streets.

When the United States entered World War I

in 1917, Philadelphia industry was boosted yet again. Almost overnight, mills and factories were retooled for wartime production. The Baldwin Locomotive Works turned out artillery shells, the Ford Motor Company made steel helmets, and the giant Hog Island shipyard, the world's largest, cranked out the better part of a navy.

Philadelphia, once described as the "workshop of the world," was quickly transformed into the "arsenal of democracy."

## Depression and war

The industrial boom came to a screeching halt when the bottom fell out of the American stock

market on October 24, 1929 – Black Thursday. The Great Depression dawned slowly on Philadelphia, but no less painfully than in other cities. When the Mummers paraded down Broad Street on New Year's Day 1930, there were still few signs of the hardships to come. Income was slashed. Unemployment skyrocketed. People were robbed of their livelihoods, their homes, their dignity. Makeshift Hoovervilles sprang up in parks and alleyways, labor strikes turned violent, and bread lines snaked along sidewalks. By 1933, 50 local banks had failed, and many of the city's most prominent industries were forced to shut down.

Then, in 1941, the nation entered World War II, and the city was swept into the war effort. In order to meet labor demands, women and African Americans were encouraged to work in factories churning out airplanes, ships, uniforms and weapons. By 1944, women accounted for nearly 40 percent of the labor force, and the number of African-American workers had doubled.

## Postwar years

When Japan surrendered in 1945, Philadelphians celebrated as never before. Thousands gathered around City Hall; parties broke out in the streets; fireworks streaked across the sky. But underlying the jubilation were disturbing questions about Philadelphia's future. The city itself was in bad shape. Neighborhoods were rundown, buildings dilapidated. Old City – home to Independence Hall and the Liberty Bell – was literally falling apart. With the exception of the Benjamin Franklin

## A TIME FOR DYING

Philadelphia was a hazardous place to be in October 1918. It was the time of the influenza pandemic that killed millions worldwide – far more than died in World War I – and the city felt its full impact.

Little noticed at first by Pennsylvania health officials, the outbreak began raging as September turned to October and the state was compelled to report a disease of epidemic proportions taking place in densely populated Pittsburgh and, with its 1½ million inhabitants, Philadelphia.

Public and private resources were overtaxed by the effects of the mass illness, which seemed to target young adults as well as children and seniors. Philadelphians took

to wearing gauze masks to ward off a disease that began with a cough and could ultimately turn stricken bodies a terminally dark color. Hundreds of policemen failed to report for work, and firemen and other municipal workers stayed home in droves as well. Large gatherings were prohibited, schools and churches closed, the city morgue filled to overflowing, and convicts were pressed into service as gravediggers.

Before running its course by late October, the so-called "Spanish flu" caused more than 12,000 deaths in Philadelphia alone. That toll was the highest among American cities.

Parkway, Philadelphia had seen almost no new development or rehabilitation.

Industry was slipping, too. Without the demands of a war to sustain them, Philadelphia's manufacturers were forced to close down, cut back or move out, leaving a glut of wartime laborers without a livelihood. Many companies left altogether, relocating to the South or West where taxes were lower and nonunion labor was plentiful. Automobiles and inexpensive housing lured thousands of predominantly white middle-class families into the suburbs. While the population of neighboring Bucks, Montgomery and Chester counties swelled, the city's population declined.

in the city's corruption-riddled government. After exposing widespread graft, embezzlement and patronage, the reformers pushed for a new Home Rule Charter curbing government excesses and establishing an independent mayoralty and city council.

The newly installed Democrats also embarked on an ambitious program of redevelopment. The old Chinese Wall – the elevated railway that blocked development north of Market Street – was torn down and the gleaming towers of Penn Center were erected. The dilapidated Dock Street Market was relocated to a new distribution center in South Philadelphia, clearing the way for a thorough rehabili-

With its tax base eroding and social services on the rise, the city was in a financial stranglehold. By the late 1960s, the administration regularly operated on a deficit. By the late 1980s, the city was on the verge of bankruptcy.

## Reform and rehabilitation

The postwar years weren't all bleak, however. Under the leadership of Richardson Dilworth and Joseph S. Clark, a coalition of activists and blue-blooded liberals pushed for reform

**LEFT:** hunger marchers protest in Philadelphia during the bleakest days of the Great Depression, 1936.
**ABOVE:** Philadelphians celebrate V-J Day, 1945.

tation of the 18th- and 19th-century homes of Society Hill. In Old City, the federal government finally took action to save Independence Hall. In 1951, the National Park Service acquired Independence National Historical Park and set to work restoring historic sites.

## Turbulent decades

As in many parts of America, the 1960s were a turbulent time in Philadelphia. A seemingly endless series of demonstrations, strikes and disturbances often paralyzed the city. Frank Rizzo, a police inspector with a reputation for strong-arm tactics, was elected mayor in 1971, promising to restore order in the streets and crack down on radicals. This optimistic law-and-order message was exactly what the working-class whites and upper-class conservatives wanted to hear. But Rizzo's tough talk also exacerbated racial, ideological and ethnic rifts.

Amid these turbulent years, however, there were several bright spots. The Bicentennial Celebration of 1976, for example, reinvigorated a spirit of civic pride and boosterism, and ignited an effort to transform Philadelphia into a world-class tourist destination. Streets were repaved, houses were renovated and closer attention was paid to the city's historic treasures. There were exciting changes in the city's food scene, too, leading to what was later

already affecting Philadelphia. While so-called yuppies gentrified Queen Village, Old City, Manayunk and other borderline neighborhoods, city services were being overtaxed by an alarming rise in homelessness. While glass-and-granite towers were erected for corporations in center city, drug abuse and related crime skyrocketed in the surrounding neighborhoods. A vicious struggle for power erupted among the mafiosi of South Philadelphia. Drug gangs and crack houses invaded blighted neighborhoods. The murder rate soared.

By far the darkest moment in the city's latter-day history came on May 13, 1985, when the Philadelphia police assaulted the members

dubbed Philadelphia's restaurant renaissance.

In 1980, after two terms in office, Frank Rizzo's grip on power came to an end despite efforts to amend restrictions on a third term. Many of the social and political tensions that vexed the city remained unresolved, as did the city's shaky financial situation. Mayor William J. Green presided over the city for four undistinguished years. And then, in 1984, W. Wilson Goode, Philadelphia's first African-American mayor, was voted into office on a platform of clean government and racial healing.

By the time Goode took the oath of office, the contradictory trends that would characterize so many other US cities in the 1980s were

of a radical back-to-nature group called MOVE, that had transformed a West Philadelphia house into an armed compound. Frustrated in their attempt to force the occupants out of the house, police dropped explosives on the roof, causing a fire that burned out of control. Eleven MOVE members (including five children) were killed in the blaze, and 61 houses were destroyed.

## Rendell's reign

In 1992 former district attorney Edward Rendell took charge of the city, which, having plunged into recession, was teetering on the verge of bankruptcy. Rizzo – a bulldog to the end – made another bid to be Philadelphia's mayor, but succumbed to a heart attack in the middle of the campaign.

Affable, hard-charging and politically savvy, Rendell took a hard line on the budget and a bullish attitude toward Philadelphia's future as a tourist destination. A $250 million deficit was rolled back, and for the first time in many years the city ran budget surpluses. Services to troubled neighborhoods were improved, and onerous business taxes – a perennial complaint of entrepreneurs – were reduced. An effort was made to spruce up center city and to enhance Philadelphia's reputation as a world-class cultural center.

Among the initiatives that came to fruition during Rendell's two terms were the opening of the Pennsylvania Convention Center, development of the Avenue of the Arts, expansion of the Delaware waterfront, planning the Kimmel Center, and invigorating the city's tourism marketing program. In an act of true bipartisanship, Rendell also succeeded in bringing the 2000 Republican National Convention to Philadelphia, despite the fact that he was serving as chairman of the Democratic National Committee at the time. In 2002, Rendell was elected governor of Pennsylvania.

## Next great city

In 2000, Mayor Rendell passed the keys of City Hall to former City Council President John F. Street, who numbered neighbourhood revitalization, safer streets and public education among the goals of his administration. Street has had his share of difficulties, not the least of which was an FBI investigation into municipal corruption that resulted in the conviction of at least one administration official.

There was no evidence that Street himself was corrupt, but the discovery of an FBI listening device in his office during his 2003 reelection campaign raised troubling questions. Street won the election, but the issue of municipal corruption – in particular the so-called pay-to-play arrangements that reward campaign contributors with city contracts – remains a vexing problem.

In the world of art and culture, however, Philadelphia continued to bloom. During his two terms, Mayor Street presided over the debut of the spectacular Kimmel Center for the Performing Arts, the construction of new sports arenas in South Philly, refurbishing the Philadelphia Water Works and Benjamin Franklin Parkway, and a $300 million revitalization of Independence Mall, including the unveiling of the National Constitution Center, the Independence Visitor Center and the new Liberty Bell Center.

In 2004, a plan was launched to establish a citywide wireless Internet network, resulting in the world's largest Wi-Fi hot spot. More

than 3,500 hotel rooms were added to the region between 1999 and 2006, including at least seven new hotels in center city. The population of full-time residents in center city increased by more than 10 percent between 2000 and 2005, and the number of shops and restaurants has grown with equal vigor.

*National Geographic Traveler* magazine declared what a good many people already knew: Philadelphia is America's "next great city." Philadelphia has had its political ups and downs in recent years and no doubt will continue to do so. But as a travel destination – or a place to settle down in – the City of Brotherly Love has more to offer than ever before. ❑

**LEFT:** President Bill Clinton and Mayor Ed Rendell, 1999.
**RIGHT:** Mayor John Street addresses a crowd at an open-air concert near City Hall.

# Decisive Dates

**Pre-1600** The Lenni-Lenape tribe lives along the banks of the Delaware River.
**Early 1600s** Delaware Bay area colonized by Swedish and Dutch traders.
**1681** William Penn receives a charter from King Charles II for a tract of land from Chesapeake Bay to Lake Erie and the Delaware River westward.
**1682** Penn negotiates peace treaties with Native Americans. With surveyor Thomas Holmes, he lays out a city between the Delaware and Schuylkill rivers, and names it Philadelphia.
**1683** Germantown founded.

**1777** Philadelphia occupied by British forces; Battle of Germantown; George Washington and his forces spend the winter at Valley Forge.
**1778** British evacuate Philadelphia.
**1779** University of Pennsylvania, the nation's first university, is established.
**1780** Pennsylvania Bank is the first bank authorized by Congress. Pennsylvania legislature passes law that no child born in the commonwealth shall be a slave.
**1781** British troops surrender at Yorktown.
**1782** Philadelphia's first synagogue is built.
**1787** Constitution of the United States of America drafted and adopted in Philadelphia. Pennsylvania is the second state to ratify it.

**1698** Swedish settlers build Gloria Dei church.
**1701** William Penn grants Charter of Privileges to Pennsylvania and leaves for England.
**1719** Benjamin Franklin, age 17, arrives from Boston and gets a job with printer Andrew Bradford.
**1728** John Bartram founds the first botanical garden in America.
**1731** Philadelphia Library, the first subscription library, founded by Benjamin Franklin.
**1751** Pennsylvania Hospital, the nation's first hospital, founded by Benjamin Franklin and others.
**1774** First Continental Congress meets in Philadelphia at Carpenters' Hall.
**1776** The Declaration of Independence is signed at Independence Hall.

**1789** George Washington is elected the first President of the United States.
**1790** Philadelphia becomes the nation's capital for 10 years. Benjamin Franklin dies and is buried in Christ Church Burial Ground.
**1792** First mint established in Philadelphia.
**1793** Yellow fever epidemic sweeps Philadelphia, causing President Washington to move his residence and his cabinet to Germantown.
**1794** First African Methodist Episcopal Church, Mother Bethel, opens on 6th Street.
**1797–8** Yellow fever deaths exceed 4,900.
**1801** US Navy yard established on the Delaware.
**1805** Pennsylvania Academy of the Fine Arts becomes the nation's first art school and museum.

**1812** Academy of Natural Sciences founded.

**1814** Athenaeum founded.

**1815** Fairmount Water Works opens as a sophisticated water-pumping facility on Faire Mount.

**1820s** Philadelphia is the largest industrial center in the United States.

**1821** College of Apothecaries is nation's first pharmacy school. Completion of Fairmount Dam allows more efficient distribution of water.

**1824** Franklin Institute founded. Pennsylvania Railroad incorporated to construct a railroad from Philadelphia to Lancaster County.

**1832** Matthias Baldwin demonstrates his steam locomotive. Railroad reaches Germantown.

**1835–45** Rioters attack African-American homes and Catholic churches; St Michael's Church and St Augustine's Church are destroyed.

**1855** Children's Hospital of Philadelphia founded, the first U.S. hospital for children. Pennsylvania Railroad opens a single track line from Philadelphia to Pittsburgh.

**1856** Republican party holds its first national convention in Philadelphia.

**1865** John Stetson founds his eponymous hat business in Philadelphia.

**1867** Fairmount Park Commission established.

**1874** Philadelphia Zoo opens, the nation's first.

**1876** Nation's first World's Fair in Philadelphia.

**1881** First electric streetlights turned on.

**1893** Reading Terminal (and market) opens.

**1900** City Hall is unveiled.

**1901** First Mummers' Parade.

**1917** Benjamin Franklin Parkway, modeled after the Champs-Elysées in Paris, is completed.

**1918** Influenza epidemic claims more than 12,000 Philadelphians.

**1926** Delaware River Bridge (renamed Benjamin Franklin Bridge in 1955) is unveiled; it is the world's longest suspension bridge.

**1928** Philadelphia Museum of Art and Curtis Institute of Music open.

**1932** PSFS building completed, the first international-style skyscraper in Philadelphia.

**1937** Philadelphia Orchestra appears in Disney's *Fantasia*, the first major symphony orchestra to be featured in a motion picture.

**1948** Both Republicans and Democrats hold political conventions in Philadelphia.

**LEFT:** the port area in the 18th century.
**RIGHT:** Kimmel Center for the Performing Arts opened in 2001 to rave reviews.

**1954** Schuylkill Expressway opens.

**1976** Bicentennial celebrations. The Please Touch Museum opens; it is the nation's first children's museum.

**1980** Phillies win the World Series.

**1985** After a gun battle, police use explosives on the MOVE house in West Philadelphia, igniting a fire that kills 11 and destroys a block of houses.

**1987** One Liberty Place is built, the first building taller than the William Penn statue atop City Hall.

**1990** First Liberty Medal is awarded to former US President Jimmy Carter.

**1992** Mayor Ed Rendell begins first of two terms.

**1993** Pennsylvania Convention Center opens. First Welcome America Festival held, celebrating

Philadelphia as the nation's birthplace. Avenue of the Arts is designated as an arts district.

**1995** Independence Seaport Museum opens.

**1998** Wachovia Center Sports Complex opens.

**2000** John Street elected mayor.

**2001** Kimmel Center for the Performing Arts opens to great acclaim.

**2003** Philadelphia International Airport opens new terminal. National Constitution Center opens. Lincoln Financial Field (home to Eagles football) opens.

**2004** Mayor John Street begins second term. Citizens Bank Park (baseball) opens.

**2005** *National Geographic Traveler* magazine declares Philadelphia America's "next great city."❑

# ART AND CULTURE

**No second fiddle to New York City, Philadelphia has long been a center for the arts, from its renowned museums and symphony orchestra to cutting-edge emerging talent**

When it comes to the arts, Philadelphia has undergone a makeover of sorts. A new wave of artists and musicians and their kind have been infiltrating the scene here, taking advantage of (relatively) low rents, a surfeit of leftover industrial space, and a more or less reasonable cost of living.

This influx of fresh creative blood, along with a host of other factors – government initiatives, world-class art schools, and a revitalized downtown – has invigorated the somewhat staid reputation of the city and raised its profile as a destination for both traditional and cutting-edge art and culture.

## Outdoors art

To enjoy fine art in Philadelphia you have only to step outside. This is due in part to the city's eclectic architecture, which runs the gamut from the sleek, Cesar Pelli-designed Cira Centre rising up like a scimitar to slice the sky to the French Empire froth of City Hall and the tidy colonial houses of Society Hill. Philadelphia launched a groundbreaking program in 1959 which requires that 1 per cent of the construction cost of all private developments, as well as a percentage of city projects, be contributed to the fine arts. The success of this effort is visible everywhere, from Claes Oldenburg's *Clothespin* near City Hall to the Alexander Calder sculptures on Benjamin Franklin Parkway. To experience fine art in

**PRECEDING PAGES:** South Street at night.
**LEFT:** Kimmel Center for the Performing Arts.
**RIGHT:** a mural adorns a South Philly building.

Philadelphia, you rarely need to pay, and you certainly don't have to go indoors.

The Mural Arts Program is another impressive component of the public arts initiative. The organization, which pairs artists with communities that request artwork, is responsible for the 2,400 or so murals painted on houses, commercial buildings and other structures around the city and is one of the country's most successful and largest of its kind. The murals focus on a wide variety of themes, including Philadelphia-born celebrities like basketball legend Wilt Chamberlain and elaborate montages that celebrate the city's immigrant heritage, artistic legacy and historic events. These colorful large-scale paintings brighten every neighborhood, from the busiest to the most blighted. Trolley tours of the murals are offered seasonally.

## Temples of art

Museums are plentiful. The Philadelphia Museum of Art, a neoclassical temple on the Schuylkill River, is a must for serious devotees – as for fans of the *Rocky* movies intent on taking their own sprint up the front steps. The Rocky statue formerly positioned at the top of the steps – to the delight of some and the disdain of others – was shifted to the Spectrum sports center in South Philadelphia before further debate erupted about resettlement at the museum. It now resides in a discreet location on museum grounds. The Rodin Museum, on Benjamin Franklin Parkway, houses the largest collection of sculptor Auguste Rodin's work outside France, including his renowned *Thinker*, *The Kiss* and *The Gates of Hell*.

On its way to join these stalwarts on the Parkway is the Barnes Foundation, which owns an impressive trove of roughly 800 Impressionist and Postimpressionist works organized according to the instructions of the eccentric collector Albert C. Barnes. One of the many stipulations in the will left by Barnes was that the collection never be moved from its custom-built gallery

## THE GALLERY SCENE

Philadelphia's gallery scene has been heating up in recent years, particularly in Old City around 2nd and 3rd streets north of Market. Here you will find galleries showcasing contemporary and experimental works in a wide range of media as well as shops dedicated to furnishings and interior decor.

The scene is especially lively on First Friday – the first Friday evening of the month – a neighborhood open house, when crowds spill out of the galleries and onto the sidewalks. Highlights are likely to include Snyderman-Works Galleries (303 Cherry St; tel: 238-9576), modern furniture and light sculptures at Bahdeebahdu (309 Cherry St; tel: 627-5002) and Minima (118 N. 3rd St; tel: 922-2002),

American artists at Rosenfeld Gallery (113 Arch St; tel: 922-1376), decorative arts at Wexler Gallery (201 N. 3rd St; tel: 923-7030) and American craft and studio furnishings at Moderne Gallery (111 N. 3rd St; tel: 923-8536).

Several galleries also offer lessons. Learn the art of glassblowing at Hot Soup (26 S. Strawberry St; tel: 922-2332), pottery at The Clay Studio (139 N. 2nd St; tel: 925-3453), or woodworking at the Wood Turning Center (501 Vine St; tel: 923-8000). There are numerous galleries elsewhere in center city, too, ranging from avant-garde collections in Chinatown and Northern Liberties to traditional American and European work around Rittenhouse Square.

on an estate in well-to-do Merion, a provision challenged in court when the Foundation was faced with bankruptcy. The legal challenge was upheld and the Barnes collection earmarked for relocation to the Ben Franklin Parkway in Philadelphia. Until then the works remain available for public viewing in Merion. Visitors should book in advance; reservations are required, and admission is limited.

Another trip to the suburbs, this time to Chadds Ford, is required to visit the Brandywine River Museum. It houses many works by the Wyeth family, that talented brood of artists who took much of their inspiration from the surrounding countryside.

### Emerging talent

Back in Philadelphia, there are plenty of places to take in art in its many incarnations. For modern works, visit the Institute of Contemporary Art at the University of Pennsylvania. Several contemporary-art collectives produce shows that crackle with the youthful energy of the burgeoning scene, in particular Vox Populi, Basekamp and Pace 1026.

The galleries at the city's esteemed art schools – the Pennsylvania Academy of the Fine Arts and the University of the Arts, Temple University's Tyler School of Art and the Moore College of Art & Design – are all excellent places to see what is taking shape in the minds of latter-day creators. The Fabric Workshop and Museum is both a functional workshop where visitors can watch artists at work and a gallery space devoted to textile arts.

The First Friday event, when galleries open their doors to the public on the first Friday of every month, is going strong after nearly 15 years. The bulk of the galleries are located in Old City and the streets spill over in good weather with browsers walking from gallery to gallery, inspecting the wares and sipping wine.

### Theater, dance, film

You can catch a bit of everything at the city's multidisciplinary arts centers. The Philadelphia Art Alliance celebrated its 90th birthday

in 2005, which makes it the nation's oldest. Housed in the graceful Wetherill Mansion on Rittenhouse Square, the Alliance presents visual, literary and performing arts.

Another arts center is The Painted Bride. It's part gallery, part theater and part social activism center where the visitor can hear jazz, see a monologuist perform in the 250-seat theater or catch a dance performance.

Modern dance is thriving in Philadelphia, with a number of small companies. The Koresh Dance Company incorporates ballet and jazz. Rennie Harris Puremovement celebrates hip-hop. Headlong Dance Theater performs avant-garde works. Then there's

Philadanco, a powerful force in contemporary dance both locally and nationally. Ballet and its hallowed tradition is kept alive by the Balanchine-inspired Pennsylvania Ballet. It performs at both the Merriam Theater and the gloriously operatic Academy of Music.

If it's dramatic art you're after, it can be experienced most famously at the Walnut Street Theater, America's oldest theater in continuous use; it's been staging productions since 1809. Both the Wilma on the recently christened "Avenue of the Arts" – a.k.a. Broad Street – and the Arden Theatre in Old City delve into more progressive theatrical works, while the Freedom Theatre produces out-

---

**LEFT:** a painting by Andrew Wyeth at the Brandywine River Museum in Chadds Ford, Pennsylvania.
**RIGHT:** the Pennsylvania Ballet performs the *Nutcracker* at the Academy of Music on Broad Street.

standing African-American dramas. New musical theater can be found at the Prince. More offbeat theatrical companies like Pig Iron and the comedy-focused 1812 Productions add an idiosyncratic flavor to the brew. The People's Light and Theatre Company, in Chester County, is consistently cited for its fine productions.

Another type of production – cinema – has become quite popular in town, thanks to a concerted effort by the Greater Philadelphia Film Office to attract Hollywood productions. Aside from yet another installment of *Rocky*, a number of films have been shot on location in Philly recently, including *In Her Shoes, Jersey Girl, Annapolis* and *12 Monkeys*. The director and writer M. Night Shyamalan, a native son, has steadfastly refused to move from the area, instead choosing to shoot his disturbing thrillers *The Sixth Sense, Unbreakable* and *Signs* in Philadelphia and the surrounding countryside.

## The Philly sound

Philly has all the sounds – classical, hip-hop, neo-soul, indie rock, opera, jazz, world beats – and some impressive venues in which to hear them. The new jewel in the crown is the Kimmel Center for the Performing Arts, completed in 2001. It's a massive construction, occupying

### A FAMILY AFFAIR

In the Brandywine Valley outside Philadelphia, one family dominates the artistic landscape – the Wyeths. The tradition began in 1902 when Newell Convers Wyeth arrived in Delaware and soon attracted notice for his work in periodicals and, later, as the illustrator of literary works. Following in his footsteps was Andrew Wyeth, the younger of his two sons. A realist in style, Andrew went on to a career as one of America's most distinguished painters, his works including the famous *Christina's World*. There are other notable artists in the family, including Andrew Wyeth's son James, a portraitist and landscape painter, and N. C. Wyeth's daughters Henriette and Carolyn.

an entire city block, topped with a spectacular 150-foot (50-meter) vaulted glass roof. It houses the 2,500-seat Verizon Hall and the 650-seat Perelman Theater and is home to the renowned Philadelphia Orchestra, lately under the baton of Christoph Eschenbach.

Kimmel, the new anchor of the "Avenue of the Arts," has stolen some of the spotlight from the Academy of Music. The Academy is the oldest opera house in America still used for that art form courtesy of the Opera Company of Philadelphia. Broadway musicals are also staged at the ornate red-and-gold Academy. The classical tradition is fortified in Philadelphia thanks in part to the presence of the Curtis Institute of Music and Academy of Vocal Arts, conservatories that provide tuition-free instruction.

Newer traditions like hip-hop and neo-soul have a firm grounding in the city. The smooth sounds of poet-songstress Jill Scott, the staccato beats emanating from infamous rapper Beanie Sigel, the explosive rhythm of The Roots, renowned DJ King Britt and even the goofy rhymes of Will Smith, formerly known as the Fresh Prince, and DJ Jazzy Jeff, now a respected producer – all have Philadelphia origins. Jazz is a potent force in the city as well, with upscale venues like Zanzibar Blue hosting big acts and smaller, funkier joints like Ortlieb's Jazzhaus, located in a former brewery in Northern Liberties, staging impromptu jam sessions.

The Philadelphia Clef Club is an important jazz landmark, the only music institution at the time of its opening in 1995 to be devoted purely to jazz. The Clef Club was founded as a union local for black musicians during the period of racial segregation. Local 274 counted on its membership rolls a veritable Who's Who of jazz, including Dizzy Gillespie, Shirley Scott, Nina Simone, the Heath Brothers and Grover Washington, Jr.

The idling rock scene has even started to gain momentum. Where 1980s favorites Hall & Oates and the Hooters were the main claims to fame in the rock arena, there are now a number of bands with Philadelphia roots that have gained national notice, like Clap Your Hands Say Yeah, The Capitol Years, and Dr. Dog. While it's not quite Seattle in the 1990s, there is a bit of a buzz these days.

You can catch up-and-coming bands in Old City at The Khyber, one of Philadelphia' oldest continuously operating bars, or at the North Star Bar in Fairmount, which is a little out of the way but worth the journey. Midsize venues like South Street's Theater of the Living Arts or The Trocadero, which is a former burlesque theater, or the Electric Factory, a former warehouse, tend to host national acts, while the sports stadiums in South Philadelphia are reserved for the heavy hitters who can pull in fans by the tens of thousands.

---

**LEFT:** artist at work in Rittenhouse Square.
**RIGHT:** a band entertains revelers at the annual Welcome America festival.

## Happenings

Arts festivals abound in Philly, and more than likely there'll be one taking place during your visit. The Philadelphia Film Festival, attracting wider notice every year, takes place around the first two weeks of April, while the Philadelphia International Gay & Lesbian Film Festival starts in mid-July.

Penn's Landing has music and culture festivals throughout the summer, and many of its events are free. The First Person Arts Festival, which celebrates the art of real-life experience through readings, films and other events, occurs at the beginning of June and overlaps with the dance festival Danceboom! The

Philadelphia Folk Festival, now in its fourth decade, attracts huge crowds with its impressive musical lineup in August.

Starting on Labor Day weekend, the Philadelphia Live Arts Festival and Philly Fringe launches a 16-day celebration of the performing arts, with hundreds of events that include everything from theater, dance and music to installation art and puppetry. If you're into the avant-garde, this is the place to be. One year, in what can only be described as a "happening," artists raced through the streets of Old City on toilets mounted on tricycles. There are plenty of opportunities to meet the artists and, if you wish, partake in the events ❏

# ARCHITECTURE: HISTORY UNDER CONSTRUCTION

**Philadelphia's architecture spans the history of the US, from Federal, Georgian and Victorian styles to a fresh crop of gleaming glass skyscrapers**

Walking west from the Delaware River through center city roughly traces the city's architectural history. Old City and Society Hill were settled first and have fine examples of Georgian architecture, such as Christ Church (1727–44) and Independence Hall (1753). Both are constructed of brick, with symmetrical design and classical details. Society Hill's narrow streets have scores of original colonial homes.

The 1800s saw the development of the Greek Revival style. Notable examples include the Second Bank of the United States (1818–24) and the Merchant's Exchange (1832), both by William Strickland. The mid-1800s gave rise to more ornate styles: the Cathedral of Sts Peter and Paul (1846–64) has a grand Italian Renaissance interior. Frank Furness's Academy of the Fine Arts (1872–76) is an idiosyncratic combination of styles. And City Hall is a monumental confection of Second Empire style.

The 20th century has spanned a range of styles, from the neoclassical Girard Trust Building (1905–8), now the Ritz Carlton Hotel, to the International-style PSFS Building (1930–31), now Loews Philadelphia Hotel. Recently, Two Liberty Place (1990) and the Bell Atlantic Tower (1991) have joined the skyline.

**RIGHT:** Independence Hall was designed in Georgian style by Andrew Hamilton and Edmund Woolley and completed in 1753.

**ABOVE:** Designed by the Philadelphia firm of Napoleon Le Brun and Gustavus Runge and completed in 1855, the Academy of Music is modeled after the grand opera houses of Europe.

**ABOVE:** Recalling the sleek profile of the Chrysler Building in New York City, the twin glass spires of Liberty Place soar above the Philadelphia skyline.

**RIGHT:** Benjamin Franklin Parkway was conceived as a grand boulevard stretching from City Hall to the Museum of Art and lined with stately public buildings.

**LEFT:** Modest colonial row houses line narrow, cobbled Elfreth's Alley, billed as the oldest continuously inhabited street in the country.

**BELOW:** Memorial Hall was built for the 1876 Centennial Exhibition, the first World's Fair in the United States. The Please Touch Museum is slated to occupy the building in 2008.

## A GRACIOUS THOROUGHFARE

In 1917, the Benjamin Franklin Parkway made a bold mark on the city, and is an outstanding example of the Beaux Arts design popular among early 20th-century architects and planners. The Parkway, both gracious and functional, created a broad green diagonal connecting City Hall to the new art museum being built atop Faire Mount, site of the city's water works.

Designed by Jacques Greber and Paul Philippe Cret, the Parkway was modeled after the Champs Elysées in Paris. It passes through Logan Circle, the site of one of Penn's original town squares, with the elegant Swann Fountain (above) in the center. The wide tree-lined boulevard ends below the museum at Eakins Oval, named after the Philadelphia painter Thomas Eakins.

The Philadelphia Museum of Art (built 1916–28) sits at the top of an expansive staircase flanked by more fountains. Influential in its design was Julian Abele, chief designer for Horace Trumbauer and the first African-American graduate of the University of Pennsylvania's school of architecture. The view down the Parkway to center city from the top of the steps is truly magnificent.

**LEFT:** City Hall was designed by architects John McArthur and Thomas U. Walter and adorned with hundreds of statues by Alexander Milne Calder, including a 27-ton cast iron figure of William Penn that stands atop the central tower. At 510 ft (145 meters), the tower is the world's tallest masonry structure.

# PHILLY EATS

**From haute cuisine to the humble cheesesteak, food – mostly glorious – is a major preoccupation in a town long noted for a hearty but discriminating palate**

Philadelphia has been on a restaurant binge since the mid-1990s, making food the talk of the town and attracting the attention of foodies nationwide. Long gone are the days when cheesesteaks were considered the height of the city's culinary achievements, though the charms of that homegrown specialty – humble as it may be – aren't lost on even the most sophisticated gourmet. To this day, the fastest way to start a debate among Philadelphians is to ask them where to find the best cheesesteaks in town. But there's far more to the city's gastronomic experience.

## Four-star and fancy

At the high end is Georges Perrier and his renowned Le Bec-Fin (1523 Walnut St; tel: 567-1000), long considered the best in fine dining in the City of Brotherly Love. The diminutive Mr. Perrier calls all the shots – he owns the place and oversees the operation from soup to nuts, and he does so in grand old-world fashion, complete with opulent décor and over-the-top service *a la française.*

The dessert cart spilleth over with extravagant sweets at Le Bec-Fin, while the wine list advertises a well-stocked cellar. These are just two reasons the restaurant has remained at the pinnacle for 35 years, weathering a location change and a total renovation. Perrier keeps a firm grip on this restaurant and – it is rumored – a portrait of Napoleon in his office.

**LEFT:** diners dig in to a gourmet meal at Buddakan.
**RIGHT:** Le Bec-Fin is regarded as one of the finest restaurants in Philadelphia.

But of course the day will come when the torch must be passed, or should we say the toque. Contenders huddle in the wings, one of them being Marc Vetri, chef-owner of his eponymous creation Vetri (1312 Spruce St; 732-3478), coincidentally housed in Le Bec-Fin's former location. A James Beard award winner (2005 Best Mid-Atlantic Chef), Vetri prepares Italian spreads of exquisite taste that bear little resemblance to the heavier fare one finds at South Philly's red-sauce joints.

There are other notable chefs in town as well, including Christopher Lee, Daniel Stern and Susanna Foo, to name three. Lee helms the venerable seafood house Striped Bass

(1312 Spruce St; tel: 732-3478). He's also a James Beard award standout (2005 Rising Star Chef of the Year) and was named *Food & Wine's* Best New Chef in 2006. Stern is chef-owner of the tiny-but-terrific Gayle (617 S. Third St; tel: 922-3850) and the soon-to-open Rae in the Cira Centre building. Susanna Foo (1512 Walnut St; tel: 545-2666) serves up Chinese fusion at the restaurant that bears her name.

## Starr and Stein

No parsing of the Philadelphia restaurant scene would be complete without a discussion of the dining juggernaut that is Stephen Starr, generally credited with jump-starting the latest restaurant renaissance. At last count, his Starr Restaurant Organization owned 12 eateries in town, each serving an entirely different cuisine, each highly stylized, and all quite successful.

Depending on which side of the napkin you fall, he's either a hospitality genius with an unerring eye for the next big thing or an evil genius who dumbs down New York concepts for a gullible Philadelphia audience. Either way, you'll be sure to find yourself dining in one of his restaurants whether you realize it or not.

His first restaurant, the swinger-esque Continental Martini Bar (138 Market St; tel: 923-6069) set in an old diner, single-handedly

### BRING YOUR OWN

Diners new to Philadelphia will notice that many restaurants are BYOB – Bring Your Own Bottle – meaning that they don't have a liquor license and can't sell wine, beer or spirits. This oddity, which favors the cost-conscious consumer, grew out of necessity more than generosity.

There are a limited number of liquor licenses in the city, and they are extremely costly. (The current market value of a liquor license is around $60,000.) Most independent restaurateurs choose to forgo the expense and allow customers to bring their own wine or beer instead. While diners may pay slightly more for food at BYOBs, they save a bundle on alcohol. In order to compete, many restaurants *with* liquor licenses allow diners to bring their own wine or beer for a so-called corkage fee – usually around $10.

There is one drawback. Wine and spirits sales in Pennsylvania are state-controlled, so if you do bring your own, you'll find yourself at the mercy of the not very interesting stock and not especially informed employees of the state-run Wine & Spirits Shoppes. Any wine can be ordered, but this must be done through a time-consuming bureaucracy. Pennsylvania is the country's largest purchaser of wine, but its customer service hasn't quite caught up with its buying power.

created the happening scene that now exists in Old City. When he opened it in 1995, the area had little to offer in the way of nightlife. Suddenly there was a reason to stay after dark.

He followed up his success with the perennially popular Buddakan (325 Chestnut St; tel: 574-9440), remarkable at the time for its giant Buddha statue, water wall and high-concept design. He followed with (in no particular order) Tangerine (232 Market St; tel: 627-5116), a Mediterranean-themed lounge; Alma de Cuba (1623 Walnut St; tel: 988-1799), a Nuevo Latino eatery; Morimoto (723 Chestnut St; tel: 413-9070), a collaboration with Iron Chef Masaharu Morimoto; Pod (3636

Street exactly what the first one did for Old City, and, finally, Striped Bass, a high-end fish house, which he took over from Neil Stein, another veteran restaurateur who was also something of a notable character. Unfortunately, Stein wasn't much of a businessman and, convicted of embezzling from his own restaurants, was forced to sell the Bass to his rival.

Stein still retains partial ownership of the frequently packed Rouge (205 S. 18th St; tel: 732-6622) overlooking Rittenhouse Square, which is the place to see and be seen for the fabulous set. Starr has since opened branches of Buddakan and Morimoto in Manhattan and a Con-

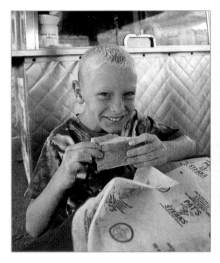

Sansom St; tel: 387-1803), another sushi spot; Jones (700 Chestnut St; tel: 223-5663), a comfort food spot; Barclay Prime (237 S. 18th St; tel: 732-7560), a luxury steakhouse; Washington Square (210 W. Washington Sq; tel: 592-7787), a South Beach-style small plates lounge; El Vez (121 S. 13th St; tel: 928-9800), a kitschy Mexican joint; a second branch of the Continental (1801 Chestnut St; tel: 567-1800), which did for the west end of Chestnut

**LEFT:** Continental Martini Bar; a chef at work at Petit 4 Pastry Studio.
**ABOVE:** enjoying a cheesesteak at Pat's King of Steaks; dinner and drinks under the Ritz-Carlton's rotunda.

tinental and Buddakan in Atlantic City. He hasn't abandoned Philadelphia entirely. A new restaurant, Parc, is scheduled to open on Rittenhouse Square, just down the block from Rouge.

## Independent eateries

The corporate behemoths aren't the only dining game in town. In fact, there's a lively offering of independent restaurants that challenge the big guns in terms of originality and cuisine. Many of these restaurants are BYOB, a phenomenon that started out of necessity but has become a signature feature of the restaurant scene. It's so prevalent at this point that many Philadelphians, now accustomed to not paying a significant mark-up on liquor, begrudge a restaurant that actually does have a liquor license.

Many BYOBs are husband-and-wife owned, with the spouses splitting the chef and front-of-the-house duties. Most are small, located in quirky storefronts or odd spaces that have been charmingly reconfigured into inviting places to dine. Matyson (37 S. 19th St; tel: 564-2925), Marigold Kitchen (501 S. 45th St; tel: 222-3699) and Chloe (232 Arch St; tel: 629-2337) all are consistently cited for their creative takes on New American cuisine. For a Mediterranean touch, head to Melograno (2201 Spruce St; tel: 875-8116) or Mercato

(1216 Spruce St; tel: 985-2962). Bring your own tequila to contemporary Mexican spot Lolita (106 S. 13th St; 546-7100) and they'll provide a pitcher of their excellent house-made margarita mix.

For those who prefer a built-in bar at a restaurant, there are plenty of excellent independent places that do have liquor licenses. Fork (308 Market St; tel: 625-9425) and Southwark (701 S. 4th St; tel: 238-1888) both merit a visit for dinner or for a well-mixed cocktail at their respective bars. For small-plates grazing along with a glass of wine, both Ansill (627 S. Third St; tel: 627-2485) and tapas spot Amada (217-219 Chestnut St; tel:

## READING TERMINAL MARKET

If you're looking for farm-fresh Pennsylvania produce, roast pork sandwiches, handmade chocolates, artisan pastries, old-fashioned butchers, traditional Amish foods, Pakistani, Greek, Thai, Mexican, Middle Eastern or vegetarian fare and, of course, Philly favorites like cheesesteaks and scrapple, then make sure to visit historic Reading Terminal Market.

The market, housed in a shed under elevated train tracks, has been in operation since 1892. Although the days are long gone when vendors packed up a basket of food for suburban housewives and sent it home on the evening train (the train terminal above the market is also

long gone), the revitalized market is thriving after a difficult spell in the 1970s and 80s that almost led to its demise.

More than 80 vendors sell their wares to residents and tourists, who pour in from the Convention Center across the street. Enjoy a sit-down meal at the Down Home Diner or the Dutch Eating Place. For a bite on the go, the piping hot soft pretzels at Fisher's are one of life's great pleasures. For fresh and local produce, the Fair Food Project transports regional farm products to the city.

The market shuts down by 6pm; Amish vendors attend only Wednesday to Saturday and close early. The market is closed Sunday.

625-2450) are great choices. To recover from a hangover, there's no better Bloody Mary and no prettier place to drink it than Beau Monde (624 S. 6th St; tel: 592-0656), an authentic Breton creperie.

### Beer here

Pennsylvania's peculiar liquor laws can make it difficult to find interesting or unusual wines, but the beer selection in Philadelphia is world-class. The city was a major brewing center before Prohibition put a lid on the booze business and is now slowly returning to its former glory.

Beers from breweries in and around the tri-state area – including Yards, Nodding Head,

Sly Fox, Triumph and Dogfish Head, to name a few – are widely available at local bars. Yuengling, the oldest brewery in the country, is still in operation in the Philadelphia suburb of Pottstown and is the ubiquitous fallback beer – the Budweiser of Philadelphia. If you want to sound like a local, go to a bar and ask for a "lager." What you'll get is a pint of Yuengling, which, though you'll rarely have to say it, is pronounced *ying-ling*.

**LEFT:** hockey fans gather for beer and companionship at a center city bar.
**ABOVE:** fresh fish, produce, cheese, meats and a variety of ethnic foods are plentiful at the Italian Market.

It's not just local beer that makes drinking so interesting. Philadelphia is rumored to consume the largest quantity of Belgian beer in the world outside of Belgium. To experience a truly mind-blowing beer bar, head to Monk's Café (626 S. 16th St; tel: 545-7005), a Belgian beer emporium that boasts anywhere from 200 to 300 beers at any given time.

An excellent (if smaller) beer selection can also be found at Tria (123 S. 18th St; tel: 972-8742), a beer, wine and cheese bar, as well as Nodding Head (1516 Sansom St; tel: 569-9525), which has an on-site brewery, and Eulogy (136 Chestnut St; tel: 413-1918). For high-quality "gastro-pub" cuisine to go along with the beer, check out Standard Tap (901 N. 2nd St; tel: 238-0630) or North 3rd (801 N. 3rd St; tel: 413-3666), both in Northern Liberties.

### Ethnic eats

Philadelphia is home to two vibrant markets: One of them is Reading Terminal Market (12th and Arch sts; tel: 922-2317), an indoor site with 80 vendors, ranging from Amish farmers to Thai stir-fryers. The other is the Italian Market, the oldest and largest outdoor market in the country. While the stretch of 9th Street between Fitzwater and Wharton is technically the market, most of the action is between Washington Avenue and Christian Street. There are vegetable vendors, butchers, cheesemongers, Italian specialty shops and a host of shops where you can grab a sandwich or snack.

This section of South Philly, once heavily populated by Italian immigrants, is now home to a burgeoning population of immigrants from other countries, particularly Mexico and Vietnam, and has the eats to match.

Just around the corner from where you'll find killer hoagies at Sarcone's (734 S. 9th St; tel: 922-1717) and the famous cheesesteaks of Pat's (1237 E. Passyunk Ave; tel: 468-1547) and Geno's (1219 S. 9th St; tel: 389-0659), you can also try banh mi, the Vietnamese version of the hoagie, at O! Sandwiches (1205 S. 9th St; tel: 334-6080), a tasty taco at Mexican taqueria La Lupe (1201 S. 9th St; tel: 551-9920), or a falafel-stuffed pita at Bitar's (947 Federal St; tel: 755-1121).

Whatever your tastes, the influx of new cultures makes for excellent eating. ❑

# A PASSION FOR SPORTS

Philly fans are a temperamental lot, as quick with a
cheer as a boo. They have had their ups and downs
over the years, but their loyalty never wavers

Three cheers for Philly sports fans! And,
oh yeah, lots of jeers, too. Fans at the
city's various sports venues have
achieved a good deal of notoriety over the
years for their unsporting behavior. You want
anecdotes? There's the one about the double-
header at old Shibe Park on an Easter Sunday
many years ago that was supposed to have featured an Easter egg hunt for kids in between
games. So who incurred the fans' jeers? Why,
who else but the poor kids who couldn't find
any eggs! That's the story, anyway. True or
false, they tell it with relish in Philadelphia.

There's more "truthiness" involved in the
incident at Franklin Field in 1968 wherein
fashion-conscious fans pelted a poorly costumed Santa Claus, slightly out of uniform,
with snowballs. Same with the World Series
game in 1930 that pit the local Athletics against
the St. Louis Cardinals, at which a forlorn
President Herbert Hoover was roasted by fans
soured on both the Depression and Prohibition.
"We want beer," they chanted. "We want beer."

Of course, it doesn't help matters that the
city's professional sports teams haven't been in
the custom of racking up championship seasons
for quite a while. They've been running dry
since 1983, when the 76ers pulled down a
National Basketball Association title. As for the
Phillies, that baseball franchise has dropped a
total of some 10,000 games since they took to
the field in 1883. Meanwhile, on ice, the

Philadelphia Flyers were swept aside in their
last trip to the Stanley Cup finals. And on the
gridiron, the Philadelphia Eagles of the National
Football League lost three straight conference
championship games before managing to reach
the Super Bowl in 2004 – only to implode.

## For the birds

The Eagles reign as the city's most popular
team. Philadelphia paints itself green on Sundays in the fall, especially when the Eagles
have home games at Lincoln Financial Field –
aka "The Linc" – in South Philadelphia. The
team has never won a Super Bowl trophy, but
it did win NFL championships in the pre-Super

---

**LEFT:** college athletes compete at the Penn Relays,
one of the largest track and field events in the US.
**RIGHT:** Phillies fans at Citizens Bank Park.

Bowl era – in 1948, 1949 and 1960. The 1960 championship game was played at Franklin Field in West Philadelphia, and it was the only time the legendary Green Bay Packers coach Vince Lombardi lost in the playoffs. The Eagles previously played at the notorious Veterans Stadium, known for its loud, fanatical fans in the "700 Level" and its unforgiving artificial turf.

The Eagles were also the benefactors of one of the most freakish moments in sports history. On the last play of a 1978 game against the division rival New York Giants at the Meadowlands in New Jersey, Giants quarterback Joe Pisarcik attempted to hand the ball off – even though a kneeldown would have preserved a

close Giants' win – and fumbled. It was picked up by Eagles defensive back Herman Edwards and returned for a touchdown. The gaffe – or divine intervention, for Eagles fans – is known as the Miracle at the Meadowlands.

## Going, going, gone

That isn't the *de facto* greatest moment in Philadelphia sports history, though. That would be the 1980 World Series championship by the Phillies, its first and only, achieved a mere 97 years after the team was founded. The famous scene of Tug McGraw striking out Willie Wilson to clinch the series at the Vet is burned into the brain of every Philadelphia sports fan.

The Vet, which was knocked down in 2004, was also the previous home of the Phillies, who now play at Citizens Bank Park. The new baseball park is much more fan-friendly than the old one, with a large food-and-games concourse called Ashburn Alley, a restaurant named after Phillies announcer Harry Kalas, and food from some of the city's famous cheesesteak and pizza joints. In its short history, the ballpark has also become notorious for turning fly-outs into home runs. The Phillies moved the left field fence back in 2006, but that has done little to stem the tide of easy homers.

Despite their status as the professional team with the most losses this side of the Washington Generals, the Phillies have a storied history of solid players (mostly on losing teams). The team claims 31 Hall of Famers, including 1930s slugger Chuck Klein, center fielder Richie Ashburn, third-baseman Mike Schmidt and right-hander Robin Roberts. In 1972,

### THE SWEET SCIENCE OF BRUISING

Boxing is big in the City of Brotherly Love, even if fight mania is not quite what it was at the height of the sport's popularity. The best known pugilist associated with Philadelphia is probably Rocky Balboa, the fictional character portrayed by Sylvester Stallone in the wildly popular film *Rocky*. In the real world, however, Philly's most famous practitioner of the "sweet science" is "Smokin' Joe" Frazier, the erstwhile heavyweight champ famous for his mano-a-mano encounters with the legendary Muhammad Ali. Others of local renown include Bernard Hopkins, who fought his way to the middleweight title before finally hanging up the gloves in 2006.

A pivotal place in Philadelphia's ring history is the venerable Blue Horizon, a Broad Street arena with a history that goes back a full 135 years. "The Blue," as it is known to fans, has been hosting boxing matches since 1964. It's known for tough-love crowds that will boo a Philly product if he's not giving it his all, as well as for no-frills fights and boxers who put on a good show. More than 30 world champions have performed here, and in 1997 the Blue Horizon played host to its first world title match. It's an intimate place with no bad seats, leading *Ring* magazine to rank it the best place in the world to take in a fight.

Phillies Hall of Fame pitcher Steve Carlton led the team with a 27-6 record, 30 complete games, 310 strikeouts and a 1.97 ERA, despite playing for a team that won only 59 games.

The city's other two major sports teams share an arena at the same South Philadelphia sports complex that is home base for all the city's big pro teams. Philadelphia's youngest sports franchise is the Philadelphia Flyers, formed in 1967. As new as it is, the team has a rock-solid fan base rivaling that of the Eagles. Known somewhat infamously as the Broad Street Bullies, the Flyers won Stanley Cups in 1974 and 1975. They were led by Hall of Famers Bernie Parent and Bobby Clarke, who later served as the team's general manager. In the 1979-80 season, the Flyers went undefeated for a record 35 straight games.

## Hardwood heroes

The Philadelphia 76ers are best known for a parade of superstars who have graced the hardwood over the years, though with little team success. The 76ers have won only two world championships while in Philadelphia – in 1967 and 1983 – despite the services of such legends as Wilt Chamberlain, Julius "Dr. J" Erving, Moses Malone, Charles Barkley and Allen Iverson.

Philadelphia's most famous basketball moment — and perhaps the greatest individual effort in sports history — didn't involve the 76ers. On March 2, 1962, playing for the Philadelphia Warriors, Wilt Chamberlain scored 100 points in a game against the New York Knicks in Hershey, Pennsylvania. No one has come within reach of 100 points since then.

## The Big 5

The 76ers aren't the city's only beloved basketball squad. Games between teams of the Big 5, an informal city series among five Division I colleges, pit brother against brother and mother against daughter. The five schools — La Salle, the University of Pennsylvania, St. Joseph's, Temple and Villanova – have played against each other since 1955. Although Big 5 contests are non-conference games, they are routinely played with the highest level of intensity. Big 5

schools have won two national championships: La Salle in 1954 and Villanova in 1985.

Despite all that, the largest sporting event in the city remains the Penn Relays, the annual track and field carnival held in April at Franklin Field on the Penn campus. The three-day meet attracts runners from grade-school level to Olympic champions and is the oldest track meet in the United States. And no round-up of Philly sports is complete without mentioning two other events: the annual Pro Cycling Championship, which features a grueling climb up the "Manayunk wall," and the Army-Navy football game, which is traditionally played in Philadelphia in late fall. ❏

### THE SCHUYLKILL NAVY

The best place to row, row, row your boat, if you're a local collegian, is along the Schuylkill River, the dividing line between center city and West Philadelphia. Indeed, the nation's largest intercollegiate rowing event takes place here annually – the Dad Vail Regatta.

At center stage is Boathouse Row, a strip of rowing team headquarters along Kelly Drive (named for rowing legend John Kelly). At night, the houses along Boathouse Row illuminate the banks of the Schuylkill. Other major river events include the Navy Day, Stotesbury Cup and Independence Day regattas and the Head of the Schuylkill.

**LEFT:** Citizens Bank Park opened in 2004.
**RIGHT:** a racing scull slices through the Schuylkill River.

# PLACES

A detailed guide to Philadelphia and its
surroundings, with the principal sites clearly
cross-referenced by number to the maps

**P**hiladelphians think of their home as a "livable city" – not too hectic,
not too crowded, manageable. It is a town with roots, old by American
standards, but progressive, too – a colonial city with a modern attitude. And, thanks to William Penn, getting around the place is a snap. Center city, the river-to-river rectangle laid out by Penn in 1682, is designed like
a giant checkerboard. North–south streets are numbered from the Delaware
River to the Schuylkill River. East–west streets are named, many after trees,
with house numbers corresponding to the numbered cross streets.

Within this area – known as center city – are Philadelphia's colonial
neighborhoods, Old City and Society Hill. This is where Benjamin Franklin
settled, the Liberty Bell rang out in celebration, and the Framers of the Constitution forged a new nation governed by "We, the People." Spreading
west from this colonial core are neighborhoods that settled as the city grew.
As the 20th century dawned, the mammoth City Hall was built on Center
Square at the intersection of center city's two main streets, Broad and Market.
Today, the four districts surrounding City Hall are like four panes in a
window: the Museum and Convention Center districts north of Market
Street, and Rittenhouse and Washington Square to the south.

Beyond center city, Greater Philadelphia is a study in contrast and color
– from the ethnic enclaves of South Philly to the diverse communities of
University City and North Philadelphia. Envisioned as a "greene countrie
towne," the urban landscape is laced with open spaces, including 8,000-acre
(3,200-hectare) Fairmount Park, the largest municipal park in the country.
Once known as the "Athens of America," the city exhibits its love of culture
at distinguished universities, galleries and numerous museums.

And there's much more beyond the city limits. In little more than an
hour, you can be shooting craps at an Atlantic City casino, eating shoofly
pie in Pennsylvania Dutch country, checking into a historic inn in the
Brandywine Valley or soaking up Bucks County's natural beauty.

This is a livable city, indeed – a town of cobblestone alleys and gleaming
skyscrapers, of tight-knit communities and vital traditions. It is a treasure
house of history, a modern metropolis, a "city to be happy in."     ❑

---

**PRECEDING PAGES:** Pennsylvania Hospital; a glass vault arches over the
Kimmel Center for the Performing Arts.
**LEFT:** a view of the Benjamin Franklin Parkway from Eakins Oval to City Hall.

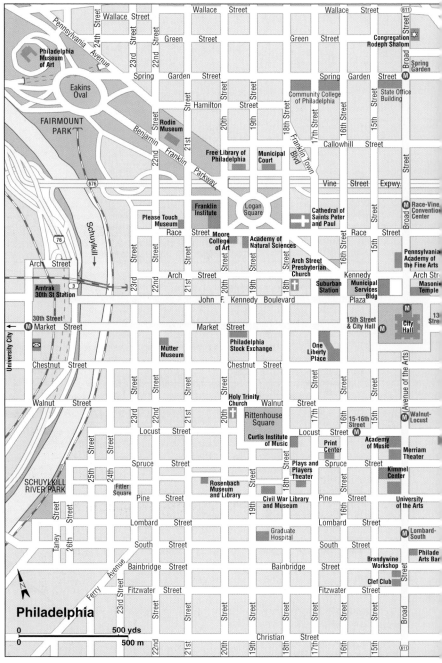

Philadelphia

# OLD CITY

America's "most historic square mile,"
where the Founding Fathers brought forth a
new nation, is home to some of the Republic's
most hallowed shrines and symbols

I n Philadelphia, it seems, everything old is new again. Take Old
City. Here in the heart of the city's
historic district, where the Founding
Fathers debated the fate of a nation,
three new facilities have revitalized
the long neglected expanse of Independence Mall and re-invigorated
the tourist experience of "the most
historic square mile in America."

In a sense, the three new buildings
– the Independence Visitor Center,
the National Constitution Center
and the Liberty Bell Center – extend
an initiative that was launched in the
early 1950s, when the National Park
Service took over much of the district,
cleared away the dreck and restored
the area's historic sites. Rehabilitation
spawned a fresh generation of shops,
restaurants and hotels. In fact, in
recent years, Old City has become
downright hip, with a lively art
gallery district on 2nd and 3rd streets
and a slew of smart new restaurants
and nightclubs.

History remains the big attraction.
One need only walk the narrow streets
and cobblestone alleys to be drawn
into Philadelphia's illustrious past.
This is where a young printer named
Benjamin Franklin set up shop, where
Thomas Jefferson composed the Dec-
laration of Independence, where the
Constitution was drafted and a new
kind of nation created.

## A good start

The best place to start a tour is at the
**Independence Visitor Center** ❶
(6th and Market sts; tel: 800-537-
7676 or 965-7676; www.indepen-
dencevisitorcenter.com; open daily
8.30am–7pm), a new building on
Independence Mall designed as a
gateway to the historic district and
Philadelphia at large. Park rangers
and concierge staff distribute maps,
literature and excellent advice about
what to see and do. There are free
short films about the city's history;

Map
on pages
62–63

**LEFT:** tourists enjoy a
carriage ride around
Independence Square.
**BELOW:**
"George and Martha
Washington" welcome
visitors to Old City.

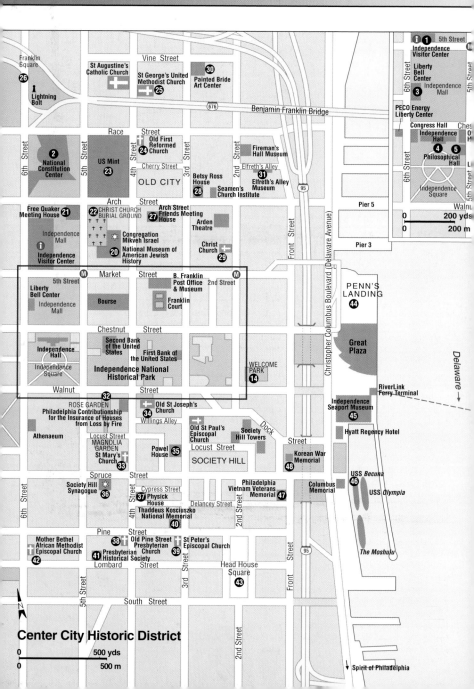

Center City Historic District

0 _____ 500 yds
0 _____ 500 m

computer kiosks with tourist information; a well-stocked gift shop; a coffee bar; costumed "interpreters" who chat with visitors in character; information about daily events; a reservation service for restaurants and hotels; and a ticket desk where you can purchase tickets to a wide variety of tours and attractions.

This is also the place to obtain free tickets for Independence Hall. Tickets are required March to December and can be acquired on the morning of your visit. Tours are often fully booked by about 1pm during peak season, so come early for the widest selection of tour times. Tickets can also be booked up to one year in advance for a nominal fee. Call 800-967-2283 for reservations or book online at http://reservations.nps.gov.

## We the people

Directly north of the Visitor Center is the **National Constitution Center** ❷ (6th and Arch sts; tel: 409-6600; Sun–Fri 9.30am–5pm, Sat to 6pm; entrance fee), the only museum dedicated solely to the US Constitution. Before entering the exhibition hall, stop at the information desk for a schedule of upcoming lectures, debates, panel discussions and author events. The museum tour starts with a multimedia presentation narrated by a live actor. Called "Freedom Rising," it tends to be a bit flashy for those who prefer history straight up, but it makes a suitably rousing preamble to the exhibits that follow.

The exhibition space is loosely divided into sections devoted to the making of the Constitution, the workings of the federal government, and the ongoing debate about such constitutional issues as freedom of speech, the separation of church and state, and the right to privacy.

The displays are beautifully designed, with a seamless combination of film, still photos, audio and text, plus numerous interactive features

**TIP**

Parking is available in an underground lot beneath Independence Mall. Entrances are at 5th and 6th streets between Market and Arch. Parking is also available at the National Constitution Center at 5th and Arch streets.

*A young patriot celebrates Independence Day in Old City.*

*A detail from John Trumbull's painting showing a draft of the Declaration of Independence being presented to the Continental Congress, meeting in Independence Hall in June 1776.*

**BELOW:**
the Liberty Bell is exhibited in a new glass pavilion across the street from Independence Hall.

that are aimed mostly at children. Perhaps the most affecting experience, however, is a relatively small, unadorned gallery populated only by life-sized statues of the 42 delegates who attended the Constitutional Convention. Wandering among the figures, coming face-to-face with George Washington, James Madison, Ben Franklin and the many lesser known delegates is a poignant reminder that for all their brilliance and bold vision, the Founding Fathers were, in the end, ordinary men.

**Liberty Bell**

To the south of the Independence Visitor Center, across Market Street, is the **Liberty Bell Center** ❸ (Independence Mall, 6th St between Market and Chestnut; usually open 9am–5pm; for exact times call the Park Service, tel: 965-2305, www.nps.gov/inde), a spacious facility opened in 2003 designed to accommodate the iconic bell and the more than 2 million people who visit annually. Tickets are not necessary, but visitors are required to pass through an airport-like security

checkpoint. A series of video displays traces the history of the bell from its creation and subsequent cracking (see sidebar below) to its elevation as a symbol, first by abolitionists in the years before the American Civil War and later by women suffragists and civil rights leaders.

**Independence Hall**

Cross Chestnut Street to **Independence Hall** ❹ (Chestnut St between 5th and 6th sts; usually open daily 9am–5pm; for exact hours call tel: 965-2305, www.nps.gov/inde) and walk through the arcade into lovely, shaded Independence Square, an excellent place to take a break and get your bearings. Touring Independence Hall requires a timed ticket, available at no charge at the Independence Visitor Center on the morning of your visit. Tours can also be booked in advance by phone (800-967-2283) or on the Web (http://reservations.nps.gov).

Independence Hall was built between 1732–56 as the Pennsylvania State House and played a key role in the birth of the nation. Here

## The Making of an Icon

The circumstances surrounding the very making of the Liberty Bell represent a kind of comedy of errors. Originally intended for the State House tower, the Liberty Bell was first cast in London by the venerable Whitechapel Bell Foundry and shipped to Philadelphia in 1752. Before it could be installed, someone decided to put it to the test and, perhaps ineptly, gave it a ring that promptly produced its famous crack. The bell was recast by two Philadelphia craftsmen, John Stow and John Pass. To their chagrin, bell number two sounded a rather unmelodious bong, and Pass and Stow recast it once again – immortalizing themselves with the inscription "Pass and Stow."

The bell tolled several times in honor of momentous events: for the joyous news of Cornwallis's surrender at Yorktown in 1781 and the signing of the Treaty of Paris two years later; for the sad news of George Washington's death in 1799 and again for Lafayette's in 1834. The bell cracked again in 1835 while being rung for the death of Chief Justice John Marshall. It tolled once more, to commemorate Washington's birthday in 1846. Since then it has stayed mute except for a handful of occasions on which it has been gently tapped.

the Second Continental Congress convened in 1775 to make their case against the British and, ultimately, to draft a revolutionary Declaration of Independence. Eleven years later, the Constitutional Congress met to amend the irresolute Articles of Confederation and ended up forging an entirely new government.

Tours of Independence Hall start in the east wing and guide visitors into the Assembly Room, where John Hancock presided over his rebellious countrymen in 1776 and Washington served as a guiding light during the secretive proceedings of the Constitutional Convention in the summer of 1787.

Although most of the original furnishings were destroyed by the British during the American Revolution, a few original touches remain, including the "rising sun chair" used by Washington. The rest of the furniture dates to the late 1700s. Independence Hall also houses period restorations of the Pennsylvania Supreme Court and, on the second floor, the Governor's Chamber and the Long Room,

which was used as a prison hospital for US soldiers after the Battle of Germantown, a reception hall for foreign dignitaries in the 1790s and, later, as Charles Willson Peale's museum of art and science.

The **West Wing** of Independence Hall has a small "Great Essentials Exhibit" of some of the original documents critical to the founding of the United States, including the Declaration of Independence, annotated drafts of the Constitution and Articles of Confederation, and the silver inkstand used to sign them.

The bell tower, which is now closed to the public, was designed by William Strickland and erected in 1828, about 37 years after the unsteady original was torn down. The bell hanging in the steeple is of course not the Liberty Bell but a substitute – the John Wilbanks bell – first installed in 1828 and still rung on national holidays.

## Congress Hall

To the west of Independence Hall, at the corner of 6th and Chestnut streets, is **Congress Hall** (9am–5pm), which

Map on pages 62–63

*The Liberty Bell wasn't always the beloved icon it is today. Colonial Philadelphians often grumbled about its insistent ringing at inopportune moments. And later, in the 19th century, plans to scrap it as an antiquated heap of metal were considered more than once.*

**BELOW:** the interior of Independence Hall appears much as it did at the signing of the Declaration of Independence in 1776.

**BELOW:**
the Lights of Liberty show illuminates the Second Bank of the United States.

housed the federal legislature between 1790 and 1800. It was here that the Bill of Rights was adopted and the second president was inaugurated, demonstrating that peaceful transition of power under the new country's system of government worked. Inside, the Senate and House chambers are replete with fine studded leather, mahogany furnishings and other 18th-century fineries.

Standing off Independence Hall's east shoulder is **Old City Hall** (9am–5pm), home of the Supreme Court from 1791 to 1800 and to city government between 1800 and 1870.

Next door on 5th Street is **Philosophical Hall ❺** (104 5th St; tel: 440-3440, www.amphilsoc.org; Fri–Sun 10am–4pm), headquarters of Ben Franklin's American Philosophical Society, which has occupied the building since 1789. A portion of the building now serves as a museum, with changing exhibits drawn largely from the Society's collection.

The Society also occupies **Library Hall ❻** on the opposite side of 5th Street. Open only to researchers, the structure serves as the Society's library and contains all sorts of historical goodies, including letters and documents written by Franklin, Jefferson and other eminent Americans.

## Biddle's bank

From Independence Hall, walk about a block east (toward the Delaware River) on Chestnut Street to the **Second Bank of the United States ❼**, a Greek Revival temple designed by architect William Strickland in 1824. This is the house that Biddle built. An influential diplomat and legislator, Nicholas Biddle administered the Second Bank for some 20 years until President Jackson, a fervent anti-elitist, launched a fierce campaign to close it down.

Today, the bank serves as Independence Park's **Portrait Gallery** (Chestnut St between 4th and 5th sts; 9am–5pm; free), housing formal portraits of the Founding Fathers by Charles Willson Peale, one of the premier US painters of his day. The gallery also features graphics and sculptures of ordinary citizens to convey what 18th-century Philadelphia was really like. The trio of

ornate buildings across the street once served as banks, too. This stretch of Chestnut Street, the city's financial center in the late 19th century, was known as Bank Row. Next to the Second Bank is a small park with a statue called *The Signer*, honoring the delegates who signed the Declaration of Independence.

## National Liberty Museum

A block east on Chestnut is the **National Liberty Museum ❽** (321 Chestnut St; tel: 925-2800; open Tues–Sun, 10am–5pm winter, daily in summer; entrance fee). A theme collection rather than one tied to historical events, the collection is presented in eight galleries organized broadly around the topics of diversity, conflict resolution, faith and freedom.

Several exhibits focus on heroes and exceptional individuals ranging from world leaders such as Mohandas Gandhi, Nelson Mandela and the Dalai Lama to celebrities like Oprah Winfrey. One gallery is devoted to the world's most notorious tyrants. The museum's art collection includes numerous works in glass, a

reminder of the fragility of liberty.

Adjacent to the museum, about 20 paces down a narrow cobblestone alley is **Franklin Court ❾**, site of Benjamin Franklin's last home. Franklin started work on the house in 1763 but didn't move in until 1785, when he retired from his diplomatic posts in Britain and France. All the while he sent letters home to his wife, Deborah, instructing her on everything from fireplace design to curtain hanging. "'Tis a very good house that I built so long ago to retire into," Franklin wrote.

Even in retirement, Franklin had little rest. He served as President of Pennsylvania for three years and, at the ripe old age of 80, as a delegate at the Constitutional Convention.

The house was torn down in 1812 by Franklin's grandchildren. Lacking plans for the structure, the National Park Service hired architect Robert Venturi to design a steel "ghost structure" representing the outline of Franklin's house and his grandson's printing office. Beneath the steel frames, viewing bays let visitors peek down into the remains

Map on pages 62–63

**TIP**

Staying for a few days? Consider buying a City-Pass, which grants admission to six attractions, including the National Constitution Center and Franklin Institute. More extensive is the Philadelphia Pass, which covers 30 attractions. The passes are sold at the Independence Visitor Center.

**BELOW:** Dale Chihuly's glass sculpture *Flame of Liberty* is displayed at the National Liberty Museum.

## An Inconvenient Truth

George Washington slept here, along with Martha, in those pre-White House days (1790–1800) when Philadelphia was the national capital. They occupied a residence on Market Street that had been offered to the federal government by financier Robert Morris, a place dubbed the President's House in which Washington and his successor John Adams took care of the nation's business.

The location is directly across from the entrance to the Independence Visitor Center. A public furor resulted when a researcher in 2002 came up with an exhaustive report, "The President's House in Philadelphia: The Rediscovery of a Lost Landmark."

The report shed light on the fact that the site accommodating the slave quarters added under President Washington's direction were directly adjacent to the Liberty Bell Center. Advocacy groups stirred to action by the revelation of this odd-couple juxtaposition of liberty and involuntary servitude clamored for public recognition of the historic truth, and the National Park Service was persuaded to reconfigure its programs accordingly. A memorial on the site will call attention to these newly highlighted realities of history.

*The First Bank of the United States was founded by Secretary of the Treasury Alexander Hamilton.*

**BELOW:** a steel "ghost structure" traces the outline of Ben Franklin's house.

of Franklin's underground kitchen and privy pit.

## Memories of Franklin

At the opposite end of Franklin Court, facing Market Street, a row of homes built by Franklin in the late 1780s now houses **Franklin Court Museum Shop** (314 Market St; 9am–4.30pm); a working Post Office (which uses a "Benjamin Franklin" cancellation stamp) and postal history museum (316 Market St); the four-story archaeological display **Fragments of Franklin Court** (318 Market St) in a building Franklin rented; and the **Franklin Court Printing Office** (320–22 Market St), an 18th-century printing shop where Franklin's firebrand grandson, Benjamin Franklin Bache, once published an influential newspaper named *The Aurora*. Visitors can see the printing press in action.

The exhibits continue in Franklin Court's **Underground Museum** (entrance in Franklin Courtyard), which features a portrait gallery, replicas of Franklin inventions such as the glass "armonica" and library chair, a display detailing Franklin's life and work as a scientist, statesman, philosopher, printer and social organizer, an illuminated index of quotations, and an audio "drama" explaining Franklin's part in the American Revolution and the Constitutional Convention. You can also pick up a telephone at the "Franklin Exchange" and hear what George Washington, Mark Twain, D.H. Lawrence and others had to say about "the wisest American" – not all of it kindly, either. The exhibits are interesting although, in the spirit of the habitually forward-looking Franklin, could use some sprucing up.

## History unearthed

Return to Chestnut Street and continue to 3rd Street. Here the **Independence Living History Center** ❿ (3rd and Chestnut sts; tel: 629-4026; Mon–Fri 9am–5pm) houses a team of archaeologists who are cataloging and analyzing a million artifacts recovered during the excavation of the National Constitution Center. The excavation site encompassed the homes of a diverse cross-section of

18th-century Philadelphia society, including the home of James Dexter, a former slave who purchased his own freedom and a founder of the city's first African-American church and the nation's first African-American self-help organization.

The building is also the starting point for tours run by **Once Upon a Nation** (tel: 629-4026; www.once-uponanation.org), whose costumed "colonials" you may see throughout the historic district. Tours and performances include "An Evening with Thomas Jefferson" and encounters with such historic figures as Ben Franklin and Edgar Allan Poe. In addition, visitors are invited to stop at more than a dozen free "storytelling benches" around the neighborhood to learn more about the life and times of colonial Philadelphians.

Standing in "lonely grandeur" across 3rd Street is the **First Bank of the United States** ⓫ (closed to the public). Completed in 1797, this neoclassical structure is a monument to the political vision of Alexander Hamilton who, as the nation's first Secretary of the Treasury, insisted that

government finances be handled by a central institution. The bank's charter lapsed in 1811 and was purchased by French-born merchant Stephen Girard, who used his resources to finance the US government during the War of 1812.

## The first stock exchange

Diagonally south of the First Bank is the **Philadelphia (Merchant's) Exchange** ⓬ (3rd and Walnut sts; closed to the public), a magnificent Greek Revival structure designed by William Strickland and opened in 1834 as the nation's first stock exchange. Be sure to walk to the rear of the building for a look at the graceful curved portico. The wide cobbled way that wraps around the Exchange is **Dock Street**, formerly Dock Creek, where ships tied up to unload their cargo in the late 1700s.

A short walk along Walnut Street to the corner of 2nd Street brings you to the **City Tavern** ⓭ (138 S. 2nd St; tel: 413-1443; open lunch and dinner), a fully functioning reconstruction of the 18th-century inn where Franklin, Washington, Adams

Map on pages 62–63

TIP

Visitors can learn more about life in colonial Philadelphia at free "storytelling benches" stationed throughout the historic district. Storytellers give free talks about the people and events – some well known, others less so – associated with the city's rich history.

**BELOW:** costumed "interpreters" offer visitors a mixture of entertainment and education.

*Old City has become such a hip neighborhood that MTV filmed its fall 2004 Real World reality show in the former home of Old Seamen's Church Institute at 3rd and Arch streets.*

**BELOW:** completed in 1774, Carpenters' Hall served as a temporary home for the First Continental Congress, Library Company, American Philosophical Society, and First and Second Banks of the United States.

and other luminaries wrangled over the issues of the day. It is a terrific place to enjoy traditional American cuisine served by costumed waiters in colonial-era surroundings.

Across 2nd Street, **Welcome Park** ⓮ is a plaza built in tribute to William Penn, who occupied a slate-roof house on this site during his second and final visit to the colony. Designed by Philadelphia architect Robert Venturi, the park is a model of Penn's original plan for the city. Next door, the Thomas Bond House is an 18th-century restoration run by the Park Service as a bed-and-breakfast inn.

Rising like an Art Deco fortress from the corner of 2nd and Chestnut streets, the US Customs Building towers over the eastern end of Chestnut Street and Old City's unofficial restaurant row. There are numerous eateries on Chestnut between 4th and Front streets and along 2nd and 3rd streets. Choices range from sushi to spaghetti, fish to French, and high-class Italian, Middle Eastern and Afghan cuisine. The Corn Exchange Building situated at the corner of 2nd and Chestnut

streets is an architectural confection of checkerboard Flemish-bond brickwork, fanciful pediments and a miniature clock tower.

## How the wealthy lived

Return to Walnut Street and turn right toward the lovely row houses and gardens between 3rd and 4th streets. Here you'll find two residential houses which give a glimpse into family life in the 1790s: the **Bishop White House** and **Todd House** ⓯ (309 Walnut and 4th sts; tour tickets available at the Visitor Center; entrance free). The Bishop White House was built in 1786 and occupied until 1836 by Episcopal Bishop William White, rector of Christ Church.

Fully restored, the house is the very picture of 18th-century affluence, with a beautifully appointed dining room in which Washington, Jefferson, Franklin and other leading figures dined, the bishop's well-stocked library, and – a sign of real wealth – an indoor privy.

At the other end of the block is the Todd House, built about 10 years earlier and, judging by the tiny rooms, modest furnishings and outdoor privy, meant for a less privileged family. John and Dolley Todd lived here for two years before John, an attorney, died in the yellow fever epidemic that swept the city in 1793. Dolley later married "the mighty little Madison" – James Madison, that is – "master builder of the Constitution" and the nation's fourth president. She was later celebrated for her graciousness as a hostess in the nation's capital and also for her heroic evacuation of the White House during the War of 1812.

The **Polish-American Cultural Center** ⓰ (308 Walnut St; tel: 922-1700; Jan–Apr Mon–Fri, May–Dec Mon–Sat, 10am–4pm; free admission) – a modest exhibition space with displays featuring famous Poles, the Polish military and folk

art – is among the row of handsome buildings across Walnut Street.

From the Todd House, it's a short walk through the Park Service's 18th-century garden into a lovely mall shaded by willow and dogwood trees. Straight ahead is **Carpenters' Hall** ⓱ (off Chestnut St between 3rd and 4th sts; Tue–Sun 10am–4pm), a beautifully proportioned Georgian structure designed by Robert Smith in 1770–74 for the carpenters' guild. The First Continental Congress met here in September 1774 to air their grievances against George III. The building later served as a hospital during the American Revolution. The hall is still owned by the Carpenters' Company; the first floor is open to the public and features a display on the hall's construction.

At the front of Carpenters' Court, two smaller buildings face Chestnut Street. The **New Hall Military Museum** ⓲ (Chestnut between 3rd and 4th streets; daily 2pm–5pm; entrance free), a reconstruction of New Hall built in 1791 and used by the War Department until 1792, houses Revolution-era muskets,

sabers, uniforms and cannonballs. It details the development of the Continental Marines, Army and Navy with dioramas, a reconstruction of a frigate gun deck, and exhibits of flintlocks and other instruments of 18th-century warfare. Across the walkway, in a reconstruction of a 1775 house built by Quaker Joseph Pemberton, is **America's National Parks Museum Shop** (Chestnut St between 3rd and 4th; open 9am–5pm), which sells souvenirs from many national parks.

### East of Independence Mall

Double back on Chestnut Street toward Independence Hall and turn right on 5th Street. About halfway up the block is the **Bourse** ⓳ (111 Independence Mall East; tel: 625-0300), a block-long Victorian beauty built in 1893–95 as a commodities exchange and now a shopping mall dedicated mostly to souvenir shops and fast-food joints. Illuminated by a domed skylight, the three-tiered arcade makes a convenient place to pick up a gift, grab a bite to eat or cool off on a hot day.

Map on pages 62–63

*Numerous shops and restaurants are located in Old City's "gallery ghetto."*

**BELOW:** the Bourse is a shopping mall housed in a restored 19th-century commercial building.

*Completed in 1744, Christ Church was for many years the tallest structure in Philadelphia.*

**BELOW:** a militiaman musters the "troops" near the Second Bank of the United States.

Continue north on 5th Street (known here as Independence Mall East) across Market Street. Tucked into a quiet brick walkway on this block is the **National Museum of American Jewish History** ㉟ (55 N. 5th St; tel: 923-3811, www.nmajh.org; open Mon–Thur 10am–5pm, Fri 10am–3pm, Sun noon–5pm; free). A modest gallery is given over to changing exhibits on American Jewish history and culture.

Sharing the building is the historic Congregation Mikveh Israel, founded in 1740, whose early members included Haym Salomon, a financier of the American Revolution, and Nathan Levy, whose ship, the *Myrtilla*, carried the Liberty Bell to America.

A greatly expanded museum is scheduled to open in 2009.

### Sacred ground

The **Free Quaker Meeting House** ㉑ (5th and Arch sts; tel: 629-5801; daily 9am–5pm; free admission) and Christ Church Burial Ground are opposite each other a little farther north on 5th Street. The meeting house was built in 1783 for the "Fighting Quakers," a splinter group that broke from the pacifist Society of Friends in support of the Revolution. **Christ Church Burial Ground** ㉒ (5th and Arch streets; www.old-christchurch.org; open Mon–Sat 10am–4pm, Sun noon–4pm; entrance fee) is the final resting place of Benjamin and Deborah Franklin, signatories to the Declaration of Independence, and a number of prominent early Americans.

Across Arch Street stands the **US Mint** ㉓ (151 N. Independence Mall East; www.usmint.gov; Mon–Fri 9am–3pm). A free, self-guided tour allows visitors to view the production line and exhibits about the Mint's history. Photo identification is required to pass through security.

From the Mint, it's a short block on Race Street to the **Old First Reformed Church** ㉔ (4th and Race sts; tel: 922-4566), built in 1837, taken over by a paint factory after 1882, reclaimed by its congregation 80 years later, and now beautifully restored. A block north, the Benjamin Franklin Bridge intrudes

on a pair of historic churches. **St George's United Methodist Church** ㉕ (235 N. 4th St; tel: 925-7788; Mon–Fri 10am–3pm), the oldest Methodist church in the US, contains a small museum relating the history of American Methodism. **St Augustine Catholic Church** (4th St between Race and Vine; tel: 627-1838) was established in 1796, burned down by anti-Catholic rioters in 1844, and rebuilt a few years later by architect Napoleon LeBrun.

About two and a half blocks west is **Franklin Square** ㉖ (Race St between 6th and 7th sts; Sun–Thu 11am–7pm, Fri–Sat 11am–9pm, extended summer hours), one of William Penn's original five town plazas. Situated at the entrance to the Benjamin Franklin Bridge, which arches more than 8,000 ft (2,500 meters) across the Delaware River, the square was recently transformed into a pocket-sized amusement park. With an old-fashioned carousel, mini-golf and playgrounds, it makes a welcome respite for families traveling with young children.

## The first flag

Double back to Arch Street for a look at the **Arch Street Friends Meeting House** ㉗ (320 Arch St; tel: 627-2667; Mon–Sat 10am–4pm; donation), built in 1804 on land granted to the Quakers by William Penn. Dioramas inside feature scenes from Penn's life.

Continuing down Arch Street – past the firehouse, the giant bust of Benjamin Franklin (which is made of thousands of pennies but looks like chopped liver), and the lovely homes hidden away in Loxley Court – is the **Betsy Ross House** ㉘ (239 Arch St; tel: 686-1252; open Nov–Mar Tues–Sun 10am–5pm, Apr–Oct daily; donation). The seamstress Betsy Ross and her husband John are thought to have lived and run their upholstery business here from 1773 to 1786, though some dispute this assertion and the claim that she sewed the first flag. Whatever the truth, the restored rooms give a fascinating glimpse into a seamstress's busy (and cramped) life in this tiny 1740 house. Costumed interpreters portray Betsy and demonstrate such

 Map on pages 62–63

**TIP**

Costumed actors at the Betsy Ross House perform a series of interactive demonstrations, including a comedic sword fighting show and presentations about the contributions of colonial women and the lives of soldiers in the Continental Army.

**BELOW:** colonial reenactors chat with young visitors near Christ Church.

**TIP**

The Old City Art Association sponsors First Friday. On the first Friday evening of every month, galleries host open houses. The event is followed by First Saturday, when artists, curators and gallery owners offer workshops, lectures and other informal get-togethers.

**BELOW:** crowds gather for a night of gallery-hopping on First Friday.

colonial skills as lace-making, wool spinning and dulcimer playing.

It's a short walk from the Betsy Ross House to **Christ Church** 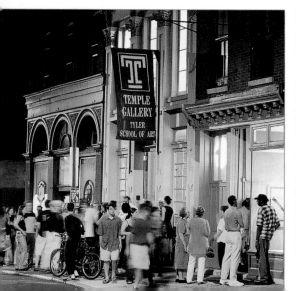 (2nd St between Market and Arch sts; tel: 922-1695; Mon–Sat 9am–5pm, Sun 12.30pm–5pm; donation). With its soaring white steeple, elegant arched windows and magnificent interior, Christ Church is one of Philadelphia's most handsome colonial buildings and was the city's most prominent structure well into the 1800s. Washington, Franklin and Betsy Ross worshipped here, and several signers of the Declaration of Independence are buried in the brick courtyard.

### The gallery scene

Walking north on 2nd Street takes you past the **Arden Theatre** (40 N. 2nd St; tel: 922-1122; www.ardentheatre.org), and a few of the new art galleries that have opened in recent years. Many are housed in airy old factories, some with ornate cast-iron facades dating back to the 1890s. This section of Old City is clearly a neighborhood in transition, with

handsome colonial buildings standing shoulder to shoulder with sooty, 19th-century warehouses, many of them transformed into artists' lofts and upscale condominiums. You'll find clusters of galleries on 2nd Street between Market and Race, and on 3rd and Cherry streets between Market and Vine. Many specialize in contemporary art or ethnic works. There are also quite a few shops dedicated to furniture and interior design.

To the north, the **Painted Bride Art Center** 30 (230 Vine St; tel: 925-9235; www.paintedbride.org) showcases provocative contemporary artists in a variety of media, ranging from film, dance, music and the spoken word to performance art and the visual arts.

### Colonial enclave

**Elfreth's Alley**, a hidden enclave of early 18th-century houses said to be the nation's oldest continuously inhabited street, is two blocks north between 2nd and Front streets. The alley began as a pathway for carts to and from the waterfront. The first houses were built in 1713 by Jeremiah Elfreth, a blacksmith who rented homes to seafarers and craftsmen. Today, all but one of the homes are privately owned.

No. 124 is a gift shop and No. 126 is the **Elfreth's Alley Museum** 31 (tel: 574-0560; open Mar–Oct Mon–Sat 10am–5pm, Sun noon–5pm, Nov–Feb Thur–Sat 10am–5pm, Sun noon–5pm; entrance fee for 15–20 minute guided tour).

A few steps away, **Fireman's Hall Museum** (147 N. 2nd St; tel: 923-1438, open Tues–Sat 10am–5pm; entrance free) is packed with old fire engines, helmets, water cannons and other equipment documenting the history of firefighting from 1731, a few years before Benjamin Franklin founded the Union Fire Company, the nation's first, in 1736. ❑

# The Wisest American

He walked into town an impoverished teenager in 1723, and in a scant 25 years Benjamin Franklin had turned himself into a celebrity. By the time he died in 1790, he had attained icon status, an international legend who had charmed the darlings of the Paris salons and helped steer the fledgling United States on its historic course.

Ben Franklin was a self-made man par excellence who embodied the very essence of democratic meritocracy. He was a voracious improver, a child of the Enlightenment, an early American Renaissance man who, as printer, scientist and statesman, plied an uncanny mix of common sense and inspiration.

And yet, for all the mythology that swirls about the figure, Franklin the man has always seemed something of a puzzle. Is the Ben Franklin who, in *Poor Richard's Alamanack*, espoused such pragmatic virtues as thrift, moderation and industry the same man whose flights of imagination gave us the Franklin stove, the bifocal lens and the kite-flying experiments in electricity? A genius he may have been, but where is the grandeur, the kind of reckless elan that appealed to the romantic fancies of hero-worshippers like Thomas Carlyle and D.H. Lawrence, two of his severest critics. He was derided as a "crafty and lecherous old hypocrite" by William Cobbett. John Keats called him "a philosophical Quaker full of mean and thrifty maxims." And both Nathaniel Hawthorne and Herman Melville regarded him as something of a mountebank, a quack dispenser of warmed-over aphorisms.

He was crafty, cautious, and sometimes conformist. Even his celebrated remark at the signing of the Declaration of Independence – "Gentlemen, we must now all hang together, or we shall most assuredly hang separately" – bespeaks a certain timorous calculation. None of that "Give me liberty or give me death!" flair.

It is not easy to square the image of Franklin the moralist, the dour didact, the "maxim-monger," with the equally evocative image of Franklin the visionary, the audacious thinker, the "party-animal" who delighted French society, the lover of food, drink and women who were not his wife.

His dalliances in France – especially with Madame Helvetius, a rich widow to whom he vainly proposed marriage, and the younger Madame Brillon de Jouy, who liked to perch coquettishly on the lap of her "cher Papa" – are legendary, if never fully disclosed in intimate detail. His affairs in London produced at least one child, a son who, much to his father's displeasure, became an ardent Loyalist.

Franklin left his mark all the same. In addition to his inventions and civic reforms, Franklin served as postmaster general and President of Pennsylvania, published books and newspapers, was honored by Harvard, Oxford, the Royal Society and French Academy, represented the colonies in London, helped draw up the Declaration and the Constitution, and negotiated peace with Britain.

George Washington may have been first in the hearts of his countrymen, but Benjamin Franklin was Mr. America to the world at large. When he died in 1790, at the age of 84, his funeral drew the largest crowd – 20,000 people – ever to assemble in early Philadelphia. He was, to borrow Horace Greeley's words, "the consummate type and flowering of human nature under the skies of colonial America."❏

**RIGHT:** the Benjamin Franklin National Memorial is set within the rotunda of the Franklin Institute.

# RESTAURANTS & BARS

## Restaurants

### Amada
217-219 Chestnut St. Tel: 625-2450. Open: L Mon–Fri, D nightly. $$–$$$
www.amadarestaurant.com
Philadelphia's only authentic Spanish tapas restaurant is also one of its best. Graze on a few small plates for a light snack or put together a full meal of traditional dishes like Spanish tortilla with saffron aioli and salt cod croquettes. Don't miss the cocktails named after Almodovar films.

### Buddakan
325 Chestnut St. Tel: 574-9440. Open: L Mon–Fri, D nightly. $$$–$$$$
www.buddakan.com
This perennial favorite

for the "see and be seen" set serves modern pan-Asian cuisine under the serene gaze of a giant Buddha. Dishes like tea-smoked spare ribs and lobster fried rice have stood the test of time, as have the inventive cocktails.

### Bistro 7
7 N. 3rd St. Tel: 931-1560. Open: D Tues–Sun. $$
Fresh and local food, simply prepared, is the main attraction of this open kitchen BYOB. The spare décor features cute touches like mismatched heirloom silver.

### Cafe Spice
35 S. 2nd St. Tel: 627-6273. Open: L Mon–Fri, D nightly, Sat & Sun brunch. $$

www.cafespice.com
Part of a mini-chain, this colorful Indian bistro has a sleek design, a sexy vibe and a selection of well-prepared, if familiar, Indian dishes like tandoori. A long martini list and occasional DJs make the bar scene here lively.

### Campo's Deli
214 Market St. Tel: 923-1000. Open: L & D Daily. $
www.camposdeli.com
A superior version of the chicken cheesesteak can be found at this deli, a family business since 1947, along with worthy hoagies, sandwiches and "regular" cheesesteaks. It's a wallet-friendly and delicious alternative in a pricey neighborhood.

### Chloe
232 Arch St. Tel: 629-2337. Open: D Wed–Sat. $$
www.chloebyob.com
This tiny cash-only, no reservations spot was one of the first to jumpstart the chef-driven BYOB trend and remains one of its top examples. The kitchen, run by a husband and wife team, prepares a creative New American menu.

### City Tavern
138 S. 2nd St. Tel: 413-1443. Open: L & D daily. $$$
www.citytavern.com
Feel like a patriot at this colonial tavern. Costumed waiters and historically

accurate recipes like West Indies Pepperpot Soup create an authentic 18th-century ambiance.

### The Continental
138 Market St. Tel: 923-6069. Open: L & D daily, Sat & Sun brunch. $$
www.continentalmartinibar.com
The first in restaurateur Stephen Starr's expansive stable offers a menu of "global tapas," but it's the swinging lounge vibe, complete with skewered olive light fixtures and clever cocktails – like the Dean Martini, served with a Lucky Strike – that continues to draw crowds.

### Cuba Libre
10 S. 2nd St. Tel: 627-0666. Open: L Mon–Fri, D nightly, Sat & Sun brunch. $$–$$$
www.cubalibrerestaurant.com
A spot-on re-creation of 1950s Havana, known for mojitos made with freshly pressed sugar cane and an extensive rum bar. The menu highlights Latin American classics like ropa vieja, chicharrones and Cubano sandwiches.

### Fork
306 Market St. Tel: 625-9425. Open: L Mon–Fri, D nightly; Sun brunch. $$–$$$
www.forkrestaurant.com
This acclaimed New American bistro, complete with an attached gourmet take-out shop, is consistently cited as one of the city's best restaurants for

its locally-inspired fare and award-winning wine list. Late night and mid-day menus served.

### Franklin Fountain
116 Market St. Tel: 627-1899. Open: daily (closed in winter, call for details) $
Save room for dessert at this period-perfect soda fountain. Ice cream sundaes, fresh waffle sandwiches and thick milkshakes are served on antique dishes by white-coated soda jerks.

### Petit 4 Pastry Studio
160 N. 3rd St. Tel: 627-8440. Open Tues–Sun. $
A dainty spot for a quick coffee and a tasty home-made dessert for those browsing nearby galleries and shops. Sit at a vintage table and watch the bakers at work in the kitchen "studio" behind the display counter filled with tarts and cookies.

### Radicchio
314 York Ave. Tel: 627-6850. Open: D nightly. $$
www.radicchio-cafe.com
A slightly off-the-beaten-path BYOB worth seeking out for its simple, well-prepared and affordably priced Italian fare.

### Society Hill Hotel Bar & Restaurant
301 Chestnut St. Tel: 923-3711. Open: L & D daily. $$
Renovated in 2005 and

under new ownership, this longtime hotel bar serves tasty gastro-pub fare and has an affordable selection of wines and local beers.

### Soho Pizza
218 Market St. Tel: 625-3955. Open: L & D daily. $
Crowds spill out of the bars and into this sliver of a shop on weekends, when it serves slices to hungry revelers till 3:30am. The shop also has a liquor license, just in case you're not ready to call it a night.

### Tangerine
232 Market St. Tel: 627-5116. Open: D nightly. $$–$$$
www.tangerinerestaurant.com
The room is spacious, but the glow of hundreds of candles and carved lanterns makes it feel like an intimate Moroccan salon. The menu gets its inspiration from across the Mediterranean. Expect to taste a variety of Middle Eastern, Spanish and North African influences.

## Bars

### Five Spot
1 S. Bank St. Tel: 574-0070, www.thefivespot.com
More sophisticated than most warehouse clubs, the Five Spot serves up a mixture of DJs, live bands, salsa lessons and swing dancing.

### Khyber
56 S. 2nd St. Tel: 238-5888. One of Philly's oldest bars, full of character and characters. An impressive selection of beers, plus live music nightly.

### Lucy's Hat Shop
247 Market St. Tel: 413-1433. A dive and proud of it, Lucy's is known for its "Drunken Monkey" Sunday brunch and booze-fest. Drink specials and a high-energy crowd make this a louche but reliably fun destination.

### Paradigm
239 Chestnut St. Tel: 238-6900. Settle in for drinks at the 50-foot granite bar in this South Beach-esque spot. Don't miss the bathrooms, which are notorious for their see-through glass doors that frost over in the nick of time.

### Sassafras Cafe
48 S. 2nd St. Tel: 925-2317. A tried-and-true Old City hangout that often gets overlooked in the shadow of the neighborhood's glitzier places. Stop in for a beer and a burger or a respite from trendy nightlife seekers.

### The Plough and the Stars
123 Chestnut St. (Entrance on 2nd St.) Tel: 733-0300. With a blazing fireplace and rich Irish coffee, this bi-level bar in the historic Corn Exchange Building is packed on weekends. Irish music on Sundays.

| PRICE CATEGORIES |
| --- |
| Prices for three-course dinner per person with a half-bottle of house wine:<br>**$** = under $25<br>**$$** = $25–$40<br>**$$$** = $40–$50<br>**$$$** = more than $50 |

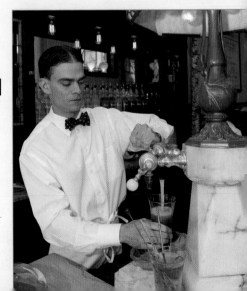

**LEFT:** swing dancers cut a rug at the Five Spot.
**RIGHT:** a soda jerk pours something sweet at Franklin Fountain, a decidedly old-fashioned ice cream parlor.

# SOCIETY HILL AND PENN'S LANDING

**Philadelphia's loveliest neighborhood has the biggest
concentration of 18th-century homes in the country.
Down on the waterfront, the city's maritime
history is preserved at Penn's Landing**

**N**amed for the Free Society of
Traders, to whom William
Penn granted land between
Walnut and Pine streets, this chiefly
residential neighborhood emerged
in the late 1700s, shared by both
working-class and wealthy families
in a lively milieu of craftsmen, merchants, shopkeepers and seamen. The
finest churches were within earshot
of the rowdiest taverns, the most
prestigious homes within smelling
distance of the open-air market.

When well-heeled families
started moving into more fashionable homes around Rittenhouse
Square *(see page 125)*, the old
neighborhood began a long decline
that turned much of it into a slum.
Had it not been for the efforts of
preservationists in the 1950s, many
of the historic homes would have
fallen to the wrecking ball. The
many years of rebuilding and renovating, painting and primping, have
paid off grandly.

Today, Society Hill contains
some of the most charming streets,
lovely homes and priciest real
estate in the city. It's a walker's
paradise, with cobbled alleyways
and hidden courtyards, brick sidewalks and tree-shaded lanes, and
historic houses, large and small,
that have been lovingly and accurately restored.

## House and garden

You can slip into Society Hill
through the iron gate of the **Rose
Garden** ㉜, on the 400 block of
Walnut Street behind the Second
Bank of the United States. The brick
walkway leads to the type of quiet
courtyard that makes strolling
through Society Hill such a delight.
Uncovered here is a section of original cobblestone. As the marker
alongside explains, while William
Penn laid out the streets in 1681, the
city did not assume responsibility

**Map
on pages
62–63**

**LEFT:**
dining aboard
the *Moshulu*, a
tall ship moored at
Penn's Landing.
**BELOW:**
spring blossoms
add color to the
Magnolia Garden.

*The metal brackets outside some second-story windows hold "busybody mirrors," which let upper-floor occupants see who is at the front door. It is said that Ben Franklin invented the mirror so he could see his wife coming down the street while he "entertained" young ladies in the upstairs parlor.*

**BELOW:** Society Hill is honeycombed with hidden courtyards and alleyways.

for paving until 1762. Follow the path across Locust Street into the smaller Magnolia Garden, planted in modern times in deference to George Washington's fondness for magnolias. Here, in early spring, magnolia and azalea blossoms surround the flagstone walk with splashes of red, white and sherbet-pink. It's a wonderful place to read the Sunday paper and sip coffee, or to take a few restful moments before pressing on.

The **Philadelphia Contributionship for the Insurance of Houses from Loss by Fire**, the oldest fire insurance company in the country, founded by Ben Franklin, is headquartered around the corner at 212 4th Street. Franklin and his pals started the "hand-in-hand" company in 1752. Its firemark – four hands locked in a fireman's carry – still hangs on buildings throughout Society Hill and Old City. Franklin's company refused to insure houses with trees nearby, so a competitor, the Mutual Assurance Company for Insuring Houses from Loss by Fire, the second oldest insurance company in America, filled the gap. The

Green Tree Company was once at Locust and 4th streets in buildings occupied by the Shippen, Wistar and Cadwalader families, the cream of Philadelphia society. It was frequented by John Adams, George Washington and a host of the city's most distinguished guests. Now the Episcopal Diocese of Pennsylvania, organized in 1784, uses the place as its Church House (240 S. 4th St; tel: 627-6434; open 9am–4.45pm, by appointment).

Next door to the Church House is **St Mary's Church** ㉝ (4th St between Locust and Spruce; tel: 923-7930; Mon–Sat 9am–4.30pm; entrance free). Founded in 1763 when St Joseph's around the corner became too small for the congregation, St Mary's is the city's oldest Catholic church still in use. Take a look inside for the two-tiered stained-glass windows. A brick walkway on the north side of the church leads to the cemetery, where Revolutionary naval commander John Barry is buried along with a number of prominent Philadelphians.

Across the street from St Mary's Church, narrow St James' Place leads into **Bingham Court**, a generous plaza surrounded by modern townhouses designed by the noted architect I.M. Pei. The north entrance leads across Willings Alley to the courtyard of **Old St Joseph's Church** ㉞ (Willings Alley, between Walnut and Locust, 4th and 3rd sts). Founded in 1733, St Joseph's is Philadelphia's oldest Catholic parish. As an inscription at the door explains, this was the only place in the British empire where the Catholic Mass was permitted by law – a tribute to William Penn's policy of tolerance. Although enjoying legal status, Catholics were looked on with suspicion if not outright contempt. According to tradition, Ben Franklin advised the Catholic fathers to protect their church behind an iron gate.

## How the other half lived

Return to Bingham Court and follow St James' Place across to 3rd Street. To the right, just past two handsome houses adorned with ornate wrought-iron balconies, is **Powel House 35** (244 S. 3rd St; tel: 627-0364; tours Thur–Sat noon–5pm, Sun 1–5pm, and by appointment; entrance fee), one of the grandest colonial homes in Philadelphia, built in 1765 and a classic example of Georgian style.

As mayor of Philadelphia and one of the wealthiest men in town, Samuel Powel entertained Washington, John Adams, the Marquis de Lafayette and other friends in the lavish reception room, dining room and ballroom. And the Powels knew how to party. John Adams – always the starched-collar Bostonian – described a Powel fête as "a most sinful feast… [with]… everything that could delight the eye or allure the taste; curds and creams, jellies, sweetmeats of various sorts, twenty sorts of tarts, fools, trifles, floating islands, whipped sillibub, &c., &c."

Nearly demolished in the 1930s, Powel House has been restored in painstaking detail from the splendid crystal chandelier, Chippendale chairs (George Washington liked them so much he ordered 20 for Mount Vernon) and Nanking china (a gift from the Washingtons), to the rack upon which Samuel hung his wig before going to bed. Before leaving, be sure to stroll through the 18th-century garden in the rear courtyard.

Take a few steps south on 3rd Street for a look at the beautiful old brownstones once owned by Michel Bouvier, great-great-grandfather of Jacqueline Kennedy Onassis, then retrace your steps to **Old St Paul's Episcopal Church** (225 S. 3rd St), built in 1761, redesigned by William Strickland in 1830, and now used as offices for the Episcopal Community Services.

St James' Place continues past a row of modern townhouses to I.M. Pei's **Society Hill Towers**, a trio of apartment buildings conspicuously out of sync with the neighborhood's colonial style. The Free Society of Traders once kept an office on this knoll overlooking Dock Creek, where

*Society Hill has the country's largest concentration of 18th-century houses.*

**BELOW:** horse-drawn carriages tour the neighborhood at a leisurely pace.

**BELOW:** the Head House stands at the north end of Head House Square, an area of shops and restaurants.
**RIGHT:** St. Peter's Episcopal Church.

ships arriving from Britain and the West Indies unloaded their freight. Years later, the area was occupied by the sprawl of Dock Street Market, since relocated to a modern facility in South Philadelphia.

Heading downhill on 2nd Street brings you back to the 18th century in a hurry. The first brick building on your right is Abercrombie House (270 S. 2nd St), a handsome Georgian home built for a Scottish sea captain in 1759.

Across the street, the modest brick building that seems to lean to one side is A Man Full of Trouble Tavern. Constructed in 1759 and, sadly, now closed, this endearing little building was typical of the taverns that once huddled around the waterfront where a sea-dog could find dinner, a few tankards of grog and a place to stay the night.

## Delightful detour

Before continuing to Head House Square, you can stroll down **Spruce Street** into the residential heart of Society Hill, where lovely 18th- and 19th-century homes have

been brought back to life with interesting contemporary touches. Some of the larger houses, like the Davis-Lenox House (No. 217) and the Wharton House (No. 336), were occupied by the well-to-do. But many homes are fairly modest, with two or three stories and relatively tight interior space.

Peek down the alleyways at Philip and American streets (between 2nd and 3rd streets). On the next block, St Joseph's Walkway returns to Bingham Court, passing a pocket of houses on the left named Bell's Court. These homes have only one room on each story – Philadelphians call them Father, Son and Holy Ghost, or Trinity houses – and are typical of working-class dwellings of the early 1800s.

On the opposite side of Spruce Street, St Peter's Way crosses to a lovely playground known as Three Bears Park between Cypress and Delancey streets. **Delancey Street**, one of the most charming and secluded in the city, is lined with 18th-century homes such as the Alexander Barclay House and

Trump House, tiny private court-yards (Drinker's Court) and imaginative modern conversions.

## Church tour

Farther along Spruce Street, between 4th and 5th, is the impressive white mass of the **Society Hill Synagogue** ㊱ (426 Spruce St; tel: 922-6590; open by appointment, Mon–Fri 10am–3pm; entrance free). Originally a Baptist church from 1829, the building has an 1851 facade designed in the Greek Revival style by Thomas U. Walter, architect of the Capitol dome in Washington, D.C.

Next to the synagogue, narrow Lawrence Street leads into a snug courtyard with modern townhouses. Have a look at the courtyard, then exit via Cypress Street to 4th Street, where you will find the **Physick House** ㊲ (321 S. 4th St; tel: 925-7866; hourly tours June–Aug Thur–Sat noon–4pm, Sun 1–4pm, Sep–May 11am–3pm; entrance fee).

Built in 1786 by Henry Hill, this magnificent freestanding mansion – one of the finest Federal-style homes in the country – is fully restored. Furnishings date from 1815 to 1837, when the house was occupied by Philip Syng Physick, "father of American surgery." Among the doctor's many innovations are surgical devices displayed upstairs, including a ghastly looking gall bladder remover that was used without the benefit of anesthesia.

South of Spruce Street, Society Hill is graced with a number of historic churches. The **Old Pine Street Presbyterian Church** ㊳ (4th and Pine St; tel: 925-8051; open Mon–Fri 10am–4pm; entrance free) has stood, in one form or another, since 1768. Originally, the church looked like its Georgian-style neighbor, St Peter's, but it was badly damaged during the Revolutionary War. A renovation in the 1800s turned it into a Greek

Revival temple, with Corinthian columns and a second-story entrance. John Adams worshipped here and, during the British occupation, redcoats used the church as a hospital. Several Revolutionary War veterans are buried in the cemetery, including 100 Hessians – German mercenaries hired by the British to put down the Yanks.

A block away, **St Peter's Episcopal Church** ㊴ (3rd and Pine St; tel: 925-5968, open for tours, Mon–Fri 8.30am–4pm, Sat 8.30am–3pm, Sun 1–3pm; guides on duty Sat 11am–3pm and Sun 1–3pm; entrance free) retains the simple dignity of its original Georgian design. Built between 1758 and 1763 by Robert Smith, master builder of both Carpenters' Hall and Christ Church, this "chapel of ease" was established for well-to-do parishioners who were tired of slogging through the mud to Christ Church.

Apart from the six-story steeple, which was added in 1852 by William Strickland, St Peter's looks much as it did more than 200 years ago. The high-backed box pews are

*Come to the Old Pine Street Presbyterian Church for Jazz Vespers, a series of live performances mixed with readings and brief sermons.*

**BELOW:** Penn's Landing.

*On August 1, 1842, a white mob attacked a parade celebrating Jamaican Independence Day near Mother Bethel Church. The Lombard Street Riot, as the episode came to be known, resulted in the burning of an African-American church and many houses and the brutal beating of several people.*

**BELOW:** RiverLink ferries passengers between Penn's Landing and the Camden waterfront.

original (Washington sat in No. 41), and the church's unusual layout, with the chancel in the east end and the pulpit in the west, remains intact. Outside, a brick path wanders past the graves of painter Charles Willson Peale, naval hero Stephen Decatur and a delegation of Indian chiefs who died in the yellow fever epidemic of 1793.

Across the street sits a National Park building: the **Thaddeus Kosciuszko National Memorial ⓬** commemorates the Polish patriot who aided the American cause in the Revolution. After an illustrious career as a military engineer in America, Kosciuszko led a failed revolt against the Czarist occupation of Poland. Wounded, imprisoned and later exiled by the Russians, he returned to Philadelphia and boarded at this modest house in 1797–98, where he received distinguished visitors, among them Vice-President Thomas Jefferson. The exhibit, which includes a slide program and a re-creation of Kosciuszko's bedroom, details the career of the man who, in Jefferson's

words, was "as pure a son of Liberty as I have ever known."

Around the corner on Lombard Street, there are three church buildings of note. The **Presbyterian Historical Society ⓭** (425 Lombard St; tel: 627-1852), the national archives and research center for the Presbyterian Church, is a balanced Federal structure set in a walled garden. In the garden are statues by Alexander Stirling Calder of important figures in church history. About a block west, Congregation Bnai Abraham (527 Lombard St; tel: 374-9280; open for services) is an imposing building with an arched arcade and stained-glass rosette over the entrance.

Around the corner, **Mother Bethel African Methodist Episcopal Church ⓮** (6th St, between Pine and Lombard; tel: 925-0616; open Tues–Sat 10am–3pm, Sat by appointment; entrance free) is believed to be the oldest property continuously owned by African-Americans in the country. The church was founded in 1787 by Richard Allen, a former slave and preacher who broke with Old St George's Methodist Church when he and other black parishioners were relegated to the upstairs gallery.

The new congregation's first church was an old blacksmith shop that Allen had hauled to the site on a horse-drawn wagon. Allen and his followers won the city's respect for their selfless efforts during the yellow fever epidemic of 1793. Later, as the center of Philadelphia's largest black neighborhood, Mother Bethel hosted abolitionists such as Frederick Douglass and runaway slaves along the Underground Railroad. Allen's tomb is in the basement.

## Retail therapy

From Mother Bethel, it's a short walk down Pine or Lombard streets to **Head House Square ⓯**, a covered marketplace which at the south

end turns into the eclectic South Street strip. In colonial times, the brick shed in the center of 2nd Street sheltered the town's "New Market," started in 1745. (The first market was on the east end of High Street, now called Market Street, in Old City.) The little brick house at the end – Head House – was added in 1804 and used as a meeting place for volunteer firemen. A fire bell once hung in the cupola. Today, Head House Square has smart shops and restaurants. The bank across 2nd Street from the Head House – strikingly out of place with its arched windows, ornate cornices and cast-iron pilasters – was modeled after the Loggio Consiglio in Padua, Italy, although it is now greatly altered.

## On the waterfront

In Benjamin Franklin's day, Philadelphia's waterfront was a hive of sailing ships, warehouses, taverns and counting houses. But, like New York, Baltimore and Boston, Philadelphia tore down the rotting piers and seedy whiskey joints that once choked its waterfront and turned it into a river-side park dubbed **Penn's Landing** ㊹ (121 N. Columbus Blvd, between Market and South; tel: 629-3200). Pedestrian walkways connect the riverfront to center city at Market, Walnut and South streets.

Between Market and Walnut is the **Great Plaza**, filled with markers detailing river geology, population growth and other facts about the city. The Great Plaza is also the site of an open-air amphitheater where pop groups perform free concerts on summer weekends and where other special events and festivals are held.

At the southern end of the Great Plaza is the **Independence Seaport Museum** ㊺ (211 S. Columbus Blvd; tel: 925-5439; daily 10am–5pm; entrance fee). The collection focuses on the history of the port, with displays on 19th-century shipbuilding and navigation and a fascinating array of nautical gadgets, model ships, scrimshaw and other artifacts as well as exhibits on undersea exploration and submarine technology. A workshop in the museum is dedicated to traditional wooden boat building.

As part of your museum admis-

Map on pages 62–63

TIP

On summer weekends, the market shed at Head House Square is occupied by a lively crafts fair.

**BELOW:** the Benjamin Franklin Bridge arches gracefully over the Delaware River.

Map on pages 62–63

*Katmandu is one of several nightclubs on the Delaware River waterfront.*

**BELOW:** Independence Seaport Museum.

sion, you can check out the **USS Becuna** 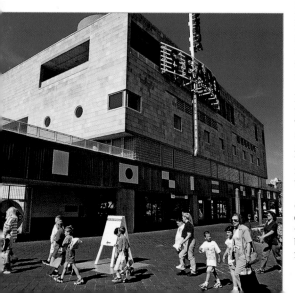, a guppy-class World War II submarine that served in 1944 under General Douglas MacArthur and later in the Korean and Vietnam wars, and the **USS Olympia**, a 19th-century cruiser pressed into service during the Spanish-American War. Also moored at Penn's Landing is the **Moshulu** (tel: 923-2500), a four-masted sailing ship christened in 1904 as a cargo vessel and now serving as a floating restaurant in the style of a 19th-century luxury liner.

For a tour of the Delaware River, make reservations for a dinner cruise aboard the *Spirit of Philadelphia* (S. Columbus Blvd at Lombard Circle, office Pier 3 at Penn's Landing; tel: 923-1419).

Nearby, the **Philadelphia Vietnam Veterans Memorial** (Front and Spruce sts) is modeled after the "Wall" in Washington, D.C. A short walk away is the **Korean War Memorial**, dedicated to the sacrifices of servicemen and women in America's "forgotten war."

The Delaware River waterfront is a hotspot for nightclubs and restau-rants, as well as a departing place for boat tours. A few places north of Penn's Landing include Dave and Buster's (325 N. Columbus Blvd, Pier 19 North; tel: 413-1951), a casual restaurant/arcade with billiards, Iwerks Theater and golf simulators, and Captain Lucky Cruises (Columbus Blvd at Callowhill St; tel: 629-8687; narrated tours daily at 10.30am and 1pm). Also north of the bridge is **Festival Pier**, a venue for concerts, festivals and special events.

### The Jersey side

Also on Penn's Landing is the **River-Link ferry terminal** (tel: 925-5465; daily 9am–5.40pm Apr–Dec), where you can catch a ride across the river. On the New Jersey side of the Delaware sits the new **Adventure Aquarium** (Mickle Blvd, Camden; tel: 800-616-5297; daily hourly admissions 9.30am–5.30pm; entrance fee), the **Camden Children's Garden**, and the **Tweeter Center**, a year-round facility with an amphitheater capable of accommodating up to 25,000 patrons.

The Aquarium has huge fish tanks, a "4D theater," seals, penguins, hippos and various other marine creatures as well as a shark tunnel that allows you to walk through a tank of some 40 sharks. There's even an opportunity for a few brave souls to swim with the sharks.

South of the Tweeter Center is the **Battleship *New Jersey*** (Clinton St at the Waterfront, Camden; tel: 856-966-1652; daily Apr–Sept 9am–5pm, shorter autumn and winter hours; guided tours and separate flight simulator ride; entrance fee). Launched in 1942, it is the most decorated battleship in US Navy history.

Also on the Camden waterfront is **Campbell's Field**, home of the Camden Riversharks baseball team, where you can watch minor league baseball in a dramatic setting at the foot of the Ben Franklin bridge. ❑

## RESTAURANTS & BARS

### Restaurants

**Dave & Buster's**
Pier 19, 325 N. Columbus Blvd. Tel: 413-1951. Open: L & D daily. $$
www.daveandbusters.com
Kids (and kids at heart) love this cavernous chain, filled with video games and pool tables, and serving standard corporate restaurant fare. For adults, there's a bar and plenty of TV screens.

**La Famiglia**
8 S. Front St. Tel: 922-2803. Open: L Tues–Fri, D Mon–Sat. $$$–$$$$
www.lafamiglia.com
A baroque setting of marble and gold, an impressive wine cellar and old-fashioned upscale Italian fare like rack of lamb for two makes this a special occasion spot with prices to match.

**La Veranda**
Pier 3, 5 N. Columbus Blvd. Tel: 351-1898. Open: L Mon–Fri, D nightly. $$$
Dine here for river views and solid Italian food. It's decidedly old school, with waiters in tuxedos and Sinatra on the stereo.

**Moshulu**
401 S. Columbus Blvd. Tel: 923-2500. Open: L & D daily, Sun brunch. $$$–$$$$
www.moshulu.com
You'll be dining on the Delaware aboard the *Moshulu*, a handsomely restored 1904 ship. This is no booze cruise; the vessel is permanently docked at Penn's Landing. Expect to see plenty of surf and turf dishes on the New American menu.

**Old Original Bookbinder's**
125 Walnut St. Tel: 925-7027. Open: D nightly. $$$–$$$$
www.bookbinders.biz
This historic seafood house reopened in 2005 after a multimillion-dollar renovation, complete with a huge lobster tank. You'll still find the famed snapper soup, but now it's served with trendier fare like yellowfin tartare.

**Positano Coast**
212 Walnut St., 2nd Floor. Tel: 238-0499. Open: L Mon–Sat, D nightly. $$
www.lambertis.com
This cozy evocation of the Amalfi Coast is an ideal spot for a snack before catching a movie at the Ritz Theatre across the street. It serves Italian "small plates" meant for sharing, as well as pasta, seafood and crudo, the Italian version of sushi.

**Swanky Bubbles**
10 S. Front St. Tel: 928-1200. Open: D nightly. $$
www.swankybubbles.com
If a celebration is in order, you've come to the right place. Champagne is the specialty of the house, offered by the glass, by the bottle or in a cocktail. There's a fun pan-Asian menu and a selection of sushi to go. Open to 2am.

### Bars

**Il Bar at Ristorante Panorama**
Penn's View Hotel, Front & Market Sts. Tel: 922-7800.
www.pennsviewhotel.com
A must for serious oenophiles, Il Bar features the world's largest custom-built wine preservation and dispensation system, offering 120 wines by the glass. Stop by just to admire the handsome wood contraption or to page through the thick binder of wine and champagne flights.

**Dark Horse**
421 S. 2nd St. Tel: 928-9307.
www.darkhorsepub.com
Hidden in plain sight on Head House Square, this pub features multiple bars in its warren of rooms, but manages to maintain a cozy pub atmosphere. A favorite watering hole for U.K. expats. Open to 2am.

---

**PRICE CATEGORIES**

Prices for three-course dinner per person with a half-bottle of house wine:
**$** = under $25
**$$** = $25–$40
**$$$** = $40–$50
**$$$** = more than $50

**RIGHT:** alfresco dining aboard the *Moshulu*.

# CELLULOID CITY: PHILADELPHIA ON FILM

**In recent years, Philadelphia's many urban and suburban locations have made it a favorite with film directors searching for realistic settings**

Once upon a time, people who had never traveled to Philadelphia might have had few images of the city beyond the Liberty Bell. Today, thanks to Hollywood, an aggressive marketing effort by the local film office and a five-county landscape full of location choices, Philadelphia's many vistas have been seen on screens around the world.

*Rocky* made a star of Sylvester Stallone and turned the steps of the Museum of Art into a magnet for joggers and tourists alike. Other films made here were Brian de Palma's 1980 thriller *Blow Out*, with John Travolta, and the romantic comedy *Mannequin* (1986), filmed in the palatial Lord & Taylor (now Macy's) department store. The opening scene of Martin Scorcese's 1993 film *The Age of Innocence* was filmed in the Academy of Music. Prolific writer and director M. Night Shyamalan shot his atmospheric thrillers in the city and surrounding countryside, including *The Sixth Sense* (1999), *Signs* (2002) and *The Village* (2004). Other recent films shot in the area include *The Woodsman* (2004) with Kevin Bacon, *National Treasure* (2004) with Nicolas Cage, *In Her Shoes* (2005), with Cameron Diaz, and Disney's *Annapolis* (2006).

**LEFT:** The 1983 comedy *Trading Places* starring Eddie Murphy and Dan Aykroyd light-heartedly explored the life of down-and-outs on Philadelphia's streets.

**ABOVE:** *Rocky* won an Academy Award for best picture in 1976 and showcased South Philly's Italian neighborhood and the Blue Horizon boxing club in North Philadelphia.

**ABOVE:** *Twelve Monkeys* (1995), with Bruce Willis and Brad Pitt, turned the Eastern State Penitentiary into an asylum.

**RIGHT:** When asked what he would like on his tombstone, native comedian W.C. Fields delivered the famous stinger: "On the whole, I'd rather be in Philadelphia."

## PHILADELPHIANS IN HOLLYWOOD

Philadelphians have always made their mark on the arts so it is not surprising that, as the film and television world grows ever larger, Philadelphia names have become part of the Hollywood scene.

*Rocky* star Sylvester Stallone is one of Philly's most famous sons. Grace Kelly grew up in East Falls, the daughter of Olympic rower and local businessman Jack Kelly, and went on to star in *High Society* and many other films before becoming a real-life princess. Comedian W.C. Fields also made it big in Hollywood but had less respect for his home town. Actor Kevin Bacon is the son of city planner Edmund Bacon and grew up in center city. Comedian and actor Bill Cosby, one of Temple University's most famous alumni, used his life growing up in North Philadelphia as fodder for many of his comedic monologues.

Also raised in the area were film director Brian de Palma, actor Will Smith (above), and writer and director M. Night Shyamalan, who continues to live and make films in his native city.

**RIGHT:** The flings and foibles of Main Line blue-bloods is the focus of *The Philadelphia Story* (1940), a romantic comedy starring Katharine Hepburn, Cary Grant and Jimmy Stewart.

**BELOW:** *Witness*, a 1984 thriller starring Harrison Ford and Kelly McGillis, explored traditional Amish life in nearby Lancaster County, although some members of the community objected to the film's portrayal.

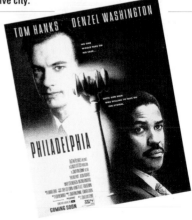

**ABOVE:** Tom Hanks and Denzel Washington starred in *Philadelphia* (1993), a film about homophobia and AIDS discrimination. The film garnered two Academy Awards – Hanks for best actor and Bruce Springsteen for best song.

# SOUTH STREET AND QUEEN VILLAGE

Although it has lost some of its Bohemian edge, the "hippest street in town" still draws a lively, youthful crowd to its shops, bars and restaurants

**W**hat's the hippest street in town? The answer used to be, unequivocally, **South Street ❶**. Today, it's a bit more complicated.

South Street is still the main tourist attraction of the Queen Village neighborhood, but it's lost some of its funky, punky luster in the past 15 years. What was once a collection of artsy, occasionally weird, always interesting shops and restaurants has suffered a series of setbacks: the invasion of corporate chains, an increasingly negative reputation due partly to a riot that occurred during Mardi Gras 2001, and the explosive growth of nightlife in other areas, such as Old City and Rittenhouse.

## Cruising the strip

While the South Street "stroll" once meant meandering up and down the stretch from Front to 5th Streets, you can now continue up South Street all the way to 10th and still find points of interest. In fact, the most interesting part of South Street is now mostly west of Broad, where independent restaurants and pubs have sprung up to accommodate a neighborhood (cumbersomely referred to as "Graduate Hospital") that has experienced tremendous rebirth.

Still, tourists and teenagers alike flock to the east end of the street to see what the legendary fuss is all about. While the stroll can sometimes feel more like a crawl, considering the crowds, it's infinitely better than the glacial drive. Customized cars "cruise" the strip, inching along while the bass thumping from tricked-out stereo systems makes the sidewalks tremble. It's best to leave the car in the lot, especially on weekends, and explore the area on foot.

It's helpful to remember that South Street exists in a perpetual

Map
on page
92

**LEFT:**
South Street florist.
**BELOW:** South Street attracts big crowds on weekend nights.

state of adolescence, attracting actual teens and those with a youthful state of mind. While the expressions of youth may change – body piercings, baggy clothes and bling have gradually replaced tie-dye and mohawks as the rebellious outerwear du jour – the neighborhood still stands as a place where such expressions can be made.

## The renaissance

South Street wasn't always a nightlife center. In the latter part of the 19th century it served as the commercial hub for a neighborhood of Jewish immigrants from eastern Europe. A taste of this exists just off South Street on **Fabric Row** ❷ – 4th Street between Bainbridge and Catharine. These blocks have long been the go-to destination for all things textile and are still populated with storefront fabric shops, seamstresses and tailors, many of which have stood for generations.

South Street was threatened with demolition in the 1950s, when city officials planned to build a crosstown expressway in its place. The project languished for years, as residents fought against it, until it was abandoned in 1973. In the interim, the available space and low rents had attracted artists who moved in and set up shop, and the South Street renaissance began.

While it was once home to numerous galleries and independent restaurants and cafes, the retail mix these days tends toward a large number of cheap, trendy clothing boutiques, junky jewelry stores, and T-shirt and tchotchke emporiums. There are still worthwhile shops to visit, you just have to work a little harder to find them. Some chains have moved in and, curiously, moved back out again – McDonald's was one that couldn't hack it – but Starbucks, Dairy Queen, Reebok, Adidas and Foot Locker all maintain a retail presence.

**TIP**

Hungry for a quick take-out meal? Stop at the Chef's Market (231 South St; tel: 925-8360) for a selection of prepared gourmet foods. An in-store cafe and a few sidewalk tables are also available.

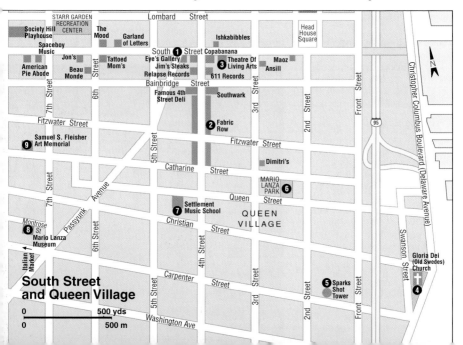

South Street and Queen Village

Many of the original stores remain, but some that were an essential part of the neighborhood have gotten the boot as rents have skyrocketed. Zipperhead, the punk-rock store brought to fame in the Dead Milkmen's song "Punk Rock Girl," closed in 2005, to be reborn again around the corner as **Crash, Bang, Boom** (528 S. 4th St; tel: 928-1123). You can still see the famous zipper and giant ants attached to the facade of its former location at 407 South.

### Snack and shop

Starting at Front Street, at the foot of the bridge connecting South Street with Penn's Landing, you'll pass Head House Square and the beginning of the real strip, at 2nd Street. Sample an excellent falafel from tiny **Maoz** (248 South St; tel: 625-3500), perfect to grab-and-go while on your stroll. **Jon's** (606 S. 3rd St; tel: 592-1390), which you can't miss – it's the one with the enormous mural on it of Queen Village native Larry Fine, aka Larry of the Three Stooges – has a

large patio and makes a nice spot for people-watching. Stop for fries at the **Ishkabibbles** (337 South St; tel: 923-4337) takeout window and a margarita at the original **Copa-banana** (344 South St; tel: 238-1512), a rollicking, tropical-themed joint that anchors the corner.

### An ear for music

Music lovers will be especially happy on this block, as it's home to the **Theatre of Living Arts ❸** (334 South St; tel: 922-1011), a South Street landmark that has survived a number of incarnations. During the hippie heyday, it was a theater operated, for an infamous season, by André Gregory of *My Dinner with André* fame. It later became a revival house showing foreign and domestic movies. After a failed attempt to turn it back into a playhouse, it's now one of the city's prime venues for touring bands that can't quite fill the city's larger concert halls.

Just around the corner on 4th Street are several indie record stores, including **611 Records** (611

*A walkway leads from Penn's Landing to South Street.*

**BELOW:** the neighborhood abounds with colorful characters.

*Oversized sculptures adorn the pedestrian bridge from Penn's Landing to South Street.*

S. 4th St; tel: 413-9100) and **Relapse Records** (608 S. 4th St; tel: 629-1090). If those aren't enough, **Repo Records** (538 South St; tel: 627-3775) and **Spaceboy Music** (704 South St; tel: 925-3032) are farther up the strip.

Stop by the **Eye's Gallery** (402 South St; tel: 925-0193), a folk art emporium that opened in 1969. The mosaic facade is the work of co-owner Isaiah Zagar, whose mirrored murals are instantly recognizable up and down the block and culminate in the exuberant *Magic Garden* on the 1000 block of South Street (see box). It's easy to spot, directly next door to the black-tiled **Jim's Steaks** (400 South St; tel: 28-1911), which cheesesteak aficionados say is one of the city's best.

Between 5th and 6th, things start to quiet down, although there's still the sideshow atmosphere of dive bar **Tattoed Mom's** (530 South St; tel: 238-9880), the New Age atmosphere of the **Garland of Letters** book shop (527 South St; tel: 923-5946), and the racy atmosphere of sex shop **The Mood** (531 South St;

tel: 413-1930) to explore. Continue farther west and you'll pass the American craft furnishing store **American Pie Abode** (718 South St; tel: 923-5333), a block-long **Whole Foods** (929 South St; tel: 733-9788) market, and, just past 14th Street, the **Jamaican Jerk Hut** (1436 South St; tel: 545-8644), the garden restaurant made famous in the 2005 movie *In Her Shoes*.

## Queen Village

Philadelphia's oldest section – although technically not part of the city until 1854 – is **Queen Village**. Nestled between posh Society Hill and the increasingly upscale Bella Vista neighborhood, it runs from Front Street west to 6th Street and from Lombard south to Washington Avenue. The area was originally known as Wiccaco, a Lenni-Lenape Indian word for "pleasant place."

Swedes were the first to occupy the area, in 1638, as part of New Sweden, although they didn't claim the territory for long. English settlers quickly overtook the Swedes, and the British Crown granted the

## Magic Garden

**W**alk along South Street and you're sure to notice the brilliant mosaics adorning the facades of numerous buildings. The exuberant murals are the work of Isaiah Zagar, who has been creating mosaics on the block since 1968, when he covered the exterior of the Eye's Gallery at 402 South Street. Zagar is a co-owner of the gallery.

These colorful works incorporate shards of mirrors, colored glass and pottery into swirling, riotous patterns that teeter joyously at the threshold of chaos. Zagar has created over 70 mosaic works over the past 30 years, including *The Skin of the Bride*, the dazzling exterior of the Painted Bride Arts Center in Old City. His most beguiling work may very well be *Magic Garden*, a sculpture garden next to his studio at 1022-24 South Street. The garden incorporates bottles, bicycle wheels and other found items, along with fragments of glass and pottery, into a surreal landscape that is both curiously soothing and totally delightful.

*Magic Garden* is open Sat–Sun noon–4pm. On a weekday, it's worth stopping by as much of the garden is visible from the outside.

land to William Penn along with the rest of Pennsylvania. Penn promptly changed Wiccaco's name to Southwark, after a London neighborhood. The Queen Village moniker didn't come along until the 1970s, when the name was changed once again to honor Sweden's Queen Christina.

The neighborhood is heavily residential and there are few attractions, aside from the South Street thoroughfare, to intrigue the out-of-town visitor. If you enjoy walking and house-ogling, you'll undoubtedly enjoy a stroll up and down its handsome blocks. Residents keep their charming homes unfailingly tidy. Red brick, freshly painted shutters and well-kept window boxes are the hallmarks of these attractive homes, both old and new.

## New Sweden's old church

There are a few sights worth seeking out. **Gloria Dei (Old Swedes) Church ❹** (Columbus Blvd and Christian St; tel: 389-1513; open daily 9am–5pm) is the oldest church in Pennsylvania, in continuous use since construction was completed

in 1700. As early as 1640, more than 40 years before William Penn arrived with his Quaker immigrants, Swedish settlers erected log cabins in this area as well as a crude blockhouse that served as the area's first church. The colony eventually outgrew its first house of worship, and Gloria Dei was built. While the original congregation was comprised of Swedish Lutherans, they joined the Episcopal Church in 1845 and remain an active congregation today.

A red brick wall surrounds the grounds, which includes outbuildings, tall, shady trees and a cemetery with tombstones dating as far back as 1708. The church itself is quite petite, built for the smaller physiques of yesteryear. Inside you'll find a wooden carving of a pair of cherubs, which was brought from the original log church, as well as an 18th century baptismal font still in use. Models of the ships that transported the first Swedish colonists, the *Fogel Gryp* and the *Kalmar Nyckel*, are suspended from the ceiling. A small plaque on

Map on page 92

*The first governor of New Sweden, established in what is today Queen Village, was Johan Printz, a spirited fellow of some 300 pounds known to the colonists as "Printz the Tub."*

**BELOW:** customers line up at Jim's Steaks, considered by some aficionados to be the city's best cheesesteak stand.

**BELOW:** South Street is lined with shops, bars and restaurants.

the wall informs the viewer that Betsy Ross married her second husband at the church.

## Bullet tower

Just south of the church, at Front and Carpenter streets, is the **Sparks Shot Tower ⑤**, the first structure of its kind (and one of the last still standing) in the U.S. Built in 1808, the 142-foot-high (43-meter) brick tower produced lead ammunition for nearly a century. It was owned by Thomas Sparks and John Bishop until Bishop, a Quaker, sold his half of the business after realizing that the shot would be used to kill people in the War of 1812, rather than just for hunting. It's no longer open to the public and sits smack in the middle of a community center.

## Art and music

A short walk away, on the 200 block of Catharine Street, you'll find the tiny, tranquil environs of **Mario Lanza Park ⑥**, named for the late, great tenor, a Queen Village native. Lanza was also a student at the nearby **Settlement Music School ⑦**

(416 Queen St). What began in 1908 as a social services center for newly arriving immigrants morphed into a community music school that has continued to expand its reach over the past century. Albert Einstein once sat on its advisory board; it continues to boast alumni in every major symphony in the United States. Other alumni include actor and musician Kevin Bacon, singer Chubby Checker and members of the hip-hop group The Roots.

Until recently, Settlement housed the **Mario Lanza Museum ⑧**, a collection of Lanza paraphernalia, which is now located a few blocks away (Columbus House, 710 Montrose St; tel: 238-9691; open Mon–Sat, 10am–3pm, closed Sat–Sun Jul–Aug; entrance free).

Another notable arts institution is the **Samuel S. Fleisher Art Memorial ⑨** (719 Catharine St; tel: 922-3456; open Mon–Fri 11am–5pm and, while school is in session, Mon–Thu 6.30–9.30pm, Sat 10am–3pm, closed Aug), the nation's oldest tuition-free community arts school. Housed in a connected series of buildings on the

700 block of Catharine Street, including a deconsecrated Romanesque church, Fleisher offers free instruction to whoever wants to learn. Classes are wildly popular and usually have long waiting lists.

Founded by Samuel S. Fleisher, an arts-loving member of a well-to-do family of textile merchants, the nonprofit organization continues to expand. His descendant, Suzanne Roberts, née Fleisher, along with her husband, Comcast founder Ralph Roberts, donated a gallery. The school features several annual exhibitions of emerging local talent, supplemented by a collection of Russian icons and 14th- to 16th-century European paintings housed in the Italian-style Fleisher Sanctuary.

### Good eats

One of the best reasons to go to Queen Village is to eat. Some of the city's best dining can be found here, much of it just off of or close to South Street. **Famous 4th Street Deli** (700 S. 4th St; tel: 922-3274), at 4th and Bainbridge, is a Philadelphia institution. Its black and white

tiled dining room is still ground zero for city politicos and heavy-hitters, although ownership changed hands in 2005. The new owner mercifully scrubbed down the restaurant (without changing any of its retro appeal) and upgraded the food from mediocre to much better classic Jewish deli fare.

Just across 4th Street, at the entrance to Fabric Row, you'll find **Southwark** (701 S. 4th St; tel: 238-1888), whose bar was named one of America's top 50 by *Esquire* magazine. The block of 3rd Street between South and Bainbridge has experimental, arty **Gayle** (617 S. 3rd St; tel: 922-3850) and small-plates haven **Ansill** (627 S. 3rd St; tel: 627-2485). Greek BYOB **Dmitri's** (795 S. 3rd St; tel: 625-0556) is a long-time favorite for locals.

While you're waiting for a table, you can grab a drink at the funky **New Wave Cafe** (784 S. 3rd St; tel: 922-8484) across the street.

Up at 6th and Bainbridge, the handsome **Beau Monde** (624 S. 6th St; tel: 592-0656) creperie is popular for those who brunch. ❑

*A colorful storefront brightens the South Street strip.*

# RESTAURANTS & BARS

## Restaurants

### Ansill

627 S. 3rd St. Tel: 627-2485. Open: D nightly, Sun brunch. $$

www.ansillfoodandwine.com

Sophisticated "small plates" for foodies – everything from bone marrow crostini to venison tartare. Wines are served by the glass, carafe, bottle – BYOB diehards can even bring their own for a reasonable corkage fee. There's a full bar as well.

### Beau Monde

624 S. 6th St. Tel: 592-0656. Open: L Tue-Fri, D Tues-Sun, Sat & Sun brunch. $$

www.creperie-beaumonde.com

This authentic Breton-style creperie, serving made-to-order savory and sweet crepes, is one of Philly's most charming restaurants. It's an especially popular spot for brunch, partially due to the draw of its potent, dill-spiked Bloody Mary. In warm weather, outdoor tables are highly coveted.

### Django

526 S. 4th St. Tel: 922-7151. Open: D Tues-Sun. $$

This place is often credited as both the genesis and finest expression of the chef-driven BYOB movement. Ownership has changed hands since it opened. Detractors say

the creative American cuisine has lost some of its edge; others insist it's just as good as ever.

### Dmitri's

795 S. 3rd St. Tel: 625-0556. Open: D nightly. $$

This beloved Greek stalwart is chugging along nicely, serving up simple and fresh Mediterranean favorites. Nearly everything comes from the grill in the open kitchen – from pita to feta. The octopus is a consistent crowd pleaser, as is the hummus. It's BYOB and the wait can be extremely long. Head to New Wave across the street for a drink while you wait.

### Downey's Restaurant

526 S. Front St. Tel: 625-9500. Open: L, D daily, Sun brunch. $$$

www.downeysrestaurant.com

Sit at tables overlooking the parade on South Street or enjoy Delaware River views from the top deck. The menu runs the gamut from steak, seafood and pasta to pub specialties like corned beef and cabbage, bangers and mash, and shepherd's pie.

### Famous 4th Street Deli

700 S. 4th St. Tel: 922-3274. Open: B, L, D daily. $-$$

Authentic Jewish deli fare, from the sensational house-made pastrami and corned beef to

the smorgasbord of smoked fish. Prices are high, but the portions, especially the sandwiches, are, as the menu says, "zaftig." Desserts are homemade and hefty. Try a slab of carrot cake or a black-and-white cookie.

### Gayle

617 S. 3rd St. Tel: 922-3850. Open: D Mon-Sat. $$$

www.gaylerestaurant.com

A tiny storefront coated with avocado green paint is the new stage for former Le Bec-Fin chef Daniel Stern, who turns out sophisticated contemporary fare with a sense of whimsy. Menu descriptions are often puzzling, but the servers are well informed. A well-pruned wine list and a full bar set this apart from the sea of BYOBs.

### Gianna's Grille

507 S. 6th St. Tel: 829-4448. Open: L, D Tues-Sun. $

www.giannasgrille.com

Even vegetarians aren't deprived of cheesesteaks in Philly; they head to this low-key pizza joint for a satisfying take on the city's official sandwich. Both vegans and vegetarians are easily accommodated here: the vegan desserts, baked by owner Babs Aguirre, are delicious and difficult to distinguish from the real thing.

### Jamaican Jerk Hut

1436 South St. Tel: 545-8644. Open: L Mon-Sat, daily. $-$$

Summertime is the best time to enjoy this easy-going spot, when it's possible to dine on the back porch, an inner city oasis overlooking a garden. The terrific Jamaican dishes can be eye-wateringly spicy, but there are delicious and tamer alternatives for the less adventurous. It's BYOB, so tote along a six-pack to quench those flames.

### Jim's Steaks

400 South St. Tel: 928-1911. Open: daily. $

www.jimssteaks.com

Aficionados will tell you that the best cheesesteak in town is not in South Philly but right here on South Street at the minimalist, black-and-white-tiled Jim's. The line can be long, snaking right out the door, but it moves quickly. Order it with "Whiz" (Cheez Whiz, that is) to experience the cheesesteak in its pure, unadulterated glory.

### Latest Dish

613 S. 4th St. Tel: 629-0565. Open: D daily. $$

www.latestdish.com

A laid-back spot just off the hustle and bustle of South Street that offers an eclectic menu –

everything from crab and cheese wontons to fish and chips – most of which is reliably good. While the Fluid nightclub is located just upstairs, the Dish often has its own DJs spinning funky tunes to dine by.

### Little Fish
600 Catharine St. Tel: 413-3464. Open: D Thur–Sun. $$
The dining room may be small, but the flavors are big at this tiny seafood BYOB. The menu varies depending on what's fresh that day, but it's always imaginatively prepared.

### Maoz Vegetarian
248 South St. Tel: 625-3500. Open: L, D daily. $
The South Street branch of the Dutch chain serves up first-rate falafel late into the night. Service can be surly, even when it's not packed. There's not much space to sit, so grab one of Maoz's signature stuffed pita sandwiches, garnish it at the fixin's bar and eat it on the go.

### Pink Rose Pastry Shop
630 S. 4th St. Tel: 800-767-3383. Open: B, L, D daily. $
www.pinkrosepastry.com
As adorable as a tea sandwich, this chintz-and-floral dessert shop is charmingly retro. Pop in for a homemade éclair, tart or cookie.

### Salt & Pepper
746 S. 6th St. Tel: 238-1920. Open: D Tues–Sun, Sun brunch. $$
This restaurant is as simple and basic as its moniker. It contains a scant 10 tables and a kitchen that's so open you feel more like you're dining in someone's house. The menu is brief, but the chefs are thoughtful in their use of seasonal and local ingredients. BYOB.

### Shouk
622 S. 6th St. Tel: 627-3344. Open: D Tues–Sun. $
Israeli mezza (small plates) are creatively prepared in this handsome, Middle Eastern-themed spot. Hummus gets a dose of ground beef, and chicken is marinated in pomegranate molasses. Head upstairs for a post-meal smoke at the intimate hookah salon.

### Southwark
701 S. 4th St. Tel: 238-1888. Open: D daily. $$
Named after a Philadelphia neighborhood, this smart corner bistro serves an eclectic menu, with everything from crab beignets and fondue to veal cheeks. It has, without a doubt, one of the city's handsomest bars and its most attentive, knowledgeable and cordial bartenders.

### Tamarind
117 South St. Tel: 925-2764. Open: D Tues–Sun. $$
This small, cozy family-run BYOB serves up tangy Thai dishes. The curries are especially tempting. There's a wide selection of vegetarian and seafood choices.

## Bars

### New Wave Cafe
784 S. 3rd St. Tel: 922-8484
www.newwavecafe.com
A neighborhood favorite that often serves as the de facto waiting room for nearby Dmitri's restaurant, although its tasty pub grub often convinces diners to forgo a table across the street. Lots of beers on tap, TVs so you don't miss the game and weekly Quizo nights keep the regular crowd coming back.

### O'Neal's
Third & South sts. Tel: 574-9495.
www.onealspub.com
Open to 2am, this Irish pub has nearly 20 beers on tap, plus a slew of microbrews and imports.

### L'Etage
624 S. 6th St., 2nd Fl. Tel: 592-0656.
www.creperiebeaumonde.com
The upstairs lounge of Beau Monde is as chic as a Parisian salon. Occasional burlesque performances and nightly DJs keep things interesting.

### PRICE CATEGORIES

Prices for three-course dinner per person with a half-bottle of house wine:
$ = under $25
$$ = $25–$40
$$$ = $40–$50
$$$ = more than $50

**RIGHT:** friends gather for drinks at Beau Monde, a French creperie just off South Street.

# WASHINGTON SQUARE

In this neighborhood of varied charms, you'll find historic houses, hip restaurants, an antiques district and the epicenter of Philadelphia's gay community

A placid patch of green shaded by sky-high walnut and sycamore trees, **Washington Square ❶** is the anchor of a mostly residential neighborhood known for fine historic houses, colorful shops, and a labyrinth of alleyways as well as being the hub of Philadelphia's gay community.

One of William Penn's original town plazas, Washington Square served as a potter's field during the American Revolution. The 5,000 British and American soldiers who were laid to rest here are memorialized by the **Tomb of the Unknown Soldier**, where an inscription reads: "Liberty is a light for which many men have died in darkness." Later, during the tragic yellow fever epidemic of 1793, hundreds of victims were interred in the square in unmarked graves.

By the middle of the 1800s, Washington Square had become a high-class residential neighborhood. A few of the fine homes still stand on Washington Square West and Walnut Street, although most are now occupied by businesses.

## Printing center

Some years later, the square became the center of Philadelphia's prestigious publishing industry. The massive **Curtis Center ❷** (6th and Walnut sts; tel: 238-6450; open Mon–Fri 9am–5pm, Sat 8am–5pm; entrance free), once the headquarters of the *Ladies' Home Journal* and *Saturday Evening Post*, still dominates the northeast corner of the square and is the home of the publishing house W.B. Saunders, an original tenant. Inside the lobby you can see **The Dream Garden**, an impressive 15 by 50-ft (4 by 14-meter), 260-color glass mosaic mural created in 1916 by Louis C. Tiffany Studios on the basis of a

**LEFT:** Pennsylvania Hospital was founded in 1751 by Benjamin Franklin and Dr. Thomas Bond.
**BELOW:** Antique Row.

**Center City West**

0 _____ 500 yds

0 _____ 500 m

N

painting by Maxfield Parrish. Lea and Febiger, the oldest publisher in the US, was once located in the palazzo on Washington Square South, now home to the **Locks Gallery** (600 Washington Square South; tel: 629-1000) and its collection of contemporary art.

The grand Renaissance-style palazzo on 6th Street is the **Athenaeum** ❸ (219 S. 6th St; tel: 925-2688; gallery open Mon–Fri 9am–5pm; entrance free; tours and research by appointment), a member-supported library built in 1845 and one of the country's foremost repositories of architecture and design documents. Filled with antique art and furnishings, the building looks much as it did 100 years ago, when bibliophiles came here to read, study and chat with other members. A changing exhibit is displayed on the first floor.

The Colonial-style reconstruction next door to the Athenaeum was the residence of the late Mayor Richardson Dilworth, a Democratic reformer described by a colleague as "D'Artagnan in long pants and a double-breasted suit." The **Penn**

**Mutual Building**, at Walnut and 6th streets, is a rambling, classically oriented composition with a towering glass-and-concrete addition. (Note the original Egyptian Revival facade of the old Pennsylvania Insurance Company still standing on Walnut Street.) The Italianate bank standing directly across the square was built for the Philadelphia Savings Fund Society in 1869.

## North of the Square

With jewelry stores of every type, **Jewelers Row** ❹, between 7th and 9th streets north of Walnut, has been Philadelphia's diamond district since 1851.

The austere-looking **Atwater Kent Museum of Philadelphia** ❺ (15 S. 7th St; tel: 685-4830; open Wed–Sun 1–5pm, first Friday of the month 5–8pm) interprets the history of Philadelphia from its Quaker roots to the present with exhibits of household objects and other materials used by local citizens through the years. A children's wing displays toys, dolls and games. Fans of Norman Rockwell will be attracted by

Map
on page
102

*Small quirky shops are found throughout the neighborhood.*

**BELOW:** the Tomb of the Unknown Soldier memorializes thousands of American and British soldiers buried in unmarked graves in Washington Square.

the museum's varied collection of *Saturday Evening Post* covers and posters by the celebrated artist who captured so much of the homely nature of American life.

Across the street from the Atwater Kent Museum, the **Graff (Declaration) House** ❻ (7th and Market sts; open daily 9am–noon, but hours vary – for exact times, call the Park Service, tel: 597-8794, www.npr/gov/inde; entrance free) is a reconstruction of the house where Thomas Jefferson wrote the Declaration of Independence. When Jefferson rented the upstairs parlor in 1776, the house, built and owned by bricklayer Joseph Graff, was located on the quiet outskirts of town. A short film is shown on the first floor, while Jefferson's rooms are re-created on the second.

### Footlights and fanfare

A quick walk west on Walnut Street brings you to two theaters. The **Walnut Street Theatre** ❼ (825 Walnut St; tel: 574-3550) is the oldest continuously used theater in the US. Before Broadway stole the show,

thespians such as Edwin Forrest, Edwin Booth, Sarah Bernhardt and Ethel Barrymore regularly walked the boards at this venerable hall, now fully modernized. These days the Walnut Street Company keeps busy with a series of dramas, musicals and Shakespeare on its main stage and smaller, contemporary or experimental work in its studio.

Farther along Walnut, the **Forrest Theatre** ❽ (1114 Walnut St; tel: 923-1515) packs in the crowds with big-time touring Broadway shows such as *Phantom of the Opera* and *Les Misérables*. The Forrest is named after stage idol Edwin Forrest, a Philadelphian whose passionate style and fiery disposition made him a national sensation.

It's difficult to imagine just how popular Forrest was in his day. When he was panned by London critics, for example, his fans in Philadelphia retaliated by pelting a rival British actor, William Macready, with rotten eggs and tomatoes. When Macready later appeared in New York City, Forrest partisans stormed the theater, sparking a riot that killed 22 people

in the blackest moment in American stage history.

Return to 8th Street and walk south for a look at some of the neighborhood's architectural landmarks. The townhouse at No. 225 South 8th Street is **Morris House**, built in 1786 when this area was still on the outskirts of town. The large fanlight over the door, heavy cornices, and black-and-red brickwork – known as Flemish bond – are hallmarks of the late Georgian style.

The **Musical Fund Hall**, just around the corner on Locust Street, was designed by Philadelphia architect William Strickland in the 1820s. In its brief career as the city's principal concert hall, it sponsored engagements by Charles Dickens, William Makepeace Thackeray, singer Jenny Lind and many other artists. In 1856, it hosted the first Republican National Convention, only two years after the formation of the party. The nominee, John C. Fremont, lost to James Buchanan in the general election. The building has since been converted into condominiums.

A block south, at 8th and Spruce streets, **St George's Greek Orthodox Church** ❾ (open for worship) is housed in a Greek Revival structure originally designed for an Episcopal congregation by the Philadelphia architect John Haviland, who is entombed beneath the church. The interior is a heady Byzantine transformation of the original conservative Episcopal style, replete with gold-foil iconography, ornate woodwork and glowing stained glass.

### Rest in peace

Walking east on **Spruce Street** ❿ will take you past two blocks of beautifully restored 19th-century houses. At least they look like houses. In fact, between 7th and 8th streets they are facades only, with a modern office building behind.

**Holy Trinity Roman Catholic Church**, erected by German immigrants in 1789, stands at 6th and Spruce streets. The church's small cemetery contains the graves of Acadian (French-Canadian) refugees who were kicked out of Nova Scotia by the English in 1755 and eventu-

*"I like this Philadelphia amazingly, and the people in it."*
—Mark Twain

**LEFT:** a saxman serenades passersby.

### First in Flight

It's not widely known, but aviation history was made a long time before the Wright brothers got off the ground at Kitty Hawk in 1903. First to penetrate the American skies was a 42-year-old Frenchman named Jean Pierre Blanchard, who lifted off in his hot-air balloon in Philadelphia in 1793.

Dressed in blue knee breeches and plumed hat, and accompanied by a small black dog, the short-statured Blanchard launched his yellow silk balloon from a yard inside the Walnut Street Prison near present-day Washington Square. Brisk winds carried the hydrogen-filled gas projectile southeasterly across the Delaware River to New Jersey, where Blanchard steered it to a safe landing 46 minutes later in a field near the village of Woodbury.

This was the first aerial voyage in the New World. Just before lift-off, Blanchard received a send-off from the young nation's most distinguished citizen, President George Washington. The one-time Revolutionary War commander-in-chief stepped from the carriage that brought him to the prison yard, walked over and shook Blanchard's hand, and wished the intrepid adventurer a bon voyage.

The striking mural at 13th and Locust streets (across from the Historical Society of Pennsylvania) is one of the dozens of art works created by the Mural Arts Program, which employs some 300 artists every year.

**BELOW:** a flower shop brightens a street corner.
**RIGHT:** Camac Street is one of the many alleys that crisscross the neighborhood.

ally found refuge in Philadelphia.

To the west on Spruce Street, between 8th and 9th streets, is tiny **Mikveh Israel Cemetery** ⓫ (tel: 922-5446 for visiting information), consecrated in 1740 and one of America's oldest Jewish cemeteries.

The congregation now has its synagogue at 44 North 4th Street on Independence Mall East, sharing a building with the National Museum of American Jewish History. Haym Salomon, an exiled Polish Jew who helped finance the American Revolution, is buried here, as is Nathan Levy, whose ship, the *Myrtilla*, transported the Liberty Bell from England.

The cemetery's most celebrated occupant is Rebecca Gratz, a friend of Washington Irving and model for the character of Rebecca in Sir Walter Scott's popular novel *Ivanhoe*.

The handsome brick houses on the 900 block of Spruce Street – each with a marble portico at the entrance – are known as **Portico Row** ⓬ and were designed by the distinguished Philadelphia architect Thomas U. Walter.

## Into the alleys

You can begin to explore the neighborhood's cozy alleys farther along Spruce Street, past the weathered brownstones between 10th and 13th streets. Many of these alleys are tree-lined, with brick sidewalks and "streets" no wider than a large cart.

First try **Quince Street** ⓭, where the University of Pennsylvania's Mask & Wig Club (No. 310) – a bizarre yellow chateau – is tucked away amid tiny brick homes and ivy-covered cul-de-sacs. To the north of Spruce Street, Quince leads into the labyrinth of Sartain, Manning, Irving and Jessup streets. To the south, it cuts across Pine Street to a corridor of trim homes at Waverly Street and another at Addison Walk.

The maze of alleyways entered at **Camac Street** ⓮ (between 12th and 13th), dubbed the Avenue of the Artists, is even more complex, with side alleys branching off every few steps. According to the *WPA Guide to Philadelphia*, published in 1937, this sheltered byway was "the scene of brawls by day and crimes by night... lined with brothels and

taverns [and] rotted in a mire of debauchery."

Camac Street was also known for the many clubs, including the **Philadelphia Sketch Club** (235 Camac St; tel: 545-9298), which once counted artists N.C. Wyeth and Thomas Eakins among its members, and which presents shows in its gallery from time to time.

You can follow Panama Street to 13th Street, where the 1839-built **Church of St Luke and the Epiphany** (Pine and Spruce sts; tel: 732-1918; open by appointment) stands in Greek Revival splendor.

A short walk north brings you to the **Library Company of Philadelphia** ⑮ (1314 Locust St; tel: 546-3181; reading room and gallery open Mon–Fri 9am–4.45pm) and the **Historical Society of Pennsylvania and Balch Institute** (Locust St between 12th and 13th sts; tel: 732-6200; open Tues & Thur 12.30–5.30pm, Wed 12.30–8.30pm, Fri 10am–5.30pm; doors close 45 minutes earlier; entrance fee), which have complementary collections.

The Library Company, now a working research library, was founded in 1731 by Benjamin Franklin and was the first circulating library in America. Documenting US history through the printed word from the colonial period to about 1880, it also has a print department and collections on African-American and women's history. A modest gallery space showcases exhibits.

The Historical Society (HSP) offers resources for educators and researchers preserving and exploring the origins, diversity and development of Philadelphia, Pennsylvania, and the nation. In 2002 the Balch Institute for Ethnic Studies merged with the HSP, bringing with it a wealth of materials relating to immigrant and ethnic experiences.

## The "gayborhood"

You can wrap up this tour by walking two blocks south to **Pine Street**, known in this area as **Antique Row** ⑯. There are a couple of dozen antiques shops between 13th and 8th streets, not to mention a number of shops and boutiques specializing in jewelry, folk art and vintage clothing.

Map on page 102

*Antique Row encompasses five blocks of shops, boutiques and eateries.*

**BELOW:** Meg Saligman's *Philadelphia Muses*, at 12th and Locust streets, is one of many works produced by the Philadelphia Mural Arts Program.

Map on page 102

*A statue of William Penn stands outside Pennsylvania Hospital.*

**BELOW:** shopping on Antique Row.

**Giovanni's Room** (345 S. 12th St), a highly regarded bookstore specializing in gay, lesbian and feminist material, serves as the informal hub of the area's gay community. Dubbed the "gayborhood," the area encompasses a number of gay nightclubs and cafés, a gay community center and other gay-owned and gay-friendly businesses. For a list of the latest happenings, pick up a copy of the *Philadelphia Gay News* at a nearby newsstand or newspaper box.

A detour south on 10th Street brings you to the **Henry George School and Birthplace Museum** ⓱ (413 S. 10th St; tel: 922-4278; museum open by appointment), birthplace of the visionary economist whose *Progress and Poverty* was a bestseller in the 1880s. George believed that a "single tax" on land would narrow the gap between rich and poor. At the height of his single-tax movement, he nearly became mayor of New York City, running as the candidate of the United Labor Party. He died in 1897, just four days before the election. Although few people remember him these days, there are still faithful Georgists who feel that the self-educated economist's ideas are as valid now as 100 years ago. The school houses a modest museum of memorabilia and offers seminars.

## Franklin's hospital

Backtrack on 10th Street just north of Pine for a quick look at **Clinton Street**, one of the neighborhood's prettiest and most exclusive thoroughfares. The walled complex of buildings at Clinton and 9th streets is **Pennsylvania Hospital** ⓲ (entrance at 8th and Spruce sts; tel: 829-3971; Welcome Center open Mon–Fri 8.30am–5pm, guided tours of 10 or more by appointment with 2–4 weeks notice; entrance free).

The oldest hospital in the country, it was founded in 1751 by Benjamin Franklin and Dr. Thomas Bond. You can get a good look at the original buildings by walking along the iron fence on Pine Street and then entering through the 8th Street gate. The east wing was completed in 1775; the west wing and central pavilion – a masterpiece of Federal architecture – were finished about 30 years later.

The statue of William Penn was given to the hospital by Penn's grandson John, who found the piece in a London junkyard and had it shipped to Philadelphia. It's said that at the stroke of midnight on New Year's Eve, the statue steps off its pedestal for a stroll around the grounds. A tour of the hospital takes you through the historic medical library and surgical amphitheater where distinguished physicians such as Benjamin Rush, Philip Syng Physick and Caspar Wistar made breakthroughs in the healing arts.

The hospital's treasures include a collection of surgical instruments, a chair used by Penn, several Thomas Sully portraits, and Benjamin West's painting *Christ Healing the Sick in the Temple*. ❏

# RESTAURANTS & BARS

## Restaurants

### Bonte
922 Walnut St. Tel: 557-8510. Open: B, L, D daily. $
www.bontewaffles.com
Crisp street-style Belgian waffles made to order and coated with imported pearl sugar are the best reason to eat here, but salads and sandwiches are served as well.

### Capogiro Gelato Artisans
119 S. 13th St. Tel: 351-0900. Open: daily. $
www.capogirogelato.com
Fanatics wax poetic about the fabulous gelato and sorbetto at this stylish shop. The flavors change daily and incorporate local fruits, herbs and milk from a special herd of cows in Lancaster County.

### Deux Cheminées
1221 Locust St. Tel: 790-0200. Open: D Tues–Sat. $$$$
www.deuxchem.com
Housed in a historic Frank Furness-designed building, its old-world elegance makes this a special occasion throwback. Chef Fritz Blank's cookbook collection is as impressive as his cuisine.

### El Vez
121 S. 13th St. Tel: 928-9800. Open: L Mon–Sat, D nightly. $$
www.elvezrestaurant.com
Go for the margaritas, the colorfully kitschy décor (including a gold-plated low-rider) and the guacamole prepared tableside. Stay for the well-executed Mexican fare – and to sample the 30 premium tequilas.

### Jones
700 Chestnut St. Tel: 223-5663. Open: L & D daily, Sat & Sun brunch. $$
www.jones-restaurant.com
The groovy rec room vibe, complete with freestanding stone fireplace and American comfort foods like fried chicken with waffles, draw crowds, especially at brunch.

### Lolita
106 S. 13th St. Tel: 546-7100. Open: D nightly. $$
www.lolitabyob.com
Inventive Mexican fare with some unexpected twists. The goat cheese cheesecake is one of the finest desserts around. Bring your favorite tequila. The owners sell pitchers of margarita mix; the watermelon-mint variety is especially good.

### Morimoto
723 Chestnut St. Tel: 413-9070. Open: L Mon–Fri, D nightly. $$$–$$$$
www.morimotorestaurant.com
The Iron Chef's original outpost is worth a peek for its striking interior, complete with light-filled booths that change colors – and worth a stay for its exceptional sushi. Sit at the sushi bar for front row seats on the expert knife action.

### Vetri
1312 Spruce St. Tel: 732-3478. Open: Sept–May D Mon–Sat, June–Sept D Mon–Fri. $$$$
www.vetriristorante.com
James Beard award-winning chef Marc Vetri's dollhouse of a restaurant is consistently on "best of" lists for its ethereal upscale Italian. This is no red sauce joint. It has the excellent service, food and prices of what it is – a spectacular fine dining establishment.

## Bars

### Fergie's Pub
1214 Sansom St. Tel: 928-8118
An Irish pub known for its beer, its quixotic owner, Fergus McCarey, and its tough "quizo" contests.

### Las Vegas Lounge
704 Chestnut St. Tel: 592-9533
A colorful dive with "Swingers" kitsch and generous drink specials.

### PRICE CATEGORIES
Prices for three-course dinner per person with a half-bottle of house wine:
**$** = under $25
**$$** = $25–$40
**$$$** = $40–$50
**$$$** = more than $50

**RIGHT:** Morimoto's sleek, contemporary interior helps make it a popular dining spot.

# CITY HALL, AVENUE OF THE ARTS AND CONVENTION CENTER

**Business and pleasure coexist in the shadow of City Hall. In this busy neighborhood, you'll find a vibrant arts district, a bustling indoor market and a massive convention center, as well as Chinatown, shopping malls and Philadelphia's financial center**

They started working on it back in 1871, it took no less than 30 years to complete, and about halfway through the project somebody tagged it "the biggest and ugliest building in America." City Hall, at once monstrous and magnificent, sits squarely on the bull's-eye of downtown Philadelphia like an urban version of some inscrutable Egyptian pyramid, evoking ambivalent awe. Walt Whitman sized it up as "a magnificent pile ... weird, silent, beautiful," and the American Institute of Architecture later pronounced it "the greatest single effort of late 19th-century architecture."

Love it or hate it, you'll find it hard to ignore this endearing hangover from the gaudy age of architectural excess. It stands in the heart of center city, at the intersection of the two major thoroughfares of Broad and Market streets, former site of William Penn's 8-acre (3-hectare) Center Square. To the west is Philadelphia's business district, bristling with a fresh wave of glass-and-granite skyscrapers. To the east is a cavernous Convention Center and the city's largest shopping area. And to the north and south along Broad, the Avenue of the Arts is the home of world-class cultural institutions, including the oldest opera house and art school/museum in the United States.

## Heart of the city

Designed by John McArthur and Thomas U. Walter, and adorned with hundreds of sculptures by Alexander Milne Calder, Philadelphia's **City Hall ⑲** (Broad and Market sts, tour office in East Portal, room 121; tel: 686-2840; tower open Mon–Fri 9.30am–4.15pm for six people at a time, 2-hour tours, including tower, 12.30pm; entrance free) is the largest municipal building in the country. Its style is classified as Second Empire – reflecting,

Map on page 102

**LEFT:** the City Hall observation deck stands about 500 ft above street level. **BELOW:** Robert Indiana's *Philadelphia LOVE* at JFK Plaza.

*City Hall is adorned with about 250 allegorical statues. Around the west portal – originally designated the Prisoner's Entrance – are representations of Sympathy, Hope, Repentance and other themes intended by sculptor Alexander Milne Calder to instruct and comfort criminals being brought to trial.*

**RIGHT:**
City Council caucus room in City Hall.

perhaps, a sense of optimism that bespeaks the American romance with Victorian architecture in the latter part of the 19th century. Its massive granite walls are 22 ft (6 meters) thick at the base, and its central tower, the world's tallest masonry structure without steel reinforcement, rises 510 ft (145 meters) above street level. Calder's famous 27-ton statue of William Penn adds another 37 ft (10½ meters).

## To the top of the tower

The city has spent millions scrubbing decades of soot and grime from the building's exterior. Walk through any of the four entrances into the inner courtyard to get an idea of how truly elaborate the building is. Many of the splendid details – tiles, mosaics, caryatids and human figures – that decorate the building are visible from the ground level.

Until the 1980s, a gentlemen's agreement prevented the construction of any building whose height would exceed the top of William Penn's hat, but with the construction

of developer Willard G. Rouse's Liberty One in 1987, quickly followed by others, Philadelphia's skyline has grown over recent years to reflect its place as a contemporary city alive with change.

The observation deck atop City Hall Tower is just below William Penn's toes, and though it is no longer the highest point in the city, the panorama is still wonderful, giving a great sense of how Penn's city plan has evolved. To reach the observation deck, get a free ticket from room 121, take the elevator from the northwest corner (15th St and JFK Blvd) to the seventh floor, then follow the red lines. A second elevator takes you the rest of the way. But be prepared to wait. During peak season and weekends, it can take an hour or more before you get lifted into the heavens.

If you'd like a closer look at some of City Hall's splendid public rooms, take the free 90-minute tour. It includes, among other sights, Conservation Hall, the City Council Chambers, the Supreme Court and the Mayor's Reception Room.

## A Clean Slate

It is constructed of 88 million handmade bricks and thousands of tons of granite and marble, and encompasses 27 acres (11 hectares) of floor space divided into nearly 700 rooms. Little wonder that it's been under one type of renovation or another since 1984. The interminable scaffolding that has crept slowly around the building has become a familiar sight to Philadelphians, almost to the point where it's difficult to remember what City Hall looked like without it.

One thing that is definitely noticeable: it looks a heck of a lot cleaner. Thanks to the efforts of engineering, architecture and historic preservation firms, the grimy facade has been scrubbed to a pearly white. The color of the clock tower appears darker not because it's still dirty, but because it is not made of stone like the rest of the building but iron and steel. During renovations, much of the original cast iron had to be replaced with steel. The tower was then weatherproofed with a paint available in limited colors, thus the pale gray that doesn't match the rest of the building. The original building cost $24.5 million in the late 1800s; the renovations may end up costing upwards of $70 million when the work is complete, sometime in 2010.

## Two temples

The imposing medieval-style building to the north of City Hall is **Masonic Temple** ⑳ (1 N. Broad St; tel: 988-1916; tours Tue–Fri 11am, 2pm and 3pm, Sat 10am and 11pm except Jul–Aug; entrance free). This is the headquarters of the Grand Lodge of Free and Accepted Masons of Pennsylvania and one of the most spectacular Masonic structures in the world. Designed in 1868 by 27-year-old James Windrim, the building is a monumental patchwork of architectural styles.

A free tour guides the visitor through seven lavishly decorated lodge halls, each reflecting a major architectural style – Oriental, Gothic, Ionic, Egyptian, Norman, Renaissance and Corinthian. The scale of the place is dazzling, the workmanship masterful, and the Masons' predilection for arcane symbols is evident throughout the building. Oriental Hall is an almost exact replica of the Alhambra in Spain, while Egyptian Hall contains hieroglyphs so accurate that visiting Egyptologists have

claimed to be able to translate them. Also remarkable is the abundance of plasterwork, much of it ingeniously disguised to look like wood or marble. For example, what appears to be elaborately carved wood in the Norman room is actually plaster painted with turkey feathers to accurately replicate a wood grain surface.

The tour ends at the Masonic Museum, which features all sorts of paraphernalia, much of it originally owned by prominent Masons such as the Marquis de Lafayette, Andrew Jackson, Ben Franklin and George Washington.

Walk north on Broad Street past the Gothic spires of the Arch Street Methodist Church, erected in 1865, to the **Pennsylvania Academy of the Fine Arts** ㉑ (118 N. Broad St; tel: 972-7600; open Tue–Sat 10am–5pm, Sun 11am–5pm; entrance fee), the oldest art school and museum in the country. Frank Furness' Victorian tour de force is as much a work of art as the paintings it contains. Highly eclectic and idiosyncratic, this building is a fine example of the

*A Mummer struts down Broad Street during the New Year's Day parade.*

**BELOW:**
Pennsylvania Academy of the Fine Arts.

**TIP**

Although best known for 18th- and 19th-century American works, the Pennsylvania Academy of the Fine Arts also has an impressive collection of 20th-century modernists, including works by Georgia O'Keeffe, Stuart Davis, Charles Demuth and Marsden Hartley.

**BELOW:**
Zanzibar Blue has live music nightly.

stylistic mix-and-match that became Furness' hallmark. The interior is a riotous counterpoint of deep-blue ceilings, red-veined marble floors, Moorish arcades, gilt accents and purplish walls with a gold floral pattern. You might expect the building to overpower the art, but it doesn't. The Pennsylvania Academy is fortunate to own one of the strongest collections of early American art in the country.

Exhibitions change regularly, but you're more than likely to find works by Charles Willson Peale, Benjamin West, Gilbert Stuart, Washington Allston, Mary Cassatt, Winslow Homer, Andrew Wyeth and the Academy's most celebrated student and teacher, Thomas Eakins, who was dismissed from the faculty for his insistence on using female nude models in a class that included women. The Academy also shows contemporary work, much of it by students or faculty members, particularly in the first-floor Morris Gallery. Call ahead for details on gallery talks, receptions and daily tours.

## South on Broad

Retrace your steps to City Hall, looping around 15th Street for a look at downtown's best-known (if not best-loved) public sculptures, including Joseph Brown's *Benjamin Franklin, Craftsman,* Jacques Lipchitz's *Government of the People,* Claes Oldenburg's colossal *Clothespin,* and Robert Engman's pretzel-like *Triune.* Much of the artwork here is a product of Philadelphia's one percent rule, which earmarks a percentage of development costs for public art.

Heading south on Broad Street, you'll pass the domed and gleaming white neoclassical **Ritz-Carlton** ㉒ (10 Ave of the Arts; tel: 735-7700), formerly the Girard Trust Company and later Mellon Bank. Built between 1905 and 1908, it is a loose adaptation of Rome's Parthenon, designed by Stanford White and Frank Furness. Take a look into the luxurious lobby, where giant columns loom like redwood trees, and the central rotunda looks down (through a glittering chandelier) on the ballroom below. Ask at the desk about the availability of tours.

The **Land Title Building**, an early skyscraper built in 1897, is on the next corner. And the **Union League** (1865) – a private club organized by well-to-do patriots during the Civil War – is housed in a Second Empire brownstone mansion with a sweeping double staircase at the corner of Sansom Street.

At the corner of Walnut Street, anchoring the Rittenhouse Row shopping district, the venerable old Bellevue-Stratford Hotel has been reborn as the **Park Hyatt at the Bellevue ㉓**. The ground floor is now devoted to luxury retail space, where upscale stores like Williams-Sonoma, Polo Ralph Lauren and Tiffany & Co. do business in marble and mahogany digs. The hotel also accommodates several fine restaurants, including a branch of **The Palm** steakhouse (200 S. Broad St; tel: 546-7256), where high-powered politicos can usually be found schmoozing and boozing. **XIX (Nineteen)** (200 S. Broad St; tel: 790-1919), the restaurant and lounge on the top floor offers wonderful views of the skyline, while **Zanz-ibar Blue** (200 S. Broad St; tel: 732-4500), a sublevel supper club, is one of the city's top jazz spots. Visit the restored lobby to see the Gilded Age mosaics, then head up the winding staircase to a massive two-tiered ballroom with Tiffany stained glass and light fixtures designed by Thomas Edison, still the venue of choice for the city's elite.

## Avenue of the Arts

Jazz is just one of the musical forms you'll hear on Broad Street, recently tagged the "Avenue of the Arts." The proliferation of theaters and other performance venues, particularly south of City Hall, has been intense. One of the most interesting is the **Prince Music Theater** (1412 Chestnut St; tel: 569-9700), specializing in new and innovative music and drama, just west of the avenue on Chestnut.

At the corner of Locust and Broad is the **Academy of Music ㉔** (232–46 Broad St; tel: 893-1999 box office/ 893-1935 for one-hour tour information and reservations). Sometimes referred to as the Grand

Map on page 102

*Claes Oldenburg's oversized* Clothespin *stands in City Hall Plaza.*

**BELOW:**
Academy of Music.

*In 2006 the Kimmel Center inaugurated the Fred J. Cooper Memorial Organ – the largest concert hall organ in the United States. The instrument has nearly 7,000 pipes and weighs about 32 tons. The largest pipe is 32 ft (10 meters) long; the smallest is the size of a pencil.*

**BELOW:** Verizon Hall at the Kimmel Center for the Performing Arts seats 2,500.

Old Lady of Broad Street, the Academy opened in 1857 and is the oldest music hall in the US still in use. Designed by Napoleon Le Brun and Gustave Runge, and renowned for its fine acoustics, the Academy has welcomed a host of illustrious speakers and musicians, among them Abraham Lincoln, Tchaikovsky, and conductors of the Philadelphia Orchestra, including Leopold Stokowski, Eugene Ormandy, Riccardo Muti and Wolfgang Sawallisch.

Next door, the **Merriam Theater** (250 S. Broad St; tel: 732-5446), formerly the Shubert Theater, features Broadway blockbusters and is home to the Pennsylvania Ballet. Also on this block is Philadelphia International Records, birthplace of the soulful Sound of Philadelphia in the 1960s and 70s. On the sidewalk is a mini "walk of fame" dedicated to hometown musical heroes like DJ Jazzy Jeff and jazzman Pat Martino. Across Broad Street, the **Wilma Theater** (265 S. Broad St; tel: 546-7824; www.wilmatheater.org) presents innovative contemporary theater in a splashy new venue.

## New kid on the block

Described by the *Philadelphia Inquirer* as "a world-class arts center … for a world-class city," the **Kimmel Center for the Performing Arts** ㉕ (260 S. Broad St; tel: 893-1999; www.kimmelcenter.org) opened to rave reviews in December 2001. Designed by architect Rafael Viñoly, the Kimmel Center's soaring glass dome encompasses the cello-shaped, 2,500-seat Verizon Concert Hall for the Philadelphia Orchestra as well as the 650-seat Perelman Recital Hall, home to the Chamber Orchestra of Philadelphia and numerous other companies. Whether you attend a performance or not, stop in for a stroll through the expansive atrium plaza and rooftop garden. A free, hour-long tour is offered at 1pm Tuesday to Sunday; make reservations at the information desk.

The curious neoclassical building at the corner of Broad and Pine is the **University of the Arts**, a visual and performing arts school. The building was originally designed by architect John Haviland in 1824 as

the Pennsylvania Institute for the Deaf and Dumb and has later additions by William Strickland and Frank Furness. The school shows work by students and guest artists in the main hall and at the Rosenwald-Wolf and Mednick galleries across the street. Across Pine Street is the future site of the **Suzanne Roberts Theater**, new home of the Philadelphia Theatre Company, which has outgrown its digs in the historic but tiny Plays and Players Theater near Rittenhouse Square.

Farther south on Broad Street, the **Philadelphia Clef Club for Jazz and the Performing Arts** (736–8 S. Broad St; tel: 893-9912) is dedicated to jazz education. The **Brandywine Workshop** (730 S. Broad St; tel: 546-3675) shows the work of printmakers and graphic artists in a former firehouse. The **Philadelphia High School for Creative and Performing Arts** occupies the former Ridgway Library, a stately temple that stood empty for decades. The **Rock School for Dance Education** is a training center affiliated with the Pennsylvania Ballet.

## Corporate muscle

Big changes have been made in the business district west of City Hall, too. A fresh crop of office towers on Market Street has pumped new vigor into an area that hasn't seen much action since the early 1960s. The twin towers of I.M. Pei's Commerce Square at 20th and Market streets and the granite-and-glass towers of both the Mellon Bank Center and 1919 Market Street are among the most conspicuous additions to the skyline. But the real headturner in this area is **Liberty Place** ㉖ (17th and Market sts), a pair of glass-plated towers (Liberty One and Liberty Two) reminiscent of New York City's Chrysler Building.

The two-level shopping arcade at Two Liberty Place (entrance at 16th and Chestnut sts) is a glossy addition to the neighborhood, with lots of marble tiles, brass trim and a sunlit central rotunda, as well as an upstairs food court with a vast array of choices for a quick lunch. The shops and eateries are predictably trendy.

Unfortunately, security concerns mean that you can no longer visit the

Map on page 102

**TIP**

The interior of the Academy of Music is modeled after La Scala in Milan. The Academy is home to the Opera Company of Philadelphia.

**LEFT:** center city architecture ranges from traditional to modern.

## No Love for Skateboarders

About a block and a half from City Hall is JFK Plaza, better known as LOVE Park after Robert Indiana's famous word-sculpture *Philadelphia LOVE*. To skateboarders around the world, however, LOVE Park is famous as one of the top skateboarding destinations in the United States. That is, at least, until a skateboarding ban was passed in 2000 (but not enforced until 2003), much to the dismay of skaters who traveled to Philadelphia for the sole purpose of skating the legendary park.

ESPN, which had hosted its X Games extreme sports tournament in Philadelphia two years in a row, pulled out after the ban. Critics called the ban shortsighted, as the park was a draw to the young tourists and residents whom the city was desperately trying to attract. Even legendary city planner Edmund Bacon, who originally conceived of the park, and architect Vincent Kling, who designed it, attended a demonstration in support of skateboarding.

Despite periodic protests (some of which have degenerated into scuffles with police), the skateboarding ban remains in effect and is vigorously enforced. The city has announced plans to build a new skateboard park near the Art Museum, but for diehard skateboarders only LOVE Park will do.

**BELOW:**
open-air arts festival on Broad Street.

**Philadelphia Stock Exchange** (1900 Market St; tel: 496-5000) two blocks away. Dating from 1790, this is the oldest stock exchange in the US. The trading floor is built around an eight-story atrium that contains a small "forest" complete with waterfalls, fountains and thousands of plants.

## Market East

To the east of City Hall, Market Street used to be dominated by discount shops and department stores, reflecting, perhaps, its early history as the locus of city shopping. As development moved westward towards the center of the city, large departments stores opened.

The granddaddy of all department stores was the former John Wanamaker, now **Macy's** ❷ (13th and Market sts), a Philadelphia institution since the 1870s, when department store pioneer John Wanamaker (the first merchant to introduce the use of price tags) moved his dry-goods shop into the old Pennsylvania Railroad depot. The current building was completed in 1911 and features a magnificent five-story

Grand Court where Wanamaker's old mascot, a giant bronze eagle, keeps an eye on shoppers. The airy Grand Court is the site of spectacular Christmas light shows and a great place to stroll during the daily organ concerts (except Sunday), performed on a 30,000-pipe organ – said to be the largest in the world, and maintained by two full-time curators.

**St John the Evangelist Catholic Church** (13th St between Market and Chestnut sts; tel: 563-4145; open Mon–Fri 9am–5pm) is located around the corner on 13th Street. Built in 1832, it served as Philadelphia's Roman Catholic cathedral before completion of the Cathedral of Saints Peter and Paul .

Since the arrival of the Pennsylvania Convention Center, east Market Street has continued to change dramatically, including the opening of several hotels and a Hard Rock Café on the corner of 12th and Market streets adjacent to the Convention Center. The **PSFS Building** at 12th and Market – now the home of Loews Philadelphia Hotel (1200 Market St, tel: 627-1200), built

between 1930 and 1932 and long known for its giant neon sign, was the first American skyscraper to be built in the International style, the forerunner of the glass-skinned monoliths that sprang up in the country in the 1950s and 1960s.

## Convention Center district

The **Pennsylvania Convention Center 28** (Visitor Services at the Convention Center, tel: 418-4735 for free tours of its contemporary art collection, by appointment only), a 1.3 million-sq-ft (121,000-sq-meter) facility hosting major exhibition shows and events, runs along Arch Street from 11th to 13th streets, with its main entrance at 12th and Arch. There is also a grand entrance on Market Street, where the head house for the Reading Terminal Railroad used to be. Inside the center an escalator leads up into the cavernous Grand Hall, which was formerly the railroad's train shed. As enormous as the Convention Center is, it's about to get bigger. The state has granted funding for an expansion that will double its size. The expansion is

expected to be completed by 2009.

The Convention Center passes over **Reading Terminal Market 29** (12th and Arch sts; tel: 922-2317; open Mon–Sat 8am–6pm; Pennsylvania Dutch Merchants open Wed 8am–3pm, Thu–Sat 8am–5pm), a boisterous food bazaar that has existed in one form or another for more than 100 years. Today, vendors offer a bewildering array of everything from sushi to scrapple, bok choi to baklava. In addition to fresh produce, meats and seafood, you'll find a slew of Philadelphia specialties: chocolate-chip cookies from the Famous 4th Street Cookie Co., Rick's Philly Steaks, related to the original Pat's King of Steaks, Bassetts' ice cream and the Termini Brothers' Italian pastries – not to mention hearty meats, sweets and baked goods brought to Philadelphia by members of the Pennsylvania Dutch community.

And that's only the beginning. In the mood for seafood? Try Pearl's Oyster Bar. Fancy a blue-corn enchilada? Have a bite at the 12th Street Cantina. How about an ice-

Map on page 102

*The Wanamaker Organ is the first pipe organ to be designated a National Historic Landmark.*

**BELOW:** Amish vendors at Reading Terminal Market.

Map on page 102

**TIP**

For an off-the-beaten-path treat, follow alley-like Juniper Street south from Macy's to hidden Drury Lane and McGillin's Olde Ale House, the oldest tavern in Philadelphia, in continuous operation since 1860. This workingman's bar has a longtime tradition of serving free soup, so it's a good spot to visit if you're on a tight budget.

**BELOW:** Chinese Friendship Gate.

cold brew at the Beer Garden? Rib-sticking Southern cuisine at the Down Home Diner? Scrapple and eggs at the Dutch Eating Place? And be sure to save enough room for one of Fisher's famous pretzels.

Having satiated yourself, shopping is next on the agenda at **The Gallery ⓿** (entrance on 9th and Market sts; tel: 625-4962; open Mon–Sat 10am–7pm, Wed and Fri to 8pm, Sun noon–5pm), a four-block mall stretching from 12th to 8th streets with three major department stores and some 200 shops and restaurants in an airy, skylit atrium.

Between 8th and 7th streets, the old Lit Brothers Department Store – a beautiful white cast-iron structure – has been transformed into **Market Place East**, a mixed-use complex of shops, restaurants and offices. You'll find even more shopping opportunities a block away on Chestnut Street.

### Chinatown

If you're still hungry, drift over to **Chinatown**, where about 45 restaurants are packed between 9th and 11th streets on one side, and Vine and Arch streets on the other. Nearly all are Chinese, of course, but there are also excellent Vietnamese, Thai and Malaysian places, and most are reasonably priced. Gift shops and grocery stores carry a bonanza of exotic Asian goodies. You can stock up on fortune cookies at the Chinese Cookie Factory (155 N. 9th St; tel: 922-7288), Chinese pastries at K.C.'s Pastries (109 N. 10th St and 145 N. 11th St; tel: 351-1177), Chinese noodles at any number of cafés, or traditional Chinese herbs, teas and medicines at the Long Life Herb Store (1011 Arch St; 625-9302).

While you're in the neighborhood, be sure to see the 40-ft (11-meter) **Chinese Friendship Gate ⓿** at 10th and Arch streets, built by craftsmen in 1984 as a sign of friendship between Philadelphia and Tianjin. The **Chinese Cultural and Community Center** (125 N. 10th St; tel: 923-6767) is modeled after a Mandarin palace and is the site of a traditional 10-course banquet in celebration of the Chinese New Year.

### The black experience

Just east of Chinatown is the first major museum devoted exclusively to African-American culture, the **African-American Museum in Philadelphia ⓿** (701 Arch St; tel: 574-0380; open Tue–Sat 10am–5pm, Sun noon–5pm; entrance fee). Exhibits explore the African-American experience and influence in American life, including the arts, architecture, sports, politics, religion, technology and medicine.

Previous shows have chronicled the history of the slave trade, migration of African-American families to various Philadelphia neighborhoods, and the role of Philadelphia's black community in the Civil Rights movement. A comprehensive program of events includes art workshops, storytelling, films, lectures and musical performances. ❏

# Colonial Landlord

L ike some benevolent padrone, William Penn has perched serenely atop City Hall since 1894, overseeing the real estate he acquired in 1681 from Charles II in satisfaction of a debt the king owed Penn's father. But if this statue – 37 ft (11 meters) tall and 547 ft (165 meters) above street level – strikes the visitor as precarious, it is an apt impression: Penn's grip on Philadelphia was never too firm. Who owned what, how the place was to be governed, theological hairsplitting that pitted Quaker against Anglican and Quaker against Quaker – it was at times an unbrotherly stew that mired the affairs of the Founder, who didn't spend all that much time here anyway.

Turmoil was nothing new to Penn. He lived through civil strife and regicide, fire and plague. Born in 1644 in London, he was sufficiently nonconformist (after embracing Quakerism, he was expelled from Oxford) for Admiral Penn to dispatch his upstart son on a Continental tour. But Quakerism stuck with Penn, providing the touchstone for his utopian designs on Pennsylvania.

A religious liberal, Penn preached and pamphleteered and got into familial and civil hot water. Confined to the Tower of London for a spell, he churned out more tracts in prison. In 1672, he married Gulielma Maria Springett, who was pregnant eight times in their first 13 years of marriage. She died in Penn's arms in 1694. Two years later he married another Quaker, 24-year-old Hannah Callowhill, begetting seven children by her.

Penn first visited his colony in 1682, just after his 38th birthday. He had promoted it so well that a couple of thousand settlers were already on hand to greet him. Penn named Philadelphia and shaped its block pattern along orderly grid lines, made land deals with the Indians and went back to England in 1684. He returned for his second, and final, visit 15 years later.

Although remembered for his tolerant leanings, Penn had his complexities. The free-holding aspirations of his settlers clashed with his own seigneurial impulse. Although he insisted on fair-dealing with Indians, he regarded them as little more than noble savages. While Quakers were among the earliest to denounce slavery, Penn himself was a slaveholder. Yet Penn's "holy experiment" laid the foundation for America's first melting pot, predating by nearly a century Jefferson's declaration that "all men are created equal" and laying the foundation for a society in which all citizens are free to worship as their conscience dictates.

From the very beginning, however, Penn was vexed by changing political and economic fortunes. Mired in debt, he considered selling the colony back to the British crown in 1712 for less than its original value, but the deal was dropped when he suffered a stroke. It would take another 64 years and a revolution to bring an end to the Penn arrangement.

The statue atop City Hall, crafted by Scottish-born Alexander Milne Calder, adorns a French Renaissance-style building presided over by a succession of Americans tending the affairs of a polyglot community. The city is the legacy of a man who took his final leave of it in 1701. In all, Penn had spent less than four years in Pennsylvania, but his influence is felt to the present day. ❑

**RIGHT:** a young William Penn, already a fervent Quaker and reformer.

# RESTAURANTS & BARS

## Restaurants

### Bliss

220-224 S. Broad St. Tel: 731-1100. Open: L Mon–Fri, D Mon–Sat. $$$–$$$$
www.bliss-restaurant.com
A breezy California aesthetic and chef Francesco Martorella's sophisticated, Asian-accented fare make this spot popular with crowds heading to shows at the nearby Kimmel Center or the Academy of Music.

### The Capital Grille

1338 Chestnut St. Tel: 545-9855. Open: L Mon–Fri, D nightly. $$$$
The local branch of this steakhouse chain is awash in politicos during lunch due to its proximity to City Hall.

Even if you're not a major wheeler-dealer, the servers are well-trained, the wine list expansive and the steaks substantial.

### Cherry Street Vegetarian

1010 Cherry St. Tel: 923-3663. Open: L & D daily. $–$$
Mock meat, a kosher menu and Chinese food all rolled into one hole-in-the-wall. There's something on the menu for every non-meat eater.

### Happy Rooster

118 S. 16th St. Tel: 963-9311. Open: L & D Mon–Sat. $$$
www.happyrooster.com
It's easy to miss the Rooster and that might be the point. This dimly lit corner bar, filled with rooster bric-a-brac, is

something of a clubhouse for its regulars. Booths are not easy to come by, but the basic bistro food tastes just as good at the bar. Thursday night karaoke is popular.

### Ly Michael's

101 N. 11th St. Tel: 922-2688. Open: L & D daily. $$–$$$
www.lymichaels.com
It's possible to get everything from kung pao chicken to prosciutto-wrapped pork at this polished fusion spot near the Convention Center.

### Nan Zhou Hand Drawn Noodle House

927 Race St. Tel: 923-1550. Open L & D daily. $
What it lacks in décor, this bare-bones shop makes up for in inexpensive and satisfying noodle dishes and soups. Watch the noodles being prepared in the back; it's impressive to see the chef stretch, twist and slap them into shape.

### Palm

Bellevue Hotel, 200 S. Broad St. Tel: 546-7256. Open: L Mon–Fri, D daily. $$$–$$$$
www.thepalm.com
Many of Philly's movers and shakers make the scene at this clubby steakhouse chain; the really important ones end up with a caricature on the wall. The bar was

recently renovated for optimum schmoozing.

### ¡Pasion!

211 S. 15th St. Tel: 875-9895. Open: D nightly. $$$
www.pasionrestaurant.com
While the Nuevo Latino menu receives raves, it's the ceviche that has made chef and cookbook author Guillermo Pernot's restaurant a destination. Sample several different types in a ceviche tasting.

### Rangoon

112 N. 9th St. Tel: 829-8939. Open: L & D daily. $–$$
Philly's only Burmese restaurant is a Chinatown favorite. The "thousand layer bread" is a real crowd-pleaser, as are the sweetly accommodating servers.

### Reading Terminal Market

12th & Arch sts. Tel: 922-2317. Open: Mon–Sat 8am–6pm. $
www.readingterminalmarket.org
There is a wondrous range of options for intrepid eaters at this historic market, from roast pork sandwiches to pad Thai. If you're planning on trying anything from the Pennsylvania Dutch, make sure to visit Wednesday to Saturday when they're on site. It can be crowded during lunch and especially during conventions; the Convention Center is across the street.

### Saint Honore Pastries

935 Race St. Tel: 925-5298.
Open daily. $
Bubble teas, dainty
desserts and meat-
stuffed pastries are good
for a quick, satisfying bite
while touring Chinatown.

### Sang Kee Peking Duck House

238 N. 9th St. Tel: 925-7532.
Open L & D daily. $–$$
It's not much to look at,
but the food is reliably
delicious at this China-
town stalwart. Try the
signature duck or
dumplings. There's a
second outpost in Read-
ing Terminal Market.

### Sansom Street Oyster House

1516 Sansom St. Tel: 567-
7683. Open L Mon–Sat, D
nightly. $$–$$$.
www.sansomoysters.com
If you crave shellfish, this
seafood spot has it to
spare. The raw bar over-
flows with a multitude of
freshly shucked oysters
flown in from far and
wide. Solid fish-house
fare has kept them in
business since 1947.

### Shiroi Hana

222 S. 15th St. Tel: 735-
4444. Open: L Mon–Fri, D
nightly. $$
High-quality sushi and
other Japanese special-
ties have won this serene
spot a loyal following. An
upstairs sake bar is open
Thursday to Saturday.

### Vietnam

221 N. 11th St. Tel: 592-
1163. Open: L & D daily. $$
www.eatatvietnam.com
A favorite of chefs, locals
and suburbanites, it's
hard to find anyone who
doesn't like Benny Lai's
busy, casually elegant
spot. The Vietnamese cui-
sine is flavorful and a bargain. Go on Friday or
Saturday when Bar
Saigon, the upstairs
lounge, is open, and sam-
ple zany tropical drinks
like the Suffering Bastard.
And don't confuse it with
the similarly named
eatery across the street.

### Zanzibar Blue

The Bellevue, 200 S. Broad
St. Tel: 732-4500. Open: D
nightly, Sun brunch. $$–$$$
www.zanzibarblue.com
Sophisticated and sleek,
this restaurant and
lounge in the Bellevue
Hotel is the place for jazz
fans to catch stars like
Pat Martino and Arturo
Sandoval. There's live
music 7 nights a week to
go along with the eclectic
menu, which is influ-
enced by everything from
bistro fare to soul food.

### Bars

### Chris's Jazz Cafe

1421 Sansom St. Tel: 568-
3131.
www.chrisjazzcafe.com
A favorite with jazzheads
and beboppers for its
intimate, smoky scene.

### Good Dog

224 S. 15th St. Tel: 985-9600.
www.gooddogbar.com
Great pub grub and an
old-time atmosphere
draw in a continuous
crowd, from nine-to-fivers
letting off steam after a
hard day at work to
restaurant workers relax-
ing after a hard night.

### Ludwig's Garten

1315 Sansom St. Tel: 985-
1525.
www.ludwigsgarten.com
Beer is the best reason
to visit this Bavarian-
themed brew hall.
They've got lots of it from
all over the world, and
it's all served by dirndl-
clad waitresses.

### McGillin's Olde Ale House

1310 Drury St. Tel: 735-5562.
www.mcgillins.com
It's Philly's oldest continuously operating bar and
it has the documentation

to prove it. Hidden down
a grungy alley, it's an
oasis of pubby warmth. If
you can't spring for the
pub grub, take advantage
of a free crock of soup, a
McGillin's tradition.

### The Vault at the Ritz-Carlton

Ritz-Carlton Philadelphia, 10
S. Broad St. Tel: 523-8000.
Drinks in the vast
Rotunda Bar at the Ritz
are always pleasant, but
the more intimate Vault
bar is a stellar spot to
spend an evening – and
some bucks. Cigar smok-
ing is permitted.

### PRICE CATEGORIES

Prices for three-course
dinner per person with a
half-bottle of house wine:
**$** = under $25
**$$** = $25–$40
**$$$** = $40–$50
**$$$** = more than $50

# RITTENHOUSE

The former epicenter of Philadelphia's blue bloods is now a neighborhood of swanky shops, fine restaurants, distinguished architecture and fascinating, though often overlooked, museums

**R**ittenhouse is the grande dame of Philadelphia – handsome, haughty and resolutely upper-crust. This was the Philadelphia of old families and old money, an enclave of Victorian splendor in a sea of "Quaker gray," a place where one finds, in novelist Henry James's polished description, a "bestitching of the drab with pink and green and silver." It is also, in recent years, the site of a resurgent dining, shopping and gallery scene known for smart, youthful style and upmarket prices.

## Rittenhouse Square

At the heart of the neighborhood is **Rittenhouse Square ❶**, named in honor of colonial clockmaker-astronomer David Rittenhouse who, like his predecessor Benjamin Franklin, was president of the American Philosophical Society and a major figure in both science and government. Rittenhouse Square hit its stride in the late 1800s when the wealthy families that once occupied the narrow streets of the colonial city moved into more spacious and stylish homes west of Broad Street. It was a period of explosive growth in Philadelphia. Energized by the meteoric rise of an industrial elite, a new breed of architects like John Notman, Wilson Eyre and Frank Furness were compelled toward

ever more exuberant and eclectic designs that were more in keeping with the city's new status as an industrial giant.

While many of the old-line well-to-do families have moved away to Chestnut Hill or the suburban comforts of the Main Line, a few remain to keep the home fires burning, and new residents with means continue to settle in the area. Although many of the grand Victorian mansions that once surrounded Rittenhouse Square have been replaced by contemporary

Map on page 126

**LEFT:** an artist at work in Rittenhouse Square.
**BELOW:** service with a smile at Brasserie Perrier.

The layout of Rittenhouse Square is the work of noted French architect Paul Philippe Cret, who also designed Philadelphia's Rodin Museum and the Barnes Foundation Gallery in Merion, Pennsylvania.

apartment buildings, this is still one of the most prestigious addresses in the city, and community groups are eager to keep it that way.

Rittenhouse Square, with its 6 acres (2.5 hectares) of green intersected by shaded benches and curving walkways, is both a geographical and social crossroad that brings together a cross-section of neighborhood residents. Young professionals can be seen power-walking in the morning and power-lunching in the afternoon; fur-clad dowagers walk their dogs; homeless people hang out in the shade; mothers (or nannies) watch children play on the bronze goat and dip their feet in the reflecting pool. People on their lunch breaks picnic on the benches, and some of the surrounding restaurants have been reported to deliver sandwiches to patrons ordering from here by cellphone. During the May Flower Market, the square is a rainbow-colored sea of petals and

pollen. In spring, the Rittenhouse Square Fine Arts Annual transforms it into an enormous open-air gallery where artists pin up their work in the hope of catching a collector's eye.

## Strolling the square

As you walk the perimeter of the square, you can see traces of the old glory days coexisting gracefully with the new. At 18th and Walnut streets, the **Van Rensselaer Mansion ❷**, one of the country's great Beaux Arts mansions, is currently occupied by the upscale Anthropologie (tel: 800-309-2500), selling clothing and household items with exotic designs from other cultures. Although much of the interior has been gutted, the ornate mantels, domed stained-glass skylight and the unusual ceiling paintings remain intact.

Next to the Van Rensselaer Mansion, the **Presbyterian Ministers' Fund**, the oldest life insurance company in the country, is housed in

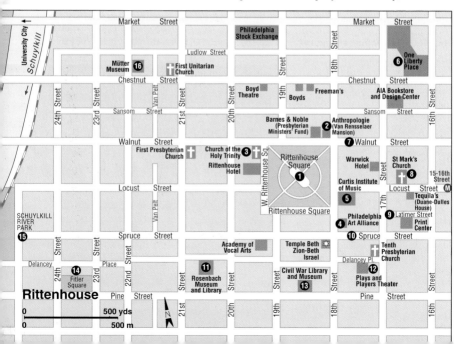

Map on page 126

the dignified Alison Building, the ground floor of which is a rambling Barnes & Noble store, where you can browse, sip cappuccino and listen to readings by noted authors.

Further down is the facade of the former **Rittenhouse Club**, one of the most prestigious of the city's famously exclusive clubs and a haunt of author Henry James when he stayed in Philadelphia. Sadly, much of the building was demolished to make way for a condominium tower after years of heated debate.

On the northwest corner of the square, John Notman's Romanesque **Church of the Holy Trinity** ❸ (Walnut St between 19th and 20th sts; tel: 567-1267; open by appointment), once the city's most fashionable congregation, is overshadowed by the modern sawtooth profile of the **Rittenhouse Hotel** (210 W. Rittenhouse Sq; tel: 546-9000), where afternoon tea is a tradition at the cozy Cassatt Lounge, which has its own outdoor garden. Smith & Wollensky Steak House (545-1700) beckons at street level and views of Rittenhouse Square can be found in Lacroix at the

Rittenhouse (tel: 790-2533), specializing in American and French cuisine.

The southwest nook of the square is occupied by a cluster of Victorian mansions, including the massive home (actually several interconnected properties) of the late art collector and bon vivant Henry McIlhenny. Continuing along the south side of the square, you'll pass the **Ethical Society**, a "humanist religious fellowship" dating from 1920 that offers "Sunday platforms" on a wide range of topics and issues. At the southeast corner, Barclay Prime, a high-end steakhouse run by ubiquitous restaurateur Stephen Starr, is on the ground floor of the former **Barclay Hotel**.

## Art and music

The Barclay is flanked by two important arts institutions. To the south is the **Philadelphia Art Alliance** ❹ (251 S. 18th St; tel: 545-4302; open Tue–Sun 11am–5pm; entrance free), housed in the grand old Wetherill Mansion. Exhibits change about every eight weeks and range over the spectrum of fine arts – painting, sculpture, crafts, photography,

*Several restaurants offer alfresco dining with views of Rittenhouse Square.*

**BELOW:**
relaxing on the lawn in Rittenhouse Square.

**TIP**

The Curtis Institute presents dozens of performances by students, alumni, faculty and distinguished guests. For a schedule of upcoming events, go to www.curtis.edu or call the ticket line at 893-7902.

**BELOW:** student and teacher at the prestigious Curtis Institute of Music.

drawing – by well-known and emerging artists. Call ahead for a schedule of free readings, recitals, performances and lectures.

To the north is the **Curtis Institute of Music ❺** (18th and Locust sts; tel: 893-7902), a highly selective, tuition-free conservatory established in 1924 by Mary Louise Curtis Bok Zimbalist, daughter of publishing magnate Cyrus Curtis. The Institute counts Leonard Bernstein, Gian-Carlo Menotti and Samuel Barber among its alumni and Ignat Solzhenitsyn among its current faculty.

Continuing north along 18th Street, you'll find a row of fashionable restaurants on the square: **Bleu** (227 S. 18th St; tel: 545-0342), **Rouge** (210 S. 18th St; tel: 732-6622) and **Devon Seafood Restaurant** (225 S. 18th St; tel: 546-5940), which in good weather open onto the sidewalk for alfresco dining.

## Rittenhouse Row

Continue north on 18th Street to Chestnut for a winding journey through the shopping district. This strip of **Chestnut Street**, a longtime ugly duckling to Walnut Street's swan, has gotten a much-needed facelift in the past several years, thanks to rising rents and a demand for retail space.

The **Continental Mid-Town** (1801 Chestnut St; tel: 567-1800), restaurateur Stephen Starr's tri-level cocktail house with a decidedly groovy vibe, anchors the corner (head up to the third-floor deck for a specialty drink and a bird's-eye view), while the **DiBruno Bros** (1730 Chestnut St; tel: 665-9220) capacious gourmet market across the way is a mecca for foodies, who sample hundreds of cheeses aged in the on-site cave and attend events at the demonstration kitchen upstairs.

A quick stroll on the 1800 block of Chestnut brings you past 200-year-old **Freeman's** (1808 Chestnut; tel: 563-9275), America's oldest auction house, and **Boyds** (1818 Chestnut; tel: 564-9000), a menswear emporium for the sartorially inclined (and financially endowed), known for its fine tailoring and VIP customer service. On the 1900 block you'll encounter the

art deco splendor of the **Boyd The-atre**, currently being restored as a stage for touring Broadway musicals and film revivals.

Continue east on Chestnut past the shimmering tower of **Liberty One** ❻ on 17th Street, the first structure to surpass the unwritten rule of not standing taller than the William Penn statue atop City Hall.

Turn south on 15th Street and head west on **Sansom Street**. The small scale and funky vibe of Sansom is a pleasant change from the crowded hustle of Chestnut and the temples of commerce on Walnut. Bookstores, tea shops, boutiques and casual restaurants line the street.

## Smart and swanky

If it's luxury you desire, **Walnut Street** ❼ between Rittenhouse Square and Broad Street is Philly's version of Rodeo Drive, with a bevy of smart shops that include ritzy clothing emporium Joan Shepp (1616 Walnut), Kenneth Cole, the flagship store for upscale jeweler Lagos (1735 Walnut), and national chains like Burberry (1705 Walnut St; tel: 557-

7400), Coach (1703 Walnut St; tel: 564-4558) and Tiffany (1414 Walnut St; tel: 735-1919). If you're a book-lover, you can choose between Barnes & Noble on Walnut or visit a local landmark, the family-run Joseph Fox Bookshop (1724 Sansom St; tel: 563-4184).

The restaurants on Walnut Street are equally swanky. When it comes to fine dining, there's no matching **Le Bec-Fin** (1523 Walnut St; tel: 567-1000), one of the country's most highly regarded French restaurants, or **Susanna Foo** (1512 Walnut St; tel: 545-2666), cited by critics for consistently imaginative Chinese cuisine. There are many other dining options, including several for budget travelers.

A short jaunt south on 17th Street past the opulent **Warwick Hotel** brings you to Locust Street, where **St Mark's Church** ❽ (Locust between 16th and 17th sts; tel: 735-1416; open for worship, group tours by appointment), a Gothic Revival masterpiece designed by John Notman, has stood since 1851.

The fanciful mishmash of build-

Map on page 126

*Thirsty? Drinking establishments around Rittenhouse Square range from corner taverns to sophisticated nightspots.*

**BELOW:** Walnut Street is in the heart of the upscale Rittenhouse Row shopping district.

**TIP**

See the Rosenbach Museum website (www.rosenbach.org) for a list of upcoming events, including the month-long Dracula Festival, children's theater inspired by the works of Maurice Sendak, and the annual observance of Bloomsday, a daylong reading of James Joyce's *Ulysses* by notable Philadelphians.

**BELOW:** an orchestra brings music to Rittenhouse Square during the Welcome America festival.

ings across the street comprise the former home of the venerable **Locust Club** (1612-16 Locust St), which has sadly fallen into disrepair, the victim of a battle among developers, zoning boards and historical advocates who are debating whether or not more condos can be constructed on the site. Farther east, the **Duane-Dulles House** (1602 Locust St), another Notman design, is home to Mexican restaurant Tequila's. The original moldings, fireplaces and other architectural details are still in place and provide a lovely, if mildly incongruous, backdrop for sipping a margarita.

Head south on 16th Street and slip into **Latimer Street** , little more than a back alley but brimming with jewel-box gardens, small-scale mansions and old-line clubs like the Pennsylvania Society of the Colonial Dames of America and the Cosmopolitan Club. The **Print Center** (1614 Latimer; tel: 735-6090; open Tue–Sat 11am–5.30pm; entrance free) is a nonprofit organization founded in 1915 devoted to printmaking and photography; its

gallery is free and open to the public. At the corner of 17th Street, take a peek at the **Edward Wood** double house (245-47 S. 17th St.), an idiosyncratic Queen Anne-style dwelling designed by Frank Miles Day that now houses a clamorous English pub.

## South of the square

To the south of Rittenhouse Square, the neighborhood is largely residential, with an occasional florist, antique shop or doctor's office at street level. **Spruce Street** is the most interesting architecturally, with a fine row of brownstones between 20th and 21st streets, and homes by Frank Furness (2132–34 Spruce St and 235 S. 21st St), Wilson Eyre (315–17 S. 22nd St) and George Hewitt (2100 Spruce St).

The **Tenth Presbyterian Church** (17th and Spruce sts; tel: 735-7688; open by appointment), a combination of styles and materials, is a paragon of Victorian eclecticism, with a prominent belltower. Built in 1855, the extravagant structure was designed by architect John McArthur,

Jr., who was later chosen to design City Hall. The sanctuary contains two original Tiffany stained-glass windows installed in the 1890s.

The mansion behind the church was once owned by Harry K. Thaw, who, in a scandalous episode, shot his wife's lover, the New York architect Stanford White. It seems that White flaunted the affair by using Mrs. Thaw as the model for his nude sculpture *Diana*, which stood atop New York's first Madison Square Garden. The statue is now housed at the Philadelphia Museum of Art. A block away, at 18th and Spruce streets, Temple Beth Zion-Beth Israel (tel: 735-5148; open Mon–Thu 9am–5pm, Fri 9am–3pm, Sun by appointment) is an imposing structure built of a lustrous local stone.

## Rare books

The 2000 and 1800 blocks of **Delancey Place** – the quietest and most exclusive street in the neighborhood, if not the entire city – have long been associated with Philadelphia's oldest families. The genteel atmosphere makes a perfect setting for the

## Rosenbach Museum and Library

⓫ (2008–10 Delancey Pl; tel: 732-1600; open Tues–Sun 10am–5pm, Wed to 8pm; entrance fee), a collection of some 30,000 rare books, 275,000 manuscripts, and a houseful of art and antiques.

Tours are led by knowledgeable guides and are tailored to visitors' interests. If there is something special you would like to see, call a few days in advance and the curators will try to have it on display.

Exhibits change frequently, but highlights are likely to include original drawings by Honoré Daumier and William Blake; 15th-century illuminated manuscripts of *The Canterbury Tales;* a page or two of James Joyce's handwritten draft of *Ulysses;* the *Bay Psalm Book* (the first book printed in America); rare editions of Melville, Defoe and Carroll; drafts of poetry by Ezra Pound, Wallace Stevens and Marianne Moore; and letters by Franklin, Washington, Jefferson, Roosevelt and hundreds of others.

The work of Maurice Sendak is featured in a new gallery named after

Map on page 126

TIP

Check the Print Center gift shop for one-of-a-kind prints, stationery and handmade books.

**BELOW:**
DiBruno Brothers gourmet shop is filled with Italian delicacies.

## Where Sendak's Wild Things Are

Alongside the original manuscript for James Joyce's *Ulysses,* Bram Stoker's notes for *Dracula* and first editions of Dickens and Shelley is a collection of over 10,000 works by noted children's book illustrator Maurice Sendak. Sendak was introduced to the Rosenbach brothers in the 1950s, and they developed a friendship over a shared affinity for collecting Herman Melville. Inspired by his New York neighbor, the poet Marianne Moore, who donated her entire living room to the Rosenbach, Sendak contributed his own works. Original artwork and notes from classic books like *Where the Wild Things Are* and *Chicken Soup with Rice* are stored at the Rosenbach. A rotating display of Sendak's whimsical, inspired works in watercolor, ink and marker is always on view in the Maurice Sendak Gallery on the second floor of the museum (where Sendak is still, coincidentally, neighbors with Marianne Moore – her living room is exhibited across the hall) along with his drafting table and a cabinet once owned by Melville himself. Sendak is a trustee of the museum. Not all items are on display at all times in the Rosenbach, so if there's an illustration you're interested in seeing, call ahead and it will be brought out for viewing.

TIP

Civil War enthusiasts will appreciate the Old Baldy Civil War Round Table, a lecture series featuring authors and historians at the Civil War Library and Museum.

**BELOW:** skulls at the Mütter Museum are labeled with the individual's nationality and cause of death.

the celebrated children's book author and illustrator, a longtime supporter of the museum.

Also on Delancey, you'll find the **Plays and Players Theater** ⓬ (1714 Delancey St, tel: 735-0630), historic home to the city's oldest community theater group. The **Philadelphia Theatre Company** (box office, tel: 569-9700), a company renowned for its bold new work, is also based here, but is building a new home on the Avenue of the Arts at Broad and Pine streets.

### War remembered

Another of Philadelphia's little-known jewels resides about two blocks away at 1805 Pine Street. It's the **Civil War Library and Museum** ⓭ (tel: 735-8196; open Thu–Sat 11am–4.30pm; entrance fee) of the Military Order of the Loyal Legion of the United States, a three-story repository of Civil War artifacts, documents and paraphernalia, and a 12,000-volume library. Over the years, the Loyal Legion has accumulated hundreds of firearms, swords, broadsides, pho-

tographs and paintings as well as such curiosities as Ulysses S. Grant's death mask, a lock of Abraham Lincoln's hair, and the stuffed head of Major General George G. Meade's trusty war horse, Old Baldy, wounded five times in battle and now the museum's mascot.

To the west, Pine Street runs past townhouses and stores to a tidy pocket park called **Fitler Square** ⓮. **Schuylkill River Park** ⓯, a pleasant patch of trees and benches with a playground and dog run, is just two blocks beyond. The newly landscaped **Schuylkill River Trail** runs about 1¼ miles (1.9 km) from the north end of the park to the Museum of Art. Plans are afoot to extend the trail south along the river to Fort Mifflin.

If you're in the area, you can wander through some of the neighborhood's quiet alleyways. Panama Street, between 18th and 19th streets, is a tree-lined hideaway of ivy-covered homes (check out the Tudor conversion at No. 1920); tiny Addison, Smedley and Croskey streets are worth exploring, too.

---

## The Soap Lady

Among the many grisly specimens at the Mütter Museum, perhaps the most curious is the Soap Lady, a woman whose corpse has been transformed into soap, or, more precisely, a waxy soap-like substance known as adipocere that results when fat undergoes a particular chemical reaction. The Soap Lady arrived in 1874, when museum director Dr Joseph Leidy learned that two peculiar corpses were unearthed at a nearby construction site. The site's foreman was reluctant to give the bodies to Leidy, so the good doctor claimed the soap couple were his grandparents, forked over $7.50 and brought them to the museum. (The Soap Man now resides in the Smithsonian.)

Leidy identified the Soap Lady as a victim of a 1792 yellow fever epidemic with the surname Ellenbogen. Research by another curator in the 1940s revealed that there was no yellow fever outbreak in 1792 and no Ellenbogens listed in the city. A 1987 X-ray confirmed the misinformation, revealing the presence of a certain type of straight pin and button, neither of which were manufactured until 1824. So who is the Soap Lady and how did she arrive at her present predicament? For the moment, these questions remain as slippery as ever.

Head north on 22nd Street, turn right on Spruce Street and then left on Van Pelt, which is lined with renovated carriage houses. Follow Van Pelt across Locust Street and pass through the archway into **English Village**, an enclave of Tudor-style homes built around a flagstone plaza. Return to 22nd Street and continue north to the **First Unitarian Church** (2125 Chestnut St; tel: 563-3980; open Mon–Fri 8am–4pm; entrance free), the only center city church designed by Frank Furness.

### Grisly treasure

A half-block away, at 22nd and Ludlow streets, is yet another of Philadelphia's little-known, and somewhat grisly, treasures: the **Mütter Museum**  (19 S. 22nd St; tel: 563-3737, ext. 242; open daily 10am–5pm; entrance fee), with its curious collection of medical instruments, artifacts and specimens. There are fairly innocuous exhibits on technology – an early heart-lung machine, obstetrical instruments, and a doctor's office from the early 1900s, among other things.

Things get a bit stickier in the pathology section. There are graphic displays of just about every eye and skin disease one would care to imagine, a plaster cast made at the autopsy of Chang and Eng, the original Siamese twins, a mummified "Soap Lady" from the early 1800s, an ovarian cyst the size of a bowling ball, a human horn (that's right, a horn), the skeleton of the so-called Kentucky giant, and a variety of organs, limbs and decapitated heads pickled in formaldehyde, including the brain of murderer John Wilson and the liver shared by Chang and Eng.

And if you think that's weird, how about hundreds of foreign objects (buttons, pins, bones and bullets) that Dr Chevalier Jackson pulled from his patients' throats with a special device invented for the task, vesicles removed from Chief Justice John Marshall's bladder by renowned Philadelphia doctor Philip Syng Physick, a chunk of John Wilkes Booth's thorax, and a tumor removed from President Grover Cleveland's jaw. This is not a museum for the faint of heart. ❑

*"[I] liked poor dear queer flat comfortable Philadelphia almost ridiculously."*
—Henry James

**BELOW:** specimens at the Mütter Museum illustrate the effects of genetic anomalies and illness.

# RESTAURANTS & BARS

## Restaurants

### Alma de Cuba
1623 Walnut St. Tel: 988-1799. Open: D nightly. $$$
www.almadecubarestaurant.com
Ubiquitous restaurateur Stephen Starr paired up with superstar chef Douglas Rodriguez to create this dark and sexy Cuban-themed eatery. As with most Starr spots, the drinks, tropical in this case, are as good a reason to go as the menu of ceviches and Nuevo Latino specialties.

### Barclay Prime
237 S. 18th St. Tel: 732-7560. Open: L Mon–Fri, D nightly. $$$$
www.barclayprime.com
A modern take on the steakhouse right on Rittenhouse Square. Marble tables, book-lined walnut shelves and massive couches upholstered in neon green create a 1970s vibe. Skip the gimmicky $100 cheesesteak and instead opt for one of the excellent dry-aged steaks or kobe mini-burgers. The clubby lounge is one of the neighborhood's classiest watering holes.

### Brasserie Perrier
1619 Walnut St. Tel: 568-3000. Open: L Mon–Sat, D nightly. $$$
www.georgesperriergroup.com
The slightly more affordable sibling of Le Bec-Fin offers the same impeccable quality of food, but in a less rarefied atmosphere. The lively lounge is a hot spot for swanky Rittenhouse types. The superb steak frites is always satisfying and a relative bargain.

### Devil's Alley
1907 Chestnut St. Tel: 751-0707. Open: L & D daily, Sun brunch. $–$$
The chic industrial décor of the Alley belies its true identity as a comfort food haven. Big burgers, salads and sandwiches make it a favorite with the business lunch crowd. A mezzanine bar and lounge are popular for get-togethers after work.

### Friday, Saturday, Sunday
261 S. 21st St. Tel: 546-4232. Open: D nightly. $$–$$$
www.frisatsun.com
An oldie-but-goodie that has weathered the storm for the past 30 years due to a creative American menu and a commitment to sell wine for only $10 over cost. Squeeze into the teeny Tank Bar on the second floor of this charming townhouse for a pre-dinner cocktail.

### La Colombe
130 S. 19th St. Tel: 563-0860. Open daily 8am–8pm. $
While this locally roasted coffee has grown far beyond its roots at this bustling cafe, fans agree that this joe is best when sampled at the source. The baristas are expert, the lattes are exceptional and the people watching is unparalleled.

### Lacroix at the Rittenhouse
The Rittenhouse Hotel, 210 W. Rittenhouse Sq. Tel: 790-2533. Open: B daily, L Mon-Sat, D nightly, Sun brunch. $$$$
www.rittenhousehotel.com
Chef Jean-Marie Lacroix's exceptional fare incorporates French techniques, American flavors and local ingredients. Foodies can reserve the chef's table in the kitchen for a front row seat at the behind-the-scenes show. The Sunday brunch buffet is a glorious, gut-busting affair, but any meal in this elegant, serene dining room feels like a special occasion.

### Le Bec-Fin
1523 Walnut St. Tel: 567-1000. Open: L Mon–Fri, D Mon-Sat. $$$$
www.georgesperriergroup.com
The grande dame of the Philadelphia dining scene is undoubtedly Le Bec-Fin, run by renowned chef-about-town and professional perfectionist Georges Perrier. This tres formal, tres fabulous temple of French cuisine got a facelift a few years back, but much remains the same, including its legendary dessert cart, which staggers under the weight of a multitude of fanciful pastries.

### Matyson
37 S. 19th St. Tel: 564-2925. Open: L Mon–Fri, D Mon–Sat. $$
www.matyson.com
One of the top BYOBs in town, Matyson serves an eclectic menu of creative American dishes. Chef Matt Spector's soups are excellent and wife Sonjia's homemade desserts are outstanding. Unlike most BYOBs, this one is open for lunch and it's just as good as dinner. Make reservations, it's always busy.

### Melograno
2201 Spruce St. Tel: 875-8116. Open: D Tues–Sun. $$
Locals start lining up long before the doors open to grab a table at this simple, Tuscan-style trattoria. Once this BYOB fills up it stays that way. Waits can be lengthy as diners linger over their fresh pasta and seasonal salads.

### Monk's Cafe
264 S. 16th St. Tel: 545-7005. Open: L & D daily. $$
This much-loved beer emporium is utterly unique. The owners, an expat Irishman and a local bartender, offer hundreds of beers from around the world and one of the best selec-

tions of Belgian beers in the U.S. The menu is full of beer as well. Don't miss the Brussels mussels or the famous frites served with mayo that packs a garlic wallop.

## Rouge

205 S. 18th St. Tel: 732-6622. Open: L & D daily, Sun brunch. $$$
For those who must be seen, there is no other restaurant in town. Grab an outdoor table (if you can) overlooking Rittenhouse Square, sip a glass of wine and people-watch the day away. The food is as good as the scenery, especially the award-winning Rouge burger.

## Striped Bass

1500 Walnut St. Tel: 732-4444. Open: D nightly, Sun Brunch. $$$$
www.stripedbassrestaurant.com
A change of ownership, a renovation and a James Beard-award-winning chef have only served to enhance the profile of this contemporary seafood-centric restaurant. Located in a former bank, the muted elegance, outstanding cuisine and superior service make this one of the most coveted reservations in the city.

## Susanna Foo

1512 Walnut St. Tel: 545-2666. Open: L Mon–Fri, D nightly. $$$–$$$$
www.susannafoo.com
A graceful fusion of Chi-

nese ingredients with French technique, courtesy of chef-owner and cookbook author Susanna Foo. Expect to see unusual pairings like tea-smoked Peking duck breast with Szechuan peppercorn sauce at this Walnut Street fixture, where the surroundings are as sophisticated as the food.

## Tria

123 S. 18th St. Tel: 972-8742. Open L & D daily. $–$$
www.triacafe.com
A contemporary cafe celebrating the "fermentation trio" of beer, wine and cheese along with tasty snacks and sandwiches. It's great for grazing, as the cheeses are all offered by the piece and the wines are all offered by the glass. The witty menu descriptions are as much fun to read as they are to sample.

## Twenty Manning

261 S. 20th St. Tel: 731-0900. Open: D nightly. $$–$$$
www.twentymanning.com
A study in minimalist chic, this sleek black-and-silver bistro is at its best in warm weather, when the French windows are flung open. The eclectic menu draws its influences from Asia and beyond.

## Bars

## Continental Mid-town

1801 Chestnut St. Tel: 567-1800.
www.continentalmidtown.com

Take the elevator upstairs and head straight for cocktails on the roof deck, serving most of the same specialty drinks that made its Old City sibling famous.

## Nodding Head Brewery & Restaurant

1516 Sansom St, 2nd Floor. Tel: 569-9525.
www.noddinghead.com
The second beer venture from the owners of Monk's has an on-site brewery with a rotating selection of beers and a fine pub menu. Open to 2am.

## Walnut Room

1709 Walnut St, 2nd Floor. Tel: 751-0201.
www.walnut-room.com
Sleek, sexy and fun, this second-floor spot has specialty cocktails, hip DJs and, on weekends, a velvet-roped line.

## Loie

128 S. 19th St. Tel: 568-0808.
www.loie215.com
This art nouveau-style brasserie transforms into a lounge late at night and gets quickly packed with Rittenhouse-ites grooving to a rotating cast of DJs.

## Tequila's

1602 Locust St. Tel: 546-0181.
www.tequilasphilly.com
It's a full-service restaurant in a beautifully restored townhouse, but the 75 tequilas are the best reason to visit.

| PRICE CATEGORIES |
|---|
| Prices for three-course dinner per person with a half-bottle of house wine: |
| **$** = under $25 |
| **$$** = $25–$40 |
| **$$$** = $40–$50 |
| **$$$** = more than $50 |

**RIGHT:** alfresco dining at Rouge.

# MUSEUM DISTRICT AND FAIRMOUNT PARK

World-class museums are strung along a grand boulevard running from City Hall to Fairmount Park. The collections range from European masters and modern art to dinosaurs and space science

**P**hiladelphia's museum district stretches down **Benjamin Franklin Parkway ❶**, a grand European-style boulevard that runs from City Hall to the Philadelphia Museum of Art, urging travelers toward the bucolic space of Fairmount Park. This is Philadelphia's Champs Elysées, a swath through Penn's orderly street grid adorned with fountains, flags, flowerbeds and more than 25 outdoor sculptures.

Designed in 1917 by French-born architects Jacques Greber and Paul Philippe Cret – exponents of the City Beautiful movement of the early 1900s – the Parkway was conceived as a sign of civic maturity, a declaration that the Quaker City had shed its mundane persona and was poised to take on the trappings of a great urban center.

## Love and skateboarding

The **John F. Kennedy Plaza ❷**, or LOVE plaza in reference to Robert Indiana's word-sculpture *Philadelphia LOVE*, had become a hot spot for skateboarders, engendering heated public debate about the appropriate use of the square.

Despite a strong movement to keep the plaza "skateboard-accessible," the City decided instead to ban skateboarding there (which can damage surfaces not designed for it)

and to add greenery, creating a park that would be more welcoming to pedestrians and office workers on their lunch break.

In return, Mayor Street promised that the City would create other venues for skateboarding, the first of which opened in South Philadelphia. Another skateboarding park is planned for a space overlooking the Schuylkill River near the Art Museum. Across the street from LOVE Plaza is Suburban Station, a busy commuter station built in 1929.

Map on page 138

**LEFT:** Philadelphia Museum of Art stands regally at the end of the Benjamin Franklin Parkway.
**BELOW:** schoolgirls celebrate the school year's end in Swann Memorial Fountain.

## Logan Square

From JFK Plaza, it's a 10-minute walk to **Logan Square ③**, one of William Penn's original town plazas, now girdled by a busy traffic circle. Originally the site of a cemetery and gallows, old Northwest Square was renamed in 1825 in honor of James Logan, who came to Pennsylvania as William Penn's secretary. Logan was not only a first-rate businessman – he made a fortune in the fur trade and in real estate – but a man of uncommon learning. His personal library was one of the most extensive in the colonies and is now maintained by the Library Company of Philadelphia. The parkway plan transformed the square into a circle to facilitate traffic around the area.

## Father, Son and Holy Ghost

At the center of Logan Square is **Swann Memorial Fountain**, an evocative rendering of three reclining nudes (representing Philadelphia's three rivers – the Delaware, Schuylkill and Wissahickon) executed by Alexander Stirling Calder. His father, Alexander Milne Calder, sculpted the statue of William Penn perched at the top of City Hall. In turn, Stirling Calder's son, Alexander Calder, continues the tradition. His mobile *Ghost* hangs in the Museum of Art, and local wits have said this makes the Calder family the Father, Son and Holy Ghost of the Parkway. An initiative to build a Calder museum on the Parkway was launched by then-mayor Ed Rendell in the late 1990s, but the effort has since lost steam and its future is uncertain at best.

On the east side of the square is the **Cathedral of Saints Peter and Paul ④** (tel: 561-1313; open daily 8am–3pm, small group tours by appointment; entrance free), a venerable Italian Renaissance structure designed by Napoleon Le Brun and

*A walk-through model of a human heart is one of the Franklin Institute's oldest and most popular exhibits.*

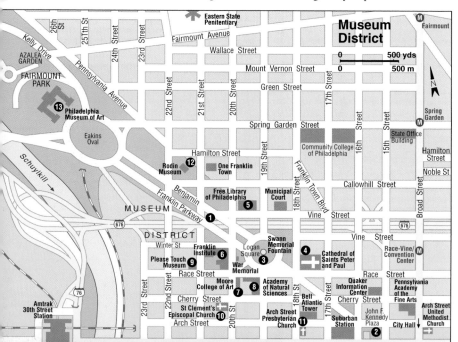

John Notman. Begun in 1846, the cathedral is one of the only major buildings on the square that predates the Parkway.

The twin neoclassical structures on the north side of the square are the **Free Library of Philadelphia ❺** (19th and Vine sts; tel: 686-5322; www.library.phila.gov; open Mon–Wed 9am–9pm, Thu–Sat 9am–5pm) and **Municipal Court**, built between 1917 and 1927 and modeled after matching palaces on the Place de la Concorde in Paris. Bibliophiles should check for special exhibits at the library's Rare Book Department, as well as a great collection of Dickens memorabilia at the William Elkins Library and the world's largest library of orchestral music.

## Art and science

Walk clockwise around the square to the **Franklin Institute ❻** (20th and Parkway; tel: 448-1200, www.fi.edu; open daily 9.30am–5pm; entrance fee), one of the premier science museums in the country, with acres of exhibition space and hundreds of

Map on page 138

interactive displays. Everywhere you turn, there's something to touch, explore, discover or play with. The Science Center is the core of the museum, covering ecology, aviation, astronomy, physics, mathematics and just about everything else of interest to budding scientists. Walk through a giant heart, climb into a jet fighter, "freeze" your shadow, have a look at "liquid air," and see how a four-story Foucault's pendulum demonstrates the Earth's rotation. A new Space Command exhibit simulates a space research station where visitors can "watch" astronauts at work, and look out onto the universe as seen from space.

Don't miss the **Tuttleman IMAX Theater**, which shows spectacular IMAX films on a four-story domed screen with 56 speakers. And if you've got the time, go stargazing at the state-of-the-art **Fels Planetarium**. The Franklin Institute is also home to the **Benjamin Franklin National Memorial** which, in addition to a fascinating collection of Frankliniana, features an enormous marble statue of the institute's

*Celebrating Independence Day on the Ben Franklin Parkway.*

**BELOW:** the Franklin Institute encompasses an interactive science museum, planetarium and IMAX theater.

**TIP**

An expanded *Butterflies!* exhibit has reopened at the Academy of Natural Sciences, where visitors can stroll a 1,200-sqfoot (111-sq-meter) recreation of a tropical garden filled with dozens of fluttering butterflies.

**RIGHT:** kids cool off in Swann Memorial Fountain, designed by sculptor Alexander Stirling Calder.

namesake and inspiration. The Memorial is in the Franklin Institute's rotunda.

Around the square, the **Moore College of Art ❼** (20th and Parkway; tel: 965-4027; thegalleriesatmoore.org; open Tue–Fri 10am–5pm, Sat–Sun noon–4pm winter only; entrance free), an art college for women, shows changing exhibits of contemporary art, sculpture, photography and architecture.

The **Academy of Natural Sciences ❽** (19th and Parkway; tel: 299-1000; www.acnatsci.org; open Mon–Fri 10am–4.30pm, Sat–Sun 10am–5pm; entrance fee) is easy to find, with a pair of bronze dinosaurs near the entrance. Founded in 1812, the Academy is the nation's oldest science research museum of natural history. At the core of the museum is Dinosaur Hall, which features the skeletons of ancient predators like *Gigantosaurus* and *Tyrannosaurus Rex* as well as an extensive collection of smaller species, dinosaur eggs, footprints, a working fossil lab, and numerous interactive exhibits detailing the evolution of

the ancient beasts and the science of paleontology.

Other permanent exhibits include a Live Animal Center, where visitors can watch through large observation windows the care of a diverse collection of wild animals that have been injured or orphaned, and a hands-on children's nature center called Outside/In, where kids can explore local habitats, examine fossils and handle live animals.

### Kid stuff

If you're traveling with young children, be sure to visit the **Please Touch Museum ❾** (210 N. 21st St; tel: 963-0667; www.pleasetouchmuseum.org; open daily 9am–4.30pm, extended summer hours; entrance fee), dedicated to children aged seven years and younger.

The museum is slated to move to a much larger space at historic Memorial Hall in Fairmount Park in spring 2008. In the meanwhile, kids are encouraged to let their imaginations run wild on three floors of hands-on exhibits, games and educational play. Children can shop in a

## Battle of the Bones

In some ways, Edward Drinker Cope was an anomaly. Raised a devout Quaker in Philadelphia, where he was born in 1840, he got turned on to mother nature's material blessings at a tender age – his childhood notes and drawings are preserved by the Academy of Natural Sciences. And when it came to describing dinosaurs, this naturalist wunderkind turned out to be a most un-Friendly warrior.

Cope climbed to the top. A prolific author, he became a museum curator and taught geology at the University of Pennsylvania. Unfortunately, his work clashed with the achievement of another leading specialist, Yale University paleontologist Othniel C. Marsh.

Between them, they named 130 dinosaur species. But their clash over nomenclature became a bitter rivalry – Marsh ridiculed Cope, in one famous incident, for mounting a skull on the wrong end of a dinosaur. Why the feud? It was one part ego, one part cantankerousness, one part philosophy – Marsh adhered to Darwin's theory of natural selection whereas Cope detected a design in nature that went beyond "mere" evolution. Whatever its cause, the feud persisted for 20 years, terminating with Cope's death in 1897.

mini supermarket, visit "Where the Wild Things Are" (an exhibit based on Maurice Sendak's best-selling book), get behind the steering wheel of a bus, and much more. The Education Store carries all sorts of nifty items for busy hands and inquisitive minds and is a great place to shop for the kids back home.

### Religious architecture

While you're in the neighborhood, make a short detour to **St Clement's Episcopal Church** ❿ (Cherry and 20th sts; tel: 563-1876; open Mon–Fri 6.30am–6pm, Sat 7am–1pm, Sun 7am–2pm, 4–5pm, check for service times during these hours), a picturesque brownstone structure designed by John Notman in 1855. A "high" Episcopal church, St Clement's has a great musical program at High Mass every Sunday.

Four blocks away, the **Arch Street Presbyterian Church** ⓫ (18th and Arch sts; tel: 563-3763; open Sun only for services) is also worth a look. Built in 1855, the church is a harmonious blend of styles brought together with massive

Corinthian columns, a copper dome and cheerful orange trim. The interior is a study in classical proportion.

Across the street, the splendid **Bell Atlantic Tower** steps skyward in a cascading series of setbacks. Its two smart neighbors – One and Two Logan Square – are worth a look, too.

### Temples of art

Back on the Parkway, just past Logan Square, the twin pylons of the **Civil War Soldiers and Sailors Memorial** stand sentinel on either side of the boulevard, acting as a gateway to the Philadelphia Museum of Art.

A block away, the **Rodin Museum** ⓬ (22nd and Parkway; tel: 568-6026; open Tue–Sun 10am–5pm; donation) is an island of tranquility set behind an elegant portal, a replica of the gateway Rodin constructed for his home in France. Given to the city by movie-house mogul Jules Mastbaum, who commissioned Paul Cret and Jacques Greber to design the building, the museum houses the largest collection of Rodin's work outside France, including *The Thinker, The Gates of Hell* and *The Burghers of Calais*.

Map on page 138

The Thinker *greets visitors near the entrance to the Rodin Museum.*

**BELOW:** technicians clean fossils at the Academy of Science.

**BELOW:** the Great Stair Hall of the Philadelphia Museum of Art.

The Rodin Museum is administered by the larger **Philadelphia Museum of Art ⑬** (26th and Parkway; tel: 763-8100; www.philamuseum.org; open Tue–Sun 10am–5pm, Fri to 8.45pm; entrance fee), which stands like a modern-day acropolis atop Faire Mount, its monumental staircase inviting visitors into the cavernous lobby. These are the same stairs on which Sylvester Stallone made his triumphant trot in the wildly popular film *Rocky*. The museum has an extensive collection of European art, as well as an Asian wing and impressive American and 20th-century collections.

A collection of European paintings from the 14th to 20th centuries contains highlights such as Van der Wyden's *Crucifixion with Virgin and St John* and Van Eyck's *Saint Francis Receiving the Stigmata*, Peter Paul Rubens' *Prometheus Bound*, Poussin's *The Birth of Venus*, Renoir's *The Bathers* and Van Gogh's *Sunflowers*, not to mention works by Rousseau, Monet, Gauguin, Manet and other latter-day masters.

## Modern masters

Elsewhere in the museum, an entire wing dedicated to 20th-century art traces the influence of innovators like Picasso, Klee, Brancusi and Duchamp on the postwar work of Warhol, Oldenburg, Johns, Stella and others. A renowned American collection features the work of Pennsylvania Dutch and Shaker craftsmen, period rooms, and well-known Philadelphia painters such as Charles Willson Peale, Thomas Eakins and Mary Cassatt.

A 16th-century Hindu temple and Japanese teahouse are but a few of the treasures in the Asian wing. A fascinating gallery of arms and armor details the extraordinary talents of Renaissance metalworkers, and an excellent photography exhibit features the work of Alfred Stieglitz.

The museum is enormous, and it's impossible to see everything in a single visit. Be selective. A good way to start is to join one of the free gallery tours offered several times a day. Check the schedule for films and lectures. And visit the shop for the city's best collection of art books.

## Fairmount Park

The backyard of the Philadelphia Museum of Art is the **Azalea Garden ⑭**, a 4-acre (1.5-hectare) bouquet of azaleas, rhododendrons and magnolias that opens onto the vast expanse of **Fairmount Park** (tel: 685-0000). The Fairmount Park System, the largest part of which is Fairmount Park itself, spreads over 8,900 acres (3,600 hectares) and is the largest municipal park in the country, with 100 miles (160 km) of hiking trails and bridle paths, 3 million trees, hundreds of statues, 105 tennis courts, 73 baseball fields, six pools, six golf courses, amphitheaters, a zoo and more than 20 historic homes. (The entire system includes parkland throughout the city, including Pennypack Park in the northeast,

Cobbs Creek in West Philadelphia, the original squares in center city and numerous pocket parks.)

Fairmount Park spreads over 4,400 acres (1,780 hectares) on both sides of the Schuylkill River, stretching up into the northern reaches of the Wissahickon Valley. The park is so large, it's necessary to drive or take the Fairmount Park trolley-bus, which departs from the JFK Plaza visitor center every 20 minutes most days of the week. The trolley-bus stops regularly along the 17-mile (27-km) loop around the park.

### At the water's edge

If you're walking from the museum, you can wander down to the **Fairmount Water Works ⓯** (www.fairmountwaterworks.org; Interpretive Center open Tue–Sat 10am–5pm, Sun 1–5pm), a glorious old pumping station that looks like a cluster of Greek temples on the river's edge.

When the efficiency of the city's first water pumping facility on Center Square (now the site of City Hall), operational from 1801 to 1815, proved less than ideal, the operation was moved to beautiful neoclassical structures on the higher ground of Faire Mount, where distribution of water could be assisted by gravity.

With the completion of the Fairmount Dam in 1821, the operation of the Fairmount Water Works was regarded as a technological marvel. It became, for a time, the second most visited tourist site (after Niagara Falls) in North America and operated until 1909. However, soon there was no room to add sand filtration beds to purify the river water which had become heavily polluted by upstream industry and the city's growing population.

The Water Works were then used as an aquarium from 1911 to 1962 and a public swimming pool from 1962 to 1973. In the 1970s, the site was declared a National Historic

Maps: pages 138, 143

*It's a 5-minute walk beyond the boathouses to the Samuel Memorial, a terraced sculpture garden featuring the work of several artists, including Jacques Lipchitz and Waldemar Raemisch.*

**BELOW:**
the Museum of Art overlooks the Fairmount Water Works and Schuylkill River.

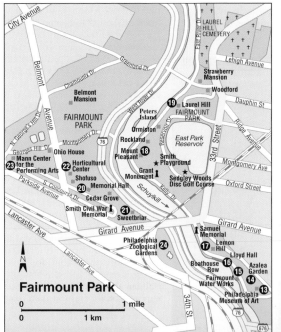

Landmark and fund-raising efforts for its restoration as a historic site began. The project is now nearly complete, with the restoration of the old Engine House, the two Mill Houses, the Caretaker's House and Gazebo. Also on site is an Interpretive Center (640 Water Works Dr; tel: 685-4908).

### River walk

The Water Works is a wonderful place to view the city, the river and the boathouses. On a nice day, you're liable to see cyclists and in-line skaters taking a break, and people stopping for a snack at **Lloyd Hall** (1 Boathouse Row; tel: 684-3936; open Mon–Fri 10am–10pm, Sat–Sun 9am–5pm), a Fairmount Park recreational facility with a gymnasium, café and bicycle rentals.

Here also is the **Schuylkill River Trail**, a level bike path that runs most of the way from the Museum of Art to Valley Forge. The trail follows Kelly Drive through the park, to Main Street in Manayunk, and then to the unpaved Manayunk Canal Towpath before continuing on through Conshohocken and Bridgeport.

*A boater paddles on the Schuylkill River near Kelly Drive.*

**BELOW:** Shofuso, also known as the Japanese House, is set within Fairmount Park.

**Boathouse Row** has been home to boathouses since the early 1800s. The boathouses were built after the 1868 Fairmount Park Commission was granted authority to approve plans for their construction. Now a historic landmark, Boathouse Row is home to high school and university crew teams.

### Historic houses

Fairmount Park is dotted with historic houses, some of which are open for viewing, but they can be difficult to locate along the winding roads that run through the park. The Philadelphia Museum of Art conducts tours of seven houses that are fully renovated: Laurel Hill, Lemon Hill, Sweetbriar, Strawberry Mansion, Woodford, Mount Pleasant and Cedar Grove; the last two are administered by the museum and staffed by park guides (Park House Guides Office, west foyer Museum of Art; tel: 684-7926; open Tue–Fri 9am–5pm). The Philadelphia Trolleyworks company (tel: 925-TOUR) also runs a trolley-bus tour Tuesday to Sunday through the park with stops at the houses.

If you plan to continue your explorations on foot, you can carry on along the river or take Lemon Hill Drive to **Lemon Hill** (Poplar Dr, East Fairmount Park; tel: 232-4337; open Tue–Sat 10am–4pm; entrance fee), the only historic home within walking distance of the Museum of Art. The property was originally owned by Revolutionary financier Robert Morris until he ran afoul of his creditors and landed in debtor's prison. Henry Pratt bought the estate at a sheriff's sale and built the present house in 1800. Named after Pratt's hothouse lemon trees, the property is a graceful example of Federal design with large, lacy fanlights, unusual oval parlors overlooking the river, and a collection of period furnishings.

From Lemon Hill, it's a short drive along the river (turn at the Grant

Monument) to **Mount Pleasant** ⓲ (Mt. Pleasant Dr; tel: 235-7469; open Tue–Sun 10am–5pm; entrance fee), a Georgian mansion constructed in 1761 by a Scottish sea captain, John Macpherson, who made a fortune as a "privateer" – a pirate in service of the monarch – a line of work that cost him an arm. Macpherson occupied his later years as a farmer, publisher and inventor of a "vermin-proof bed."

In 1779, Benedict Arnold bought the house for his bride, Peggy Shippen, but was convicted of treason before either could move in. Described by John Adams as "the most elegant seat in Pennsylvania," Mount Pleasant remains a masterpiece of Georgian style, with restored woodwork, Chippendale furniture, portraits by Benjamin West and Charles Willson Peale, and a lush garden.

You'll pass more modest **Rockland** (1810) and **Ormiston** (1798) along the road to **Laurel Hill** ⓳ (E. Edgely Dr, tel: 235-1776; call for opening times; entrance fee), a summer estate built in 1760. Farther along the loop, **Woodford** (33rd and Dauphin sts, tel: 229-6115; Tues–Sun

10am–4pm; entrance fee) is a Georgian manor house built in 1756 by William Coleman, a member of Franklin's Junto, and later occupied by David Franks, who turned the house into a center of Tory activity during the British occupation. Home of the Naomi Wood collection of American antiques, Woodford is brimming with 18th-century furnishings, including household items such as foot warmers, wind harps, wick trimmers and antique books.

Nearby, Strawberry Mansion (near 33rd and Dauphin sts, tel: 228-8364; Wed–Sun 10am–4pm) was built in two stages: the central section in 1798 and the matching wings in the 1820s. The largest house in the park, it got its name in the 1840s when strawberries and cream were served to visitors. Today, the house is fully restored with a variety of period furnishings.

### The west side

The green dome you see looming over the trees belongs to **Memorial Hall** ⓴ (Belmont Ave and Concourse Dr, West Fairmount Park; tel:

Map on page 143

*Memorial Hall is the future home of the Please Touch Museum.*

**BELOW:** Boathouse Row is home to college crew teams and rowing clubs.

Map on page 143

*Visitors can have a close encounter with exotic birds in the Philadelphia Zoo's lorikeet enclosure.*

**BELOW:** Kids get an underwater view of the polar bear tank at the Philadelphia Zoo.

685-0000; open Mon–Fri 9am–5pm), a monumental exhibition hall built as a museum in 1875 for the Centennial Fair and one of only two buildings that remain from the celebration. The other is **Ohio House**, a modest Victorian structure made out of Ohio stone at States Drive and Belmont Avenue. Both buildings are now used for offices, but visitors can get information at Memorial Hall and view its breathtaking central hall.

From the rear of Memorial Hall, it's a short way on North Concourse Drive through the twin spires of the **Smith Civil War Memorial** to two very different historic homes. **Cedar Grove** (Lansdowne Dr; tel: 235-7469; Tue–Sun 10am–5pm; entrance fee), a farmhouse built in 1745 and moved stone by stone from its original Northern Liberties site, is a fine example of Quaker simplicity. Nearby **Sweetbriar** ㉑ (Lansdowne Dr; tel: 222-1333; open Wed–Sun 10am–4pm; entrance fee) is the neoclassical home of merchant Samuel Breck, built in 1797 as a sanctuary from a yellow fever epidemic.

Also not far from Memorial Hall is

the **Horticultural Center** ㉒ (Horticultural Dr; tel: 685-0096; visitor center open daily 9am–3pm, grounds daily 7am–6pm; entrance free), which includes a greenhouse complex and a 22-acre (9-hectare) arboretum. Nearby is **Shofuso** (Lansdowne Dr; tel: 878-5097; May–Oct Tues–Sun; entrance fee), known as the Japanese House. Originally built for display in 1954–55 at New York's Museum of Modern Art, it was moved to Philadelphia when the exhibit ended. Shofuso is a replica of a 17th-century Japanese home behind a walled garden. Guides are happy to show you around, and tea ceremonies are occasionally conducted.

West of Belmont Avenue is the **Mann Center for the Performing Arts** ㉓ (George's Hill; box office tel: 893-1999; Jun–Sep), an outdoor amphitheater where you can hear the Philadelphia Orchestra, as well as touring rock, jazz and pop shows. There are outdoor restaurants at the top of the hill and the view of the city skyline is wonderful.

## Animal planet

The last stop on the tour is yet another Philadelphia first. Founded in 1859, opened in 1874, the **Philadelphia Zoological Gardens** ㉔ (3400 W. Girard Ave; tel: 243-1100; daily; entrance fee) is the oldest zoo in the US. The 42-acre (17-hectare) site is home to nearly 2,000 animals, many in re-created habitats.

Highlights include the 5-acre (2-hectare) African Safari Quest, a Primate Reserve, a Reptile and Amphibian House, Jungle Bird Walk, a Children's Zoo, and the "Treehouse," an 1876 building transformed into six different environments. Exhibits featuring rare or exotic species are brought in each season. To get an overview of the park, try the new Zooballoon, a balloon ride that takes visitors 400 ft (120 meters) up, wind conditions permitting. ❏

# RESTAURANTS & BARS

## Restaurants

### Figs
2501 Meredith St. Tel: 978-8440. Open: D Tues–Sun, Sat & Sun brunch. $$
www.figsrestaurant.com
A neighborhood bistro with North African influences, courtesy of Moroccan chef-owner Mustapha Rouissiya. You'll find dishes like brie baked in a clay pot with lavender and honey alongside filet mignon with gorgonzola. BYOB.

### Fountain at the Four Seasons Hotel
One Logan Sq. Tel: 963-1500. Open: B, L, D daily, Sun brunch. $$$$
Everything you'd expect from this storied name – exquisite food, flawless service and an immaculate interior. Try chef Martin Hamann's upscale cheesesteak wrapped in a spring roll. The less formal Swann Lounge is a popular spot for cocktails.

### Illuminare
2321 Fairmount Ave. Tel: 765-0202. Open: L Mon–Sat, D nightly, Sun brunch. $$
Serving Italian classics in a casual setting, this neighborhood spot is best known for its tasty brick oven pizza.

### Jack's Firehouse
2130 Fairmount Ave. Tel: 232-9000. Open: L Mon–Sat, D nightly, Sun brunch. $$–$$$
www.jacksfirehouse.com
Southern-inflected fare and smoked and grilled meats are served in this restored firehouse. Although the cuisine veers towards Dixie, chef-owner Jack McDavid is committed to using local ingredients.

### London Grill
2301 Fairmount Ave. Tel: 978-4545. Open: L Mon–Fri, D nightly, Sun brunch. $$
www.londongrill.com
Chef-owner Michael McNally's eclectic menu spans the globe at this Fairmount favorite but comes home to roost with the tasty London burger. The black-and-white tiled bar is original to the space and a cozy place to fritter away an afternoon with a few beers.

### Mugshots
21st & Fairmount Ave. Tel: 267-514-7145. Open: B, L, D daily. $
www.mugshotscoffeehouse.com
Across the street from the Eastern State Penitentiary, this bustling coffeehouse serves smoothies, salads and sandwiches made with local and organic ingredients. There are ample vegan and vegetarian options and cozy couches and chairs.

### Rembrandt's
741 N. 23rd St. Tel: 763-2228. Open: L & D daily, Sun brunch. $$
Entering its third decade, this neighborhood spot now includes a second, smoke-free tavern and private rooms. The best dishes are the thin-crust pizzas baked in a wood-fired oven.

### Rose Tattoo
1847 Callowhill St. Tel: 569-8939. Open: L Mon–Fri, D Mon–Sat. $$
www.rosetattoocafe.com
This Fairmount bistro oozes a vaguely Southern charm, from the wrought-iron balcony dripping with hanging greenery to the elaborate flower arrangements. Serving New American cuisine, it's a favorite for romantics.

## Bars

### The Bishop's Collar
2349 Fairmount Ave. Tel: 765-1616.
Live music and TVs, plus a casual neighborhood vibe near the Art Museum.

### Bridgid's
726 N. 24th St. Tel: 232-3232.
A lengthy Belgian beer list is the main draw at this hideaway. Full menu.

### PRICE CATEGORIES
Prices for three-course dinner per person with a half-bottle of house wine:
$ = under $25
$$ = $25–$40
$$$ = $40–$50
$$$ = more than $50

**RIGHT:** a hot dog vendor offers the specialty of the house.

# THE FRANKLIN INSTITUTE

**Multimedia shows and interactive exhibits give museum-goers a high-tech – and high-touch – experience of science and technology**

IN HONOR OF B

The Franklin Institute is usually described as a museum, but it's more like a playground for the mind, where kids and their adult companions learn about science and technology from a kaleidoscopic array of hands-on exhibits.

Highlights among the scores of permanent installations include the "Train Factory," which features a working 350-ton locomotive, and the "Franklin Air Show," which investigates aviation technology with a flight simulator, a Wright brothers Model B Flyer and a jet fighter. "Sports Challenge" uses virtual technology to explore the physics of curve balls, surfing, rock climbing and other sports-related phenomena. The renovated "Giant Heart" gives children a chance to walk through a two-story model of the human heart, watch a video of cardiac surgery and learn about the latest breakthroughs in robotic surgery and high-tech imaging. In "Sir Isaac's Loft" a dizzying array of Rube Goldberg contraptions illustrate concepts such as motion, kinetic energy and force.

Equally exciting are the temporary exhibits, which in recent years have included blockbusters like "King Tut," "Body Worlds" and "The Titanic."

**ABOVE:** Dedicated to educating the public about science and technology, the Franklin Institute was established in 1824 and moved to its present location on the Benjamin Franklin Parkway in 1934.

**LEFT:** Clever exhibits, like this skeleton on an exercise machine, demonstrate the internal mechanics of the human body.

**LEFT:** The experience starts at the Benjamin Franklin Memorial in the cavernous rotunda, where visitors are greeted by a 20-ft-high (6-meter) statue of the institute's namesake. An exhibit chronicles Franklin's career as a scientist and inventor.

**RIGHT:** The hall of colors leads to a display of optical illusions.

**ABOVE:** The Fels Planetarium employs a state-of-the-art star-field projector to guide viewers on a journey through the galaxy. The system produces a wide variety of computer graphics and a dazzling repertoire of audio and visual effects.

## THE SKY'S THE LIMIT

Like a window on the cosmos, the Fels Planetarium introduces visitors to the wonders of the universe. Recently outfitted with a new dome, a digital projector and a viscera-shaking sound system, the Planetarium offers state-of-the-art star shows as well as special programs on such topics as the search for extraterrestrial life.

Surrounding the Planetarium is "Space Command," a gallery with 30 interactive stations that explore the science behind spacesuits, satellite imaging and other space-age technology. Other exhibits include a chunk of a meteorite that crashed into northern Arizona some 50,000 years ago and moon rocks collected by Apollo astronauts in 1972.

On the roof of the Franklin Institute is the Joel N. Bloom Observatory, where visitors using high-powered telescopes and protective filters can view sunspots and solar flares. Venus is another favorite daytime target.

For a visual experience of a very different sort, the Institute also has an IMAX theater with a domed screen 4½ stories high.

**BELOW:** A giant walk-through model of the human heart is one of the most popular, and oldest, exhibits at the Franklin Institute.

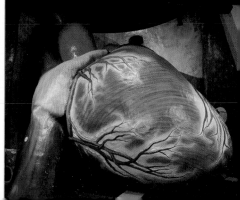

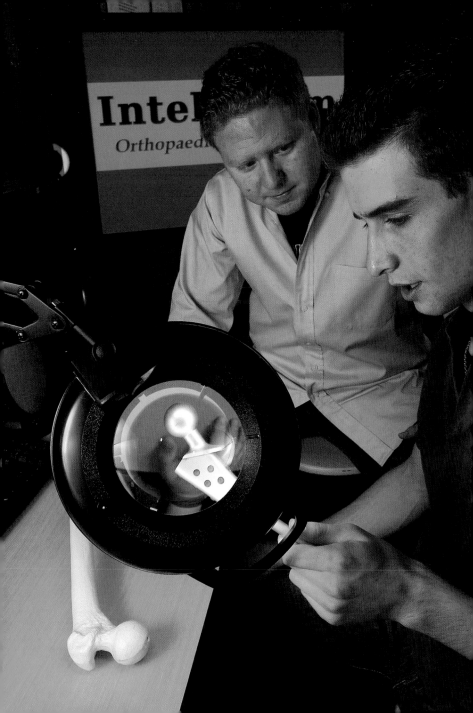

# UNIVERSITY CITY

Like a college town set within the city, this
neighborhood is known for fine Victorian
architecture, excellent museums and galleries,
and a lively collegiate atmosphere

The saga of the University of Pennsylvania begins in 1740 with the campaign for a Charity School at 4th and Arch streets "for the instruction of Poor Children Gratis ... and also for a House of Publick worship." Unfortunately, the school never did get solidly off the ground, financially speaking, and a few years later the ubiquitous Benjamin Franklin stepped in to spearhead a drive to transform the benevolent school into a less secular, more public oriented institution. The academy that was founded evolved into the College of Philadelphia and then into the nation's first university in 1779; it shifted its place of operations in 1802 to 9th Street, between Chestnut and Market.

## Second city

This second home sufficed for seven decades, until a new provost took over and denounced the location as a "vile neighborhood, growing viler every day." Fashionable Philadelphians had already begun abandoning center city and heading west. And so did the university. "Penn" shifted its campus across the Schuylkill River to the west bank, some 15 blocks from the paternal glance of William Penn atop City Hall. Construction of a bridge in 1805 had created easier access from the east, but it was the university's relocation that quickened the developmental pace. And in 1892, the founding of what became Drexel University nearby designated the area as University City.

Today, aside from its academic attractions, University City is home to several medical centers, museums, a variety of restaurants, and historic residential communities. Bridges connect University City to center city on five streets: JFK Boulevard (both

Map
on page
152

**LEFT:** Penn students study prosthetic joints.
**BELOW:** the Fine Arts Library, designed by celebrated architect Frank Furness, is on the University of Pennsylvania campus.

ways), Market (westbound), Chestnut (eastbound), Walnut (westbound) and South (both ways).

## College town

A walk through the neighborhood, following a roughly circular route, discloses much of the area's character – the cloistered campuses, ivy-covered halls, exuberant collegiate atmosphere, grand Victorian architecture, and ethnic diversity – like a little college town against the backdrop of a modern city. The boundaries of the neighborhood run roughly from the Schuylkill River to 45th Street and from Baltimore Avenue to Market Street. As in center city, the streets are laid out in a grid, making orientation easy.

The **30th Street Station ①** (30th St and JFK Blvd), which can be reached by any SEPTA (Southeastern Pennsylvania Transportation Authority) subway-surface trolley or Market Street subway train, acts like a sort of

*A Penn student competes at the Penn Relays, one of the country's largest and most prestigious track and field events.*

reception hall for University City. Occupying nearly a full city block, the station, of Greek design and faced with Alabama limestone, was opened in 1933 by the once mighty but now vanished Pennsylvania Railroad. Today, the recently renovated station (complete with a food court and stores) has been handed over to Amtrak and is that line's second busiest depot.

**Drexel University ②** (tel: 895-2000) is near the station, with many of its buildings clustered between Market and Chestnut, 31st and 33rd streets. Although much of the campus is recently but unimaginatively constructed, there are some older buildings of note. The Paul Peck Alumni Center at 32nd and Market streets is a Frank Furness building that opened in 1876 for the first World's Fair. The **Peck Center Gallery** is open to the public (tel: 895-0480, Mon–Fri 10am–5pm; entrance free). It shares the Drexel

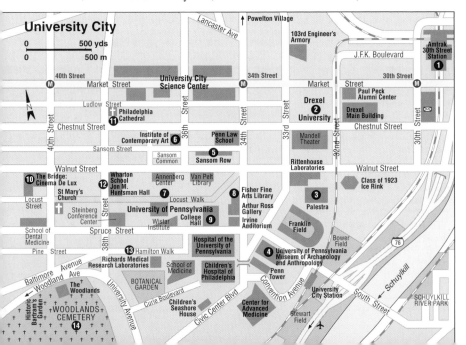

Collection, established in 1892 by the university's founder Anthony J. Drexel, with the **Westphal Picture Gallery** (tel: 895-0480; Mon–Fri 3.30–5.30pm; entrance free), which is housed in the most important of Drexel's original buildings to remain in use – the Main Building at 32nd and Chestnut streets, now a National Historic Landmark. The structure, built in a classic Renaissance style with terracotta decorative touches and a truly heroic interior court, is a stunning example of late 19th-century design.

## History and art

The **University of Pennsylvania** is the dominant presence in University City and the largest employer in West Philadelphia. The university's athletic facilities are along the Schuylkill River between Walnut and South streets. They include the **Class of 1923 Ice Rink** (3130 Walnut St; tel: 898-1923; open Sep–Mar; entrance fee), tennis and squash courts, the **Palestra ❸**, the university's indoor basketball and track arena, and **Franklin Field**, the

site of Ivy League football, the Penn Relays and other sport events.

Of particular interest in this area is the University of Pennsylvania **Museum of Archaeology and Anthropology ❹** (3360 South St; tel: 898-4000; www.museum.upenn.edu; open Tue–Sat 10am–4.30pm, Sun 1–5pm, closed summer Sundays; entrance fee). The University Museum has one of the most distinguished archaeological collections in the world, with 32 exhibition galleries and a special emphasis on the arts and cultures of classical Old World civilizations as well as the native people of Polynesia, Africa and the Americas. The museum building itself is significant – a huge, though incomplete 19th-century building designed in a dizzying variety of architectural styles.

South of the museum is the Penn Tower hotel and its pedestrian bridge to the University of Pennsylvania's hospital. Beyond the bridge on the southeast side of the street sits Convention Hall, which has been used as a sound stage for a number of films, including *The Sixth Sense* in 1999.

*Penn's ubiquitous founder, Ben Franklin, memorialized on a park bench.*

**BELOW:** Penn students take a break under a statue of university founder Benjamin Franklin.

## Center of Learning

Higher education in Philadelphia goes back to 1749. Benjamin Franklin founded a preparatory school that would become, in 1755, the College of Pennsylvania. In 1779, a medical school was added, qualifying it as the nation's first university, the University of Pennsylvania, where nine signers of the Declaration of Independence would either teach, study or serve as trustees.

Penn, as the school is known, was only the beginning. Drexel University, founded in 1891, is nearby, and Temple University in North Philadelphia, founded in 1884, educates more than 31,000 students in 14 schools and colleges. The Philadelphia area has the largest concentration of higher educational institutions in the country, with 88 colleges and universities, 27 of them within city limits. They include five medical schools; 24 teaching hospitals; the renowned Curtis Institute of Music, established in 1924; the Pennsylvania Academy of the Fine Arts; the University of the Arts; and schools established by the Quakers – Bryn Mawr, Haverford and Swarthmore. Just 45 miles (72 km) from the city is Lincoln University, the first institution of higher learning to provide education to African-American men.

Walk back north on 34th Street (passing on the northwest corner of 34th and Spruce the Irvine Auditorium, a ziggurat-like 1929 building designed by Horace Trumbauer) to Sansom Street just west of 34th Street, known as **Sansom Row** ❺.

The south side is a lovely block of row houses built around the time of the Civil War. No. 3420 was for a time the home of the famous 19th-century spiritualist Madame Helena Blavatsky.

The building, divided into small dining rooms, now houses the **White Dog Café** (tel: 386-9224; www.whitedog.com), named in honor of the white dog Madame Blavatsky successfully draped over her infected leg as a cure. It is one of the most stylish and characteristic restaurants in the neighborhood. More than an eating place, the White Dog hosts lectures and discussion groups, throws parties to celebrate local causes, and produces a tri-annual newsletter on its activities. It also has music in its piano parlor on weekends.

At the west end of Sansom Row, at 36th Street, is **Sansom Common**, a shopping and dining area anchored by the University of Pennsylvania Bookstore at 36th and Walnut streets.

The **Institute of Contemporary Art** ❻ (118 S. 36th St; tel: 898-7108; open Wed–Fri noon–8pm, Sat–Sun 11am–5pm; entrance fee) features cutting-edge photography, performance and plastic arts.

## Penn campus

The Penn campus begins in earnest at 34th and Walnut streets. A stroll down **Locust Walk** ❼, a pedestrian extension of Locust Street running from 34th to 40th streets, offers a splendid way to examine the university's central campus. Architecturally, it is a patchwork of many styles, as if the school's trustees had decreed that each building had to represent an entirely different school of design. The result is an architectural grab bag, whose contents, if pleasing individually, are unsettling en masse.

Some of the most intriguing buildings are clustered at the east end of Locust Walk. Notable among them

*The fanciful sculpture in front of the Fine Arts Library is Claes Oldenburg's* Split Button. *Associated with the Pop Art movement of the 1960s, Oldenburg is best known for huge reproductions of everyday objects.*

**BELOW:** ancient Egyptian artifacts at the University of Pennsylvania Museum of Archaeology and Anthropology.

is the old University Library, built in 1888–90, and now the **Fine Arts Library**  (34th and Walnut sts). The building, perhaps the master-work of Philadelphia architect Frank Furness (whose buildings are found throughout University City), is as richly ornamented as a fairytale castle. It was named a National Historic Landmark in 1985. Part of the library is devoted to the **Arthur Ross Gallery** (220 S. 34th St; tel: 898-2083; www.upenn.edu/ARG; open Tues–Fri 10am–5pm, Sat–Sun noon–5pm; entrance free), which features changing exhibits from the university's art collection.

## Victorian style

**College Hall** , a fine example of the Victorian Gothic style, lies across the court from the Van Pelt Library. Built in 1871–72 to house the university upon its move from 9th and Chestnut streets, it reflects the influence of John Ruskin, the eminent English art historian and critic, who championed the decorative use of contrasting colored stone and other materials.

Locust Walk runs west, alternately a shaded enclave between ivy-covered stone, an open bridge over busy 38th Street, and a walk through a high-rise dormitory complex, before ending at 40th Street. Around the corner at 40th and Walnut streets is **The Bridge: Cinema De Lux** , a state-of-the-art theater complex featuring first-run and some high-profile independent movies on six screens with stadium seating and digital surround-sound, as well as pre-show live entertainment, a restaurant and outdoor terrace, and a "media immersion room" with giant plasma screens.

**Philadelphia Cathedral**  (38th St, between Chestnut and Market sts; tel: 386-0234; www.philadelphia-cathedral.org; Mon–Fri 10am–2pm) is worth a special look. Built in 1906 for the Pennsylvania Episcopal Diocese, the cathedral is reminiscent of a 5th-century Christian basilica, with its vaulted ceilings, stained-glass windows (one by Tiffany), and a wide open nave.

In 2002 **The Wharton School**  of the University of Pennsylvania,

Map on page 152

**TIP**

During the school year, the Leonard Pearlstein Gallery behind Nesbitt Hall at 33rd and Market streets, shows student work in various media. (tel: 215-895-2548; open Mon–Fri 11am–5pm).

**BELOW:** Penn is a leader in the training of young scientists.

## Meals on Wheels

Some of the tastiest food in University City comes from the mobile vendors around the Penn and Drexel campuses. It's an international buffet on asphalt, where you can sample Chinese, Korean, Middle Eastern and other cuisines at wallet-friendly prices.

Carts have loyal followings – and long lines. Yue Kee, which parks on 38th Street between Walnut and Spruce, was well reviewed by the *Inquirer's* food critic Craig Laban, while The Greek Lady turned her cart into a brick-and-mortar restaurant. There are rivalries – don't confuse Le Ahn Chinese Food with The Real Le Ahn, on the same block. For a list of food trucks go to www.dailypennsylvanian.com

Map on page 152

**TIP**

Combine a cruise on the Schuylkill River with a visit to Historic Bartram's Garden. Tour boats depart from the foot of the Walnut Street bridge along the Schuylkill River Trail. Call 888-748-7445 for reservations.

**BELOW:** Penn students chat on the Quad between classes.

one of the world's best business schools, opened Jon M. Huntsman Hall at 38th and Walnut streets. The state-of-the-art facility is a striking addition to the Penn campus.

Locust Walk between 36th and 38th streets is paralleled two blocks south by **Hamilton Walk** ⓫. Another of the many leafy walkways that cut through the campus, Hamilton Walk is bordered by the former Men's Dormitories, which run along Spruce Street. A sprawling structure adorned with gables and gargoyles, the building is a beautiful evocation of a medieval English university. Across the walk are the starkly vertical lines of the Alfred Newton Richards Medical Research Laboratories. Hidden away just south of the Richards building is a Botanical Garden, an unexpected pleasure in this otherwise urban academic environment.

### Beyond the campus

South and west of Penn the neighborhood becomes mostly residential. Many streets are lined with architecturally interesting houses in various states of repair. Across Woodland Avenue is **Woodlands Cemetery** ⓮, burial ground for many of Philadelphia's distinguished families.

**Powelton Village**, tucked into the northeast corner of University City several blocks directly north of the Drexel campus, is characterized by large Italianate and Victorian homes as well as several blocks of charming row houses.

South of University City on a patch of green hugging the Schuylkill River lies **Historic Bartram's Garden** (54th St and Lindbergh Blvd; tel: 729-5281; garden open daily 10am–5pm; house tours Mar–Dec Tues–Sun at 12:10, 1:10, 2:10 and 3:10pm; entrance fee for house tour only). John Bartram, friend of Benjamin Franklin (with whom he founded the American Philosophical Society) and one-time botanist to King George III, established this 44-acre (18-hectare) farm in 1728. Visitors can tour Bartram's house, barn and cider press, wander through the gardens, stroll the river trail, and view archaeological excavations dating as far back as the 15th century. ❏

# RESTAURANTS & BARS

## Restaurants

### Dahlak
4708 Baltimore Ave. Tel: 726-6464. Open: D nightly. $–$$
www.dahlakrestaurant.com
Homey, funky and laid-back, Dahlak serves the richly flavored cuisine of Eritrea, which you eat with injera, a spongy pancake used for scooping and sopping. Have a drink at the lively, speakeasy-like bar while you wait.

### Greek Lady
222 S. 40th St. Tel: 382-2600. Open: B, L, D daily. $
A longtime street vendor, the Greek Lady put down roots at the Shops at Hamilton Village. The menu is familiar; egg sandwiches and cheesesteaks are augmented by Greek specialties like gyros and moussaka.

### Kabobeesh
4201 Chestnut St. Tel: 386-8081. Open: L & D nightly. $
This old dining car has been transformed into one of the area's best options for cheap, delicious Pakistani fare. It's frequented by homesick cab drivers, Penn students and budget diners.

### La Terrasse
3432 Sansom St. Tel: 386-5000. Open: L Mon–Fri, D nightly, Sun brunch. $$$
This French bistro has long been the go-to spot in University City for romantic dinners, especially on the patio. There are other options in the area, but Le Terrasse still packs them in.

### Marigold Kitchen
501 S. 45th St. Tel: 222-3699. Open: D Tues–Sat. $$–$$$
www.marigoldkitchenbyob.com
An old Victorian house is the location of what many consider to be one of the city's top chef-driven BYOBs. The menu features a range of artfully prepared dishes with global influences. If you can't make up your mind, try a tasting menu.

### Nan
4000 Chestnut St. Tel: 382-0818. Open: L Tues–Fri, D Tue-Sat. $$–$$$
www.nanrestaurant.com
This spare Thai-French fusion BYOB is a quiet neighborhood favorite. The exterior may indicate otherwise, but there's serious upscale cooking going on inside, combining French technique with Asian ingredients.

### Penne Restaurant & Wine Bar
The Inn at Penn, 3611 Walnut St. Tel: 823-6222. Open: L Mon-Fri, D nightly. $$$
www.pennerestaurant.com
Fresh pasta made in house is the draw of this Italian spot in the Hilton Hotel, although there are many meat and fish entrees to choose from as well. The wine bar offers mostly Italian wines and tasting flights.

### Picnic
3131 Walnut St. Tel: 222-1608. Open: Mon–Sat B, L, D. $
If you're in need of a quick bite to go, the gourmet fare here is an upscale alternative to the area's street vendors. Ask them to pack a picnic basket for you.

### Pod
3636 Sansom St. Tel: 387-1803. Open: L Mon–Fri, D nightly. $$$
www.podrestaurant.com
Supremely mod, Pod's white interior is part Austin Powers, part Clockwork Orange. Dine from the pan-Asian menu while sitting in futuristic "pods" or pick sushi off a conveyor belt.

### Rx
4443 Spruce St. Tel: 222-9590. Open: D Tues–Sat, Sat & Sun brunch. $$
www.caferx.com
This cute apothecary-themed BYOB in a former pharmacy is appreciated by locals and University types, especially for brunch. The eclectic American cuisine incorporates organic ingredients.

### White Dog Cafe
3420 Sansom St. Tel: 386-9224. Open: L Mon–Sat, D nightly, Sun brunch. $$$
www.whitedogcafe.com
A commitment to using local, sustainable and organic ingredients is what distinguishes the White Dog from the rest of the pack. Each dish lists the pedigree of its ingredients, from purveyors to farmers. The homespun interior gives it a rambling country house feel; the bar serves mostly American wines and boutique beers.

## Bars

### World Cafe Live
3025 Walnut St. Tel: 222-1400.
www.worldcafelive.com
One of the city's premier (and newest) venues for live music. Acts range from established bands to up-and-coming local talent. Full menu.

### Marbar
40th & Walnut sts. Tel: 222-0100.
Upstairs from the bustling Marathon Grill and Bridge theater, this vast space is slightly more sophisticated than the average Joe College bar. Nightly drink specials and DJs.

### PRICE CATEGORIES
Prices for three-course dinner per person with a half-bottle of house wine:
$ = under $25
$$ = $25–$40
$$$ = $40–$50
$$$ = more than $50

# SOUTH PHILLY

With an immigrant history dating back to the 17th century, this sprawling blue-collar neighborhood attracts visitors to a colorful open-air market, dozens of ethnic eateries, and the city's professional sports complex

O n balance, Friedrich Nietzsche said, the most admirable of all Europe's people are the Italians, the most perfect humanists. Their American cousins have exhibited this genius for humanism in enclaves like South Philadelphia since around 1880, when the migratory urge began the depopulation of Italy's Mezzogiorno. These ragged *paesani* were poor in possessions but rich in culture, determination and family spirit.

Lots of others – Irish, Germans, Jews from Eastern Europe, African-Americans – came to South Philly too, and in recent years there has been an influx of new faces – Vietnamese, Cambodian, Chinese, Mexican – sinking roots into the row house terrain, building new lives in a strange land.

South Philly is a tight-knit community. Kids play stickball in the streets, old folks perch on stoops, church bells chime all day, and the smells of countless delis, bakeries and pizzerias permeate the air.

## Little Italy

At the heart of the neighborhood, in all of its bustling, ramshackle glory, is the **Italian Market** ❶, six blocks of butchers, bakers and pasta-makers strung along 9th Street between Christian and Washington. There's

a slew of discount stalls, too, hawking everything from bootleg CDs to cut-rate shoes. And yes, this is the market Sylvester Stallone jogged through in *Rocky*.

Touring this Little Italy in the early 1920s, Christopher Morley wrote that the market "breathes the Italian genius for good food." And so it does, although these days you're also likely to find Chinese, Vietnamese and black hucksters. The merchandise is much the same as it was 80 years ago. There are

Map on page 160

**LEFT:** Geno's Steaks, longtime rival of across-the-street competitor Pat's.
**BELOW:** Valente's Barbershop, a South Philly institution for more than 70 years.

## TIP

Most shops in the Italian Market are open Monday to Saturday, but the best time to visit is Saturday morning, when chefs, amateur and professional, stock up for the week, and the vendors, eager to sell produce before the weekend, offer the best deals.

piles of fruit and vegetables, wriggling crabs, miles of fresh linguine, and everything from 6-ft (1.5-meter) salamis to suckling pigs hanging in storefront windows.

Starting at the northern end of the market, a quick tour might include a taste of crusty, brick-oven bread at **Sarcone's Bakery** (734 S. 9th St; tel: 922-1717), a sackful of herbs, teas and coffee beans at **Spice Corner** (904 S. 9th St; tel: 925-1660), a wedge of provolone at **DiBruno Brothers** ( 930 S. 9th St; tel: 922-2876), a bowl of moist mozzarella at **Claudio King of Cheese** (926 S. 9th St; tel: 627-1873), a look at the latest culinary gadgets at **Fante's** (1006 S. 9th St; tel: 800-443-2683), and then fresh linguine at **Talluto's** (944 S. 9th St; tel: 627-4967).

At the end of the market, reward yourself with one of Geno's or Pat's cheesesteaks or one of a dozen restaurants within walking distance of the market.

## High kicks

You'll find another cluster of shops and restaurants on Passyunk Avenue. An old cow path, Passyunk swerves through the street grid and intersects

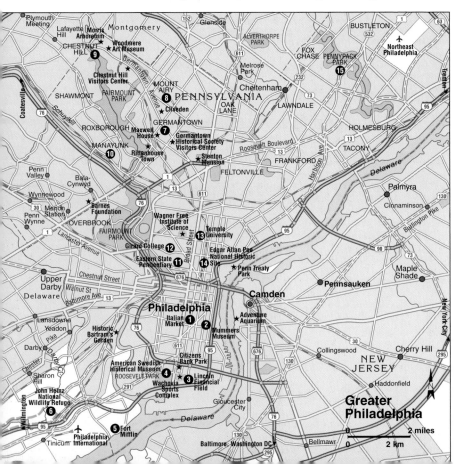

Map
on page
160

Broad Street, which, as any true-blue South Philadelphian can tell you, is the path of the Mummers New Year's Day Parade. If you can't wait until New Year's Day, you can get a taste of the Mummer experience at the **Mummers Museum ❷** (1100 S. 2nd St; tel: 336-3050; open Tues–Sat 9.30am–4.30pm, Sun noon–4.30pm, May–Sep open Tue to 9.30pm; entrance fee). Housed in an unusual building that is supposed to represent the strutters' flamboyant outfits, the museum chronicles the tradition and history of Philadelphia Mummery. The famous Mummers string bands offer concerts at the museum on Tuesday evenings between May and September and at special events throughout the city.

At the south end of Broad Street, three large arenas draw fans of major league baseball, football, basketball and hockey, as well as rock concerts, ice shows, the circus and various other sports events. **Lincoln Financial Field ❸**, new home to the Eagles football team, opened in 2003 and also hosts pop concerts. Just south of Pattison Avenue, the

**Wachovia Sports Complex** (events tel: 336-3600; box office open Mon–Fri 9am–6pm, Sat–Sun of event 10am–4.30pm) is home to the Flyers (hockey), 76ers (basketball), Wings (lacrosse ), Kixx (soccer) and Phantoms (AHL hockey) as well as Comcast SportsNet, a sports cable network. Tours of the Wachovia Center, including the Comcast SportsNet, the press box and locker rooms, are available for groups of 15 or more with advance reservations. Individuals are added to tours as space allows (tel: 389-9543; entrance fee). A new ballpark for the Phillies, **Citizens Bank Park** (tel: 463-5000 for ticket information), opened in 2004. With its classic ballpark design and great views of the skyline, the park is a huge improvement over its now-demolished predecessor, Veterans Stadium.

### The earliest immigrants

Of course, Italians weren't the first immigrants to settle in these parts. Way back in the 1640s, four decades before William Penn stepped foot on American soil, a hardy bunch of

*Mummers were originally masked actors whose mimes were popular in England in the 18th and early 19th centuries. The first official Mummers Parade was held in Philadelphia in 1901. Until 1964, when civil rights groups objected, black face paint was often worn.*

**BELOW:** a produce vendor mans a stall at the Italian Market.

Map on page 160

**TIP**

Guides in period costume lead weekend tours of Fort Mifflin. Call 685-4167 for a tour schedule.

**BELOW:** a young patriot at historic Fort Mifflin, site of a heroic defense of Philadelphia during the American Revolution.

Swedish pioneers hacked out farms and built log cabins in the place where row houses and family grocery stores now stand.

You can learn more about the brief but fascinating history of New Sweden at the **American Swedish Historical Museum** ❹ (1900 Pattison Ave; tel: 389-1776; www.american-swedish.org; Tue–Fri 10am–4pm, Sat–Sun noon–4pm; entrance fee). Set on the edge of Roosevelt Park in a building modeled after Sweden's 17th-century Eriksberg Castle, the museum features a collection of artifacts and artworks displayed in galleries designed in a variety of Swedish architectural styles. The museum also sponsors annual festivals such as Valborgsmassoafton in April, a crayfish party in August, and Lucia Fest, with a candlelight procession, in December.

## A valiant defense

History buffs may want to travel even farther south to old **Fort Mifflin** ❺ (Island and Fort Mifflin Rd, near the airport off I-95; tel: 685-4167; open Apr–Dec Wed–Sun 10am–4pm;

entrance fee), site of the gallant but failed defense of Philadelphia during the American Revolution.

Construction of the fort was started by the British in 1772, but it was abandoned to the Americans after the Declaration of Independence. In 1777, the rebel force at Fort Mifflin was instrumental in preventing the British fleet from reaching Philadelphia. Hundreds of Americans died during two weeks of bombardment, and the redcoats finally broke through. But the delay was sufficient to protect General Washington's army at Valley Forge. The fort was rebuilt in 1795 and used as a prison for Confederate soldiers during the Civil War. Now a National Historic Landmark, many of the buildings inside the thick stone walls have been restored.

## Walk on the wild side

The **John Heinz National Wildlife Refuge** ❻ at Tinicum (86th and Lindbergh Ave; tel: 365-3118; open daily 8am–sunset; entrance free) is a short drive from Fort Mifflin. Thanks to the efforts of local conservationists, 1,200 protected acres (480 hectares) have been set aside along the woods, tidal marshes and mud flats of Darby Creek. The **Cusano Environmental Education Center** (open daily 8am–4.30pm), built according to principles of sustainable design, is a valuable addition to the refuge, and has exhibits, a library and classrooms.

Tinicum was first settled in 1643 by Johann Printz, who put his village on what was then an island at the mouth of Darby Creek. Today, Tinicum is among the last unspoiled areas in the environmentally rich wetlands around the metropolitan area. The reserve serves as a nesting ground for more than 70 species of bird and a stopover for migratory birds. The 3-mile (5-km) loop trail and boardwalk lead hikers across the lagoon and into the woods. ❑

# The Cheesesteak War

They have been locking horns for more than 30 years: **Pat's King of Steaks** (1237 E. Passyunk Ave; tel: 468-1546) and **Geno's** (1219 9th St; tel: 389-0659), South Philly's cheesesteak champs, facing off like opposing chess pieces across the intersection. There are other – some heretics even say better – cheesesteak stands in Philadelphia (Jim's Steaks at 400 South St is often mentioned as a contender), but the rivalry between Pat's and Geno's has catapulted them to legendary status.

Publicly, the owners downplay the issue. "There's a rivalry between the two of us," says Frank Olivieri, Jr, grand-nephew of Pat, the founder. "Sure, we're always looking out the window to see what the other guy is doing, but it's mostly media hype. We're friends on the battlefield and we're friends off the battlefield." Geno's owner agrees: "Competition is healthy," Joe Vento says. But the rivalry is "not what people think. We're friends."

Still, like longtime sparring partners, the two can't help but throw a few jabs. Olivieri says his cheesesteaks are the people's choice. The secret, he says, is the well-seasoned, nearly 70-year-old grill. He claims that Pat's outsells Geno's 12–1. Vento challenges this and says that Geno's is a larger operation. "You put 10 people over [at Pat's], it looks packed. You put 30 people at my place, and it's nothing. We can push 'em out faster and keep the lines down." He's also proud of his cleanliness. "I don't buy that greasy spoons make better steaks."

About the only thing the two agree on is who started selling steak sandwiches first. "Pat's did it first," concedes Vento, who opened his stand in 1966 – although who first added cheese is still debatable. It all began in 1930. Pat's founders, brothers Pasquale and Harry Olivieri, then hot-dog vendors, slipped grilled chopped beef into a hot-dog roll for a hungry taxi driver. The cabbie liked the newfangled sandwich so much he came back for more, and pretty soon Pasquale and Harry knew that they had a hot item on their hands. Years later, after the brothers opened shop at their Passyunk Avenue stand, one of the cooks got bored eating plain steak on a bun, so he melted some cheese on top. The rest was history.

Since then, the cheesesteak has proved a remarkably adaptable concoction. Imaginative chefs substitute pork or chicken, mozzarella or provolone, pile on mushrooms, hot sauce, tomatoes, peppers, eggplant and mounds of fried onions. A few have even created a vegetarian variety.

But the rivalry between Pat's and Geno's goes on. And loyalty is a serious matter. "Pat's is number one," customers chime, hoisting hefty sandwiches toward their mouths. "The first, the original, the best."

"Geno's is the best," customers on the opposite side of the street say. "Tastes better, friendly people. No contest. They're not chintzy with the onions, either."

Geno's owner Joey Vento stirred up a hornet's nest of a different sort in 2006 when he posted a sign outside his shop that said, "This is America ... when ordering speak English." The sign was meant as a commentary on the issue of immigration, much in the news at the time, and made the outspoken Vento a talk-show darling for several weeks. ❏

**RIGHT:** Pat's King of Steaks.

# RESTAURANTS & BARS

## Restaurants

### Carman's Country Kitchen

1301 S. 11th St. Tel: 339-9613. Open: daily B & L. $$
Diners crowd this loopy little luncheonette (and a converted pickup truck parked outside) for a small but seductive breakfast and lunch menu. A little pricey, but the eccentric atmosphere and attentive staff make it a unique experience.

### Dante & Luigi's

762 S. 10th St. Tel: 922-9501. Open: Tues–Fri L & D, Sat Sun D. $$
Solid Italian fare has been the attraction at this South Philly stalwart for more than a century. You won't be treated to any flights of culinary fancy, but it's a great place to get a feeling for the old-time neighborhood. A mafia hit some years ago adds mystique.

### Fitzwater Cafe

701 Fitzwater St. Tel: 629-0428. Open: Mon–Sun B & L. $–$$
The prettier, younger sister to the masculine Saloon just down the block, sunny Fitzwater is popular for breakfast, brunch and lunch, which features big portions of homey, Italian favorites like wedding soup. Don't skip dessert.

### La Lupe

1201 S. 9th St. Tel: 551-9920. Open: B, L & D daily. $
It's low-budget in atmosphere and cost, but intrepid eaters brave its frill-free environment for some of Philly's most authentic Mexican.

### Marra's

1734 E. Passyunk Ave. Tel: 463-9249. Open: Tues–Sun L & D. $
Squeeze into a red-vinyl booth at this classic South Philly pizzeria and restaurant and enjoy first-rate brick-oven pizza, pasta and other home-style Italian favorites.

### Melrose Diner

1501 Snyder Ave. Tel: 467-6644. Open: 24 hours daily. $
www.melrose-diner.com
Diner aficionados should make a trip to this no-frills South Philly institution. The cakes, pies and cookies are the best items on the menu, but the long-time waitresses are the real dish. Local characters abound in the wee hours.

### Morning Glory Diner

735 S. 10th St. Tel: 413-3999. Open: Mon–Fri B & L, Sat & Sun Brunch. $
www.morningglorydiner.com
In warm weather, the namesake flowers lining the windows make this updated diner one of the city's prettiest. The food attracts a loyal following. Expect crowds at weekend brunch, lining up for frittata and pancakes.

### Nam Phuong

1100-1120 Washington Ave. Tel: 468-0410. Open: L & D daily. $–$$
Enormous and inexpensive, this Vietnamese restaurant is a good choice for large groups. Sample their worthy pho and other traditional fare.

### O Sandwiches!

1205 S. 9th St. Tel: 334-6080. Open: L & D Tues–Sun. $
www.osandwiches.com
Just down the block from Philly's cheesesteak crossroads is a whole different sandwich – banh mi – aka the Vietnamese hoagie. Served on baguettes baked in-house, these delicious, inexpensive sandwiches are piled high with pâté, cilantro and veggies.

### Pif

1009 S. 8th St. Tel: 625-2923. Open: D Wed–Sun. $$
This hole-in-the-wall BYOB is as tiny as a restaurant could possibly be and still be called a restaurant. Though cramped, the single dining room is inviting and chef-owner David Ansill's excellent French bistro fare makes up for the lack of elbow room.

**LEFT:** service with a smile at Carman's Country Kitchen, a quirky South Philadelphia favorite.
**RIGHT:** fresh bread at Sarcone's Deli.

## Paradiso

1627 E. Passyunk Ave. Tel: 271-2066. Open: L Tues–Fri, D Tue- Sun. $$–$$$
www.paradisophilly.com

A relatively recent addition to the neighborhood, this elegant spot serves contemporary Italian fare and has a sophisticated selection of mostly Italian wines. Saturday nights offer up live jazz music.

## Pat's King of Steaks

1237 E. Passyunk Ave. Tel: 468-1546. Open: 24 hours daily. $
www.patskingofsteaks.com

## Geno's

1219 S. 9th St. Tel: 389-0659. Open: 24 hours daily $
www.genossteaks.com

The intersection of 9th and Passyunk is the nexus of the great cheesesteak debates: Pat's or Geno's? Whiz or provolone? Wit' or wit'out (translation: with onions or without)? For some, the answer to where to get the best cheesesteak in the city is neither of these places, but still the crowds line up at both places, especially in the wee hours of the morning. Be prepared for strict rules about ordering at both joints, which are designed to keep the long lines moving, and for a hefty dose of the famous South Philly "atty-tood" from the fast-moving staff.

## Ralph's

760 S. 9th St. Tel: 627-6011. Open: L & D daily. $–$$
www.ralphsrestaurant.com

For those seeking an authentic, red sauce experience, look no further than Ralph's, an Italian restaurant near the Italian Market that's been in operation for over a century. The food is strictly old-school spaghetti and meatballs fare; it's the atmosphere that makes Ralph's worth visiting.

## Saloon

750 S. 7th St. Tel: 627-1811. Open: L Mon–Fri, D Mon–Sat. $$$$
www.saloonrestaurant.net

An Italian steakhouse with a clubby, old-world vibe is a favorite hangout for local high rollers and their entourage. Both the steaks and the attractive, mostly female wait staff are considered a draw. Only cash and AmEx are accepted.

## Sabrina's

910 Christian St. Tel: 574-1599. Open: B, L, D Mon–Sat, Sun brunch. $$
www.sabrinascafe.com

If you're hungry for "brunch all day," Sabrina's is your place. This low-key pastel-hued cafe is packed at brunch but quieter on weekdays. Acolytes rave about the enormous stuffed challah French toast, filled with farmer cheese and fruit.

## Sarcone's Deli

743 S. 9th St. Tel: 922-1717. Open: L Tues–Sun. $

It's not much to look at, but the hoagies can't be beat at this unassuming corner deli. When it comes to sandwiches, the bread is half the battle and Sarcone's bread, which is made at their sister bakery just down the street, has some of the best around.

## Taqueria La Veracruzana

908 Washington Ave. Tel: 465-1440. Open: L, D daily. $

One of the first restaurants to spring from Philly's burgeoning Mexican community is still a favorite. It's a casual cantina, perfect for a quick snack of soft tacos while touring the Italian Market.

## Termini Bros.

1523 S. 8th St. Tel: 334-1816. Open daily; closed Sun–Tues in summer. $
www.termini.com

Termini now has four locations, but nothing beats the original for old-time atmosphere. Stop by for cannoli, sfogliet-teli, biscotti and dozens of other sweet delights.

### Chickie & Pete's Cafe

1526 Packer Ave. Tel: 218-0500.

It's jock heaven at this sports bar near the stadiums famous for its crab fries and myriad TV sets.

### Royal Tavern

937 E. Passyunk Ave. Tel: 289-6694.

Hipster haven, open to 2am every night, serving solid bar food and weekend brunch.

### PRICE CATEGORIES

Prices for three-course dinner per person with a half-bottle of house wine:
$ = under $25
$$ = $25–$40
$$$ = $40–$50
$$$ = more than $50

# URBAN VILLAGES

Philadelphia is often described as a city of neighborhoods, each with its own identity, and you couldn't ask for a better example than the "urban villages" clustered in the city's northwest corner

stablished at different times and under very different circumstances, Philadelphia's urban villages, Germantown, Chestnut Hill, Mount Airy and Manayunk, have little more in common than their general location. Once separate towns with discrete borders, the area was annexed by Philadelphia in the 1830s. Germantown is the oldest, founded just two years after Philadelphia. While the community has struggled through hard times, it is rich with historic sites. Chestnut Hill began as a real estate development for well-to-do Philadelphians and remains an enclave of beautiful homes and ritzy shops. Manayunk started as a mill town but has, since the 1980s, undergone sweeping gentrification along its trendy, boutique-lined Main Street.

Three neighborhoods, three very different personalities. Taken together or separately, they make a terrific day trip "outside" the city. Although public transportation is available from center city, driving may be more convenient, especially if you plan to visit more than one neighborhood.

## Germantown

Lying about 6 miles (10 km) northwest of Philadelphia, **Germantown** ❼ was founded in 1683 by Quaker and Mennonite immigrants who were invited by William Penn to join his "holy experiment" in the New World. Led by Pietist scholar Francis Daniel Pastorius, the original 13 families – mostly Dutch or German-speaking Swiss – laid out the village on a gentle rise along Wissahickon Creek. The little town grew quickly, gaining an early reputation in weaving, printing and publishing. When the British captured Philadelphia in 1777, Lord Howe stationed the bulk of his army in Germantown. George Washington

Map on page 160

**LEFT:** sidewalk dining on Main Street in Manayunk.
**BELOW:** portrait of Manayunk.

launched a daring attack against the redcoats from here, but fog and poor timing scuttled the plan, and despite fierce combat along Germantown Avenue, Washington was forced to retreat to Valley Forge. In 1793, Philadelphians fled to Germantown to escape another invader – a yellow fever epidemic. Many returned later, building summer retreats in the surrounding countryside.

Germantown grew in waves as technology made it more accessible to the city. In the 1870s, when the railroad line from center city to Chestnut Hill reduced the trip to Germantown to a mere half-hour commute, prosperous Philadelphians could afford to live there year-round and mansions sprung up near every train stop. Around the turn of the 20th century, row houses appeared as housing for factory workers.

Sadly, Germantown today is a poor and troubled neighborhood, not the sort of place most tourists will feel safe exploring. Your best bet is to stick to the historic buildings strung along Germantown Avenue at some distance from each other.

**TIP**

Hours at historic homes in Germantown are maddeningly irregular, so call in advance if you would like a guided tour. A few are open only by appointment.

**BELOW:** the 1777 Battle of Germantown is reenacted around Cliveden.

## Exploring Germantown

William Penn's brilliant secretary, James Logan, was among the first to build a Germantown retreat, and it is the farthest east of the group. **Stenton Mansion** (4601 N. 18th St; tel: 329-7312; open Tues–Sat 1–4pm and by appointment; entrance fee), a Georgian house built in 1728, was Logan's refuge from his professional obligations – a place where he could entertain Indian friends, indulge his interest in science, and delve into his 2,000-volume library, one of the largest in the colonies. Only five of the original 500 acres (200 hectares) remain in this partially blighted neighborhood, but the barn, greenhouse and much of the Logan family's furnishings are intact. Washington camped here before confronting the British at the Battle of Brandywine, and the British commander Lord Howe chose it as his headquarters before the Battle of Germantown.

The **Germantown Historical Society** on Market Square is a good next stop. Market Square, once the village center and site of the firehouse, stocks and market shed, is now occupied by an imposing Civil War monument. An 1888 Presbyterian church stands on the site of what was the Church of German Reformed Congregation of Germantown, dating from 1733.

The Federal-style Fromberger House, which dates from the late 1790s, now houses the **Historical Society Visitors Center, Museum and Library** (5501 Germantown Ave; tel: 844-1683; www.germantownhistory.org; visitors center and museum shop open Mon–Fri 9am–5pm, Sun 1–5pm; museum and library open Tues, Thur 9am–5pm, Sun 1–5pm; entrance fee for museum and library). The museum offers an overview of local history and displays a large collection of 18th- and 19th-century tools, toys, household goods

and textiles. The library contains archives and books relating to the history of Germantown, Mount Airy and Chestnut Hill.

Down the street, **Grumblethorpe** (5267 Germantown Ave; tel: 843-4820; open Apr–Dec Tues, Thur, Sun 1–4pm; entrance fee) is a solid stone house built as a country home for wine importer John Wister in 1744 and employing a style of Georgian architecture unique to the Germantown area.

## The other White House

Across the street from the Historical Society, the **Deshler-Morris House** (5442 Germantown Ave; tel: 596-1748; for hours, call 597-1293; entrance fee) sheltered President Washington during the yellow fever epidemic. Cabinet meetings were held here, prompting the nickname "Germantown White House." Maintained by the National Park Service, the house has been restored with period furnishings and a garden.

Continue north to **Wyck** (6026 Germantown Ave; tel: 848-1690; www.wyck.org; open Apr–mid-Dec

Tues–Thur 12–4.30pm, Sat 1–4pm and by appointment; entrance fee), a modest Quaker home built in 1700 with original furnishings and a fascinating 200-year-old garden.

About a half-block north, the **Germantown Mennonite Historic Trust** (6133 Germantown Ave; tel: 843-0943; open by appointment; entrance fee) is next to a meetinghouse built in 1770 on the site of the sect's first American house of worship. During the Civil War, Germantown residents participated in the Underground Railroad by hiding runaway slaves. The **Johnson House**, several blocks north (6306 Germantown Ave; tel: 438-1768; www.johnsonhouse.org; open by appointment Thur, Fri 10am–4pm, Sat 1–4pm; entrance fee), built in 1768, saw heavy fighting during the Battle of Germantown and was a safe house in the Underground Railroad.

Across the street, the **Concord Schoolhouse** (6309 Germantown Ave; tel: 844-8845; open by appointment; entrance fee), constructed in 1775, contains original desks, chairs, books and an old school bell.

Map on page 160

*Artifacts at the Germantown Mennonite Historic Society include a table on which the first written protest against slavery in the New World was signed. The document was signed on February 18, 1688, nearly two centuries before the Emancipation Proclamation freed slaves in the southern states.*

**BELOW AND LEFT:** Wyck housed nine generations of the Wistar and Haines families, who owned it from 1689 to 1973.

A block away, **Cliveden** (6401 Germantown Ave; tel: 848-1777; www.cliveden.org; open Apr–Dec Thur–Sun noon–4pm; entrance fee), Germantown's most lavish 18th-century mansion, occupies a 6-acre (2.5-hectare) park. Built in 1763 by Benjamin Chew – a Loyalist, and the last Chief Justice of the colonial period – the house was used as a fortress by the British during the Battle of Germantown. The house is beautifully maintained and, thanks to the reams of documentation saved by the Chew family, is a thoroughly accurate renovation. During the assault on Cliveden, Washington placed his artillery on a knoll across the street, where the lovely Federal-style Upsala has stood since 1798.

## Mount Airy to Chestnut Hill

Although the neighborhoods no longer have definitive boundaries, **Mount Airy** ❽ extends roughly from Upsal Street north to Cresheim Valley Drive. Mount Airy is the largely residential neighborhood between Germantown and Chestnut Hill and has become known as one of the most integrated communities in the region, with numerous inter-faith, interracial and gay couples living among traditional nuclear families. Two churches here are historically significant. The **Church of the Brethren** (6611 Germantown Ave), erected in 1770, is the first of the Dunkard sect, a branch of the Mennonites named for their distinctive practice of baptism.

Nearby, **St Michael's Lutheran Church** (6671 Germantown Ave), founded in 1717, is the country's oldest Lutheran congregation. The existing structure is the third on the site, although the Lutheran school-house, built in 1740, still stands.

Turning south off Germantown Avenue (back near the Mennonite Historic Trust) onto Tulpehocken Street, you will find large Victorian homes, built in the mid- to late-1800s with prosperity from the rail-road line. The **Ebenezer Maxwell Mansion** (200 W. Tulpehocken St; tel: 438-1861; open Fri–Sun 1pm–4pm; entrance fee) is an elaborate Victorian home built in 1859 and furnished with a clutter of Philadel-

*Cliveden's 2-ft-thick (60-cm) stone walls still bear pockmarks left by musket balls and grapeshot fired during the American Revolution.*

**BELOW:** Japanese tea ceremony at the Morris Arboretum.
**RIGHT:** *Tierra,* by Sidney Goodman, on the grounds of the Wood-mere Art Museum in Chestnut Hill.

phia furniture and Victorian decor.

If you continue north on Germantown Avenue, you'll come to **Chestnut Hill** ❾, the city's most exclusive residential district. Chestnut Hill was a remote area of farmland and forest until Henry Houston, a director of the Pennsylvania Railroad and the area's largest landholder, arranged a commuter line.

Houston constructed a grand country inn (now Chestnut Hill Academy) and church (St Martin's in the Field), both on West Willow Grove Avenue, as well as scores of fashionable homes intended to lure well-heeled Philadelphians to the suburbs. Houston's son-in-law, Dr George Woodward, continued the work well into the 1900s. Woodward drew inspiration from English and French country homes in an effort to develop comfortable housing for both affluent and working families.

The **Chestnut Hill Historical Society** (8708 Germantown Ave; tel: 247-0417; open Mon–Fri 9am–5pm) is a good source of information, offering rotating exhibits of local interest, an archive of documents, and architecture guides for local tours. There is also a **Chestnut Hill Visitors Center** (8426 Germantown Ave; tel: 247-6696; open Mon–Fri 8.30am–5pm, Sat 10am–3pm) with information on local attractions, restaurants and businesses.

## Art and nature

**Woodmere Art Museum** (9201 Germantown Ave; tel: 247-0476; open Tues–Sat 10am–5pm, Sun 1–5pm; donation requested), housed in Charles Knox Smith's magnificent Victorian mansion, features changing exhibits from a permanent collection of 19th-century art as well as work by contemporary Delaware Valley artists.

Farther north, at the very edge of Chestnut Hill, the University of Pennsylvania maintains the serene **Morris Arboretum** (100 Northwestern Ave; tel: 247-5777; open daily 10am–4pm, until 5pm on weekends Apr–Oct; admission fee). Developed by John and Lydia Morris (heirs to the Morris Iron Works fortune) in the late 1800s on their summer estate, the 92-acre (37-

Map on page 160

TIP

Among the best examples of the Houston-Woodward architectural style in Chestnut Hill are Houston's private castle, Drum Moir, at West Willow Grove Avenue, and the houses around Pastorius Park.

**BELOW:** Germantown Avenue, Chestnut Hill.

## Rittenhouse Town

While in Chestnut Hill, consider visiting Rittenhouse Town (206 Lincoln Dr, enter from Wissahickon Ave; tel: 438-5711; www.rittenhouse-town.org; open May–Sept Sat–Sun noon–4pm, or by appointment; entrance fee). This small community was founded in 1690 by Mennonite leader and papermaker William Rittenhouse. Site of the first paper mill in British North America and birthplace of notable astronomer, clockmaker and political leader David Rittenhouse (1732–96), the National Historic Landmark encompasses original homesteads, mills and outbuildings as well as a contemporary papermaking studio. Tours on summer weekends.

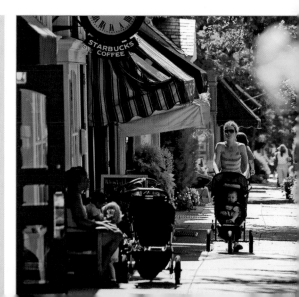

Map
on page
160

**TIP**

If you're in the area on Thursday, Friday or Saturday, be sure to stop at the Chestnut Hill Farmers Market (Thu–Fri 9am–6pm, Sat 8am–5pm) behind the Chestnut Hill Hotel at 8229 Germantown Avenue.

**BELOW:** the Manayunk Towpath is a favorite of bicyclists.

hectare) arboretum maintains nearly 2,000 kinds of plants and includes a fragrant rose garden, Japanese gardens and a swan pond as well as outdoor sculptures and an exhibit about medicinal plants.

## Manayunk

It was once a big jump from blue-blooded Chestnut Hill to blue-collar **Manayunk ⑩**, but not anymore. Since upscale stores and eateries have opened on Main Street, this compact working-class burg has been drawing fresh crowds of city and suburban folk alike. Built on a steep hillside rising from the Schuylkill River, Manayunk was once one of Philadelphia's most productive industrial neighborhoods.

With the swift current of the Schuylkill River to power its factories and the mule-drawn barges of the Schuylkill Canal to transport materials, Main Street's 14 mills turned out blankets, upholstery, cloth and other textiles by the ton.

Although the textile industry was decimated by the Great Depression, a few manufacturers survived and

many of the old mills have now been converted into fancy condominiums or office buildings. The sons and daughters of the original Polish, Irish and Italian immigrants are still here, very often occupying the same modest row houses as their parents. At the top of the hill you can still see the much grander mansions that were occupied by the wealthy mill-owners in their 19th-century heyday.

The big attraction in Manayunk is **Main Street**, a strip of trendy shops and galleries tucked into a parade of colorful storefronts. Manayunk is a Lenape Indian word meaning "the place we go to drink," and with gastronomes packing local bars and eateries, the name is as fitting today as it was 300 years ago.

In good weather you're apt to see bicyclists taking ice cream breaks along the **Manayunk Towpath**. This is a gravel path that runs along the **Manayunk Canal** and is used as part of the Schuylkill River Trail, a bike path that extends from center city to Valley Forge National Historic Park.

## Special occasions

If you need even more incentive to break out of center city, keep other events in mind: In mid-May, **Canal Day** celebrates the birth of the Manayunk Canal in 1823, which helped contribute to Philadelphia's leading position in 19th-century industry. Usually quiet back streets are thronged with spectators who come to watch cyclists conquer the grueling "Manayunk Wall" during the annual **Pro Cycling Championship** in June.

Also in June is the **Manayunk Arts Festival**, a juried outdoor art show. These summertime events provide great opportunities to see Manayunk at its best and to meet the old and new "Yunkers" who have transformed a graying mill town into a thriving contemporary urban village. ❏

# RESTAURANTS & BARS

## Restaurants

### An Indian Affair
4425 Main St., Manayunk. Tel: 482-8300. Open: L & D daily. $$
Laudable Indian fare on the Main Street strip, in a contemporary bistro setting that many consider quite romantic. Nosh on nan and curry to sounds of sitar music. BYOB.

### Cafette
8136 Ardleigh St., Chestnut Hill. Tel: 242-4220. Open: L Mon–Sat, D Tues–Sat, Sun brunch. $–$$
A laid-back vibe and comfort fare make Cafette a popular choice for the Mom-and-stroller set. The patio, complete with sculpture garden, is a relaxing spot. Cash only.

### CinCin
7838 Germantown Ave., Chestnut Hill. Tel: 242-8800. Open: L Mon–Sat, D nightly. $$$
Upscale Chinese cuisine attracts hordes to this stylish spot. It can be a long wait, especially on weekends, but if you're in the mood for Chinese, you'd be hard pressed to find a better option in the neighborhood.

### Cresheim Cottage Cafe
7402 Germantown Ave., Mt. Airy. Tel: 248-4365. Open: L & D Tues–Sun, Sat–Sun brunch. $$$
www.cresheimcottage.com

The ambiance at this historic 18th-century cottage is the main reason to dine here, either indoors or out. An eclectic menu of American comfort food is augmented with local produce.

### Hikaru
4348 Main St., Manayunk. Tel: 487-3500. Open: L Wed–Sun, D nightly. $$–$$$
A standby for decent sushi and Japanese food in Manayunk. Specialty rolls are the stars here. For those who prefer cooked fare, chefs dazzle diners with their knife work at the teppanyaki grills downstairs.

### Jake's
4365 Main St., Manayunk. Tel: 483-0444. Open: L Mon–Sat, D nightly, Sun brunch. $$$–$$$$
www.jakesrestaurant.com
The top – possibly the only – fine dining destination in Manayunk is Bruce Cooper's esteemed Jake's, as famous for its brunch as for its dinner and wine list. Make reservations; walk-ins are tough, especially at brunch.

### Johnny Mañana's
4201 Ridge Ave., East Falls. Tel: 843-0499. Open: L & D nightly. $$
It's not easy to miss this colorful corner spot. Just look for the giant red chile pepper poised over the

sign. Basic Tex-Mex fare, flowing margaritas and a large list of tequilas are good reasons to visit.

### Roller's Restaurant at Flying Fish
8142 Germantown Ave., Chestnut Hill. Tel: 247-0707. Open: L Tues–Sat, D Tues–Sun, Sun brunch. $$–$$$
New digs for this Chestnut Hill favorite haven't affected its status as a beloved neighborhood fixture. Chef-owner Paul Roller serves upscale comfort food from turkey meatloaf to pumpkin ravioli. Cash only, closed Sundays in July and August.

### U.S. Hotel Bar & Grill
4439 Main St., Manayunk. Tel: 483-9222. Open: L & D daily. Sun brunch. $$–$$$
www.libertiesrestaurant.com
A classic saloon atmosphere with an upscale pub fare menu. Sit at the solid cherry bar and admire the original tin ceiling while dining on a burger or prime rib. Open to 2am.

### Winnie's Le Bus
4266 Main St., Manayunk. Tel: 487-2663. Open: B Mon–Thu, L Mon–Fri, D nightly, Sat & Sun brunch. $$
www.lebusmanayunk.com
A longtime Main Street presence, Le Bus is usually packed, but the casual atmosphere encourages quick turnover. Diners enjoy salads, sandwiches on arti-

san breads, craft brew beers and friendly service.

### Zesty's
4382 Main St., Manayunk. Tel: 483-6226. Open: L Tues–Sat, D nightly, Sun brunch. $$
www.zestys.com
This "Greek and Roman" cafe serves up tasty Mediterranean fare, but the Greek dishes are the stars. Try the taramosolata, hummus spreads and gyros. Outdoor tables are a great spot to watch the crowds promenade down Main Street.

## Bars

### McNally's Tavern
8634 Germantown Ave., Chestnut Hill. Tel: 247-9736.
An unassuming tavern full of locals, McNally's is regionally famous for its trademarked Schmitter sandwich, an artery-clogging twist on the cheesesteak.

### North by Northwest
7165 Germantown Ave., Mt. Airy. Tel: 248-1000.
A bar, restaurant and music venue rolled into one renovated storefront.

### PRICE CATEGORIES

Prices for three-course dinner per person with a half-bottle of house wine:
$ = under $25
$$ = $25–$40
$$$ = $40–$50
$$$ = more than $50

# NORTH OF VINE

**It may be off the beaten path, but there are sights of interest in the north – a reminder of the area's glory days**

Philadelphia north of Vine Street extends north of center city and then separates, reaching up like two arms northeast and northwest of the city. Nestled just north of center city are the neighborhoods of Fairmount, Spring Garden and Northern Liberties, much of which were settled in the 19th century and which have undergone successful gentrification in recent years. Here you'll find a mixture of large townhouses and smaller row houses, high-rise apartment complexes and small businesses, in addition to several prominent historic landmarks.

North Philadelphia is a rather indistinct, amorphous expanse that takes in a wide range of ethnic enclaves, sprawling suburban housing, faded industrial centers, inner-city blight and a wooded city park. It wasn't always this way. In the mid-1800s, parts of North Philadelphia were considered very fashionable. North Broad Street in particular was a magnet for the burgeoning class of industrialists seeking large lots for sumptuous new homes. Unfortunately, many of these neighborhoods have long since fallen on hard times.

Jutting to the east is the "Great Northeast." The arm west of Germantown Avenue is comprised of the "urban villages" of Germantown, Mount Airy, Manayunk and Chestnut Hill (see page 167).

## House of correction

Just a few blocks from the Museum of Art is the **Eastern State Penitentiary** ⓫ (22nd and Fairmount sts; tel: 236-3300; tours mid-Apr–Nov, Wed–Sun 10am–5pm, last entry 4pm; entrance fee except Sun 10–11.30am; no children under 7), closed as a prison facility in 1972 and reopened recently as a historic

Map on page 160

**LEFT:** Eastern State Penitentiary
**BELOW:** art students learn to express themselves at Taller Puertorriqueño.

*A mural adorns the Legendary Blue Horizon, a venerable boxing arena on North Broad Street.*

**BELOW:** Al Capone's cell at the Eastern State Penitentiary had all the comforts of home.

landmark. Designed by John Haviland and constructed between 1823 and 1836, this building was an innovative experiment in prison design, reflecting the Quaker philosophy that criminals could be reformed by isolating them in solitary confinement, allowing reflection and prayer. Tours include a look at cells, the work area and the central guard tower, as well as exhibits of inmate-made weapons, mug shots and photographs and stories of famous inmates such as the gangster Al Capone. There are also several art exhibits exploring themes of prison existence.

## Island of education

Several blocks north of the Penitentiary is **Girard College** ⑫ (Girard and Corinthian sts; tel: 787-2680; open Thur 9.30am–2pm and reserved tours by appointment other days; entrance fee), an oasis of green grass and white marble behind iron gates. The compound of classically inspired structures centers on Founder's Hall, a building of breathtaking scale designed by 29-year-old Thomas U.

Walter in 1833 and regarded as one of the finest examples of Greek Revival architecture in the US. Founder's Hall houses the Girard Collection, which preserves the household furnishings, books and papers of Stephen Girard, the college's founder and an important financier of the early American government.

Girard was born in Bordeaux, France, to a family of merchant mariners. At the age of 14, he signed on as a cabin boy aboard a merchant vessel and remained at sea for several years. At 23 he became captain on a ship that traded in the West Indies, and he then took part in the American coastal trade, building up his own business at the same time that he represented a New York mercantile company.

Britain's blockade of American ports during the stormy political period before the Revolution led Girard to settle in Philadelphia, where he launched a successful business career. He built a fleet of ships that was to provide him with a great fortune in international shipping. In 1812, he acquired the building that had been the Bank of the United States, and transformed it into the Bank of Stephen Girard. Girard and the German-born John Jacob Astor – both destined to become the richest men of their era in America – spearheaded a drive to sell government bonds to finance the War of 1812 against Britain. At the age of 75, Girard began carefully planning the administration of his estate, including large bequests to both Philadelphia and Pennsylvania, and setting aside $6 million of his fortune for the establishment of a school for poor white male orphans.

The school, Girard College, was opened in 1848, 17 years after its founder's death. Legal battles challenging the terms of Girard's will had been fought before the school was opened, and another protracted legal

conflict ensued in the mid-20th century over the stipulation that admission was restricted to white males. Finally, in 1968, non-white boys were admitted following a ruling by the US Supreme Court. Today, students are of both genders and all races, as well as children of single parents who require financial assistance.

A major anchor of the North Broad Street community is **Temple University** ⑬ (1801 N. Broad St; tel: 204-7000), founded in 1884, with more than 28,000 students in 16 schools and colleges, including professional schools in law, dentistry and medicine. Three blocks west of the Temple campus is the little-known **Wagner Free Institute of Science** (17th and Montgomery Sts; tel:763-6529; www.wagnerfreeinstitute.org; open Tues–Fri 9am–4pm; children under 18 must be accompanied by an adult; donations welcome), built in 1860. Its founder was William Wagner, a wealthy merchant with a penchant for stones, bones and stuffed animals and a desire to share the discoveries made on his expeditions. He hired John

McArthur, Jr, architect of City Hall, to design the impressive Greek Revival building to house his collection and provide space for his scientific lectures. Today, the museum remains almost exactly the same as it was over a century ago and continues to provide free educational lectures and programs on a variety of scientific subjects.

### Literary landmark

To the east of Broad Street, just north of Old City, is a neighborhood known as the **Northern Liberties**, part of the "Liberty Lands" that William Penn parceled out as bonuses to people who bought building lots in the city proper. Gentrification has crept up from center city, but the area is still peppered with factories and warehouses, many now serving as loft apartments and condominiums.

Artists have discovered the area, and the neighborhood has developed a reputation as Philadelphia's version of Soho, with a lively mix of industrial buildings and warehouses in various states of repair, some now operating as artist workshops and

Map on page 160

*Freedom Theatre is Pennsylvania's oldest African-American theater.*

**BELOW:**
a statue of Stephen Girard, founder of Girard College, makes a convenient perch.

## Eddy, Sissy and Annabel Lee

Edgar Allan Poe moved to Philadelphia in 1837 to undertake editorial work for *Burton's Gentleman's Magazine*, having already made a reputation in literary circles in Maryland and Virginia. A year earlier he had married his 13-year-old cousin Virginia, the inspiration for his immortal poem *Annabel Lee*.

It was in the house on North 7th Street that Poe composed *The Fall of the House of Usher* and *The Gold Bug*. And it was here in Philadelphia that he found domestic contentment. Poe lived at several addresses in Philadelphia, but this house is the only one that has survived. It was a happy menage: "Eddy," his beloved "Sissy" and her mother. Unfortunately, in 1842 Virginia suffered her first attack of consumption, the family moved to New York two years later, and the poet lost his "beautiful Annabel Lee" there in 1847. She was 24.

The blow was devastating, and it wasn't long before the disconsolate widower was gone as well. Poe was found lying on a Baltimore street corner on October 3, 1849, and died a few days later. Poe transformed the short story into an art form, perfected the thriller genre, and produced some of the finest literary criticism of his time.

Map on page 160

*Founded in 1843, the Seamen's Church Institute (75 N. 5th St; tel: 922-2562) first operated on a boat known as "The Floating Church of the Redeemer," ministering to Philadelphia seamen. The ministry continues today; the Institute also houses a small maritime museum.*

**BELOW:**
the bookstore at
Taller Puertorriqueño,
founded in 1974 by
Latino artists and
activists.

studios, edgy boutiques, galleries, trendy bars and restaurants, and a growing number of freshly renovated houses.

Many visitors come to the area to pay homage to a literary genius at the **Edgar Allan Poe National Historic Site** ⓮ (530–32 N. 7th St; tel: 597-8780; open Wed–Sun 9am–5pm; entrance free). The site encompasses two structures, one occupied by Poe between 1842 and 1844 and the neighboring house, which now contains a display on this famous author's life and work, as well as brief biographies of his literary contemporaries, including Charles Dickens, whom Poe met in Philadelphia.

The Poe house itself is bare and unfinished from the upstairs bedrooms to the spooky dark basement. Even the walls are stripped down to the plaster. Poe moved often when in Philadelphia, and sold most or all of his furniture when he eventually left town. This was the last residence for Poe in Philadelphia.

To the north, the area is rapidly changing, although parts can still be dicey for travelers. Philadelphia, like many large northern cities, lost much of its manufacturing in the mid-20th century, leaving large patches of blighted, abandoned homes and factories.

A bright spot here is **Taller Puertorriqueño** (2721 N. 5th St; tel: 426-3311; www.tallerpr.org; bookstore and art gallery open Tues 2–6pm, Wed–Sat 10am–1pm, 2pm –6pm), a cultural center and community workshop in the Hispanic neighborhood's colorful business district. A brilliant three-story mural is painted on the side of the building which houses a Spanish-English bookshop and an art gallery.

## The Great Northeast

The scene is somewhat different to the east of 5th Street in the old manufacturing centers such as Frankford, Richmond, Fishtown and Tacony along the Delaware River. In the earliest days of European settlement these were small agrarian villages separated from the city by farms and pastures. But by the late 1600s, small mills and workshops were springing up along Pennypack Creek, providing the area with flour, lumber, textiles and iron tools.

The steam engine freed factories from swift-running streams and, at the onset of the Industrial Revolution, this northeastern area flourished, cranking out iron, steel, textiles and other manufactured goods, and attracting thousands of immigrant laborers.

Thanks to the Fairmount Park Commission, there is a patch of green in these post-industrial neighborhoods; the 1,300-acre (520-hectare) **Pennypack Park** ⓯ runs 8 miles (11 km) along Pennypack Creek, with miles of hiking and biking trails, picnic areas, peaceful woods, a 150-acre (60-hectare) bird sanctuary and an environmental center with exhibits on the wildlife and ecology of this inner-city wilderness. ❑

# RESTAURANTS & BARS

## Restaurants

### Las Cazuelas
426 W. Girard Ave. Tel: 351-9144. Open: L & D daily. $–$$
www.lascazuelas.net
This compact BYOB is a favorite in this rapidly gentrifying neighborhood (and beyond) for its authentic Mexican fare, from corn sopes to mole poblano.

### A Full Plate Cafe
1009 Bodine St. Tel: 627-4068. Open: L & D Mon–Sat, Sat–Sun brunch. $
Expect comfort food with a creative twist at this casual BYOB, where diners tuck into fried chicken and waffles, catfish po' boys, mac and cheese, fried okra, pierogi and more. Try the fried pickles.

### Higher Grounds Cafe
631 N. 3rd St. Tel: 922-3745. Open daily. $
Bare brick walls, high ceilings, wood floors and walls covered with local art set the tone at this cafe, offering flavorful coffee drinks and a light menu. Stop by for a midday pick-me-up, or take in an evening of poetry or acoustic music.

### Honey's Sit 'n' Eat
800 N. Fourth St. Tel: 925-1150. Open: B & L Tues–Sun, Sun brunch. $
"Southern Jewish" food is the bill of fare at this cozy eatery, which serves up rib-sticking favorites like biscuits and gravy, chicken fried steak, pastrami on rye and challah French toast. Plank floors and rough-hewn beams give the place a homey rustic atmosphere.

### North 3rd
801 N. 3rd St. Tel: 413-3666. Open: D nightly, Sun brunch. $–$$
www.norththird.com
Dark, funky and fun, North 3rd, is a busy resto-bar with a seriously good menu that's served late into the night. The wasabi-spiked tuna burger on brioche is a favorite. A popular hipster haunt.

### Sovalo
702 N. 2nd St. Tel: 413-7770. Open: D $$–$$$
www.sovalo.com
Modern Italian cooking is served with a thoughtful selection of California and Italian wines. The owners are alumni of Napa Valley's famous Tra Vigne.

### Standard Tap
901 N. 2nd St. Tel: 238-0630. Open: D nightly, Sat and Sun brunch. $–$$
www.standardtap.com
A Northern Liberties pioneer that draws customers from all over the city for its gastro-pub fare, local beers and timeless corner bar ambiance.

## Bars

### Abbaye
637 N. 3rd St. Tel: 627-6711.
A casual pub with a broad Belgian beer selection. Food is served.

### The Fire
412 W. Girard Ave. Tel: 671-9298.
A neighborhood joint in Northern Liberties with local beer, local bands and local characters.

### Johnny Brenda's
1202 Frankford Ave. Tel: 739-6984.
The second venture from Standard Tap owners Paul Kimport and William Reed is just as successful as the first. Pool table and jukebox, plus good grub cooked up in an open kitchen.

### North Star Bar
2639 Poplar St. Tel: 787-0488.
Artsy and a little shaggy, with a lively crowd of regulars and live music several nights a week.

### Ortlieb's Jazzhaus
847 N. 3rd St. Tel: 922-1035.
A unique jazz venue and bar located in a former brewery. Open to 2am, seven days a week.

### PRICE CATEGORIES

Prices for three-course dinner per person with a half-bottle of house wine:
**$** = under $25
**$$** = $25–$40
**$$$** = $40–$50
**$$$** = more than $50

**RIGHT:** laying down a groove at Ortlieb's Jazzhaus.

# THE MAIN LINE

**Though far less exclusive than it used to be, the suburban corridor to the west of the city is still identified with Philadelphia's upper crust**

Philadelphia

I n the Philadelphia area, few phrases are as instantly evocative of a certain lifestyle as "Main Line." While the social scene is markedly different today than it was at its prime in the late 19th and early 20th centuries, the Main Line still conjures up visions of grand estates, cricket clubs, fox hunting, *The Philadelphia Story* and old money. The area is no longer the provenance of the super wealthy, but it remains a desirable residence for all species of the affluent, from the upper middle class to the fabulously rich. It boasts high-priced homes (many of the new "McMansion" variety), excellent schools and proximity to the city.

The Main Line refers to a series of suburban towns strung along Route 30 (Lancaster Avenue) west of Philadelphia. The name derives from the Main Line of Public Works, an early version of the current R5 railroad line, built by the state and completed in 1832. It ran from Philadelphia through Paoli and Lancaster before terminating in Columbia. The state, displeased with the cost of maintaining the line, sold it to the Pennsylvania Railroad in 1857, which, in turn, brilliantly reshaped its identity into a destination for the *crème de la crème* of Philadelphia society.

## The Welsh Tract

Much earlier, in the late 1600s, the area had been settled by Welsh Quakers, who were intent on creating an insular, Welsh-speaking "barony" in William Penn's religiously tolerant new land. Although the barony never crystallized as they had hoped, many Welsh Quakers were drawn to the area, including families such as the Cadwaladers, Robertses and Morrises who would later give rise to some of Philadelphia's most prominent figures. The

Map on page 191

**PRECEDING PAGES:** boardwalk ride, Wildwood, New Jersey. **LEFT:** ancient Roman mosaic, Glencairn Museum. **BELOW:** polo is a favorite pastime of the Main Line elite.

Map on page 191

TIP

Use this mnemonic to remember the order of stations on the Main Line: Old Maids Never Wed And Have Babies – Overbrook, Merion, Narberth, Wynnewood, Ardmore, Haverford, Bryn Mawr.

**RIGHT:** Cairnwood, in Bryn Athyn, is typical of the Main Line's guilded age mansions.

**Merion Friends Meetinghouse ❶** (615 Montgomery Ave, Merion Station; tel: 610-664-4210; merion-friends.org), built in 1695, is still in use, as is the **Radnor Meetinghouse** (Conestoga Rd and Rt 320, Radnor; tel: 610-293-1153; www.quaker.org), which was erected about 1718.

## A refuge for the rich

You might think that towns with Welsh-sounding names like Bala Cynwyd and Bryn Mawr were established during this period, but actually the names were part of a marketing scheme concocted by the Pennsylvania Railroad to refashion the Main Line in the image of the British countryside. The railroad encouraged its executives to set an example for other well-heeled Philadelphians by relocating to the corridor and saw to it that "buildings of offensive occupation" such as "taverns, drinking saloons, blacksmith, carpenter or wheelwright shops" were prohibited.

The strategy was a whopping success. The blue bloods who had once congregated around Rittenhouse Square decamped to the suburbs, and the exodus continued well into the 20th century. Mansions sprang up, although, as historian Nathaniel Burt noted, they were designed in a "quieter key" than those of the New York robber barons, "avoiding the curse of 'parvenu ostentation.'" Certain social institutions were established as well, not the least of which was the Devon Horse Show, the Radnor Hunt (a fox-hunting club), the Merion Cricket Club and the yearly round of debutante balls, all of which remain active today though in a somewhat altered form.

The **Radnor Hunt Races** (tel: 610-647-4002; www.radnor3day.org), a three-day steeplechase event, is held in autumn at the Radnor Hunt in Malvern. The **Devon Horse Show ❷** (tel: 610-688-2554; www.thedevonhorseshow.org) is held in spring at the Devon Show grounds in Devon.

Many of the grand estates of old were sold off, subdivided or razed. Only a few remain in private hands today, including Ardrossan in Radnor Township, the home of Hope Montgomery Scott, the model for ▷

## Houses of the Holy

For an inside look at some of the Main Line's lavish manors, consider visiting the Glencairn Museum (1001 Cathedral Rd, Bryn Athyn; tel: 267-502-2993; open Sat for tours, reservations suggested). The museum is housed in the former mansion of Raymond Pitcairn, who designed the fanciful Romanesque castle without the benefit of formal architectural training. Now operated by the Academy of the New Church, the museum is dedicated to educating the public about world religions with a collection of art and artifacts, ranging from ancient Egyptian, Greek, Roman and Asian sculptures to fragments of medieval European churches and monasteries. The museum tour includes a trip to the top of the mansion's tower, a visit to the Pitcairn's master bedroom and plenty of time to peruse the galleries.

Also open to the public is Woodmont (1622 Spring Mill Rd, Gladwyne; tel: 610-525-5598; open for tours Sun Apr–Oct), the opulent Gothic estate of Father Divine, the flamboyant preacher whose Peace Mission Movement attracted thousands of followers in the 1930s and 40s. Father Divine is interred in a mausoleum on the grounds. Mother Divine still resides in the house and occasionally leads visitors on tours of the property.

# Valley Forge

There were no battles fought at Valley Forge, but more Continental soldiers died here than in any single engagement during the American Revolution. The enemies at this grueling six-month encampment were hunger, cold, fatigue and disease. Driven back from their defense of Philadelphia, repelled at Brandywine and at Germantown by the better equipped and organized British army, George Washington's beleaguered troops pulled back to Valley Forge, where they built log huts and, without proper clothes, shoes or blankets, sustained themselves on "firecake," a bland mixture of flour and water. Hundreds came down with dysentery, pneumonia and typhus. At times, nearly a third of Washington's men were unable to report for duty. "Unless some great … change suddenly takes place," Washington lamented, "this Army must inevitably … starve, dissolve, or disperse." Of the 12,000 who retreated to Valley Forge in December 1777, 10,000 survived.

Only loyalty to Washington and the cause of American independence held the camp together. Yet, despite heavy losses, desertions and rumors of mutiny, the ragtag Continental Army was transformed at Valley Forge into a capable, cohesive fighting force. The tide began to turn in February, when Prussian officer Baron Friedrich von Steuben arrived from France with a letter of introduction from Benjamin Franklin. A skilled officer, von Steuben embarked on a training program that transformed the raw enlistees into an integrated army. He drilled the soldiers relentlessly, reorganizing troop structure, teaching musket volleys and shoring up discipline.

In June, the British left Philadelphia, and Washington's reinvigorated army hurried to intercept them in New Jersey, staving off a British counterattack at the Battle of Monmouth. The war dragged on for another five years, but the struggle at Valley Forge – the triumph over hunger, disease and hardship – propelled the Continental Army to victory.

Today, the site of Washington's fateful encampment is preserved at **Valley Forge**

**National Historical Park** (Rt 23 and N. Gulph Rd; tel: 610-783-1077; www.nps.gov/vafo; open daily 9am–5pm; entrance fee for historic buildings), 18 miles (28 km) northwest of Philadelphia. The **Welcome Center** has exhibits of Revolutionary War artifacts, a museum shop, an 18-minute film and free maps of the park. You can follow a 10-mile (16-km) self-guided driving tour, and there are 18 miles (29 km) of hiking and biking trails. A number of original 18th-century buildings, including Washington's headquarters, still stand on the 3,500-acre (1,200-hectare) site, as do reconstructed huts. Concerts are held in the **Washington Memorial Chapel** in summer. Near the chapel is the **World of Scouting Museum**, housed in a rustic log cabin (tel: 610-783-5311, open Sat–Sun noon–5pm), which chronicles the Boy Scout movement.

Near the park is the quirky **Wharton Esherick Museum** (Horseshoe Trail Rd; tel: 610-644-5822; open Mar–Dec Sat 10am–5pm, Sun 1–5pm, Mon–Fri groups only 10am–4pm; entrance fee), home and studio of artist Wharton Esherick (1887–1970). Esherick began his artistic life as a painter but was best known for his sculptural furnishings. The museum preserves his studio and houses a collection of over 200 paintings, ceramics, sculptures and furnishings.

**RIGHT:** National Memorial Arch, Valley Forge.

Map on page 191

**TIP**

In the mood for a shopping spree? There are more than four dozen upscale shops and restaurants as well as a lively farmers market at Suburban Square (610-896-7560), a village-style shopping mall at Anderson and Montgomery Avenues in Ardmore.

**BELOW:** the Barnes Foundation is home to scores of modern masterpieces.

socialite Tracy Lord, played so memorably by Katharine Hepburn in *The Philadelphia Story*. In Wayne, the gardens of **Chanticleer**, (786 Church Rd, Wayne; tel: 610-687-4163; open Apr–Oct Wed–Sun 10am–5pm, to 8pm Fri in summer), the former estate of pharmaceutical magnate Adolph Rosengarten, are open to the public.

Several other mansions have been given over to the campuses of the many schools in the area, including **Bryn Mawr** ❸ (101 N. Merion Ave, Bryn Mawr; tel: 610-526-5000; www.brynmawr.edu), founded in 1885 and the first women's college to offer a Ph.D. program. Bryn Mawr also happens to have one of the most beautiful campuses in the region, with grounds originally designed by landscape architects Frederick Law Olmsted and Calvert Vaux (who also designed New York City's Central Park) and buildings in the so-called Collegiate Gothic style reminiscent of Cambridge and Oxford Universities in England.

Other colleges in the area include **Villanova University** (800 Lancaster Ave, Villanova; tel: 610-519-6000; www.villanova.edu), Pennsylvania's oldest Catholic university, established by Augustinian brothers in 1842, and **Haverford College** (70 Lancaster Ave, Haverford; tel: 610-896-1101; www.haverford.edu), which was founded by Quakers in 1833. If time permits, stroll the **Haverford Arboretum**, which encompasses about a third of the 200-acre (80-hectare) campus.

## The Barnes legacy

The best reason to visit the Main Line, at least for the time being, is to see the **Barnes Foundation** ❹ (300 N. Latches Lane, Merion; tel: 610-667-0290; www.barnesfoundation .org; Sep–Jun Fri–Sun 9.30am–5pm, Jul–Aug Wed–Fri 9.30am–5pm; reservations required, call at least a month in advance of visit) before its planned – but still unscheduled – relocation to the Benjamin Franklin Parkway.

Housed in a building designed by architect Paul Philippe Cret (who also designed the Rodin Museum), the collection includes scores of works by such modern masters as Cézanne, Renoir, Matisse, Manet, Degas, Seurat and Picasso as well as works of African and Asian art, ancient classical art, and old masters such as El Greco, Rubens and Titian.

Essential to the experience is the arrangement of the art. Barnes eschewed traditional exhibition methods, choosing instead to display the work by theme or overall context. A limited number of tickets for docent tours of the collection and the adjacent arboretum are offered on a first-come, first-served basis 30 minutes before the tours begin.

For a look at the work of local artists, check out the **Main Line Art Center** (Old Buck Rd and Lancaster Ave, Haverford; tel: 610-525-0272; Mon–Thur 9am–9pm, Fri–Sat 9am–5pm, which also offers a full schedule of classes and lectures. ❏

# RESTAURANTS

## Restaurants

### Bunha Faun

152 Lancaster Ave., Malvern. Tel: 610-651-2836. Open: D Tues–Sun. $$
Don't judge a book by its cover, or a restaurant by its storefront. Inside this modest building is an inviting candlelit dining room where customers enjoy French cuisine with an Asian influence.

### Carmine's Creole Cafe

232 Woodbine Ave., Narberth. Tel: 610-660-0160. Open: D Tues–Sun. $$
www.carminescreole.com
Chef and owner John Mims dishes up the flavors of the Big Easy at this spirited restaurant. Appreciative diners tuck into creative interpretations of such classic dishes as chicken andouille fricassee, shrimp crawfish etouffee, deviled crabmeat cake and blackened shrimp.

### Georges

Spread Eagle Village, 503 Lancaster Ave., Wayne. Tel: 610-964-2588. Open: L, D Tues–Fri, D Sat–Sun, Sun brunch. $$$
www.georgesonthemainline.com
From Georges Perrier – chef, owner and overlord of Le Bec-Fin – comes this casual but stylish outpost at a Main Line shopping center. High

and low cuisine mixes freely here. Fine dishes such as herb-braised lamb shank, chicken Marsala and veal tenderloin are prepared with Perrier's usual panache. More homely, and homey, fare such as pizza, burgers, salads and cheesesteaks are also given the gourmet treatment.

### Hymie's Deli

342 Montgomery Ave., Merion Station. Tel: 610-664-3544. Open: B, L, D daily. $
www.hymies.com
When only a Jewish deli will do, head over to Hymie's, a deli and diner where you will find matzo ball soup, bagels and lox, whitefish salad, knishes, borscht, and sandwiches stuffed with corned beef, pastrami and more.

### Margaret Kuo's

175 E. Lancaster Ave., Wayne. Tel: 610-688-7200. Open: L, D Mon–Sat. $$
www.margaretkuos.com
You get two-for-one at this attractively designed restaurant: Chinese cuisine on the first floor and a Japanese restaurant and sushi bar on the second. Both are quite good, although the Chinese food wins kudos for authenticity. You may never order take-out again.

### Nectar

1091 Lancaster Ave., Berwyn. Tel: 610-725-9000. Open: L Mon–Fri, D nightly. $$–$$$
www.tastenectar.com
Asian meets French at this stylish spot, where the soothing decor and architecture are as artful as the carefully prepared dishes. A late-night sushi bar, thoughtful wine list and cocktail bar round out the offerings.

### Restaurant Taquet

139 E. Lancaster Ave., Wayne. Tel: 610-687-5005. Open: L, D Mon–Sat. $$–$$$
www.taquet.com
Contemporary French cuisine prepared with seasonal local ingredients is the attraction at this sophisticated restaurant at the historic Wayne

Hotel. Alfresco dining is available on the porch.

### Yangming

1051 Conestoga Road, Bryn Mawr. Tel: 610-527-3200. Open: L, D Mon–Sat, D Sun. $$
A cut above the typical Chinese restaurant, Yangming surprises with French, Italian and Southeast Asian influences but is no slouch when it comes to traditional Chinese dishes.

### PRICE CATEGORIES

Prices for three-course dinner per person with a half-bottle of house wine:
**$** = under $25
**$$** = $25–$40
**$$$** = $40–$50
**$$$** = more than $50

**RIGHT:** shopping at the Ardmore Farmers Market.

# PENNSYLVANIA DUTCH COUNTRY

**Within easy reach of Philadelphia is Lancaster County, home of traditional Amish and Mennonite communities, numerous historic sites and a busy schedule of special events, including a folk festival and Renaissance Fair. Side trips include a visit to the "sweetest place on Earth" and a hallowed Civil War battlefield**

Only two hours from Philadelphia, the bucolic countryside of Lancaster County makes a worthwhile trip for a day or a weekend. Religious dissenters who settled this land in the early 1700s were an independent group, and they've managed to hang onto their beliefs, traditions and language despite the constant encroachment of mainstream culture.

## The road less traveled

There's a right way and a wrong way to explore Lancaster County. If you hop on Route 30 at Philadelphia, you'll find it's a painful process, bogged down by bumper-to-bumper traffic as billboards scream their come-ons for "genuine Amish" attractions and "traditional" smorgasbords. Lancaster County is replete with tourist attractions and tourist traps, and sometimes the difference can be subtle. Sadly, too many visitors never stray from Route 30, and their only experiences of Amish culture are tacky faux farms and souvenir shops.

Fortunately, there's a better way, if you're willing to head off along meandering side roads that snake through the county. Buy a good map and you'll see countless small roads running at right angles to the major tourist arteries of routes 222,

23, 340, 30 and 741. Take any of these tiny tracks north or south, and within minutes you'll find yourself in the middle of a modern-day Brigadoon, where the only sounds are the muted lowing of the cattle, the creaking of a buggy, and the whisper of the wind across patchwork acres of summer wheat. If you've had the foresight to bring bikes, get them out now. Otherwise, park your car and take a hike along a country road and discover the measured rhythm of the real Lancaster County.

Map on pages 190–91

**LEFT:** Amish elders.
**BELOW:** vintage toys for sale at an Adamstown antique market.

*Known broadly as
the Pennsylvania
Dutch, the religious
dissenters who set-
tled Lancaster
County in the 18th
century weren't
Dutch but Deutsch,
that is, German.*

### Back in the saddle

There are many ways to get to Lancaster itself. One of the best is to take
the Pennsylvania Turnpike and jump
off at **Morgantown** ❺ (exit 22). In
the village of Morgantown, turn right
onto Route 23 and head west toward
**Churchtown** ❻, a little village of
stone mansions, cozy cottages and
antique stores. Outside Churchtown
is the Amish-owned **Smucker's Harness Shop** (2014 Main St, Narvon;
tel: 717-445-5956), known throughout the world for fine handmade har-
nesses and sleigh bells. Smucker's
outfits the Budweiser Clydesdales and
made the late singer John Denver's
wedding saddle. Take a look in the
back, where you'll see Amish saddlers
quietly stitching on antique sewing
machines as Amish tots frolic on the
floor under your feet. A stop at
Smucker's can give you a sense of
how the "real Amish" live and work.

A short detour east will bring you
to **Hopewell Furnace National**
**Historic Site** ❼ near Pottstown,
where an entire iron-manufacturing
village has been restored to its early
19th-century appearance (tel: 610-
582-8773; open daily 9am–5pm;
entrance fee). In summer, costumed guides demonstrate the
skills necessary to keep the community running.

### A taste of things Amish

As you continue west, be sure to stop
at the roadside stands to stock up on
luscious fruits and vegetables, homemade bread and pies, and canned rel-
ishes, jams and jellies. Some stands
offer quilts and other gifts.

Continue west on Route 23
toward Blue Ball, where you can
pick up Route 322 and head toward
**Ephrata** ❽, home of the **Ephrata**
**Cloister** (632 W. Main St; tel: 717-
733-6600; open Mon–Sat 9am–5pm,
Sun noon–5pm; entrance fee), where
in 1732 more than 300 celibate German followers of Pietist Conrad

Beissel built a community of log-and-stone buildings. Known for printing, basketmaking and milling, the cloister founded a school in the 1740s and nursed 500 wounded colonial soldiers during the Battle of Brandywine, but faded into unimportance by the 1800s. Then, as now, there isn't much future in celibacy.

Also at Ephrata, you'll find **The Artworks at Doneckers** (100 N. State St; tel: 717-738-9503; open Mon, Tue, Thur 10am–5pm, Fri 10am–9pm, Sat 10am–5pm; entrance free), selling the work of 50 artists and artisans. The Doneckers complex also features a top French restaurant (409 N. State St; tel: 717-738-9501), and the Inns at Doneckers (40 restored rooms in four different locations; tel: 717-738-9502).

## Antiques roadshow

At this point, if you're an antiques buff and you like fresh local food, you may want to head north on Route 272 for a visit to the market and auction house of the **Green Dragon** (955 N. State St, Ephrata; tel: 717-738-1117; open Fri 9am–10pm; entrance free), which offers everything from lace to milk cans. As the locals say, "If you can't buy it at the Green Dragon, it chust ain't fer sale!" Then move east on Route 272 to **Adamstown 9**, where on most weekends you'll find more than 30,000 dealers of 18th- and 19th-century collectibles and antiques. Three times a year they really put on a show, attracting another 4,800 dealers from around the country.

Midway between Ephrata and Adamstown you may want to stop for a bite at Zinn's Diner (Route 272), a heavily advertised eatery/gift shop/recreation park that serves decent local food. There may be a line of tourists, but locals love to come here, too.

Heading back on Route 272 south again toward Lancaster, don't miss

*Ephrata Cloister was an ascetic religious community founded in 1732 by a German-born mystic, Conrad Beissel.*

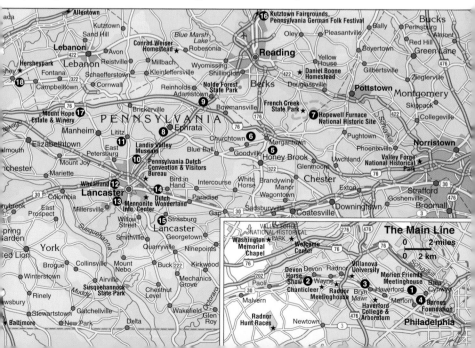

the **Landis Valley Museum**  (2451 Kissel Hill Rd; tel: 717-569-0401; open Mon–Sat 9am–5pm, Sun noon–5pm, entrance fee), a reconstructed 19th-century village of shops, workshops and houses where guides re-create the crafts, skills and day-to-day chores of the 1800s. The 1999 movie *Beloved* was filmed on location here. The museum also offers a variety of workshops and events throughout the year, including Harvest Days (fall), Herb Faire (summer) and Days of Belsnickel (winter). Across the road from the museum is the **Hands-on House Children's Museum** (721 Landis Valley Rd, Lancaster; tel: 717-569-KIDS; open Sep–May Tue–Thur 11am–4pm, Fri 11am–8pm; Jun–Aug Mon–Thur 10am–5pm, Fri 10am–8pm; year-round, Sat 10am–5pm, Sun noon–5pm; entrance fee), two floors of please-touch fun and educational activities.

A billboard painted on the side of a barn advertises a locally grown product.

**BELOW:** a farm auction holds the interest of a group of fence-sitting Amish boys.

## Sweet and salty

From there, travel west on Route 772 to **Lititz** , a peaceful 18th-century Moravian village with a tree-shaded square lined with stores and anchored by the restored Victorian General Sutter Inn (14 E. Main St). When the wind is right, you can smell the chocolate from the nearby chocolate factory. There's no factory tour, but you can visit the **Wilbur Chocolate Candy Americana Museum and Factory Store** (48 N. Broad St; tel: 717-626-3249; open Mon–Sat 10am–5pm; entrance free) to see a demonstration candy kitchen, antique signs and confectioners' tools.

Nothing goes better with chocolate than pretzels, so stop at the other end of the street at the **Sturgis Pretzel House** (219 E. Main St; tel: 717-626-4354; open Mon–Sat 9am–5pm; entrance fee), the first commercial pretzel bakery in the US. Then take your booty to the Lititz Springs Park (Main St) for a picnic near the stream.

Just outside downtown Lancaster, you can discover 250 years of local history at the **Lancaster County Historical Society** (230 N. President Ave; tel: 717-392-4633; open Tue, Thur 9.30am–9.30pm; Wed, Fri–Sat 9.30am–4.30pm; entrance free). Nearby is **Wheatland**  (1120 Marietta Ave; tel: 717-392-8721; open daily Apr–Oct, Fri–Mon in Nov, 10am–4pm; entance fee), the home of James Buchanan, the only Pennsylvanian to become President of the United States.

## Lancaster City

Convenient parking in downtown **Lancaster**  puts you within walking distance of **Central Market** (King and Queen sts, Penn Square; Tue and Fri 6am–4.30pm, Sat 6am–2pm), a great place to buy from Amish and Mennonite standholders. You'll find not just the freshest, cheapest fruits, vegetables, meat and fish around, but piles of Amish quilted goods, plain aprons and hats and Amish dolls. Three gourmet food stands offer tasty lunch takeaways, but you'll also find Pennsylvania Dutch specialties: Lebanon bologna, red beet eggs, potato chips, moon pies, whoopie pies, shoofly pies and fresh horseradish.

Surrounding Central Market on all four sides you'll find a Dickensian cobblestone alley of tiny art shops, antiques dealers and jewelers as well as the Lancaster Cultural History Museum (13 W. King St; tel: 717-299-6440; open Tue–Sat 10am–5pm, Sun noon–5pm; entrance fee), which celebrates the history and decorative arts of the area. The Lancaster Quilt & Textile Museum (37 Market St; tel: 717-299-6440; open Tue–Sat 10am–5pm, Sun noon–5pm; entrance fee) occupies a grand Beaux Arts building originally owned by the Lancaster Trust Company. Its collection includes fine 19th-century Amish quilts.

If you're a theater buff, walk one block south and check out the **Fulton Opera House** (12 N. Prince St; tel: 717-397-7725), which offers theatrical productions and performances by the Lancaster Symphony Orchestra.

## Plain folk

If you really must visit an "Amish" attraction, head out of King Street (Rt 462/Business Rt 30/Lincoln Hwy). Stop first at the **Pennsylvania Dutch Convention and Visitors Bureau** (501 Greenfield Rd; tel: 717-299-8901; open Mon–Thur 8am–6pm, Fri 8am–7pm, Sun 8am–5pm) or the **Mennonite Information Center** (2209 Mill Stream Rd just off Rt 30; tel: 717-299-0954; open Mon–Sat 8am–5pm). At the tourist bureau, you can rent an audio-tape, which gives you an in-car tour of the area's attractions. The Mennonite Center offers a tour guide service. For a minimum of two hours a guide will join you in your car for a tour of the countryside.

Continue on Route 30 a few miles east of town to the **Amish Country Homestead** (Rt 340; tel: 717-768-3600; open Jul–Oct Mon–Sat 8.30am–8pm, Sun 10.30am–5pm; Nov, Apr–Jun 10am–5pm, Sun 11am–5pm; Jan–Mar weekends only), part of The Amish Experience, an entertainment complex, with a theater and restaurant.

Your kids may also talk you into

Map on pages 190–91

*Amish boys dress much as adult men do: wide-brimmed hats, solid-color shirts and black trousers with suspenders.*

**BELOW:**
a gallery opening in downtown Lancaster.

# This Hallowed Ground

History buffs shouldn't miss a side trip to **Gettysburg National Military Park**, just two hours west of Lancaster, where in the summer of 1863 Confederate and Union forces fought the bloodiest battle in US history. When Confederate General Robert E. Lee and his 75,000 men collided with the 97,000-man northern army of General George C. Meade, the three-day fight that followed marked the turning point in the American Civil War. More men died that July than in any other battle on American soil.

The climax came when Major General George E. Pickett led 12,000 Confederate troops in a desperate charge across an open field. Blasted by artillery and rifle fire, Pickett's men could not break the Union line. When the dust cleared, 10,000 men and more than 5,000 horses lay dead. Four months later, Abraham Lincoln delivered his inspired Gettysburg Address at the adjacent cemetery where 3,500 Civil War soldiers are buried.

The Gettysburg battlefield is located in and around the town of Gettysburg, with more than 100 historic buildings radiating from the town center at Lincoln Square. One block north of the square the **Gettysburg Convention and Visitors Bureau** (31 Carlisle St; tel: 717-334-1124; www.gettysburg.com) offers information about Gettysburg attractions and various tour options, including walking, driving, bus, carriage, horseback and candlelight ghost excursions. If you drive yourself, consider hiring a licensed battlefield guide to accompany you at the National Park Service office (97 Taneytown Rd; tel: 717-334-1124; www.nps.gov/gett), next door to the Gettysburg National Cemetery.

Continue your tour at the **Wills House** (1 Lincoln Square), the spot where Lincoln worked on his address and slept the night before he delivered it. About eight blocks away, **General Lee's Headquarters Museum** (401 Buford Ave; tel: 717-334-3141; mid-Mar–Nov 9am–5pm, extended summer hours) is where General Lee struggled with his ill-fated battle plans. Next, stop by the restored Civil War era home of the only woman killed in the battle, Jennie Wade, who was struck by stray bullets in her kitchen while baking bread for Union soldiers (758 Baltimore St). The original wooden doors still carry the scars of hundreds of bullets. At the **American Civil War Museum** (297 Steinwehr Ave; daily Mar– Dec, Sat–Sun Jan–Feb) an audio-visual presentation has more than 200 lifesize figures in 30 scenes, a reenactment of the battle and an animated Lincoln giving his address.

Before venturing onto the battlefield itself, stop by the **National Military Park Visitor Center** (tel: 717-334-1124; open daily 8am–5pm with extended summer hours), which has a museum full of Civil War artifacts. Next door is the Cyclorama Center with a vast painting and a 20-minute sound and light show of the battle.

Once you've got a bit of background, you're ready to tackle the battlefield itself. The 6,000-acre (2,400-hectare) park is the most visited Civil War battlefield in the US, with over 1,300 monuments and 400 cannon. It looks very much like it did 145 years ago, with its farms, gray stone walls, and rolling pastureland. Take along a map, a guide, or a taped tour to help you navigate. ❑

**LEFT:** Confederate reenactors assemble at Gettysburg Battlefield.

stopping at **Dutch Wonderland** ⑭ (2249 Rt 30 East; tel: 866-386-2839; open May–Oct, phone for opening hours; entrance fee). This old-fashioned amusement park is no Disney World, but it's a good choice for young children.

## No puns please

East of Lancaster are the small towns of **Bird-in-Hand**, **Paradise** and **Intercourse**. You'll hear plenty of jokes about the origin of the Intercourse name, but there's no accepted explanation. Some think it's a corrupted version of "entercourse," referring to the entrance to an old racecourse outside town. Others believe the village grew up at the intercourse of two roads. The place is inundated with tourists sporting "Intercourse is for Lovers" T-shirts. Don't be too distracted – this part of the county features some of the area's most beautiful scenery.

For a more informative view of the area, try **The People's Place** (tel: 800-390-8436; open 9.30am–8pm Jun–Aug, 9.30am–6pm Sep–May;

entrance fee) on Main Street, where an interesting 25-minute film explores Amish history and customs.

## Train town

About 10 miles (16 km) south on Route 896 is **Strasburg** ⑮, where you can learn about the development of America's railroads at the **Railroad Museum of Pennsylvania** (Rt 741 East; tel: 717-687-8628; open daily, closed Mon Nov–Apr; entrance fee), and then hop aboard the Strasburg Railroad's historic steam locomotive for a 45-minute round-trip to Lancaster (tel: 717-687-7522). The town has a number of other attractions, from an "Amish village" to buggy rides and miniature golf.

While you're in the area, you might consider one of the religious shows at the **Sight and Sound Millennium Theater** on Route 896 in Strasburg (tel: 717-687-7800 for times; entrance fee). These dramatic productions (featuring scores of actors, live animals and special effects) are close to Broadway standards, but with a fundamentalist Christian orientation.

Map on pages 190–91

*An Amish boy carts a cigar-store Indian to a local auction.*

**BELOW:** the Strasburg Railroad operates vintage trains.

*Girls dig into fach-
naughts, traditional
Pennsylvania Dutch
doughnuts.*

**BELOW:** a spring
auction, or mud sale,
brings out Amish and
Mennonite folks to buy
everything from horses
to household goods.

West of Strasburg on Route 272 in the village of Willow Street you'll find the 1719 **Hans Herr House and Museum** (1849 Hans Herr Dr; tel: 717-464-4438; open Apr–Dec Mon–Sat 9am–4pm; entrance fee), the oldest meeting-house used by Swiss Mennonite immigrants.

Built in 1719 and restored in 1970, the house is also the oldest dwelling in the county. Tours provide a good introduction to early Mennonite history. The first Saturday in August is Herr House Heritage Day, where you can find demonstrations of gardening, soap-making and other activities typical of rural life.

For shoppers more interested in designer clothes, Route 30 is also home to two huge outlet malls just a few blocks apart. Tanger Outlet and Rockvale Square sell everything from brand-name clothing to power tools.

## Fairs and festivals

One of the best ways to get up close to the Amish is by traveling to one of the many local fairs. Remember that photography is not appreciated; the Amish feel that photos violate a religious injunction against graven images. The most popular of the fairs is the **Kutztown Pennsylvania German Folk Festival** ⑯ (Kutztown Fairgrounds) in early July. The fact that Kutztown isn't in Lancaster County is just a technicality – this fair is still the best way to experience Amish culture without feeling as though you are trespassing.

Summer weekends also bring the **Pennsylvania Renaissance Faire** (tel: 717-665-7021). Here, a troupe of costumed performers turn the grounds of the **Mount Hope Estate and Winery** ⑰ (off the Pennsylvania Turnpike at exit 20) into a 16th-century English country fair complete with jousting, Shakespearean performances and dancing. In winter, the estate reopens for an Edgar Allan Poe Halloween and a Charles Dickens Christmas Past.

## Hershey country

A bit farther to the west is **Hershey** ⑱ and **Hersheypark** (100 W. Hersheypark Dr; tel: 800-HERSHEY; open May–Labor Day daily; entrance fee), home of the world-famous chocolate company. Hersheypark has some serious fun for roller-coaster aficionados. New in 2005 was Turbulence, the world's first free-falling tower coaster. There are 60 other rides and more than 20 rides for the very young. Included in the admission is a stroll through the 11-acre (5-hectare) ZooAmerica, featuring 200 animals native to North America.

If all this wears you out, try a stroll through the lush 23-acre (10-hectare) **Hershey Gardens** (Hotel Road), or take a ride through **Hershey's Chocolate World** (800 Park Blvd; tel: 717-534-4900; open daily; entrance free). In 2004 Hershey's Factory World opened, giving visitors the chance to observe a chocolate manufacturing line. ❑

# RESTAURANTS

## Restaurants

### Bird–in–Hand Family Restaurant
2760 Old Philadelphia Pike, Bird-in-Hand. Tel: 717-768-1500. Open: B, L, D Mon–Sat. $
There are no tricks here, just plentiful country cooking in a family atmosphere. Tourists vie for space with local folks who come for generous helpings of roast beef and turkey drenched in gravy, chicken pot pie, chicken corn soup and other Pennsylvania Dutch specialties. The all-you-can-eat buffet is a good deal for big appetites.

### Good 'n Plenty
East Brook Road (Route 896), Smoketown. Tel: 717-394-7111. Open: L, D Mon–Sat. $
This large, spirited restaurant offers classic Pennsylvania Dutch specialties in an 1871 Amish farmhouse. It's like a family dinner for 600. Diners are served at long tables with a dozen or so people at each. The meal starts with soup or salad and then pushes on to round after round of rib-sticking favorites – huge bowls of mashed potatoes, pitchers of gravy, and huge platters of fried chicken, pork and sauerkraut, ham, meat loaf, turkey noodles, homemade bread and more. And just when you think you can't eat another bite, they start on dessert. One price covers everything.

### Inn at Twin Linden
2092 Main St. (Route 23), Churchtown. Tel: 717-445-7619. Open: D Sat. $$$
A sumptuous, four-course, fixed-price dinner is served on Saturdays in a candlelit dining area at this 19th-century inn. A creative matching of fresh, artfully prepared ingredients is the inn's hallmark. The menu changes every week, but a few highlights might include wild mushroom consommé with truffles, seared foie gras, Maine lobster and rack of lamb. It's pricey but worth it.

### Kling House
Kitchen Kettle Village, Route 772, Intercourse. Tel: 717-768-2746. Open: B, L Mon–Sat. $
When weather allows, diners lounge on the porch and watch Amish buggies pass by, much as owner Pat Burnley did as a child. Mrs. Burnley grew up in the house – now the restaurant – that anchors Kitchen Kettle Village, a collection of shops and galleries in old Intercourse village. Before heading for the shops, start your day with a breakfast of peach melba pancakes or maple cinnamon French toast. While you're waiting for your meal, you can nibble on crackers with cream cheese and Kitchen Kettle's pepper jam.

### Lemon Grass Thai Restaurant
2481 Lincoln Hwy (Route 30), Lancaster. Tel: 717-295-1621. Open: L, D Tues–Sun. $–$$
A Thai restaurant in Amish Country? Well, yes and no. Set on busy Route 30 across from the Rockvale Square Outlets, this lovely little place features Thai specialties bursting with a tangy mix of garlic, chili, cilantro, basil, curry and mint. Standards such as satay and pad Thai are complemented by less familiar choices, including many vegetarian dishes.

### Log Cabin
11 Lehoy Forest Drive, Leola. Tel: 717-626-1181. Open: D daily. $$–$$$
Set in the woods near a covered bridge, this former speakeasy offers a warren of intimate dining rooms with exposed beams, fireplaces, chandeliers, comfy armchairs and antique paintings. The menu doesn't bow to fashion, concentrating instead on classic Continental cuisine.

### Miller's Smorgasbord
2811 Lincoln Hwy (Route 30), Ronks. Tel: 717-687-6621. Open: L, D daily, B Sun. $
Eat all you like at this huge buffet. Breakfast features fresh fruit, made-to-order eggs, French toast, pancakes, scrapple and sausage. Lunch and dinner are equally substantial, with country favorites like chicken corn soup, turkey, ham and chicken pot pie. In all, there are more than 75 items.

### Plain & Fancy Farm
3121 Old Philadelphia Pike (Route 340), Bird-in-Hand. Tel: 717-768-4400. Open: L, D daily. $
Hearty country cooking and lots of it is what you'll find at this all-you-can-eat, family-style restaurant in a complex of shops and attractions just outside the village of Bird-in-Hand. Customers are seated together at large tables and pass around heaping plates of roast beef, fried chicken, chicken pot pie, mashed potatoes, desserts and more – a lot more. Not the place for an intimate dinner, but gregarious travelers will have a good time.

### PRICE CATEGORIES
Prices for three-course dinner per person with a half-bottle of house wine:
**$** = under $25
**$$** = $25–$40
**$$$** = $40–$50
**$$$** = more than $50

# DOWN THE SHORE

**Since 1801, when the New Jersey shore was first pushed as a summer resort, it has been a Philly favorite, only a 90-minute drive from center city**

The colorful beach towns along the coast from the tip of Cape May to the shoals of Long Beach Island appeal to a variety of tastes and interests. From the Victorian houses of Cape May to the revelries of Wildwood, the glitz of Atlantic City to the family ambience of Ocean City, the Jersey Shore just can't be beat.

Cape May's beach is small and, due to erosion, getting smaller every year, but there is a boardwalk and a pedestrian mall of quaint shops. Once a family community, Wildwood began luring a younger crowd in the 1970s, earning the nickname "Child-wood." It is still a rite of passage for high school graduates, and two weeks in June known as "Senior Weeks" can get hectic, but it has the best boardwalk in New Jersey.

Stone Harbor, Avalon and Sea Isle City have a lower profile than their neighbors; Stone Harbor is noted for its bird sanctuary. Next door to Margate is Ventnor, where the Atlantic City boardwalk begins. This is bicycle-riding territory, with elegant ocean-front homes.

Farther north is Long Beach Island, 18 miles (29 km) long with a series of little towns along the main boulevard. It attracts a mix of teenagers, families and well-off vacationers. At the northern tip is historic Barnegat Lighthouse, which offers magnificent views.

**ABOVE:** The baby parade is a beloved tradition in Ocean City, which was founded by Methodists in 1879 as a "moral" (if sleepy) seaside resort. It remains a popular family destination.

**ABOVE LEFT:** Keeping a cool head on the beach at Long Beach Island, a sliver of sand 18 miles long with a series of little towns strung along the main boulevard. The island stretches between the Atlantic Ocean and Barnegat Bay.

**BELOW:** New Jersey has 127 miles (204 km) of white sandy beaches. Ocean waves are often big enough for surfing, while the bays have calm, shallow water suitable for windsurfing, kayaking and fishing.

**LEFT:** A surf caster displays the catch of the day at Island Beach State Park, a narrow barrier island that stretches about 10 miles along the coast.

## PLACE YOUR BETS: ATLANTIC CITY

After two decades of slot machines inside concrete casinos, Atlantic City is getting a new lease on life. Following New Jersey's approval of casino gambling in 1976, several unlovely casinos opened, but the city never had the allure of Las Vegas.

Until now, that is. The Borgata – the first new casino for many years – opened in 2003, complete with upscale restaurants, bars, a hip dance club and full spa. It's glamorous and gorgeous and the older casinos are fighting back. First came beachfront bars and a new hotel tower at Showboat, then Tropicana's The Quarter, a dining and shopping complex designed to recall the atmosphere of Old Havana. Its new Havana Tower will be New Jersey's largest hotel. Harrah's is planning a new entertainment center and hotel with some 950 rooms. Caesar's is expanding its shopping complex. And the MGM Mirage is moving forward with a new resort and casino.

**ABOVE:** At Margate you'll find a 90-ton, six-story-high elephant named Lucy. Built as a real-estate promotion in 1881 and later used as a tavern and hotel, Lucy is now a National Historic Landmark and the object of fierce loyalty among Margate residents.

**LEFT:** Set on the northern tip of Long Beach Island, Barnegat Light – known to residents as Old Barney – was built in 1859. At a height of 165 ft (50 meters), it is the second tallest lighthouse in the United States. The light was extinguished in 1965; visitors are welcome to climb to the top.

**RIGHT:** The hazy days of summer lure huge crowds to the Jersey shore. Public beaches close when they reach capacity, so be sure to arrive early if you plan to visit on a summer weekend.

**LEFT:** On the southernmost tip of New Jersey is the town of Cape May, a family-friendly resort of Victorian inns, gingerbread homes and sandy beaches.

# BUCKS COUNTY

An hour north and a world away from center city, this region has some of the most beautiful landscapes in the Delaware Valley – a sanctuary of woods, farms, creeks and wildlife

Philadelphia

Map on page 202

No sooner did William Penn design the layout of Philadelphia than he ran off to the suburbs, choosing to make his home in the woods of Bucks County. Stressed-out city dwellers have been following in his trail ever since. "The country life is to be preferred for there we see the works of God," Penn wrote. Three centuries later, travelers seeking a peaceful getaway are still finding the place heavenly.

## Penn's home

William and Hannah Penn set up house at **Pennsbury Manor** ❶ (400 Pennsbury Memorial Rd, off Rt 13 south of Morrisville; tel: 215-946-0400; open Tue–Sat 9am–5pm, Sun noon–5pm; entrance fee), an 8,000-acre (3,200-hectare) estate situated on a bend in the Delaware River about 26 miles (40 km) north of the city. Penn spent 1682–84 and 1699–1701 at the plantation before returning to England in 1701.

"Let not poor Pennsbury be forgotten, or neglected," he wrote his servants, "keep the housen, the farme & the Gardens, till we come." But Penn never returned, and the property fell to ruin.

That might have been the end of Pennsbury had it not been for a group of historians, architects and preservationists who quite literally

brought the estate back to life. Meticulously reconstructed from archaeological studies and Penn's own detailed instructions, the property is now a working re-creation of a colonial estate, fully furnished with one of the state's best collections of 17th-century antiques. The grounds are available for self-guided viewing. During guided tours (call for times), costumed guides show visitors around the mansion, smokehouse, stable, kitchen, carpenter's shop, brew house and other out-

**LEFT:** Mercer Museum.
**BELOW:** Pennsbury Manor.

*A garden gnome keeps watch on a backyard in Bucks County.*

buildings. There is a packed schedule of special events, including children's workshops, garden tours, a 17th-century country fair, Christmas festivities and demonstrations of open-hearth cooking, beer-making, woodworking and other crafts.

## River mansions

Near Pennsbury Manor is the colonial town of **Fallsington** ❷ (4 Yardley Ave, off Rt 1; tel: 215-295-6567; tours May–Oct Mon–Sat 10.30am–3.30pm, Sun 12.30pm–3.30pm, Nov–Apr weekdays only 10.30am–3.30pm; fee for guided tours), where Penn came to worship while residing in the country. It preserves several 18th-century buildings around a charming village square, including three Quaker meetinghouses and a log cabin. Walking tour maps are available at the Historic Fallsington Information Center, and guided tours of the buildings are available.

Two other historic homes in the area are also worth a visit. The **Margaret R. Grundy Memorial Library and Museum** ❸ (610 Radcliffe St, Bristol; tel: 215-788-7891; open Mon–Thur 11am–9pm, Fri 11am–5pm, Sat 10am–4.30pm; entrance free) is an elegant Victorian home, with a fine collection of period furnishings, that overlooks the Delaware River. Tours of the house and library, which is a modern subterranean structure, are available by appointment.

**Andalusia** ❹ (1237 State Rd, Andalusia; tel: 215-245-5479; tours by appointment only; entrance fee), one of the country's finest Greek Revival homes, is also on the Delaware River. Originally a simple country house, it was redesigned by financier Nicholas Biddle, who hired Thomas U. Walter to handle the renovation. The 220-acre (90-hectare) estate is still owned by the Biddle family, which preserves the house and its magnificent furnishings.

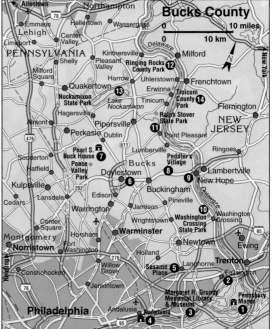

## For the children

If you're traveling with children under the age of 13, you may want to set aside a day for nearby **Sesame Place ⑤** (100 Sesame Rd, Langhorne, off Rt 1; tel: 215-752-7070; open daily mid-May–Labor Day, Sat–Sun Sep–mid-Oct, hours vary; entrance fee), a Sesame Street theme park with a range of rides, water slides, shows and other attractions such as Balloon Race, Grover's World Twirl, Vapor Trail, Slimey's Chutes, Mumford's Water Maze and the indoor Games Gallery designed to engage young minds and bodies.

## Genius Belt

**Doylestown ⑥**, the Bucks County seat, is directly north of center city Philadelphia. An important stagecoach station in the 1700s, today it is a Main Street town of gingerbread houses, interesting shops and first-rate inns and restaurants.

Most tourists come to Doylestown to see the **Mercer Mile**, three fantastic structures built between 1908 and 1916 by Henry Chapman Mercer, a brilliant if somewhat eccentric, archaeologist, artist and historian. After years of studying ancient cultures in the US and abroad, Mercer turned his attention to the tools and handicrafts of the Delaware Valley, searching the countryside for tools, utensils and other artifacts made obsolete by the Industrial Revolution. He called the collection "Tools of the Nation Maker," and with more than 40,000 objects, it remains the largest of its kind in the world.

Mercer was also an artist. While researching local crafts, he became fascinated with a nearly forgotten style of Pennsylvania German pottery. Although he himself wasn't much of a potter, he adapted the style to tile-making and developed a commercial clay shop to produce tiles and other ceramics of his own design. By 1905, Mercer's Moravian tiles had become a major exponent of America's Arts and Crafts movement, and his work was being commissioned for such varied buildings as Grauman's Chinese Theater in Hollywood, the Harvard Lam-

Map on page 202

*Mercer tiles are inspired by traditional Pennsylvania German designs.*

**BELOW:** Fonthill is constructed entirely of concrete and richly decorated with Mercer tiles.

poon building, the National Press Club in Washington, D.C., the Pennsylvania Capitol in Harrisburg, and high-class hotels all over the world.

## Concrete fantasy

During his travels in Europe, Mercer visited a number of castles and always fancied living in one himself. Back home in Doylestown, he decided to build one. The result is **Fonthill** (E. Court St and Rt 313/Swamp Rd; tel: 215-348-9461; open Mon–Sat 10am–5pm, Sun noon–5pm; entrance fee), a Tudor-style castle completed in 1910 and constructed entirely of reinforced concrete, a material he found could be molded much like clay.

He built the castle from the inside out without benefit of blueprints, improvising techniques as he went along, even pouring concrete over a farmhouse and incorporating it into the structure. The rooms are irregular, the windows unmatched and stairways sometimes go nowhere, but the overall effect of the vaulted salons, maze-like floor plan and the thousands of brilliantly colored tiles

is astonishing. It's safe to say that you have never seen anything like it. Guided tours of Fonthill are offered several times a day; make reservations a few hours in advance.

Mercer started the neighboring **Moravian Pottery and Tile Works** (130 Swamp Rd; tel: 215-345-6722; open daily 10am–4.45pm; entrance fee) even before Fonthill was completed. Modeled after several California missions, this second concrete fantasy served as a tile factory well into the 1950s.

The Bucks County Parks Department reopened the Tile Works as a working museum in the 1970s and it still turns out tiles using Mercer's original designs and techniques, although on a smaller scale. Tours of the Tile Works leave every half hour.

Mercer followed the Tile Works with yet another medieval-style castle designed to house his massive collection of pre-industrial tools and farm implements. The **Mercer Museum** (84 S. Pine St, Doylestown; tel: 215-345-0210; open Mon–Sat 10am–5pm, Tue until 9pm, Sun noon–5pm; entrance fee) is

**BELOW:** Bucks County croquet party.

## The Walking Purchase

Compared to his countrymen in New England and Virginia, William Penn was quite liberal in his treatment of the Lenape Indians, requiring that they be well-paid for land occupied by white settlers. Unfortunately, fair-dealing with Indians was not a family trait. Several years after Penn's death, his son Thomas cheated the Lenape out of prime Bucks County real estate in the so-called Walking Purchase of 1737. The Lenape agreed to sell territory in upper Bucks "as fast as a man can go in a day and a half," so the crafty younger Penn hired trained runners to do the pacing and acquired significantly more territory than the Lenape wanted to part with.

crammed with everything from old stagecoaches to sausage-makers. Much of the collection is dramatically suspended by wires in the four-story central atrium.

An iconoclast in almost everything he did, Mercer felt that the unusual display allowed visitors to see ordinary objects from a new perspective. Whatever his reasoning, the effect is jaw dropping.

## Art and literature

The **James A. Michener Museum** (138 Pine St, Doylestown; tel: 215-340-9800; Tue–Fri 10am–4.30pm, Sat 10am–5pm, Sun noon–5pm, Apr–Oct, Wed until 9pm; entrance fee), named in honor of Doylestown's renowned author, is directly across the street from the Mercer Museum.

The museum is located on the grounds of the former Bucks County Jail. Prison walls surround part of the site, and the warden's house now serves as gallery space for the museum's collection of 20th-century American art. The center's shows feature selections from the permanent collection in addition to

work by regional artists. In 2003, the museum opened a satellite location in New Hope.

You can also visit the homestead of another eminent Bucks County writer, Pearl S. Buck, author of *The Good Earth* and winner of both the Pulitzer and Nobel prizes. The **Pearl S. Buck House ❼** (520 Dublin Rd, Perkasie; tel: 215-249-0100; tours Mar–Dec Tue–Sat 11am, 1pm, 2pm, Sun 1pm, 2pm; entrance fee) is part of a 60-acre (25-hectare) spread known as Green Hills Farm. The early 19th-century farmhouse is also now headquarters of the Pearl S. Buck Foundation, an international children's-aid agency.

## Consumer culture

A 10-minute drive southeast of Doylestown on Route 202 brings you to **Peddler's Village ❽**, a complex of about 80 boutiques and restaurants specializing in antiques, folk art, fashions and handcrafted gifts. The shops are built around a landscaped "village green" with a pond, waterwheel, gingerbread-style gazebo and award-winning gardens. Bargain

Map on page 202

*The Michener Museum has a strong collection of American Impressionists, including members of the New Hope Group.*

**BELOW:**
Rice's Market is one of the largest flea markets in the region.

hunters should try nearby **Rice's Market** (6326 Greenhill Rd; tel: 215-297-5993; Tue and most legal holidays, Sat Mar–Dec), a sprawling 30-acre site where some 500 vendors sell antiques, crafts, housewares, clothing, jewelry, produce and used items of all kinds.

## New Hope

It's a 5-mile (8-km) drive on Route 202 south to the village of **New Hope ❾**, a former ferry crossing on the Delaware River that now caters to the hordes of tourists who flock here every weekend. As a result, traffic can be horrendous, so be sure to give yourself plenty of time.

A small mill town in the 1700s, New Hope boomed with the opening of the Delaware Canal in 1832. Although the railroad came along and put the waterway out of business in the early 1900s, by then New Hope was attracting a newer, different sort of crowd. The arrival of William Lathrop, Daniel Graber, Edward Redfield and other influential painters led to the growth of a lively artists' colony. And today,

*A gentle current and warm water make the Delaware River a favorite of tubers and canoeists.*

**RIGHT:** the New Hope & Ivyland Railroad runs from New Hope to Lahaska.

artists and collectors are still flocking to New Hope for the galleries and special exhibitions.

The Michener Museum's new satellite gallery – **The Michener at New Hope** (Union Square on Bridge St; tel: 215-862-7633; Jan–Mar Wed–Sun 11am–5pm, Apr–Dec Tue–Sun 11am–5pm, Sat to 6pm Memorial Day to Labor Day) – displays the growing collection of Pennsylvania Impressionist paintings and other notable contemporary and historic artists from the New Hope area.

## Historic houses

The **Delaware Canal**, named a National Heritage Corridor, is also still in operation, although the mule-drawn barges of the **New Hope Canal Boat Company** (149 S. Main St, New Hope; tel: 215-862-0758; entrance fee) now carry tourists rather than coal and lumber.

The **Locktender's House**, where you pick up the barge, has been preserved and has a small free museum (tel: 215-862-2021 for information).

You can also catch a ride on the

## Across the river in Lambertville

Just a short and scenic walk across the bridge from New Hope is the small city of Lambertville, New Jersey. Larger and less hectic than its sister city, Lambertville has become a destination in its own right, with beautifully restored Victorian buildings, dozens of shops and galleries, and some of the area's most interesting restaurants. The old factories and warehouses are long since closed, though some have been converted into retail and office space.

You'll find most of the action on Bridge and Main streets, where weekend tourists browse the shops or stop for a bite at one of the restaurants or cafes. Some 30,000 people descend on this neighborhood every spring for Shadfest, a street fair with food, music and other special happenings. This is also where you'll find some of the town's most interesting sites. Lambertville Station, for example, is the former depot of the Belvidere & Delaware Railroad. Built in 1874, the station is now a restaurant and serves as the terminus of the Black River & Western Railroad, which operates vintage locomotives. This is also a good spot to stroll along the Delaware and Raritan Canal, a historic greenway that parallels the Delaware River for some 30 miles (48 km) through Mercer and Hunterdon counties in New Jersey.

**New Hope & Ivyland Railroad** (32 W. Bridge St; tel: 215-862-2332; www.newhoperailroad.com; entrance fee) which runs vintage steam and diesel locomotives on a 9-mile (14-km), 50-minute round-trip between New Hope and Lahaska.

More than 200 historic buildings in New Hope are listed on the National Register of Historic Places. At South Main and Ferry streets, for example, the **Logan Inn** surrounds the shell of the original Ferry Tavern, which opened for business in the 1720s and is now the departure site for **Bucks County Carriages**, offering carriage rides through town (tel: 215-862-3582).

Nearby, old Town Hall, now the **New Hope Visitors Center** (Main and Mechanic sts; tel: 215-862-5880; open daily), and **Vansant House** date to the latter half of the 18th century.

Built in 1784, the **Parry Mansion** (New Hope Historical Society, 45 S. Main St; tel: 215-862-5652; open May–Dec, Sat–Sun 1–5pm, group tours by appointment; entrance fee) now serves as a museum of decorative arts, displaying rooms in five different period styles, dating from 1775 to 1900.

New Hope is also home to the **Bucks County Playhouse**, which has been offering summer stock for more than 50 years from a renovated gristmill. And don't forget New Hope's sister city across the bridge in New Jersey. **Lambertville**, filled with homey restaurants, quirky shops and a more low-key attitude is a perfect place to take shelter from New Hope's crowded sidewalks.

## Washington at war

History buffs should make a point of visiting **Washington Crossing State Park** ⑩ (1112 River Rd, Washington Crossing; tel: 215-493-4076; open Tue–Sat 9am–5pm, Sun noon–5pm; entrance fee), where George Washington launched his daring Christmas attack on the British and Hessian camp at Trenton, an event that is reenacted every Christmas Day.

The park is divided into two units. About 2 miles (3 km) south of New Hope is the **Thompson-Neely**

Map on page 202

*A mule-drawn barge floats down the Delaware Canal.*

**BELOW:** a Christmas reenactment of Washington's crossing of the Delaware.

Map
on page
202

*Set in Lumberville on
the Delaware River,
the Black Bass Hotel
was a loyalist meeting
place during the
American Revolution.*

**BELOW:**
horseback riders ford
Neshaminy Creek at
the foot of Schofield
Covered Bridge.

**House**, where the general and his officers met to plan the attack. A short drive away, the 110-ft (30-meter) **Bowman's Tower** (open Tue–Sun 9am–4.30pm), built in 1930 to commemorate a Revolutionary War lookout point, affords a spectacular view of the valley.

An 80-acre (30-hectare) **Wildflower Preserve** (tel: 215-862-2924; open daily 9am–5pm; entrance fee) surrounds the tower; a naturalist is usually on hand to answer questions and suggest tours along the many trails.

About 5 miles (8 km) south, the second unit includes the **Washington Crossing Memorial Building** where a replica of Emanuel Leutze's famous painting *Washington Crossing the Delaware* hangs.

## Covered bridges

But the real flavor of Bucks County lies along the back roads and untrammeled spaces of its many farms and natural preserves. From New Hope, River Road winds along the Delaware River to the three charming towns of **Lumberville**,

**Erwinna** and **Uhlerstown**. Along the way, at **Point Pleasant** ⓫, you can rent canoes and inner tubes for a leisurely float down the river. **Bucks County River Country** rents inner tubes, rafts, canoes and kayaks. Call 215-297-5000 or visit www.rivercountry.net for reservations.

You'll find the area's loveliest parks in the northern reaches of the county, too, including the fascinating boulder field of **Ringing Rocks County Park** ⓬; the peace and isolation of **Bull's Island State Park** in the Delaware River; the 1,450-acre (580-hectare) **Lake Nockamixon** ⓭, which is the largest body of water in the county and a haven for sailors; **Tohickon Valley County Park** and **Ralph Stover State Park** in the Tohickon Valley; **Peace Valley** just north of Doylestown; and the 19th-century **Erwin Stover House** and **Tinicum County Park** ⓮ overlooking the Delaware River in Erwinna.

Upper Bucks is also home to most of the county's 12 covered bridges, most built in the 1870s. Contact the Bucks County Conference and Visitors Bureau (3207 Street Rd, Bensalem; tel: 800-836-bucks) for a map.

A wine-tasting tour is a good way to see the countryside. Bucks County has several wineries that welcome visitors, including: **Buckingham Valley Vineyards** (1521 Rt 413, Buckingham; tel: 215-794-7188; open Tue–Sun; entrance free), **New Hope Winery** (6123 Lower York Rd, New Hope; tel: 215-794-2331; open daily) and **Sand Castle Winery** (755 River Rd, Erwinna; tel: 610-294-9181; open daily). **Chaddsford Winery** also has tastings at its retail shop (Rts 202 and 263, Peddler's Village; tel: 215-794-9655; open daily). And, of course, Bucks County is famous for its cozy inns and classy restaurants, many in historic buildings. ❑

# RESTAURANTS

## Restaurants

### Black Bass Hotel
3774 River Rd, Lumberville. Tel: 297-5770. Open: L Mon–Sat, D daily, Sun brunch. $$$
You'll be treated to a close-up view of the river from the dining room of this rustic, 18th-century inn. A display case filled with British royal memorabilia recalls the days when it was a notorious Tory hangout. A seasonal menu features creative American and Continental fare presented in a country setting with a touch of gourmet smarts. After dinner, stroll across the dramatic footbridge to Bull's Island.

### Carversville Inn
Aquetong and Carversville rds, Carversville. Tel: 297-0900. Open: L Tues–Sat, D Tues–Sun, Sun brunch. $$–$$$
The cuisine at this 1813 stone inn is largely American, although Chef Will Mathis, a Virginian, often draws on an impressive repertoire of Continental – and Southern – touches. The menu changes seasonally in order to take advantage of fresh ingredients but may include favorites like lamb chops, roast duck, and freshly made pasta. The rustic setting is nicely offset by starched linen, fine goblets and other elegant touches.

### Havana
105 S. Main St., New Hope. Tel: 862-9897. Open: L, D daily. $$
The big attraction here is the colorful crowd, the party bands and the never-ending show on Main Street. The patio is one of the best places in town to munch fries, sip beer, and soak in New Hope mania. Ambitious entrees sometimes go amiss, but simpler dishes like big juicy burgers are quite satisfying.

### Hotel du Village
2535 N. River Rd, New Hope. Tel: 862-9911. Open: D Wed–Sun. $$$
A perennial favorite, Hotel du Village has country elegance with an at-home feeling. Dress ranges from casual to chic, but the service and old-world ambiance are consistently classy. The menu has changed little over the years. Favorites like veal Madeira, sweetbreads, lamb chops and seafood are prepared in classic French style.

### Inn at Phillips Mill
2590 River Rd, New Hope. Tel: 862-9919. Open: D daily. $$–$$$
There's romance in the air and haute cuisine on the table at this inn, housed in a converted 1750s stone barn. Just when you think you can't eat another morsel, your waiter brings out a tray laden with scrumptious desserts. There's alfresco dining in the garden.

### La Bonne Auberge
1 Rittenhouse Circle, New Hope. Tel: 862-2462. Open: D Thurs–Sun. $$$$
Trying to impress a date? Look no farther than this hilltop hideaway off Mechanic Street. Elegant, romantic and profoundly French, La Bonne Auberge is dedicated to those who savor fine dining. Here's what you get: a 200-year-old farmhouse with refined ambiance, impeccable service, and exquisite cuisine. So what's not to like? Not a thing, assuming that money is no object.

### Logan Inn
10 W. Ferry St, New Hope. Tel: 862-3931. Open: L, D daily. $$$
The patio overlooking Main Street is packed with tourists on summer weekends, but the attraction at this historic inn is location rather than food. The oldest part of the inn – in fact, the oldest structure in town – was built in 1727 by New Hope's first ferryman and now houses a tavern with a long wooden bar and ancient fireplace. Lunch includes a predictable selection of burgers, sandwiches, salads and a few chicken and steak choices. The dinner menu sticks with American and Continental fare, ranging from crab cakes and filet mignon to vermouth-tinged chicken.

### Mother's
34 N. Main St., New Hope. Tel: 862-5857. Open: L, D daily, Sat–Sun brunch. $$
Casual and congenial, Mother's is a longstanding New Hope tradition with a variety of filling dishes – burgers, steaks, seafood, pizza, fajitas, veggie sandwiches and more. Or just come for dessert – cholesterol-soaked goodies that will weaken the will of the most committed dieter.

### Odette's
274 S. River Rd, New Hope. Tel: 862-2432. Open: L, D daily, Sun brunch. $$–$$$
A previous owner of this riverside restaurant was Broadway actress Odette Myrtil. The walls are plastered with show-biz memorabilia, and there's a lively bar and cabaret. The menu features Continental and American dishes. A romantic spot with river views.

### PRICE CATEGORIES
Prices for three-course dinner per person with a half-bottle of house wine:
**$** = under $25
**$$** = $25–$40
**$$$** = $40–$50
**$$$** = more than $50

# BRANDYWINE VALLEY

A short drive southeast of Philadelphia leads to a valley of historic homesteads, scenic hamlets and quiet country roads where the legacy of two celebrated American families lives on

A s you head out of Philadelphia on Route 1, you'll come to the valley of the Brandywine River, which twists through 20 miles (40 km) of rolling hills and estates. The river itself is really no more than a creek where two east and west branches meet at Chadds Ford, eventually joining the Delaware River at Wilmington. In the shadow of this babbling brook, scions of the Wyeth and du Pont families settled down to pursue their dreams.

Originally the territory of the Lenni-Lenape tribe, the Brandywine Valley was subsequently colonized by the Dutch, Swedes and English. It was river power that first attracted E.I. du Pont and his two sons, who saw a need for high-quality gunpowder in the New World and set about creating a company that would be the foundation of a worldwide industrial powerhouse.

## Chadds Ford

Much later, the valley nurtured another family's dream of quite a different sort. Decades ago, the haunting play of light and shadow on the Brandywine hills first attracted illustrator N.C. Wyeth to settle here, followed by his son Andrew and grandson Jamie. You can find the greatest collection in the world of Wyeth paintings in

Chadds Ford ❶, at the **Brandywine River Museum** (Rt 1, Chadds Ford; tel: 610-388-2700; open daily 9.30am–4.30pm except Christmas; entrance fee). The museum, housed in a renovated Civil War-era gristmill, also displays the largest US collection of English Pre-Raphaelite paintings, as well as collecting and preserving American art with an emphasis on landscape and still life. The circular glass-walled structure showcases spectacular views of the Brandywine River and the rural

Map on page 212

**LEFT:** aerial view of the Brandywine Valley.
**BELOW:** Andrew Wyeth's studio at the Brandywine River Museum in Chadds Ford, Pennsylvania.

*Tulips blossom at Longwood Gardens.*

landscape that inspired many of the artists represented in the museum. The grounds are planted with native wildflowers and a 1-mile (2-km) riverwalk that leads to the 18th-century bluestone **John Chads House** (Rt 100; tel: 610-388-7376; open May–Sep Sat–Sun noon–5pm, Oct–Apr by appointment; entrance fee). The house was built in 1725 for the innkeeper and ferry operator who gave his name to Chadds Ford (the extra "d" was a Victorian flourish), its simplicity reflecting Chads' Quaker heritage.

### Wine and war

Right across the street is the **Chaddsford Winery ❷** (632 Baltimore Pike, tel: 610-388-6221; open daily noon–6pm; free tour, entrance fee for wine tasting). This small premium winery, located in a renovated 17th-century colonial barn, first began production in 1982. Today the winery produces

**BELOW:** a pottery demonstration at a Brandywine fair.

30,000 cases of wine, making it the largest in Pennsylvania. You can take the winemaking tour, taste wines or picnic on the grounds.

While you're in Chadds Ford, don't miss **Brandywine Battlefield Park ❸** (tel: 610-459-3342; open Tues–Sat 9am–5pm, Sun noon–5pm). The park is the site of the Battle of Brandywine, which took place during the Revolutionary War. Still standing are the quarters of the Marquis de Lafayette and the spot where General Washington set up his headquarters before retreating for the dispirited winter at Valley Forge. A permanent interpretive exhibit and an audio-visual presentation tell the story of the battle and its relation to the Philadelphia Campaign of 1777.

It's a short drive to Kennett Square, a quiet town originally home to the Lenni-Lenape tribe. Named after a village in England, the town was incorporated in 1855

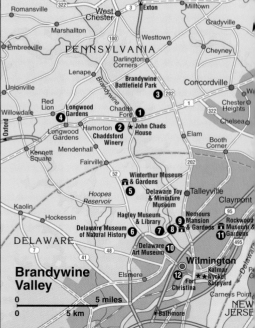

and was known for strong anti-slavery sentiments. Kennett Square was a hotbed of abolitionism – Harriet Tubman lived and worked here and Quakers helped slaves to freedom along the Underground Railroad.

## Flowers and fountains

About 3 miles (5 km) northeast of Kennett Square is **Longwood Gardens ❹** (Route 1; tel: 610-388-1000; www.longwoodgardens.org; visitors center and outdoor garden open daily Apr–Oct 9am–6pm, Nov–Mar 9am–5pm, open-air theater performances June–Aug; entrance fee). The property was sold by William Penn to Quaker farmers Samuel and Joshua Peirce, who planted a small arboretum here in 1700 known as Peirce's Park. It changed hands several times until Pierre du Pont bought the property in 1906.

Pierre was a gardening fanatic whose eclectic tastes included a love of theater. As a result, Longwood offers not only flowers and trees but fireworks, fountain displays, organ recitals, choral concerts, children's workshops and other special events.

Entering the gardens is a bit like falling down a rabbit hole into Wonderland; you enter through a low building built right into the side of a hill and emerge on the other side into the park – a great leafy world filled with bird song and wind chimes. There's no such thing as an "off season" here, where even in the dead of winter you can visit the heated conservatories for miniature walk-through eco-climates of deserts and rainforests.

The greenhouses and the conservatory are particularly colorful from November to April, but masses of flowering plants adorn the conservatory year round. May is the month of maximum blooms, when 50,000 bulbs burst into flower. Spectacular illuminated displays at the main fountain garden take place Tuesday,

Thursday and Saturday evenings June through August.

If all that exploring makes you peckish, stop for a bite to eat at the cafeteria or the formal Terrace Restaurant, both located a short walk from the conservatory. During warm weather you can eat outside.

## Du Pont treasures

To continue your tour of the Brandywine Valley, hop on Route 52 south, stopping just 30 miles (50 km) south of Philadelphia and 6 miles (10 km) north of Wilmington at the **Winterthur Museum and Gardens ❺** (Rt 52; tel: 800-448-3883; open Tues–Sun 10am–5pm; reserve tours by phone; entrance fee).

Winterthur houses the nation's largest collection of early American decorative arts, set in a mansion on 1,000 acres (400 hectares) of landscaped meadows and woods. It was home to Henry Francis du Pont, a superb landscaper and the most prodigious collector of decorative arts made or used in the US from 1640 to 1860. Du Pont inherited the original 18th-century country house

Map on page 212

**TIP**

On your way out of Longwood, check out the Chester County Visitors Center (Rt 1, near Longwood Gardens; tel: 800-228-9933) to get an idea of what's happening in the area.

**BELOW:** the water lily pond and Conservancy at Longwood Gardens.

*The Brandywine Valley is known for its historic inns and restaurants, including the Dilworthtown Inn, which has a wine cellar of some 800 labels.*

**RIGHT:** Brandywine River Museum.

in 1927 and proceeded to transform it into a 175-room home filled with US furniture, art and accessories, such as entire portions of a Philadelphia mayor's house, a Pennsylvania Dutch farm, a 19th-century Delaware inn and the family room of a 17th-century Massachusetts dwelling. A staircase and several rooms were originally part of the Montmorenci estate in North Carolina.

Each room has its own treasures – an old general store, a Chinese parlor built to showcase wallpaper hand-painted in 1770 in a continuous panorama of Chinese village life. There are about 5,000 pieces of Chinese porcelain, in addition to chandeliers, paintings, maps, statues, tapestries, silverware and more – du Pont's collection of objets d'art is the largest in the world. Interactive displays in the galleries explore the history and development of Early American decorative arts.

The spectacular gardens, which peak in early May, include rare rhododendron and azaleas and 60 acres (25 hectares) of native and exotic plants.

Still driving south on Route 52, you'll come to the **Delaware Museum of Natural History** ❻ (4840 Kennett Pike, Wilmington; tel: 302-658-9111; open Mon–Sat 9.30am–4.30pm, Sun noon–4.30pm; entrance fee). The museum, which contains a variety of natural-history exhibits in natural settings, includes an extensive shell collection, mounted African animals and extinct birds. A discovery room features hands-on exhibits and activities, and films are shown on a regular basis.

## Guns and money

A few miles south on the Brandywine River is the **Hagley Museum and Library** ❼ (Rt 141; tel: 302-658-2400; open daily Mar–Dec, weekends Jan–Mar 9.30am–4.30pm). Built on the original site of the 1802 du Pont mills, Hagley was the du Ponts' first US home. It was here that the 19th-century workers lived; today it is an outdoor museum spreading over 240 acres (100 hectares) along the Brandywine Valley.

A National Historic Landmark, this nonprofit institution is dedi-

## American Dynasty

In late 1799, the Paris-born Pierre Samuel du Pont de Nemours and *famille* set sail for America to find their fortune. Boy, did they ever! Winding up in Delaware, the family and successive generations became a capital success. Few names in the American industrial pantheon shine more luminously than that of du Pont.

Over the years, du Ponts have had a lot of irons in the fire – chemical, weaponry, automotive, aviation, rubber, food, financial – you name it, they've been into it. Family success started with a bang with, yes, gunpowder. The younger of Pierre's two sons, Éleuthère Irénée, who had trained with the royal French arsenal, produced a better grade of black powder than the stuff turned out by Americans, and he set up operations in the Brandywine area.

Profits began piling up, and the War of 1812 helped immensely. Diversification in such manufactures as textiles were to follow, and du Pont offspring began to play active roles in public affairs. The du Ponts also took up banking and finance, making possible all sorts of projects – like, for example, the world's tallest structure, the Empire State Building in New York City. By the 1920s, the du Pont enterprise had come to encapsulate American capitalism in all its fullness.

cated to America's economic and technological heritage. Exhibits and demonstrations depict the evolution of the US economy and include a wooden waterwheel, turbine-powered roll mills, an operating steam engine and a restored 1870s machine shop. Working models in the Millwright Shop demonstrate the production of black powder.

The Henry Clay Mill is an old stone cotton-spinning shop featuring dioramas, models and narrated displays tracing economic development along the Brandywine from the 17th century to the present day. A restored workers' community on nearby Blacksmith Hill features a one-room schoolhouse and a worker's house.

Overlooking the Brandywine is **Eleutherian Mills**, the Georgian-style mansion built in 1803 by company founder Éleuthère Irénée du Pont, a French nobleman and son of Louis XVI's finance minister. The mansion and its furnishings reflect the tastes of the five generations of du Ponts who lived there. The barn contains 19th-century farm tools, weather vanes, vehicles, a Conestoga wagon and antique cars.

If your kids aren't wild about manufacturing displays, they may enjoy a stop instead at the **Delaware Toy and Miniature Museum ❽** (Rt 141; tel: 302- 427-8697; guided tours by reservation Tues–Sat 10am–4pm, Sun noon–4pm, closed public holidays; entrance fee) just past the entrance to the Hagley. It offers a collection of more than 100 antique and contemporary dollhouses, as well as dolls, toy trains, boats and planes from the 18th century to the present day.

### Art and nature

Haven't had enough of the du Pont grandeur? Then continue on Route 141 to the **Nemours Mansion and Gardens ❾** (Rockland Rd; tel: 302-

651-6912 or 800-657-6912; open May–Oct Tues–Sun, tours 9am, 11am, 1pm, 3pm; no 9am tour on Sun; limited holiday tours Nov–Dec; kids under 12 not permitted). The 17,000-sq-ft Louis XVI-style estate of Alfred I. du Pont displays antiques, Oriental rugs and paintings and tapestries dating from the 15th century. Nemours is set on 300 acres (120 hectares) of woodlands and manicured gardens with examples of the family's extravagant life, including vintage automobiles and a bowling alley. You can take a bus tour through the gardens, one of the finest examples of French-style horticulture in the US.

Leaving Nemours, you can take Route 100 south to the **Delaware Art Museum ❿** (2301 Kentinere Pkwy, Wilmington; tel: 302-571-9590; open Tues, Thur–Sat 10am–4pm, Wed 10am–8pm, Sun noon–4pm; entrance fee; free guided tours Sat–Sun). Among the museum's 12,000 art works are many examples of American art from the 19th to the 21st century, including the country's largest collection of paintings by

Map on page 212

*Pennsylvania produces more mushrooms than any other state, and Kennett Square alone provides about 25 percent of the entire US mushroom crop.*

**BELOW:**
Winterthur Gardens.

Map on page 212

*A glassblowing demonstration at the Simon Pearce glass works and restaurant in West Chester, Pennsylvania.*

**BELOW:** a chef prepares dinner at a Brandywine restaurant.

John Sloan and an important collection of English Pre-Raphaelite art. There are also rooms devoted to American illustration, and the museum offers workshops for adults and children.

If you're interested in more decorative arts, you're just a short distance from an 1851 manor house, the **Rockwood Museum and Gardens ⑪** (610 Shipley Rd, Wilmington; tel: 302-761-4340; open daily 7am–7pm, tours 10am–3pm; entrance fee). Guides conduct tours of the rural Gothic house and you can also explore the gardens. A cast iron and glass conservatory is filled with tropical plants.

## Wilmington

From Rockwood, it's just a short drive to **Wilmington ⑫**, first christened New Sweden and renamed Willingtown by its Quaker founders to honor local merchant Thomas Willing in 1731. For tourist information, go to the **Greater Wilmington Convention and Visitors Bureau** (100 W. 10th St; tel: 302-652-4088 or 800-422-1181).

Just a few blocks away is the Delaware History Center, which dominates the 500 block of Market Street Mall in downtown Wilmington. The **Delaware History Museum** (504 Market St; tel: 302-655-7161 or 656-0637; open Mon–Fri noon–4pm, Sat 10am–4pm, closed public holidays; entrance fee) is located in a renovated Art Deco Woolworth store and features three galleries of interactive exhibits on Delaware history, with an emphasis on the objects of everyday life – toys, clothing and decorative arts. The Old Town Hall, built in 1798, was the hub of political and social activity in Wilmington's mercantile-milling economy. Today it's owned by the Historical Society of Delaware and used for exhibitions. Willingtown Square consists of six historic houses relocated into an urban park in 1976.

## On the waterfront

To get a feel for Wilmington before the du Ponts made it their home, head out to the waterfront to visit the *Kalmar Nyckel* **Shipyard and Museum** (823 E. 7th St, Wilmington; tel: 302-429-7447; open Mon–Sat 10am–4pm, Sun noon–4pm, closed public holidays; entrance fee). The *Kalmar Nyckel* was the ship that brought the first European settlers to the Delaware Valley in 1638. There are tours of the shipbuilding facilities led by costumed guides, plus a replica of the tall ship.

You can continue your tour of the city's Swedish roots at **Old Swedes Church** (606 Church St; tel: 302-652-5629), built in 1698 by children of Swedish Lutherans who came to the New World aboard the *Kalmar Nyckel*, and at **Fort Christina** (7th St; tel: 302-652-5629; entrance free) next to the shipyard. Here you can still see the site where the first settlers landed and some of their original log homes. ❏

## RESTAURANTS & BARS

### Restaurants

#### Chadds Ford Tavern and Restaurant
96A Baltimore Pike, Chadds Ford. Tel: 610-459-8453. Open: L & D nightly. $$
A low-key tavern with works from local artists on the walls and a cozy fireplace. The straightforward menu isn't breaking any new ground, but it's a decent and affordable alternative to pricier inns.

#### Dilworthtown Inn
1390 Old Wilmington Pike, West Chester. Tel: 610-399-1390. Open: D nightly. $$$$
www.dilworthtowninn.com
If you're hunting for the ultimate charming country inn, you might end up here. It's been around in one form or another since the Battle of Brandywine and is now a fine-dining restaurant serving new American cuisine, from house smoked salmon to rack of lamb. Wine lovers will appreciate the 800-bottle cellar.

#### Gilmore's
133 E. Gay St., West Chester. Tel: 610-431-2800. Open: D Tues–Sat. $$–$$$
www.gilmoresrestaurant.com
This 35-seater in an 18th-century townhouse is considered the top BYOB in Chester County. The whimsical French-American menu, prepared by chef-owner and longtime Le Bec-Fin chef de cuisine

Peter Gilmore, has everything from foie gras pizza to roasted baby pheasant.

#### Hank's Place
Baltimore Pike & Creek Rd., Chadds Ford. Tel: 610-388-7061. Open: B, L, D daily. $
Convenient to both the Brandywine Museum and Longwood Gardens, this old-fashioned country diner is a favorite for a quick pit stop (except on weekends, when long lines make it a more leisurely pit stop). It's rumored that artist Andrew Wyeth and Helga, his famous subject, are customers.

#### High Street Caffe
322 S. High St., West Chester. Tel: 610-696-7435. Open: L Tues–Fri, D Tues–Sun. $$–$$$
www.highstreetcaffe.com
Fun, funky and exceedingly purple, this rock and roll spot serves Cajun, Creole and "exotic" cuisine. The last one probably refers to wild game like alligator and ostrich. Less adventurous diners can choose familiar New Orleans fare like jambalaya, etoufee, gumbo and fried crawfish.

#### Iron Hill Brewery
3 W. Gay St., West Chester. Tel: 610-738-9600. Open: L Mon–Sat, D nightly, Sun brunch. $$–$$$
www.ironhillbrewery.com
For beer lovers, this

restaurant with an on-site brewery is a real find. House brand lagers, porters and ales are always available and a roster of seasonal brews rounds out the list of options. The food is a step up from your usual pub grub and includes wood oven pizza and seared scallops. Look out for nightly beer specials and beer dinners.

#### Simon Pearce on the Brandywine
1333 Lenape Rd., West Chester. Tel: 610-793-0948. Open: L & D Wed–Sun. $$$–$$$$
www.simonpearce.com
The dining room overlooks the Brandywine River, and an on-site glassblowing workshop provides all the plates and glasses in the restaurant. Dine on contemporary American cuisine with Irish accents, then visit the glass factory and shop.

#### The Green Room at the Hotel duPont
11th & Market sts, Wilmington, Delaware. Tel: 302-594-3154. Open: B & L Mon–Sat, D nightly, Sun brunch. $$$$
www.dupont.com/hotel
This luxury hotel, the brainchild of chemical magnate Pierre du Pont, opened its doors in 1913 and was intended to rival the finest Euro-

pean hotels. It had faded a bit over the years, but a rehab in 2005 restored its former opulence. In the Green Room, you'll eat fine French cuisine served on Versace china by an expert staff. Jackets are required Friday and Saturday evenings. More casual dining and afternoon tea are offered in the lobby lounge.

### Bars

#### Four Dogs Tavern
1300 Strasburg Rd., West Chester. Tel: 610-692-4367.
www.fourdogstavern.com
Located in a converted barn, this casual bar offers seasonal outdoor patio seating. Pub menu served; bar stays open to 1am nightly.

#### Half Moon Restaurant & Saloon
108 W. State St., Kennett Square. Tel: 610-444-7232.
www.halfmoonrestaurant.com
The mahogany bar downstairs features 20 taps. The upstairs bar on the rooftop deck has views of the countryside. Serves eclectic tavern fare.

#### PRICE CATEGORIES
Prices for three-course dinner per person with a half-bottle of house wine:
**$** = under $25
**$$** = $25–$40
**$$$** = $40–$50
**$$$** = more than $50

# TRANSPORTATION

## GETTING THERE AND GETTING AROUND

*Note: Unless indicated otherwise, Philadelphia telephone numbers cited here have a 215 area code.*

### GETTING THERE

#### By Air

Philadelphia is served by Philadelphia International Airport, situated about 8 miles (13 km) from center city. Most major domestic carriers do business here. International carriers include Air France, British Airways, Lufthansa, and Air Canada. For flight departure and arrival information, go to www.phl.org or call 937-6800 or 800-745-4283.

### Ground Transportation

There are several options for getting directly into the city.
**Taxis, limousines and shuttles:** Taxis are the most convenient. The flat fee for a ride to central Philadelphia is $25. Other fares are charged by the mile. There is a $10 minimum fare from the airport to any destination. Limousines and share-ride vans are also available.

For fees and departure times, speak with a representative at a Ground Transportation Information (937-6958) desk in every baggage claim area.
**Train:** SEPTA's R1 High Speed Rail Line runs from the airport to Eastwick Station, University City, 30th Street Station, Suburban

Station, and MarketEast/The Gallery. Enter the airport's train stations from the pedestrian bridges. The one-way fare is $5.50.
**Bus:** SEPTA also runs two bus lines through the airport, although neither takes passengers to Center City. The R1 High Speed Rail Line is a better option.

### Hotel Shuttle

Some hotels offer free shuttle service. Ask your hotel when you make reservations or look for the marked vans that pull up curbside, usually outside baggage claim.

### Car Rental

Unless you plan on venturing outside Center City, a car is probably unnecessary and frequently inconvenient. If you need a car, several rental agencies are available at the airport. To rent a car, you must be at least 21 years old (some companies don't like to rent to anyone under 25), have a valid driver's license and a major credit card. Be sure you are properly insured for both collision and liability. Insurance costs are usually not included in the base rental fee. You may already be covered by your own insurance or credit card company, in which case you may not need the addi-

### AIRLINES

| | | | |
|---|---|---|---|
| Air Canada | 800-361-8071 | Delta Connection | 800-221-1212 |
| Air France | 800-237-2747 | Frontier Airlines | 800-432-1359 |
| Air Jamaica | 800-523-5585 | Lufthansa | 800-645-3880 |
| Air Tran Airways | 770-996-9000 | Midwest Airlines | 800-452-2022 |
| American | | Northwest | |
|    Airlines | 800-433-7300 |    Airlines | 800-225-2525 |
| American Eagle | 800-433-7300 | Southwest | |
| America West | 800-235-9292 |    Airlines | 800-435-9792 |
| British Airways | 800-247-9297 | United Airlines | 800-241-6520 |
| Continental | | United Express | 800-241-6520 |
|    Airlines | 800-525-0280 | US Airways | 800-428-4322 |
| Continental | | US Airways | |
|    Express | 800-525-0280 |    Express | 800-428-4322 |
| Delta Air Lines | 800-221-1212 | USA 3000 | 877-872-3000 |

tional insurance sold by the rental agency.

If you are traveling from the United Kingdom, try to arrange for car rental before departing, since many rates available overseas tend to be less costly than the best US deals.

Alamo, tel: 800-327-9633
Avis, tel: 800-331-1212
Budget, tel: 800-527-0700
Dollar, tel: 800-800-4000
Enterprise, tel: 1-800-736-8222
Hertz, tel: 800-654-3131
National, tel: 800-227-7368

## By Rail

Amtrak, the national railway system, offers service from Philadelphia's 30th Street Station. Several Amtrak routes pass through Philadelphia, including the Metroliner (Washington, DC, to New York City), Pennsylvanian (Pittsburgh to New York City), Cardinal/Hoosier State (Chicago to New York), Silver Service/Palmetto (Miami to New York City). For a premium, another option is the Acela Express, a high-speed (up to 150 mph/240kph) line from Boston to Washington, DC, via Philadelphia. SEPTA subway connections and taxis are available at 30th Street Station. **Amtrak fare and schedule information:** www.amtrak.com or call 800-872-7245.

## By Bus

Greyhound Bus Terminal, the nation's largest bus network with connections to cities and small towns throughout the U.S., is at 11th and Filbert Street near Market East/The Gallery. Greyhound also has several suburban stations outside Philadelphia, including King of Prussia (234 E. DeKalb Pike, tel: 610-265-2900) and Willow Grove (800 Fitzwater Rd, tel: 659-3443). **Greyhound Bus Lines fare and schedule information:** 800-231-2222, www.greyhound.com

## By Car

All roads lead to Philadelphia, or thereabouts. From New York City, the New Jersey Turnpike (exit 4) leaves you about 20 minutes from Philadelphia, near Camden, New Jersey. From Washington, DC, and Baltimore, I-95 follows the Delaware River directly through the city.

From the west, the Pennsylvania Turnpike intersects I-76 (the Schuylkill Expressway); and from Atlantic City, the Atlantic City Expressway leads to the Walt Whitman Bridge and Benjamin Franklin Bridge.

Bridges across the Delaware River between Philadelphia and New Jersey include the Walt Whit-

man, the Benjamin Franklin, the Betsy Ross and the Tacony-Palmyra.

Three major arteries cross Philadelphia. Although often slowed by rush hour traffic, they make it easy to get from one end of the city to another during off-hours.

I-76, or the Schuylkill Expressway (known derisively as the Sure-Kill Crawlway), runs along the Schuylkill River from northwest Philadelphia to the Walt Whitman Bridge in South Philadelphia. I-95 run north-south through the eastern edge of the city. The Vine Street Expressway (676) runs east-west across center city from I-95 to I-76.

### Parking

Two words strike fear in the heart of every Philadelphia motorist: meter maid. The Parking Violations Bureau is extremely efficient. If you park illegally, you will get a ticket. And if you don't pay the fine within the allotted time, you will get slapped with a hefty penalty.

Parking meters accept coins and Smart Cards, which can be purchased online (www.philapark.org/smartcards/purchase_smartcard.aspx) and shipped to you before your visit. Take note of the regulation signs. The red signs tell you when you can't park, the green signs will tell you when and how long you can park. If you can't find a space, it is almost always cheaper to leave the car in a parking lot or garage than to pay a parking ticket.

There are garages and parking lots throughout center city, some operated by the Philadelphia Parking Authority (PPA), others by private owners. You will find PPA lots in center city at:
Parking Plaza Garage, 801 Filbert Street.
AutoPark at the Gallery Mall, Market Street East.
AutoPark at JFK Plaza, 15th & Arch streets.
AutoPark at City Center, 15th & Arch streets.

**BELOW:** with luck, you can park outside a restaurant in the old city.

Philadelphia Gateway Parking Garage, 1540 Vine Street. AutoPark at Jefferson, 10th and Ludlow streets. AutoPark at Olde City, 2nd and Sansom streets. AutoPark at Independence Mall, 5th and Market streets. Parkway Museums, 19th and Callowhill streets. Rittenhouse Square, 20th and Sansom streets.

## GETTING AROUND

Thanks to William Penn, getting around center city is fairly easy. The streets are laid out in an orderly grid. Traffic isn't too bad, except at rush hour. There is plenty of public transportation. But the best way to get around is on foot. From City Hall, you can walk just about anywhere in center city in about 30 minutes.

Otherwise, the most convenient and inexpensive way to move around town is the **Phlash**, (www.phillyphlash.com) a purple, trolley-like bus that runs in a loop from Penn's Landing to City Hall via Market Street, then to the Art Museum via the Ben Franklin Parkway. The Phlash runs daily from 10am to 6pm, March to November. It stops at 19 locations in center city and arrives about every 12 minutes. The fare is $1 per ride or $4 for an all-day individual pass. A $10 all-day

**BELOW:** information gathering at the Independence Visitor Center.

family pass (2 adults and 2 children 6–17 years old) is also available. Children under the age of five and seniors ride free. Tickets can be purchased at the Independence Visitor Center (6th and Market), the RiverLink Ferry at Penn's Landing or on the trolley.

Beyond center city, Philadelphia sprawls interminably. Public transportation is necessary to visit surrounding areas. Driving is usually convenient, too, although finding a parking spot may be difficult in some neighborhoods.

**SEPTA** (Southeastern Pennsylvania Transportation Authority) operates an extensive public transit system with buses, subways, and surface-subway cars able to take you just about anywhere in the city, and commuter rail lines linking the city with the suburbs. An unlimited day pass for all SEPTA buses, trains, and trolleys is $5.50. The two main subway lines are the **Broad Street, or Orange Line**, which runs north and south along Broad Street, and the **Market-Frankford, or Blue Line** (also known as the "El" in places where the rail is elevated above street level), which runs east and west. The **Green** subway-surface trolley lines run east and west through center city, then branch north and west to various points in and outside the city.

**SEPTA Regional Rail Lines** (www.septa.org) will take you even farther afield, with links to the suburbs in Bucks, Montgomery, Chester and Delaware counties. Board regional lines at 30th Street Station (30th and JFK Blvd), Suburban Station (16th and Market) or Market East Station (11th and Market).

**PATCO** operates a high-speed rail link across the Delaware River between Philadelphia and Lindenwold, New Jersey. Patco has four underground stations in center city: Locust Street at 16th, 13th and 10th Streets, and 8th and Market Streets. Trains run 24 hours a day, with departures every 3 to 12 minutes

during peak travel times. (PATCO 922-4600 or www.drpa.org)

Another way across the Delaware River is the **RiverLink Ferry**, which runs from Penn's Landing to the New Jersey State Aquarium in Camden from 9.20am to 6pm daily May through September, and from Friday to Sunday in April and October. Express evening service is often available for events at the Tweeter Center on the Camden waterfront.

RiverLink Ferry System 925-5465 or www.riverlinkferry.org.

### *Handicapped Travelers*

SEPTA has a good website (www.septa.org/service/accessible_septa. html), with information about accessibility for disabled travelers. SEPTA's Advisory Committee for Accessible Transportation can be reached at 610-353-6640. Or call Septa Customer Service at 580-7800.

### Taxis

Cabs are usually available at tourist spots in center city. Rates are fairly reasonable: $2.70 for the first one-seventh of a mile and 30¢ for each one-seventh of a mile or 54 seconds of wait time thereafter. A 15 percent tip is customary. Call at least 30 minutes ahead for door-to-door service anywhere in the city.

**Olde City Taxi**, tel: 338-0838
**Quaker City Cab**, tel: 728-8000
**United Cab Association**, tel: 238-9500
**Yellow Cab**, tel: 922-8400

### Carriages

Horse-drawn carriages are a romantic (but expensive) way to see the historic district. Drivers, many in costume, act as guides. You can almost always catch a carriage at Head House Square or Independence Hall.

Philadelphia Carriage: 922-6840 or www.philacarriage.com
76 Carriage: 389-8687 or www.phillytour.com

# Accommodations

## SOME THINGS TO CONSIDER BEFORE YOU BOOK THE ROOM

### Choosing a Hotel

The opening of new hotels in recent years gives travelers a wider selection of lodging than ever before and encourages competitive pricing, making Philadelphia hotels an especially good value. The most convenient, and expensive, are in center city, which encompasses the historic district, the Avenue of the Arts (South Broad Street), the museum district, Rittenhouse Square and the downtown area around the Pennsylvania Convention Center.

There are approximately 11,000 rooms in center city, ranging in size and style from ultra-modern, high-rise suites to antique-filled guest rooms in historic boutique hotels. Options for budget travelers are not extensive, but they do exist (the Chamounix Mansion hostel in Fairmount Park is a notable example). Chain hotels in and around center city can be a good deal, though what you gain in savings you lose in personal touches. Wherever you book a room, be sure to inquire about special rates and packages (asking is essential; reservation agents don't necessarily volunteer the cheapest rates). The hospitality business in Philadelphia is extremely competitive, and hotels offer a variety of special deals to boost occupancy, especially during weekends. Nearly all hotel rooms in the city are outfitted with high-speed wireless Internet and cable television. The lodging tax in Philadelphia is 14 percent.

### Bed and Breakfast

B&B lodgings have been springing up throughout the city but are particularly numerous in getaway destinations outside the city, such as Bucks County, the Brandywine Valley, Lancaster County, and Cape May, New Jersey, where historic mansions, farmhouses and cottages have been lavishly restored. The original B&B concept, in which travelers rent a room in a private home, often socializing and eating with the resident family, is long gone. Most B&Bs today are really small inns managed by dedicated professionals. Some offer modest comforts (like shared bathrooms and creaky beds) at a modest price. Others are far more elaborate, with such luxuries as whirlpool tubs, fireplaces, high-quality linens, original art, antique furnishings and state-of-the-art electronics.

As the name suggests, breakfast is included in the price of lodging. This can range from a basket of muffins and a cup of coffee to an elaborate gourmet repast. At some inns, guests are served at separate tables. In others, they dine together. A few offer breakfast in your room. Most serve one entrée only, unless a special request is made in advance.

Many small inns are not suited for young children, and some have explicit age restrictions. In most cases, smoking and pets are not permitted. A minimum of two nights on weekends and three nights on holidays may be required. Unlike business hotels in the city, rates are lowest on weekdays, highest on weekends.

Contact the agencies for B&B information and reservations:

**Bed and Breakfast Connection of Philadelphia**
Tel: 610-687-3565 or 800-448-3619. Fax: 610-995-9524
www.bnbphiladelphia.com

**Bucks County Bed and Breakfast Association**
P.O. Box 154
New Hope, PA 18938
www.visitbucks.com

**New Hope Bed and Breakfasts**
www.newhopepa.com/lodging.htm

**Authentic Bed and Breakfasts of Lancaster County**
Tel: 800-552-2632
www.authenticbandb.com

**Brandywine Valley Bed and Breakfasts**
www.bvbb.com/index.html

## ACCOMMODATION LISTINGS

# OLD CITY

### Expensive

**Best Western Independence Park**
235 Chestnut Street
Tel: 922-4443
Fax: 922-4487
www.independenceparkhotel.com
You can't beat the location of this small hotel, in a handsome 19th-century building adjacent to Independence Park and within walking distance of Old City galleries and Penn's Landing. Guest rooms are fairly generous in size, with high ceilings. Complimentary breakfast and afternoon tea are served in a glass-enclosed courtyard. Although the property is owned by motel chain Best Western, this isn't a cookie-cutter hotel.

**Omni Hotel at Independence Park**
401 Chestnut Street
Tel: 925-0000
Fax: 925-1263
www.omnihotels.com
Contemporary in style, this plush hotel offers first-rate service and attractive rooms overlooking Independence Park. Most rooms have a small sitting area and comfy touches like feather pillows and terrycloth robes. Corner rooms tend to be larger and have extra windows. If you have money to burn, ask for the penthouse suite, which features a canopy bed, marble bathroom, whirlpool tub, cathedral ceilings, and a dining area with a table for ten. Facilities include the Azalea restaurant, a fitness center and indoor lap pool.

**Penn's View Hotel**
14 N. Front Street
Tel: 922-7600
Fax: 922-7642
www.pennsviewhotel.com
This large bed and breakfast has 51 rooms in a converted 1828 warehouse with views of the Delaware River. Handsome rooms have hardwood floors, stylish period-style furnishings and comfy beds with high-quality linens. Deluxe rooms feature a whirlpool tub, fireplace and balcony. A generous continental breakfast and a morning newspaper are included in the room rate. The highly regarded Ristorante Panorama is on the first floor. The bar is a wine-lovers dream, with 120 wines by the glass.

### Moderate

**Holiday Inn – Historic District**
400 Arch Street
Tel: 923-8660
Fax: 923-4633
hiphiladelphia-historicdistrict.
felcor.com
History lovers will like being close to Independence Park, but service and facilities are mediocre at best. It's a decent choice if you're happy with moderately priced accommodations in a good location, but don't expect any frills.

**Morris House Hotel**
225 S. 8th Street
Tel/Fax: 922-2446
www.morrishousehotel.com
This historic 18th-century house near Washington Square offers 15 tastefully appointed rooms and suites with private bathrooms, televisions, and wireless Internet access. Continental breakfast is included in the room rate. A courtyard garden offers a peaceful place for relaxation.

**Thomas Bond House**
129 S. 2nd Street
Tel: 923-8523 or 800-845-2663
Fax: 923-8504
This 18th-century bed-and-breakfast has been outfitted with modern amenities, including a private bath in every room, without sacrificing period character. Some rooms have a fireplace and whirlpool tub. Breakfast is included. An excellent choice if you want to

immerse yourself in colonial ambience.

### Inexpensive

**Bank Street Hostel**
32 S. Bank Street
Tel: 922-0222
Fax:922-4082
www.bankstreethostel.com
You can't beat the price at this youth hostel set on a narrow alley in a converted warehouse off Market Street. It's cheap, safe and reasonably clean. Guests sleep in gender-segregated dormitories and share bathrooms, a kitchen, and lounge with pool table and TV. The hostel is closed much of the day, and there's a nightly curfew.

**BELOW:** the Ritz-Carlton on South Broad Street.

# SOCIETY HILL AND PENN'S LANDING

## Luxury

**Sheraton Society Hill Hotel**
One Dock Street
Tel: 238-6000
Fax: 238-6652
www.sheraton.com/societyhill
Set on a cobblestone street in a quiet corner of Society Hill, the hotel offers rooms decorated in an understated Colonial style. The atrium lobby is all shiny marble and lush greenery. There's a glass-enclosed pool, a fitness facility and three restaurants.

## Expensive

**Hyatt Regency at Penn's Landing**
201 S. Columbus Blvd

Tel: 928-1234
Fax: 521-6600
pennslanding.hyatt.com
One of Philadelphia's newer hotels, the Hyatt is a modern high-rise on the Delaware River with all the amenities one expects from a high-end property. Service is professional, and the views are magnificent. It's about a 15-minute walk on a pedestrian bridge over I-95 to the historic district. Facilities include a fitness room, pool, restaurant and café.

## Moderate

**Comfort Inn**
100 N. Columbus Blvd
Tel: 627-7900
Location and price are

the big attractions at this pleasant chain hotel on the Delaware River adjacent to I-95. Expect clean, contemporary guest rooms, some with great views of the river. Continental breakfast is included. A courtesy shuttle runs guests over to the historic area. No bells and whistles, but a good value.

**Shippen Way Inn**
418 Bainbridge Street
Tel: 627-7266
The oldest portion of this snug bed-and-breakfast was built about 1750, and the place still exudes colonial character. It is set in Queen Village about a 15-minute walk to Independence Hall. A

light breakfast is included. A brick courtyard is a pleasant place to relax.

**Ten Eleven Clinton**
1011 Clinton Street
Tel: 923-8144
Fax: 923-5757
Situated on a quiet leafy street within walking distance of Independence Hall, this stately brick 1836 townhouse offers seven guest suites with a private bathroom, kitchen and fireplace.

# RITTENHOUSE

## Expensive

**Rittenhouse Hotel**
210 W. Rittenhouse Square
Tel: 546-9000
Fax: 732-3364
www.rittenhousehotel.com
One of the city's most elegant hotels towers nine stories over Rittenhouse Square. Spacious rooms are appointed with mahogany furnishings, fine linens, marble bathrooms and terrycloth robes. Every unit has a sitting area. For even more space, ask about luxury suites, each with a kitchen. Views from the upper floors are fantastic. Facilities include a high-end salon and spa, indoor pool, fitness center, and four restaurants – the sumptuous

Lacroix at The Rittenhouse, Mary Cassatt Tea Room, and the Garden, Smith & Wollensky steakhouse, and the clubby Boathouse Row Bar. A genuine taste of the upper crust.

**Rittenhouse Square Bed and Breakfast**
1715 Rittenhouse Square
Tel: 546-6500
Fax: 546-8787
www.rittenhousebb.com
More akin to a small European hotel than a traditional bed and breakfast, this renovated carriage house is set on a quiet back street near Rittenhouse Square. Fifteen guest rooms and suites are decorated in an elegant though not fussy style, with antique reproductions, fine linens and marble bath-

rooms. Extra touches include concierge service, fluffy bathrobes, computer work stations, and a generous selection of baked goods for breakfast. Staying here is a fitting way to recall the neighborhood's elegant heyday.

**Sofitel Philadelphia**
120 S. 17th St.
Tel: 569-8300
Fax: 564-7436
www.sofitel.com
Set in the former Philadelphia Stock Exchange building, the contemporary European style of this fashionable French chain brings a welcome change of pace to Philadelphia's hotel market. Guest rooms are furnished with large desks, comfy duvets, a small sitting area, and

generous bathrooms. Facilities include the highly regarded French brasserie Chez Colette, La Bourse lobby lounge, and a fitness room. Ask for a "hot deal" and you could save a bundle on the full rate.

### PRICE CATEGORIES

Price categories are for a double room without breakfast:
**Luxury:** over $300
**Expensive:** $175–300
**Moderate:** $125–175
**Inexpensive:** under $125

## Moderate

**La Reserve – Center City Bed and Breakfast**
1804 Pine Street
Tel: 735-1137
Fax: 735-0582
www.lareserveandb.com
Guests enjoy a genuine B&B experience at this 1850s brick townhouse a few blocks south of Rittenhouse Square – a homey atmosphere (assuming your home is meticulously decorated with antiques, fine linens, and original art work) and a tasty home-

style breakfast (assuming you're in the habit of eating breakfast in a formal dining room with silver, china and a private chef). And like home, you may have to share a bathroom and television with other folks. Of the seven rooms, only the large suites have private bathrooms. If you're the B&B type, this is a fine choice.

**Latham Hotel**
135 S. 17th St.
Tel: 563-7474
www.lathamhotel.com
A block from Rittenhouse

Square in a trendy shopping district, the Latham is an old-world, high-rise hotel. Though highly regarded for its elegant Beaux Arts architecture, the building is showing its age, and travelers accustomed to modern corporate hotels may find the rooms a bit snug. Considering the price and location, it's a good value.

**Radisson Plaza Warwick Hotel**
1701 Locust Street
Tel: 735-6000
Fax: 789-6105

www.radisson.com/philadelphiapa
You'll get a taste of old-fashioned blue-blood Philadelphia at this 1926 landmark about a block from Rittenhouse Square. Designed in English Renaissance style, the hotel is listed in the National Register of Historic Places and features two restaurants, a café, and a fitness room. Some of the standard rooms may be a bit dodgy – small and in need of renovation. Spring for the Plaza Club if you can afford it.

# DOWNTOWN

## Luxury

**The Westin Philadelphia**
99 S. 17th Street
Tel: 563-1600
Fax: 564-9559
www.starwoodhotels.com/westin
Colonial style takes a luxurious turn at this winning hotel attached to the shops at Liberty Place. Public spaces are decorated with fine art, china, flowers and marble floors. Guest rooms have tasteful hardwood furnishings, neutral colors, extra comfy beds, big-screen television, marble bathrooms and generous touches like fluffy terrycloth robes and Starbucks coffee. The Grill is a warm and clubby spot for a good meal or drinks. Luxury at a fair price.

**Ritz-Carlton Philadelphia**
10 Avenue of the Arts
Tel: 523-8000
Fax: 568-6445
www.ritzcarlton.com
Housed in a restored 1908 neoclassical bank "temple" designed by

McKim, Mead, and White, the public spaces at this grand hotel are truly spectacular. The nine-story domed lobby, replete with white marble columns and antique furnishings is particularly impressive. Facilities include a spa and fitness center, three restaurants and a "bath butler." Guest rooms are attractive but tend to be snug. A grand hotel but you can get more room for the money elsewhere.

## Expensive

**Courtyard By Marriott – Downtown**
21 N. Juniper Street
Tel: 496-3200
Fax: 496-3696
http://marriott.com
Opened in 1999 in the former City Hall Annex, this 17-story hotel in the heart of the downtown district is winning kudos for its comfortable, modern rooms and the sensitive renovation of its stately architecture. Amenities

include two restaurants, an indoor pool and fitness center. Weekend rates are a good value.

**Loews Philadelphia Hotel**
1200 Market Street
Tel: 627-1200
www.loewshotels.com
The landmark 1932 PSFS Building, the first skyscraper in the international style, now serves as a hotel. Rooms are a bit snug, but the decor is a welcome change of pace – a contemporary take on Art Deco style. Creative seafood dishes are the specialty at hip SoleFood. A fitness facility has cardio equipment, steam room, spa, and indoor lap pool. Children under 18 stay for free. A hip alternative to chain hotels.

**Marriott Philadelphia – Downtown**
1201 Market Street
Tel: 625-2900
Fax: 625-6000
http://marriott.com
This massive upscale hotel is connected via "skybridge" to the Con-

vention Center. Designed for business travelers, the property is long on corporate polish, but predictably short on personal touches. Recreational facilities include a fitness center and lap pool. Dining options range from a sushi bar and steakhouse to a sports bar and café.

**Park Hyatt at the Bellevue**
Broad and Walnut streets
Tel: 893-1234
Fax: 732-8518
www.parkphiladelphia.hyatt.com
A Philadelphia landmark for more than a century, the Bellevue lives up to its reputation for old-world luxury. The bottom floors are occupied by Tiffany & Co., Williams-Sonoma and other ritzy boutiques as well as the

Zanzibar Blue jazz club. Guest rooms are generously proportioned, with high ceilings, thick moldings and other architectural details recalling the glories of the Gilded Age. Guests enjoy free access to an adjacent health club with an indoor pool, basketball, squash and racquetball courts, an indoor track, massage and sauna rooms and fitness center. A full-service spa is below the hotel. Yes, it's pricey, but you'll experience an authentic taste of old Philadelphia luxury.

## Moderate

**Alexander Inn**
12th and Spruce streets
Tel: 923-3535
Fax: 923-1004
www.alexanderinn.com
Art Deco style pervades this interesting little hotel in an attractive neighborhood near Antique Row. With original art work, stained-glass windows, fresh flowers and individually designed rooms, the property has the intimate feel of a bed and breakfast but is priced like a budget hotel. The "personal single rooms" are quite snug but an excellent value if you're traveling alone. Standards and doubles have more elbow room. A breakfast buffet and daylong snack bar are included. This property is a rare gem: A value hotel that delivers more than expected.

**Crowne Plaza Hotel – City Center**
1800 Market Street
Tel: 561-7500
Fax: 561-4484
www.ichotelsgroup.com

This 25-story hotel offers business accommodations of standard quality – reliable if not especially inspiring. The in-house business center comes in handy, and the fitness center and rooftop pool help you stay fit while on the road. The English-style Elephant and Castle serves pub food and drinks. Not thrilling, but a reasonable value.

**Doubletree Hotel**
237 S. Broad Street
Tel: 893-1600
Fax: 893-1664
www.doubletree.com
A solid, quality chain hotel, this glass-fronted high-rise has the advantage of being located on the Avenue of the Arts across from the Academy of Music. The serrated facade gives each room a bay window with excellent views of the city. The building encompasses a fitness center, indoor pool and two restaurants. Decent value, central location.

**Hilton Garden Inn**
1100 Arch Street
Tel: 923-0100
Fax: 925-0800
www.hiltongardenphilly.com
A short walk to the Convention Center, this is a favorite with business travelers. Guest rooms offer the usual corporate comforts, plus a few extra features like a mini-fridge and microwave. A 24-hour business center is handy. Amenities include an indoor pool, fitness center and restaurant.

**Hampton Inn – Convention Center**
1301 Race Street
Tel: 665-9100
Fax: 665-9200
www.hamptoninn.com
Budget travelers will

appreciate this clean, comfortable hotel across from the Convention Center. The immediate neighborhood isn't particularly scenic, but the historic district is only a 10-minute walk. Free breakfast enhances the value, especially if you're traveling with kids. The pool and fitness room are a pleasant surprise. Ask about promotional discounts.

**Holiday Inn Express**
1305 Walnut Street
Tel: 735-9300
Fax: 732-2682
www.ichotelsgroup.com
This older hotel delivers what one expects from a Holiday Inn: clean, comfortable lodging at a reasonable price. The complimentary continental breakfast and discounted parking help stretch your dollar. The neighborhood is unexciting, but it's only three blocks from the Kimmel Center, seven from Independence Hall.

**Inn at the Union League**
1450 Sansom Street
Tel: 587-5570
www.unionleague.org
And now for something completely different. The Union League is a majestic 1865 mansion just south of City Hall erected by well-to-do patriots during the American Civil War. To lodge here, however, you need to be recommended by a club member or a member of a reciprocal club. Provided you meet that requirement, what you will find inside the building is a throwback to the heyday of Philadelphia's notoriously exclusive private clubs, with millions of dollars worth

of art on the walls, a 28,000-volume library, dining rooms and – a couple of modern touches here – a state-of-the-art fitness center with spa facilities and personal trainers, and a business center with computers, copiers and wireless Internet. A full breakfast is included. Guest rooms are spacious and comfortable, though generally not equipped with the latest technology. The League has a strict dress code: Men must wear jackets in the restaurants, except at breakfast, when "business casual" is permitted.

## Inexpensive

**Antique Row Bed and Breakfast**
341 S. 12th Street
Tel: 592-7802
Fax: 592-9692
www.antiquerowbnb.com
Homey in a favorite slipper sort of way, this is not the type of B&B chockablock with fussy antiques and precious knick-knacks. Instead you'll find quilts, folk art and lots of dog-eared books – a good fit in light of the property's location just around the corner from Antique Row. Only some of the rooms have private bathrooms. For long stays, a full apartment is also available. Breakfast included.

### PRICE CATEGORIES

Price categories are for a double room without breakfast:
**Luxury:** over $300
**Expensive:** $175–300
**Moderate:** $125–175
**Inexpensive:** under $125

# MUSEUM DISTRICT

## Luxury

**Four Seasons Hotel**
18th and Race Streets,
One Logan Square
Tel: 963-1500
Fax: 963-9506
www.fourseasons.com/philadelphia
One of the city's most elegant hotels is on Logan Square near the Franklin Institute and Museum of Art. More than 350 suites and guest rooms are furnished in Federal style, with private bar and extra touches like fresh flowers and twice-daily maid service. Among the many luxury amenities are a health spa with an indoor pool, a business center and the posh Fountain Restaurant and Swann Lounge. Luxurious but a bit stiff for freewheeling travelers.

## Expensive

**Embassy Suites Hotel – Center City**
1776 Benjamin Franklin Pkwy
Tel: 561-1776

Fax: 561-1850
Each unit at this renovated hotel near Logan Square, is a two-room suite, with bedroom, living room and balcony. The kitchen includes a microwave, refrigerator and bar. Harried parents will appreciate the separate bedroom and two televisions. Breakfast is included.

## Moderate

**Best Western Center City Hotel**
501 N. 22nd Street
Tel: 568-8300
Fax: 557-0259
www.bestwestern.com
Moderate price and convenient location are the attractions of this not-terribly-attractive hotel near the Ben Franklin Parkway. A recent renovation has spruced up the rooms, and an outdoor pool and fitness room are welcome amenities. A utilitarian choice but not a good pick to pamper yourself.

**Hotel Windsor**
1700 Benjamin Franklin Pkwy
Tel: 981-5678
www.windsorhotel.com
A reasonable option if you're traveling with a family or planning an extended stay, this former apartment building offers studio and one-bedroom suites with kitchens, a rooftop pool, a fitness center and two restaurants. The building is showing its age, but guests get a lot of space for a modest price.

**Wyndham Philadelphia**
17th and Race streets
Tel: 448-2000
An impressive four-story atrium sets the tone of this large, high-end hotel. Facilities include workout rooms with aerobic and weightlifting equipment, an indoor swimming pool, tennis courts, and a jogging track. There are also meeting and banquet facilities, restaurants, and lounges. An excellent choice if you're looking for a large (if

somewhat impersonal) hotel with lots of extras.

## Inexpensive

**Chamounix Mansion – Hostelling International**
West Fairmount Park,
3250 Chamounix Drive
Tel: 878-3676
Fax: 871-4313
www.philahostel.org
An excellent option for travelers on a shoestring budget, this hostel offers bare-bones but clean dormitory lodging in a early-19th-century country estate in the leafy confines of Fairmount Park. The self-serve kitchen comes in handy. The park setting is beautiful but quite far from most center city attractions. It's about a mile to the nearest bus stop.

# UNIVERSITY CITY

## Expensive

**Sheraton University City Hotel**
3549 Chestnut Street
Tel: 387-8000
Tel: 387-7920
www.philadelphiasheraton.com
This newly refurbished campus hotel is popular with conference-goers and parents of students. Facilities include a fitness center, outdoor pool, business center and restaurant.

## Moderate

**Cornerstone Bed & Breakfast**
3300 Baring Street
Tel: 387-6065.
www.cornerstonebandb.com
A beautifully restored Victorian mansion with six rooms and suites tastefully decorated in period style. All rooms have private baths, wireless Internet and CD players. All but one have television. Convenient to University of Pennsylvania and

Drexel University. Close to bus and trolley.

**Hilton Inn at Penn**
3600 Sansom Street
Tel: 222-0200
Fax: 222-4600
This newly renovated hotel offers the usual high-end amenities associated with the Hilton chain – tasteful rooms with space for a functional work desk and personal comforts like terrycloth robes as well as a business center, workout room and two restaurants. The only

caveat is the location, which is perfect if you're visiting the University of Pennsylvania but is not especially convenient to Independence Hall and the historic district.
**The Gables Bed and Breakfast**
4520 Chester Avenue

Tel: 662-1918
www.gablesbb.com
This restored 1889 mansion has 10 rooms with period furniture, cable television and Internet access. Most have private bathrooms; some have gas fireplaces. Breakfast is included. A memorable experience for those who appreciate historic houses, if you don't mind being off the beaten path.

### Inexpensive

**Divine Tracy Hotel**
20 S. 36th Street
Tel: 382-4310
Budget travelers and those with a taste for local oddities may find this hotel interesting. Operated by the Peace Mission Society, founded in the early 1900s by the flamboyant preacher Father Divine, the hotel offers clean, basic lodging, but imposes strict rules: no smoking, alcohol or food in the rooms; no foul language; men and women stay on separate floors; women must wear dresses or modest skirts and stockings (no pants or shorts); men

**PRICE CATEGORIES**

Price categories are for a double room without breakfast:
**Luxury:** over $300
**Expensive:** $175–300
**Moderate:** $125–175
**Inexpensive:** under $125

must wear shirts with sleeves (tucked in), pants and socks. Cash or travelers checks only.

# SOUTH PHILADELPHIA/AIRPORT

### Moderate

**Courtyard By Marriott**
8900 Bartram Avenue
Tel: 365-2200
Fax: 365-6905
No surprises at this chain hotel designed for business travelers. A free shuttle transports guests to and from the airport, about a mile way. Facilities include an indoor pool and exercise room. Otherwise, you'll find a standard of comfort commensurate with most chain hotels in this price range.

**Embassy Suites Hotel – Airport**
9000 Bartram Avenue
Tel: 365-4500
Fax: 365-4803
www.embassysuites.com
Every unit of this all-suite hotel about a mile from the airport has a private bedroom, living room, two televisions, a refrigerator, microwave, and a dining/work table. Adding to the value is a nightly manager's reception with snacks and an open bar and, in the morning, a complimentary hot breakfast. Facilities include a fitness room, pool, tennis court and restaurant.

**Fairfield Inn By Marriott – Airport**
8800 Bartram Avenue
Tel: 365-2254
Fax: 365-2254
A comfortable chain hotel with such extra amenities as a complimentary continental breakfast, pool and free airport shuttle. Nothing special, but delivers a fair value for the buck.

**Hampton Inn – Airport**
8660 Bartram Avenue
Tel: 966-1300
Fax: 966-1313
www.hamptoninn.com
A cookie cutter chain hotel near the airport – clean, comfortable and wholly unexciting. The complimentary breakfast is a notable extra.

**Hilton Philadelphia – Airport**
4509 Island Avenue
Tel: 365-4150
Fax: 937-6382
A recent renovation has spruced up this older hotel, which caters mostly to business travelers during the week and to leisure travelers on weekends. The hotel encompasses a business center, restaurant, fitness facility and pool.

**Sheraton Suites – Airport**
4101 Island Avenue

Tel: 365-6600
Understated contemporary styling and an attractive eight-story atrium set off this property from other airport hotels. Guests can take advantage of a complimentary airport shuttle, 24-hour fitness center, indoor heated pool, business center, and atrium restaurant.

**BELOW:** the Loews Hotel is housed in the landmark PSFS Building in center city.

# THE MAIN LINE/VALLEY FORGE

## Expensive

**Homewood Suites**
12 E. Swedesford Road,
Malvern, PA 19355
Tel: 610-296-3500
Fax: 610-296-1941.
homewoodsuites.hilton.com
This all-suite hotel offers
accommodations with a
separate bedroom, living
room and kitchen. The
rate includes a breakfast
buffet as well as an
evening "manager's
reception." Additional
facilities include an
indoor pool, high-speed
Internet access, laundry
and fitness room.

## Moderate

**Great Valley House**
1475 Swedesford Road,
Malvern, PA 19355-8750
Tel: 610-644-6759
www.greatvalleyhouse.com
There are three bed-
rooms at this 300-year-

old farmhouse, replete
with original architectural
elements, including a 12-
foot-wide fireplace, hand-
hewn beams and stone
walls. Guest rooms have
antiques and quilts, pri-
vate bathrooms, cable
television and Internet
access. Breakfast is
served in the dining
room. The property has
gardens and a swimming
pool. It's just a short
drive to Valley Forge.
**Radnor Hotel**
591 E. Lancaster Ave.,
St. Davids, PA 19087
Tel: 610-688-5800
Fax: 610-341-3169.
www.radnorhotel.com
This four-story hotel has
171 spacious rooms
and suites. Facilities
include an outdoor pool,
a workout room, formal
gardens, a bar and
restaurant, and an adja-
cent salon and spa.
Sunday brunch is lavish.

**Shearer Elegance**
1154 Main Street, Linfield,
PA 19468
Tel: 610-495-7429 or 800-
861-0308
Fax: 610-495-7814
www.shearerelegance.com
Lovers of Victorian
style will appreciate
this gorgeous stone
mansion, built in 1897
and now beautifully
restored. The inn has
four bedrooms and
three suites, each with
a private bathroom and
period furnishings. The
nightly rate includes a
full breakfast served in
a formal dining room.
**Wayne Hotel**
139 E. Lancaster Avenue,
Wayne, PA 19087
Tel: 610-687-5000 or 800-
962-5850
Fax: 610-687-8387
www.waynehotel.com
This prim Victorian rehab
listed in the National
Register of Historic

Places has four floors of
spacious guest rooms
furnished in a comfy
update of period style.
The highly regarded
Restaurant Taquet is on
the main floor. The hotel
is a short walk to the
Wayne train station.
**Wyndham Valley Forge**
888 Chesterbrook Blvd.,
Wayne, PA 19087
Tel: 610-647-6700
An all-suite business
hotel within easy driving
distance of Valley Forge
and the King of Prussia
Mall. Facilities include a
restaurant, lounge,
indoor pool, and fitness
room with weightlifting
equipment and whirlpool.

# BRANDYWINE VALLEY

## Expensive

**Inn at Whitewing Farm**
370 Valley Road, West Chester,
PA 19380
Tel: 610-388-2664
Fax: 610-388-3650
www.whitewingfarm.com
Situated on 43 acres in
Chester County, this
bed and breakfast has
much in common with a
rustic resort. Guests
stay in spacious rooms
in various outbuildings,
including a cottage on a
pond and carriage
house. The grounds
encompass flower gar-
dens, stables and cow
pastures as well as a
pool, spa, tennis court,
and 10-hole golf course.

**Pennsbury Inn**
883 Baltimore Pike, Chadds
Ford, PA 19317
Tel: 610-388-1435 or
888-388-1435
Fax: 610-388-1436
www.pennsburyinn.com
The oldest section of this
handsome farmhouse is
nearly three centuries
old. The seven guest
rooms are carefully fur-
nished in period style;
most have a private
bath and a fireplace
with electric firestove
inserts. The Lafayette
Suite is the largest and
most elaborate unit – a
spacious bedroom with
a four-poster bed plus a
downstairs parlor with a
wood-burning fireplace.

The 8 acres have mani-
cured gardens, wooded
paths, ponds and a
reflection pool. A full
breakfast is served in
the dining area in front of
a large walk-in fireplace.

## Moderate

**Brandywine River Hotel**
P.O. Box 1058, Route 1 &
Route 100, Chadds Ford,
PA 19317
Tel: 610-388-1200 or
800-274-9644
www.brandywineriverhotel.com
Combining the homey
style of a bed and break-
fast with the size and
facilities of a business
hotel, this property
offers 40 large rooms

and such amenities as a
fitness center, business
center and lobby bar. The
suites are an especially
good deal. For only $30–
$40 more, guests get an
extra large room with a
sitting area, sofa bed,
fireplace, dining table
and whirlpool tub. Break-
fast is included.
**Cornerstone Bed and
Breakfast**
300 Buttonwood Road,
Landenberg, PA 19350

Tel: 610-274-2143
Fax: 610-274-0734
www.cornerstoneinn.net
The oldest portion of this fieldstone house was built in the early 1700s. Guests stay in nine bedrooms in the main house. All have bathrooms, period-style furnishings, air conditioning, and cable television; some have four-poster beds, fireplaces and whirlpool tubs. In addition, a detached cottage and seven suites have kitchens. Breakfast is included. The grounds have gardens and a pool.

**Hamanassett Bed & Breakfast**
115 Indian Springs Drive,

Chester Heights, PA 19017
Tel: 610-459-3000 or 877-836-8212
www.hamanassett.com
This 19th-century mansion is set on 7 landscaped acres. Seven guest rooms in the main house have antique furnishings, hardwood floors and oriental rugs. All rooms have bathrooms, televisions with VCRs, and terrycloth robes. The master bedroom has a sitting area and wood-burning stove. Common areas include a formal dining room, where guests enjoy a full breakfast served with china, silver and crystal. Also on the grounds is a detached carriage

house, with two bedrooms and kitchen.

**Harlan Log House**
205 Fairville Road, Chadds Ford, PA 19317
Tel: 610-388-1114
www.bbonline.com/pa/harlan
This 18th-century log cabin (with additions) has two rooms with bathrooms, canopy beds, fireplaces and colonial style furnishings. Breakfast is included.

### Inexpensive

**1732 Folke Stone Bed and Breakfast**
777 Copeland School Road, West Chester, PA 19380
Tel: 610-429-0310
www.bbonline.com/pa/folkestone
Three guest rooms are

available at this 18th-century manor house. Rooms are furnished with antiques and quilts, and have cable television and a private bathroom. A full breakfast is served.

**Hilton Garden Inn – Kennett Square**
815 E. Baltimore Pike, Kennett Square, PA 19348
Tel: 610-444-9100
Fax: 610-765-1029
www.brandywinehilton.com
Less than a mile from Longwood Gardens, this property offers the usual comforts of an upper-end chain hotel. Amenities include a breakfast cafe, indoor pool, fitness center and business center. It's excellent value for a relatively modest price.

# BUCKS COUNTY

### Expensive

**Barley Sheaf Farm**
P.O. Box 10, 5281 York Road, Holicong, PA 18928
Tel: 794-5104
Fax: 794-5332
www.barleysheaf.com
A half mile from Peddler's Village, this secluded property – formerly owned by playwright George S. Kaufman – feels like a world away. Set on 30 acres of fields and meadows at the end of a sycamore-lined driveway, the stone-and-plaster main house – part of which dates to 1740 – contains guest rooms decorated with country antiques and folk art, each with a private bathroom. Additional rooms and suites are situated in outbuildings. A full country breakfast is included. The grounds encompass a pool,

ponds, and plenty of room to roam.

**Bridgeton House**
1525 River Road, Upper Black Eddy, PA 18972
Tel: 610-982-5856
www.bridgetonhouse.com
If you're looking for something a bit artsy, this house on the Delaware is a good choice. Set within casting distance of the river, this 19th-century inn is furnished with an eclectic mix of contemporary and antique pieces, combining modern crafts, folk art, Victorian furniture and faux painting and murals. Rooms range in size from snug to spacious, many a balcony overlooking the river. All have private bathrooms and air conditioning. A penthouse suite on the third floor is outfitted with a marble bathroom, fireplace, leather

lounge chairs and panoramic views of the river. A two-course breakfast is served in the dining room.

**Evermay on the Delaware**
889 River Road, Erwinna, PA 18920
Tel: 610-294-9100
www.evermay.com
This grand 18th-century inn was refashioned in Victorian style in 1871. Set on 25 acres on the Delaware River, the inn offers 18 rooms furnished in a restrained period style with sturdy carved headboards, marble-top vanities, oriental rugs and wood floors. Some rooms and suites are set in the converted carriage house, barn and cottage. All have private bathrooms and air conditioning. A generous continental breakfast is served in the garden.

### Moderate

**Aaron Burr House Inn**
80 W. Bridge Street, New Hope, PA 18938
Tel: 862-2343
Fax: 862-3937
www.aaronburrhouse.com
It's claimed that Aaron Burr hid in a house at this site in 1804 after dispatching Alexander Hamilton in their infa-

TRANSPORTATION

ACCOMMODATIONS

ACTIVITIES

A – Z

mous duel – an intriguing though disputable possibility. No matter. The important thing is that this lovely 1873 Victorian – one of three properties in New Hope's Wedgewood Collection – offers warm and homey accommodations only a few blocks from Main Street. The décor is eclectic, with canopy beds and fireplaces in some guest rooms; all rooms have private bathrooms. A full breakfast is served in the dining room or in your bedroom.

**Hotel Du Village**
2535 N. River Road,
New Hope, PA 18938
Tel: 862-9911
www.hotelduvillage.com
Built in 1907 as a country estate and later occupied by a school for girls, this European-style inn stands on 10 acres less than two miles from New Hope. The slate roof, ivy-covered walls and Tudoresque details exude old-world charm. Twenty rooms are furnished in simple country style, all with bathrooms and air conditioning. A

highly regarded restaurant, tennis courts and pool are also on the grounds. Continental breakfast is included.

**Mansion Inn**
9 S. Main Street, New Hope, PA 18938
Tel: 862-1231
www.themansioninn.com
Built in 1865 and now one of the county's landmark inns, this elegant Victorian in the heart of New Hope offers the opulence of the mid-19th century with many welcome contemporary touches. The emphasis

is on details, from impeccably designed interiors to the well-tended English garden. Guests are greeted in a grand entrance hall with a mahogany staircase, crystal chandelier and large gilt mirror. The hall is flanked on either side by a parlor and drawing room appointed in period style. Guest rooms have private baths; some have a fireplace, sitting room and whirlpool. A full buffet breakfast is served in the dining room.

# PENNSYLVANIA DUTCH COUNTRY

## Moderate

**Boxwood Inn**
1320 Diamond Street, Akron, PA 17501
Tel: 717-859-3466
www.theboxwoodinn.net
Named after the gnarled 180-year-old boxwood that grows near the front porch, this stone and clapboard house was built in stages by a Mennonite family starting in 1768. Perched on a hillside overlooking Amish farmland, the inn is decorated in traditional style with thoughtful contemporary touches. The carriage house is particularly affecting, with cathedral ceilings, rich wood floors, a fireplace, and a large bathroom with

## PRICE CATEGORIES

Price categories are for a double room without breakfast:
**Luxury:** over $300
**Expensive:** $175–300
**Moderate:** $125–175
**Inexpensive:** under $125

whirlpool. A full breakfast is served in the dining room or on the patio.

**Cameron Estate Inn**
1855 Mansion Lane,
Mount Joy, PA 17552
Tel: 717-492-0111
The oldest part of the inn was built about 1805 and was later expanded by US Senator Simon Cameron, who served as Secretary of War under President Abraham Lincoln. Listed in the National Register of Historic Places, this grand manor is a symphony of late 19th-century decor, with gorgeous woodwork and period furnishings that give even the smaller, third-floor rooms a dignified ambience. Many rooms have whirlpool tubs and fireplaces. Breakfast is served on the sun porch.

**Inn at Twin Linden**
2092 Main Street,
Narvon, PA 17555
Tel: 717-445-7619
Fax: 717-445-4656
www.innattwinlinden.com
Traditional and contemporary styles meet in this

mid-19th-century inn. The suites are particularly stunning, with skylights, pellet-burning stoves and whirlpools. The same artful touch is evident in other rooms, ranging in size from cozy to spacious, many with canopy beds, whirlpools and/or gas fireplaces. A gourmet breakfast is included.

**Inns at Doneckers**
318-409 N. State Street,
Ephrata, PA 17522
Tel: 717-738-9500
www.doneckers.com
There are three inns in the Doneckers community, encompassing more than three dozen rooms and suites. Accommodations range in size, style and price, although most have a comfortable country feeling. Continental breakfast is included.

## Inexpensive

**Bird-in-Hand Family Inn**
2740 Old Philadelphia Pike,
Bird-in-Hand, PA 17505
Tel: 717-768-8271
Fax: 717-768-1117

www.bird-in-hand.com/familyinn
This family-friendly motel offers basic but comfortable accommodations within minutes of popular tourist attractions.

**Red Caboose Motel**
P.O. Box 175, 303 Paradise Lane, Strasburg, PA 17579
Tel: 717-687-5000
Railroad aficionados will be tickled by this one-of-a-kind motel composed of more than three dozen cabooses brought here from rail lines as far away as Alaska and the Northern Pacific Railroad. The cabooses offer basic comfort, with various combinations of queen, double, single and bunk beds. A little farmhouse on the property has been transformed into guest quarters. Kids will get a kick out of it.

TRANSPORTATION

# **A**CTIVITIES

# EVENTS, THE ARTS, NIGHTLIFE, SHOPPING, TOURS AND SPORTS

## EVENTS

Public holidays are marked with an 🅗. Listings and advertisements for upcoming events can be found in *The Daily News*, *Philadelphia Inquirer*, *Philadelphia Magazine*, and free papers like *The Philadelphia Weekly* and *Philadelphia City Paper*.

### *Ongoing events*

**First Friday**. An ongoing art fest held at Old City galleries on the first Friday of every month. Tel: 625-9200 or 800-555-5191; www.oldcityarts.org
**First Saturday**. A more personal follow-up to First Friday, with lectures, workshops and impromptu conversations with artists and gallery owners. Tel: 625-9200 or 800-555-5191; www.oldcityarts.org
**Art After 5**. Stroll the galleries, sip a cocktail, nibble on appetizers, and enjoy an eclectic blend of live jazz and international music in the Philadelphia Museum of Art's Great Stair Hall. Tel: 763-8100; www.philamuseum.org

### *January*

**Mummers Parade** 🅗. 30,000 high-struttin' Mummers march up Broad Street on New Year's Day. Tel: 336-3050; www.mummers museum.com

**Benjamin Franklin's Birthday**. Look for a variety of events commemorating the birth of Philadelphia's first citizen at the Franklin Institute and Independence Mall. Tel: 800-537-7676; www.independencevisitorcenter.com
**Edgar Allan Poe Birthday**. Special tours, programs and exhibits are presented at the Poe National Historic Site. Tel: 597-8780; www.nps.gov/edal
**Martin Luther King, Jr, Birthday** 🅗. Ceremonies, special performances, lectures and other observances in honor of Dr King. Tel: 800-537-7676; www.independencevisitorcenter.com
**Philadelphia Home Show**. Products and plans for remodeling, renovating, furnishing and decorating your home exhibited at the Pennsylvania Convention Center. Tel: 856-784-4774 or 800-756-5692; www.phillyhomeshow.com

### *February*

**Black History Month**. A series of special exhibits, performances and presentations at the African American Museum and other venues throughout the city. Tel: 574-0380; www.aampmuseum.org
**Philadelphia International Auto Show**. Scores of new models and spiffy foreign imports exhibited at the Pennsylvania Convention Center. www.phillyautoshow.com
**Presidents' Day** 🅗. Look for special tours and events at Independence Park, Valley Forge and other historic sites in celebration of Washington's and Lincoln's birthday. Tel: 800-537-7676; www.independencevisitorcenter.com
**Chinese New Year**. Chinatown celebrates the new year with processions, festivities and traditional 10-course banquets. Look for other events at the University of Pennsylvania Museum of Archaeology and Anthropology, Independence Seaport Museum and Philadelphia Museum of Art. Tel: 922-2156; www.chinatown-pcdc.com
**PECO Jazz Festival**. Several days of top-notch jazz at venues throughout the city featuring local talent and international jazz legends. Tel: 800-537-7676; www.independencevisitorcenter.com
**US Pro Indoor Tennis Championship**. The world's top tennis players compete at the Spectrum. Tel: 389-9560; www.comcast-spectacor.com

### *March*

**Philadelphia Flower Show**. The Pennsylvania Convention Center is transformed into a sea of petals and pollen at the largest flower show in the country. Tel: 988-8800; www.theflowershow.com
**St. Patrick's Day Parade**. Celebrate Philly's Irish heritage on Ben Franklin Parkway and Broad Street. www.philadelphiastpatsparade.com

ACCOMMODATIONS

ACTIVITIES

A – Z

**The Book and the Cook.** The city's finest chefs hitch up with cookbook authors and food critics for a celebration of fine food and drink. www.thebookandthecook.com

**Poetry Week.** The American Poetry Center honors the muse with readings, lectures, exhibits and other events for local literati. Tel: 610-617-9919; www.apc.tv

## April

**Penn Relays.** The country's oldest and largest amateur track meet is held at Franklin Field on the University of Pennsylvania campus. Tel: 898-6151; www.pennathletics.com

**Valborgsmassoafton.** A traditional Swedish rite of spring with folk music, dance and food at the American Swedish Historical Museum in South Philadelphia's Franklin Park. Tel: 389-1776; www.americanswedish.org

**Philadelphia Film Festival.** A major event in the film world, with screenings of new features, documentaries, shorts, animation and international movies by established and emerging filmmakers. www.phillyfests.com

**Philadelphia Open House.** Bus and walking tours through the homes, churches and gardens in the city's historic neighborhoods. Tel: 861-4971; www.ushistory.org

**Philadelphia Antiques Show and Sale.** Held at the 33rd Street Armory, this tradition among the area's dealers and collectors is one of the finest shows in the country. Tel: 387-3500; www.philaantiques.com

## May

**Dad Vail Regatta.** With more than 3,000 rowers, the largest collegiate regatta in the country floats down the Schuylkill River near Boathouse Row. www.dadvail.org

**Israel's Independence Day.** A celebration with a parade down the Ben Franklin Parkway plus food and entertainment. Tel: 832-0500; philadelphia.ujcfedweb.org

**Italian Market Festival.** A day of music, cooking demonstrations, street performances and outdoor food stands at the 9th Street Market. Tel: 545-4543; www.9thstreetitalianmarketfestival.com

**International Theater Festival for Children.** Five days of theater, folktales, puppet shows and dance at the Annenberg Center of the Performing Arts (University of Pennsylvania). Tel: 898-3900; www.annenbergcenter.org

**Devon Horse Show.** One of the country's largest outdoor horse shows, and a great Main Line tradition, is held at the Devon Fairground about 45 minutes from center city. Tel: 610-525-2533; www.thedevonhorseshow.com

**Jam on the River.** A three-day Mardi Gras-like blast at Penn's Landing with live rock, blues, soul and jazz. Tel: 922-2386; www.jamontheriver.com

**Memorial Day ⓗ**. Commemoration of men and women who died in military service is observed throughout the city. Look for a formal observance at Valley Forge and Independence Parks and aboard the 19th-century *USS Olympia* at Penn's Landing. Monday following last weekend in May. Tel: 800-537-7676; www.independencevisitorcenter.com

**Rittenhouse Square Flower Market.** A tradition for more than 75 years, featuring thousands of flowering plants and food stands.

**Penn's Landing Summer Season.** Dozens of concerts, ethnic festivals and other events – many free of charge – are offered at this waterfront venue. This is one of the best entertainment values in the city; weekends through September. Tel: 928-8801; www.pennslandingcorp.com

**PrideFest America.** Several days of seminars, lectures, performances, exhibits and parties in celebration of the gay and lesbian community. Tel: 732-3378; www.equalityforum.com

## June

**Elfreth's Alley Day.** The residents of the oldest residential street in the country, many in colonial dress, open their charming homes to visitors. Colonial crafts and baked goods are sold at the Museum House. Tel: 574-0560; www.elfrethsalley.org

**Midsommerfest.** A summer celebration with folk dancing, music and food at the American Swedish Historical Museum in South Philadelphia. Tel: 389-1776; www.americanswedish.org

**Rittenhouse Square Fine Arts Annual.** Many of the area's most talented artists exhibit thousands of works at this five-day open-air "clothesline" exhibit. Tel: 800-537-7676; www.independencevisitorcenter.com

**Flag Day.** Old Glory is celebrated with a parade and ceremonies at the Betsy Ross House. Tel: 686-1252; www.betsyrosshouse.org

**Head House Square Crafts Fair.** Artists and craftsmen exhibit their work under the historic market shed; Saturday–Sunday through August. Tel: 800-537-7676; www.independencevisitorcenter.com

**Mann Music Center Summer Concerts.** A series of open-air performances in beautiful Fairmount Park by the world-renowned Philadelphia Orchestra and a variety of pop, jazz and country artists. Tel: 893-1999; www.manncenter.org

**Philadelphia International Pro Cycling Championship.** The highlight of this grueling 156-mile bicycle race is the punishing climb up the Manayunk Wall. The race begins and ends in front of the Museum of Art. One of the biggest pro cycling events outside Europe. Tel: 610-676-0390; www.procyclingtour.com

**Kutztown Folk Festival.** Perhaps the area's best opportunity to experience Pennsylvania Dutch and Amish culture, crafts, food and people at this nine-day festival at the Kutztown Fairgrounds, about 15 miles northeast of Reading, Pennylvania. Tel: 888-674-6136; www.kutztownfestival.com

**Manayunk Arts Festival.** This annual open-air juried art festival lures more than 200 artists and thousands of visitors to Manayunk's hip Main Street. Tel: 482-9565; www.manayunk.com

## July

**Welcome America ⓗ**. Independence Day is a big deal in Philadelphia. In addition to parade and fireworks, there are Mummers bands, sporting events, concerts and more. Most of the week's action is centered around Independence Park, but events are held at Rittenhouse Square, the Museum of Art, Penn's Landing, Valley Forge and other venues. Check the papers for a detailed list of events.
**Pennsylvania Renaissance Faire**. Played more for fun than accuracy, this re-creation of 16th-century life at a 38-acre "English village" includes a cast of hundreds of costumed performers, jousting knights, ladies, lords, minstrels, dramas, jugglers and food merchants; weekends through October; Mount Hope Estate and Winery, 16 miles outside Lancaster. Tel: 717-665-7021; www.parenaissancefaire.com
**Philadelphia International Gay & Lesbian Film Festival**. Screenings of gay-themed features, documentaries and shorts. Tel: 267-765-9700; www.phillyfests.com

## August

**Philadelphia Folk Festival**. A tradition for more than 45 years, this three-day festival features an international roster of folk musicians at Old Poole Farm in Schwenksville, Pennsylvania. Tel: 242-0150; www.folkfest.org
**Pennsylvania Dutch Festival**. Demonstrations of arts, crafts and food from Pennsylvania Dutch country; Reading Terminal Market; Tel: 922-2317; www.readingterminalmarket.org
**Goschenhoppen Folk Festival**. A Pennsylvania Dutch festival in East Greenville, Pennsylvania. www.goschenhoppen.org

## September

**Mellon Jazz**. Some of the biggest names in jazz perform at the Kimmel Center and other Philadelphia venues in what has become a year-round series. Tel: 893-1999, www.kimmelcenter.org

**Penn's Landing Jazz on the Waterfront**. A series of performances featuring some of the region's most exciting jazz players. Tel: 922-2386; www.pennslandingcorp.com
**Dressage at Devon**. A world-class equestrian competition featuring the country's finest horses and riders in a very beautiful, very English event at the Devon Fairgrounds. www.dressageatdevon.org
**Von Steuben Day Parade**. A tribute to the German general who whipped the Continental Army into shape at Valley Forge and a salute to the city's rich German heritage. The procession runs down Ben Franklin Parkway and then heads to Independence Hall. Tel: 636-3300; www.pcvb.org
**Puerto Rican Day Parade**. Celebrate Philly's Puerto Rican community with a parade on the Parkway. Tel: 627-3100; elconcilio.net
**Philadelphia Distance Run**. Thousands of participants run this half-marathon on the Ben Franklin Parkway and along the Schuylkill River. www.philadistancerun.org
**Harvest Show**. A flower and garden show at the Horticultural Center in Fairmount Park. Tel: 683-0200; www.fairmountpark.org
**Fairmount Park Festival**. Sports competitions, special tours, exhibitions and other recreational activities; through November. Tel: 683-0200; www.fairmountpark.org
**Pennsbury Manor Fair**. A recreated 17th-century country fair on the grounds of William Penn's Bucks County estate, with costumed players, craftsmen, puppeteers, musicians and food. Tel: 946-0400; www.pennsburymanor.org
**Battle of Brandywine**. Re-enactment of the historic clash between rebels and redcoats at Brandywine Battlefield State Park in Chadds Ford, Pennsylvania. Tel: 610-459-3342; www.brandywinebattlefield.com
**Philadelphia Live Arts Festival & Philly Fringe Festival**. Sixteen days of cutting-edge performances challenge the norms of theater, dance, music, poetry and puppetry. Tel: 413-9006; www.pafringe.com

## October

**Columbus Day ⓗ**. Celebrate Columbus's voyage with a parade on Broad Street, the second Mon of the month. Tel: 800-537-7676; www.independencevisitorcenter.com
**Pulaski Day Parade**. A parade honoring the Polish patriot and the city's Polish-American community. Tel: 922-1700; www.polishamericancenter.org
**Thomas Eakins Head of the Schuylkill Regatta**. Collegiate crew teams row down the Schuylkill River in honor of the city's famed artist, who immortalized rowers in his finest works. Tel: 866-546-7573; www.pcvb.org
**William Penn's Birthday**. The Founder's birth is celebrated in period costume with a special party at Pennsbury Manor and at various events in the city. Tel: 946-0400; www.pennsburymanor.org
**Battle of Germantown**. Washington's attempt to dislodge the British from Germantown in 1777 is commemorated with a historic re-enactment at Cliveden. Tel: 848-1777; www.cliveden.org
**Philadelphia Open Studio Tours**. A great opportunity to watch artists at work and get a behind-the-scenes look at Philly's vibrant art scene. Tel: 546-7775; post.cfeva.org

## November

**Thanksgiving Day Parade ⓗ**. The parade files down Market Street and west on the Parkway, with giant balloons, colorful floats, brass bands and a cast of thousands. Tel: 800-537-7676; www.independencevisitorcenter.com
**Philadelphia Crafts Show**. A four-day juried crafts fair held at the Civic Center with the work of 100 artists from around the country.

## December

**Twelfth Night Celebration at Old Fort Mifflin**. Scores of Americans died during the siege of this fort in 1777 in order to protect Washington's army from a British attack. The annual Twelfth Night celebration features a colonial-style dinner and costumed "soldiers." Tel: 685-4167; www.fortmifflin.com

**Army-Navy Football Classic**. West Point and the Naval Academy face off in Philly for the annual gridiron grudge match. Tel: 463-2500; www.phillylovesarmynavy.com

**Christmas Tours of Historic Houses**. The mansions of Fairmount Park are decked with Christmas cheer for special tours. Tel: 925-8687

**Lucia Fest**. A Swedish winter festival with music, crafts, a candlelight procession and a Christmas fair at the American Swedish Historical Museum in South Philadelphia and Old Swede's Church in Queen Village. Tel: 389-1776; www.americanswedish.org

**A Dickens of a Christmas**. *A Christmas Carol* and other works are brought to life at the Mount Hope Estate and Winery by the same people who present the Pennsylvania Renaissance Faire. Tel: 717-665 – 7021; www.parenaissancefaire.com

**New Year's Eve Celebration ⓗ**. Ring in the new year with fireworks, music and hundreds of revelers at Penn's Landing. Tel: 800-537-7676; www.independencevisitorcenter.com

**Washington's Crossing of the Delaware**. Washington's bold river crossing in 1776 is re-enacted on Christmas Day at Washington Crossing State Park in Bucks County. Tel: 493-4076

## THE ARTS

### Theater

**1812 Productions**, 525 S. 4th Street, Suite 479, tel: 592-9560, 1812productions.org. Comedy is king for this company, which presents comic theater, cabaret and more.

**Act II Playhouse**, 56 E. Butler Avenue, Ambler, tel: 654-0200; www.act2.org. Philadelphia actors and directors stage fresh comedy, drama and musicals.

**Arden Theatre Company**, 40 N. 2nd Street, tel: 922-1122, www.ardentheatre.org. Seven productions each year include original literary adaptations, musicals, modern dramas, classics and a couple of children's shows.

**Bucks County Playhouse**, 70 S. Main St, New Hope, tel: 862-2041, www.buckscountyplayhouse.com. Musicals, comedies and dramas often featuring a number of well-known actors.

**Bushfire Theatre of Performing Arts**. 224 S. 52nd Street, tel: 747-9230. Drama, comedy and musicals – both new and classic – that reflect the experience of African Americans.

**Forrest Theater**, 1114 Walnut Street, tel: 923-1515, www.forresttheatre.com. Several big-time Broadway road shows each year.

**Freedom Theater**, 1346 N. Broad Street, tel: 978-8497, www.freedomtheatre.org. A leading African-American theater featuring original productions, classic plays and film adaptations.

**InterAct Theatre Company**. 2030 Sansom Street, tel: 568-8079, www.interacttheatre.org. Challenging plays address modern issues.

**Lantern Theater Company**, St. Stephen's Theater, 10th and Ludlow streets, tel: 829-9002, www.lanterntheater.org. Interpretations of classic theater from Shakespeare to such modern masters as Pinter and Stoppard.

**Mask & Wig Theatre**, 310 S. Quince Street, tel: 923-4229, www.maskandwig.org. This charming theater tucked away in an alley in Washington Square West is home to the University of Pennsylvania's all-male comedy troupe.

**McCarter Theater**, 91 University Place, Princeton, NJ. Tel: 609-258-2787, www.mccarter.org. A wide range of performances, including musicals, dramas, comedies and new works as well as music, dance and children's theater.

**Mum Puppettheatre**, 115 Arch Street, tel: 925-7686, www.mumpuppet.org. Challenging, imaginative works blur the lines between puppetry and, live theater.

**Painted Bride Art Center**, 230 Vine Street, tel: 925-9914, www.paintedbride.org. A major force in the alternative arts scene for more than 30 years, the center presents cutting-edge dance, performance art, music, mime and more.

**People's Light and Theater Company**, 39 Conestoga Road, Malvern, tel: 610-644-3500, www.peopleslight.org. Exciting adaptations, contemporary and classic dramas presented in a 200-year-old converted barn about 45 minutes outside center city.

**Philadelphia Live Arts Festival & Philly Fringe Festival**, 211 Vine Street, tel: 413-9006; www.pafringe.com. Sixteen days of cutting-edge performances by established and emerging artists challenge the norms of theater, dance, music and puppetry.

**Philadelphia Shakespeare Festival**, 2111 Sansom Street, tel: 496-8001, www.phillyshakespeare.org. Classic and contemporary interpretations of the Bard as well as a full schedule of lectures, discussions and parties.

**Philadelphia Theater Company**, Suzanne Roberts Theater, Broad and Lombard streets, tel: 985-0420, www.phillytheatreco.com. A polished presenter of new plays; several productions are staged each year at a new theater on the Avenue of the Arts.

**Pig Iron Theatre Company**, tel: 627-1883, www.pigiron.org. Boundary-breaking theater from a young and exciting company.

**Play and Players Theater**, 1714 Delancey Street, tel: 735-0630, www.plays-players.org. The oldest community theater in the country presents several light dramas, musicals and comedies each year.

**Prince Music Theater**, 1412 Chestnut Street, tel: 569-9700, www.princemusictheater.org. A launching pad for musical theater, the Prince is dedicated to nurturing contemporary works and artists.

**Shubin Theater**, 407 Bainbridge Street, tel: 592-0119. A small artsy venue featuring original, cutting-edge theater.

**Society Hill Playhouse**, 507 S. 8th Street, tel: 923-0210, www.societyhillplayhouse.com. There are two stages at this historic venue – a 22-seat theater and

smaller cabaret – presenting a variety of old and new fare, improv comedy, musicals, drama, comedy and dinner theater.
**Walnut Street Theater**, 825 Walnut Street, tel: 574-3550. The oldest continuously operated theater in the country presents musicals, dramas, classics and Broadway road shows as well as new plays and children's shows.
**Wilma Theater**, Broad & Spruce streets, tel: 546-7824, www.wilmatheater.org. Creatively staged drama and comedy, including adaptations and translations, are presented at this highly regarded theater on the Avenue of the Arts.

### Film

Philadelphia has a growing reputation as a film center. In addition to cinemas throughout the area, the city is host to the Philadelphia Film Festival, Philadelphia International Gay & Lesbian Film Festival, and Jewish Film Festival.

**AMC Franklin Mills Mall 14**, 903 Franklin Mills Circle, Tel: 281-2750.
**AMC Neshaminy 24**, 3900 Rockhill Drive, Bensalem, tel: 722-4262.
**AMC Orleans 8**, Cottman and Bustleton streets, tel: 722-4262.
**AMC Plymouth Meeting Mall 12**, 494 Germantown Pike, Plymouth Meeting, tel: 610-397-0784.
**AMC Woodhaven 10**, 1336 Bristol Pike, Bensalem, tel: 244-1200.
**The Bridge**, S. 40th and Walnut Streets, tel: 386-3300
**Bryn Mawr Film Institute**, 824 W. Lancaster Ave, tel: 610-527-9898.
**Clearview's Bala Theatre**, 157 Bala Ave, Bala Cynwyd, tel: 610-668-4695.
**Free Library of Philadelphia**, 19th and Vine Streets, tel: 686-5322. Free film series.
**International House**, 3701 Chestnut Street, tel: 895-6542. Independent and avant-garde cinema from around the world.
**Narberth Stadium 2**, 129 N. Narberth Ave, Narberth, tel: 610-

667-0115.
**Regal Plymouth Meeting 10**, 1011 Ridge Pike, Conshohocken, tel: 800-326-3264.
**Ritz 5**, 214 Walnut St, Tel: 925-7900. Independent, limited-run, art and foreign films.
**Ritz at the Bourse**, 400 Ranstead Street, tel: 925-7900. Independent, limited-run, art and foreign films.
**Ritz East**, 2nd Street between Chestnut and Walnut Streets, tel: 925-7900
**Roxy Theatre Philadelphia**, 2023 Sansom Street, tel: 923-6699.
**Tuttleman IMAX Theater**, Franklin Institute, 20th Street and Benjamin Franklin Parkway, tel: 448-1111. Huge screen, 70mm theater.
**UA Cheltenham Square**, 2385 Cheltenham Avenue, tel: 800-326-3264.
**UA Grant Plaza**, 1619 Grant Avenue, tel: 800-326-3264.
**UA King of Prussia Stadium 16**, 300 Goddard Blvd, King of Prussia, tel: 800-326-3264.
**UA Main Street 6**, 3720-40 Main Street, Manayunk, tel: 800-326-3264.
**UA Movies at 69th Street**, 53 S. 69th Street, Upper Darby, tel: 800-326-3264.
**UA Riverview Stadium 17**, 1400 S. Columbus Blvd, tel: 800-326-3264.

### Classical Music

**Academy of Vocal Arts**, 1920 Spruce Street, tel: 735-1685, www.avaopera.org. Performances at this distinguished school of the operatic arts are staged in a historic 150-seat theater.
**Orchestra of Philadelphia**, Kimmel Center for the Performing Arts, 260 S. Broad Street, tel: 545-5451, www.chamberorchestra. org. The Kimmel Center's resident chamber orchestra features some of the most talented musicians in the region.
**Choral Arts Society**, 1420 Locust St. Tel: 545-8634. This 100-member symphonic chorus performs at churches and other

venues throughout the area.
**Mendelssohn Club of Philadelphia**, tel: 735-9922, www.mc chorus.org. World-class chorus performs sacred music, classics and new works.
**Network for New Music**, 416 Queen Street, tel: 848-7647, www.networkfornewmusic.org. Rousing performances of contemporary works.
**Opera Company of Philadelphia**, Academy of Music, 1420 Locust Street, tel: 893-1999, www.opera philly.com. The city's premier opera company presents five operas a year at the Academy of Music.
**Orchestra 2001**, tel: 922-2190, www.orchestra2001.org. 20th-century orchestral works are presented at the Kimmel Center and Lang Concert Hall at Swarthmore College.
**Pennsylvania Pro Musica**, 844 Crestview Drive, tel: 222-4517. Chamber music and major works, both orchestral and vocal, with emphasis on the Baroque; performances at Holy Trinity, Christ Church and Old Pine Street Church.
**Piffaro**, tel: 235-8469, www. piffaro.com. A small ensemble specializing in the music of the late Medieval and Renaissance.
**Philadelphia Boys Choir**, tel: 222-3500, www.phillyboyschoir.org. An acclaimed ensemble of 90 boys and 30 men that performs at venues throughout the city.
**Philadelphia Chamber Music Society**, tel: 569-8080, philadelphiachambermusic.org. First-rate classical and occasional jazz performances are presented at venues throughout the area.
**Philadelphia Classical Guitar Society**, 416 Queen Street, tel: 567-2972, www.phillyguitar.org. A classical guitar series featuring local and touring musicians at the Settlement Music School.
**Philadelphia Folksong Society**, 7113 Emlen St, tel: 247-1300, www.pfs.org. American and international folk music presented at the Commodore Barry Club; the Society also sponsors the annual Philadelphia Folk Festival.
**Philadelphia Orchestra**, Kimmel Center, Broad and Spruce

streets, tel: 893-1999, www.philorch.org. World-famous orchestra once conducted by Leopold Stokowski, Eugene Ormandy, Riccardo Muti and Wolfgang Sawallisch, now under the baton of Christoph Eschenbach, performs at the Kimmel Center; summer concerts at the outdoor Mann Center in Fairmount Park.

**Philadelphia Singers**, Kimmel Center, Broad and Spruce streets, tel: 751-9494, www.philadelphiasingers.org. This professional chorus appears at the Kimmel Center and St. Clement's Church, sometimes with the Philadelphia Orchestra or visiting ensembles.

**Philomel**, tel: 893-1999, www.philomel.org. This distinguished early-music ensemble performs throughout the Philadelphia area and tours widely.

**Philly Pops**, 260 S. Broad Street, 16th Fl, tel: 893-1900, www.phillypops.com. Led by Peter Nero, the orchestra performs a mixed repertoire of classical, Broadway, rock, jazz and pop favorites.

**Relache**, 715 S. Third Street, Suite 208, tel: 569-9700, www.relache.org. A leader in the performance of new music, the ensemble produces 15 to 20 concerts a year, including several new commissions.

**Savoy Company**, tel: 735-7161, www.savoy.org. Gilbert and Sullivan troupe; performances at the Academy of Music and Longwood Gardens.

## Jazz

**Asociacion de Musicos Latino Americanos**, tel: 324-0746 (ext 260 or 315), www.amla.org. A cultural center presenting performances, seminars and master classes with Latin jazz, salsa and folk musicians.

**Chris' Jazz Cafe**, 1421 Sansom Street, tel: 568-3131, www.chrisjazzcafe.com. A snug, smoky bar and restaurant with top-notch local players.

**LaRose Jazz Club**, 5531 Germantown Ave, tel: 248-4415. Bar and supper club with music by top jazz musicians.

**Ortlieb's Jazzhaus**, 3rd and Poplar streets, tel: 922-1035, ortliebsjazzhaus.com. Hot jazz in a down-home, no-frills atmosphere.

**Philadelphia Clef Club of Jazz**, 736-38 S. Broad Street, tel: 893-9912, www.clefclubofjazz.com. Primarily dedicated to jazz education, the institute also organizes Jazz in the Sanctuary at the Church of the Advocate, 18th and Diamond streets.

**Zanzibar Blue**, 200 S. Broad Street, tel:732-5200, www.zanzibarblue.com. Cool, upscale nightclub and restaurant with some of the best local talent and touring acts.

## Folk

**Philadelphia Folk Festival**. A tradition for more than 45 years, this three-day festival features an international roster of folk musicians at Old Poole Farm in Schwenksville, Pennsylvania. Tel: 242-0150; www.folkfest.org

**Philadelphia Folklore Project**, 7113 Emlen Street, tel: 242-0150, www.folkloreproject.org. Performances and workshops focus on folk music, dance, storytelling and visual arts from Philadelphia and abroad.

## Venues

**Academy of Music**, 1420 Locust Street, tel: 893-1999, www.academyofmusic.org. The grand dame of Broad Street is as elegant as ever, even though the new Kimmel Center has stolen some of the limelight. The Academy is home to the Opera Company of Philadelphia and Pennsylvania Ballet.

**Annenberg Center**, 3680 Walnut Street, tel: 898-3900, www.pennpresents.org. A complex of theaters at the University of Pennsylvania that hosts the eclectic "Penn Presents" series of live music, dance and theater as well as the Philadelphia International Children's Festival.

**Boyer College of Music and Dance**, Temple University, 1715 N. Broad Street, tel: 204-8307, www.temple.edu/music. Free performances and master classes feature students, teachers and guest performers at the university's attractive 300-seat theater.

**Curtis Institute of Music**, 1726 Locust Street, tel: 893-7902, www.curtis.edu. Dozens of free concerts and recitals are held at the Institute's small concert hall.

**Electric Factory**, 421 N. 7th Street, tel: 627-1332. A relatively small venue for relatively big rock acts. Downstairs is general admission for all ages. Upstairs is a bar and seating for the over-21 crowd.

**International House**, 3701 Chestnut Street, tel: 387-5125, www.ihousephilly.org. International folk music, dance and film.

**Keswik Theatre**, 291 N. Keswick Ave, Glenside, PA 19038, tel: 572-7650, www.keswicktheatre.com. Good acoustics and a modest size (about 1,300 seats) make this an excellent spot for pop concerts.

**Kimmel Center for the Performing Arts**, Broad and Spruce streets, tel: 893-1999, www.kimmelcenter.org. This state-of-the-art performance space is the centerpiece of Philly's Avenue of the Arts. Resident companies include the Philadelphia Chamber Music Society, the Chamber Orchestra of Philadelphia, Philadanco, Philly Pops, the Opera Company of Philadelphia, the Pennsylvania Ballet and the American Theater Arts for Youth.

**Mann Center for the Performing Arts**, 52nd Street and Parkside Ave, Fairmount Park, tel: 893-1999, www.manncenter.org. Spreading a blanket on the lawn and enjoying music under the stars is a Philadelphia tradition at this outdoor amphitheater in Fairmount Park, summer home of the Philadelphia Orchestra and a series of pop, rock and jazz shows.

**Merriam Theater**, 250 S. Broad Street, tel: 732-1366. Owned by the University of the Arts, the theater stages university shows as well as touring companies and the occasional pop concert.

**Painted Bride Art Center**, 230 Vine Street, tel: 925-9914, www.paintedbride.org. A cornerstone of the alternative arts scene, the Bride presents music, dance, theater and poetry as well as a series of art exhibits.

**Penn's Landing**, tel: 928-8801, www.pennslandingcorp.com. Summer series of jazz and pop concerts, many free, at a riverfront stage.

**Settlement Music School**, 416 Queen Street, tel: 320-2600, www.smsmusic.org. Free or inexpensive performances and master classes are presented at school branches throughout the area.

**Spectrum**, Broad Street and Pattison Ave, www.comcast-spectacor.com. 17,000-seat arena, used for giant pop shows.

**Theater of the Living Arts**, 334 South St. Tel: 922-1011. Somewhat grungy South Street venue, with general admission for 800.

**Tower Theater**, 69th and Ludlow streets, Upper Darby, PA, tel: 352-2887. This venerable 3,000-seat theater, originally built as a movie and vaudeville house in 1928, is a classic venue.

**Tweeter Center**, 1 Harbour Blvd, Camden, NJ, tel: 856-365-1300, www.tweetercenter.com. In winter this riverfront performance space is an indoor venue seating 7,000 people. In warm weather, the walls come down and it is transformed into an open-air shed with seating for 25,000, much of it on the lawn.

## Dance

**Brian Sanders' Junk**, 1223 Wood Street, tel: 922-1660. Acrobatic, comic, conceptual dance in Philly's up-and-coming "loft district."

**Dance Affiliates**, 4701 Bath Street #46, tel: 636-9000, www.dancecelebration.org. A series of contemporary dance companies.

**DanceBoom!** Wilma Theater, S. Broad and Spruce streets, tel: 546-7824, www.wilmatheater.org. The Wilma Theater is host to an annual dance series presenting some of the most interesting dance troupes in Philadelphia, often in intriguing combinations.

**Group Motion**, Community Education Center, 3500 Lancaster

Ave, tel: 387-9895, www.groupmotion.org. Improvisational dance in a multimedia setting.

**Headlong Dance Theater**, 1170 S. Broad Street, tel: 545-9195, www.headlong.org. Original pieces by a small troupe dedicate to cutting-edge, contemporary commentary.

**Jeanne Ruddy Dance Company and Performance Garage**, 1515 Brandywine Street, tel: 569-4060, www.ruddydance.org. Traditional modern dance at a new venue in the Spring Garden neighborhood.

**Koresh Dance Company**, 104 S. 20th Street, tel: 751-0959, www.koreshdance.org. A highly regarded modern dance company.

**Movement Theatre International** (MTI), 3700 Chestnut Street, tel: 382-0606. Dance, mime, puppetry and cabaret at a converted "tabernacle" in University City.

**Pennsylvania Ballet**, Academy of Music, 1420 Locust Street, tel: 551-7000, www.paballet.org. Philadelphia's premier ballet company performs at the Academy of Music and Merriam Theater; the *Nutcracker* is an annual tradition.

**Philadanco**, 9 N. Preston Street. tel: 893-1999, www.philadanco.org. A premier modern dance company that tours extensively throughout the region and country.

# NIGHTLIFE

## Nightclubs

**Egypt**, 520 N. Columbus Blvd, tel: 922-6500. The Nile meets the Delaware at this riverfront club, where the young and stylish roam a warren of theme rooms.

**The Fire**, 412 W. Girard Ave, tel: 671-9298. A neighborhood joint in up-and-coming Northern Liberties with local bands, local beer and local characters.

**Five Spot**, 1 S. Bank Street, tel: 574-0070, www.thefivespot.com. Slightly more sophisticated than most warehouse clubs, the Five Spot serves up a mixture of DJs, live bands, salsa lessons, swing dancing, and other special events.

**Fluid**, 613 S. 4th Street, tel: 629-0565. A small but popular dance club near South Street with a changing roster of DJs and an intimate underground vibe.

**Katmandu**, 417 N. Columbus Blvd, tel: 629-7400. Open May–Oct only. A popular outdoor bar on the riverfront with live music, dance space and outdoor dining.

**Khyber**, 56 S. Second Street, tel: 238-5888, www.thekhyber.com. Rock club in Old City with local bands; a little rough around the edges but much beloved by regulars.

**L'Etage**, 624 S. 6th Street, 2nd Floor, tel: 592-0656. www.creperiebeaumonde.com. The upstairs lounge of Beau Monde is as chic as a Parisian salon. Occasional burlesque and nightly DJs keep things interesting.

**Loie**, 128 S. 19th Street, tel: 568-0808. www.loie215.com. This art nouveau-style brasserie transforms into a nighttime lounge and gets packed with Rittenhouse-ites grooving to a rotating cast of DJs.

**North by Northwest**, 7165 Germantown Avenue, tel: 248-1000, www.nxnwphl.com. A bar, restaurant and music venue all rolled into one renovated storefront. An impressive mix of local and national acts appear in this nightclub for grownups.

**North Star Bar**, 2639 Poplar Street, tel: 787-0488. Artsy and a little shaggy, with a lively crowd of regulars and live music several nights a week.

**Ortlieb's Jazzhaus**, 847 N. 3rd Street, tel: 922-1035, ortliebsjazzhaus.com. A city's jazz favorite for years, a casual old-time nightclub and restaurant in the Northern Liberties with local and national jazz talent and jam sessions.

**Shampoo**, 417 N. 8th Street, tel: 922-7500, www.shampooonline.com. Gay and straight mix at this cavernous hall with a viscera-shaking sound system and several breakout rooms for a semi-private tete-a tete. The unisex bathroom is interesting but not for the shy. Shaft Friday draws the biggest gay crowd.

**Theatre of Living Arts (TLA)**, 334 South Street, tel: 922-1011.

There's a bar here, but this survivor of the grungy 1980s is really more of a performance space. **Tin Angel at Serrano**, 20 S. Second Street, tel: 928-0770, www.tinangel.com. Take a walk on the mellow side at this cozy Old City bar/coffee house, which bills itself as an "acoustic café."

**Transit Nightclub**, 600 Spring Garden Street, tel: 925-8878, www.transitnightclub.com. A huge old bank serves as a nightclub with three floors of dancing, multiple bars, DJs, and theme nights.

**The Trocadero,** 1003 Arch Street, tel: 922-6888, www.thetroc.com. A former burlesque theater, the Troc has been a mainstay of the alternate rock scene for years. The upstairs bar books local bands and runs a popular Monday movie night.

**US Hotel Bar & Grill**, 4439 Main Street, tel: 483-9222. A welcoming neighborhood bar, once part of Manayunk's best hotel during this mill town's boom years.

**World Cafe Live**, 3025 Walnut Street, tel: 222-1400, www.worldcafelive.com. One of the city's premier (and newest) venues for live music from established bands and up-and-coming acts.

**Walnut Room**, 1709 Walnut Street, 2nd Floor, tel: 751-0201, www.walnut-room.com. Sleek, sexy and fun. This second floor spot has excellent specialty cocktails, hip DJs and, on weekends, a velvet-roped line.

**ZanzibarBlue**, The Bellevue, 200 S. Broad Street, tel: 732-4500, www.zanzibarblue.com. Sophisticated and sleek, this restaurant and lounge in the historic Bellevue Hotel is the place for jazz fans to catch sets by stars like Pat Martino and Arturo Sandoval. There's live music and happy hours 7 nights a week to go along with the eclectic menu.

## Gay Scene

Tourism officials have aggressively marketed the city to gay and lesbian tourists. ("Get your history straight and your nightlife gay," the slogan goes.) The hub of Philly's gay community is Washington Square West between Lombard and Walnut and 11th and 13th streets, an area dubbed the Gayborhood. Here you will find several gay nightclubs and a plethora of gay-friendly businesses.

For the latest news and information on upcoming events, pick up a copy of the **Philadelphia Gay News** (www.epgn.com), available in newspaper boxes on most street corners in the area. **Giovanni's Room** (345 S. 12th Street, tel: 923-2960, www.giovannisroom.com) is a highly regarded gay bookstore and an excellent place to meet people and learn more about the community. The **William Way Lesbian Gay Bisexual Transgender Community Center** (1315 Spruce Street, tel: 732-2220, www.waygay.org) offers a varied schedule of workshops, community forums, lectures, performances, dance parties and other events.

Several events are worth noting, too. **The Equality Forum** (1420 Locust Street, Suite 300, tel: 732-3378, www.equalityforum.com), usually held in late April or early May, is a weeklong series of symposiums, lectures, festivals, and other happenings that freely mix education, activism and fun. The event culminates with **SundayOUT Street Festival** in Old City. The longstanding **Blue Ball**, a three-day party that benefits gay and lesbian organizations, is now held at or about the same time. The **LGBT Pride Day** (875-9288, www.phillypride.org) in June features a parade and festival at the Great Plaza on Penn's Landing. The Fall **OutFest** (www.phillypride.org) is a street party, with live music, food vendors and speakers, in honor of National Coming Out Day. Also notable are the **Philadelphia Gay and Lesbian Theatre Festival**, (627-6483, www.philagaylesbiantheatrefest.org) in June and the **Philadelphia International Gay and Lesbian Film Festival** (733-0608, www.phillyfests.com) in July.

## Gay Nightclubs

**12th Air Command**, 254 S. 12th Street, tel: 545-8088, www.12thair.com. A disco, lounge, pool room and open-air rooftop bar occupy three floors at this well-known gay gathering place. Check the schedule for karaoke nights and drag shows.

**Bike Stop**, 206 S. Quince Street, tel: 627-1662. A warm and fuzzy leather bar? Sort of. The upstairs sports bar is a non-intimidating place to watch a game and have a beer. The main floor is a bit more hardcore, but serious cruising is reserved for the aptly named "Pit" downstairs.

**Bump**, 1234 Locust Street, tel: 732-1800, www.bumplounge.com. A stylish, contemporary gay club with a hip crowd, fancy drinks and so-so food.

**Key West**, 207 S. Juniper Street, tel: 545-1578. A long-time gay hotspot with dancing, drinking, a sports bar and go-go boys.

**Odette's**, 274 S. River Road, New Hope, PA 18938, tel: 862-2432. Nostalgia reigns at the piano bar and cabaret at this lovely Bucks County restaurant once owned by Broadway actress Odette Myrtil.

**Pure**, 1221 Saint James Street, tel: 735-5772. This cavernous three-story after-hours club is tricked out with high-tech lighting and sound systems and flamboyant decor, including a see-through floor that allows you to spy on dancers below. The good times roll until 4am. This is a members-only club. To enter, you need to know a member and pay a one-time admission fee.

**Shampoo**, 417 N. 8th Street, tel: 922-7500, www.shampooonline.com. Gay and straight mix at this cavernous hall with a viscera-shaking sound system and several break-out rooms for a semi-private tête-à-tête. The unisex bathroom is interesting but not for the shy. Shaft Friday draws the biggest gay crowd.

**Sisters**, 1320 Chancellor Street, tel: 922-7500, www.sistersnightclub.com. Dining, dancing, a slick bar, a pool table, giant plasma screens, live bands and a series of special events are among the attractions at Philly's best-known lesbian nightclub.

**Tavern on Camac**, 243 S. Camac Street, tel: 545-0900, www.tavernoncamac.com. A piano bar gives this place a celebratory air. There's dancing upstairs and a fine restaurant.

**Uncle's**, 1220 Locust Street, tel: 546-6660. Lively conversation and reasonably priced drinks are the main attractions at this clubby place, a longtime crossroads in the city's gay community.

**Woody's Bar**, 202 S. 13th Street, tel: 545-1893, www.woodysbar.com. Well-mannered gay club with a chatty, collegial cocktail bar, relaxed coffee bar, and second-floor dance bar.

## SHOPPING

### Malls and Marketplaces

The largest shopping mall in center city is **The Gallery at Market East** (1001 Market Street, tel: 625-4962, www.galleryatmarket east.com), which occupies more than three blocks and four levels next to the Pennsylvania Convention Center between 11th and 8th streets. There are more than 150 shops and restaurants around the airy, skylit atrium including the expected chain stores such as The Gap and Old Navy. **Market Place East** is next to the Gallery at 8th and Market Streets. Housed in a magnificent cast-iron structure once occupied by the Lit Brothers Department Store, this block-long mixed-use complex is now divided between offices and about 25 stores and restaurants.

Also in the area, facing Independence Mall, is the **Bourse**, a 19th-century commercial exchange with a six-story central hall occupied by stores, restaurants and offices. The location is perfect for a shopping or dining break close to Independence Hall.

Running parallel to Market Street, the **Chestnut Street Transitway** is closed to all traffic except buses between 6th and 18th streets. Most of the retailers on this strip are discount stores or specialty shops. The snazzy **Liberty Place** (851-9055) complex is between 16th and 17th streets. The 70 shops and restaurants are set around a two-story glass rotunda.

For even fancier pickings, try the **Shops at the Bellevue**, a posh marketplace beneath the Hotel Atop the Bellevue at Broad and Walnut streets, where retailers like Ralph Lauren Polo, Tiffany, and Williams Sonoma do business in beautifully appointed shops.

**Rittenhouse Row**, an area loosely centered around **Walnut Street** between Broad and 21st streets, has its share of fancy retailers, including Burberry's, Brooks Brothers and an abundance of trendy boutiques.

For more adventurous tastes, **South Street** is the place to go. The shops and eateries on or near South Street from 9th to Front streets include everything from punk shops and art galleries to rock bars and fine restaurants. This is a hip, edgy part of town, popular with, but certainly not limited to, young people. It tends to be a carnival on Friday and Saturday nights, but it's almost always interesting. At one time, South Street ran through a large Jewish neighborhood. A remnant of those days can still be found on **Fabric Row**, which runs along 4th Street south of South Street.

For neighborhood shopping, stroll Germantown Avenue in tony **Chestnut Hill** or Main Street in **Manayunk**, both with boutiques, restaurants and gift shops.

Shopping malls elsewhere in the metropolitan area include the following:

**Franklin Mills**
1455 Franklin Mills Circle, tel: 632-1500. A sprawling discount mall with more than 200 outlet stores, 30 fast-food counters and restaurants, and a multiscreen

cinema. Factory outlets include Ann Taylor, Banana Republic, Brooks Brothers, Gap, Nine West, Old Navy and Tommy Hilfiger.

**Cherry Hill Mall**
2000 Route 38, Cherry Hill, NJ, tel: 856-662-7440. One of the first enclosed shopping malls on the East Coast has mostly upscale stores such as Abercrombie & Fitch, Ann Taylor, Banana Republic, Brooks Brothers, Coach, Sephora and Victoria's Secret, plus department stores Macy's and JC Penney.

**Court at King of Prussia**
160 N. Gulph Rd, King of Prussia, PA, tel: 610-265-5727. The biggest mall on the East Coast has more than 350 shops, including such department stores as Bloomingdale's, Neiman Marcus, JC Penney, Macy's, Lord & Taylor, Nordstrom and Sears, ranging from high-end designer duds to discount goods.

**Neshaminy Mall**
Route 1 and Bristol Road, Bensalem, PA, tel: 357-6100. Three department stores anchor this mall, which has scores of shops and food vendors and a cinema.

**Oxford Valley Mall**
2300 E. Lincoln Hwy, Langhorne, PA, tel: 752-0221. You will find the usual mall fare at this regional shopping center in Lower Bucks County, including Aeropostale, Banana Republic, Gap, Foot Locker, Victoria's Secret and the like, plus a food court and multiplex cinema.

**Peddler's Village**
Route 202, Lahaska, PA, tel: 794-4000. Seventy specialty shops featuring crafts, antiques and handmade gifts as well as several restaurants in a pleasant country village setting.

**Plymouth Meeting Mall**
500 W. Germantown Pike, Plymouth Meeting, PA, tel: 610-825-9351. More than 100 stores, including two department stores, a food court and a 12-screen movie theater. **IKEA**, a popular Swedish furniture and housewares company, is adjacent to the mall.

## Antiques

Philadelphia is big on antiques. Once a major center of American craftsmanship, the city still attracts collectors and dealers who scour swap meets, flea markets and salvage operations in search of ancient treasures. The best place to start looking for antiques is Pine Street between 13th and 8th streets, also known as **Antique Row**. There are about 20 or so antique dealers along this strip as well as jewelers, craft shops and several interesting spots for a bite to eat. You might also want to try the nearby **Antiquarian's Delight** (615 S. 6th Street, 592-0256), an indoor antique market just off South Street with some 25 antique dealers under a single roof. If you're serious about antiques, you should also check out the "Weekend" section of the *Philadelphia Inquirer* for listings of special antique markets in and around the city as well as the yearly **Philadelphia Antiques Show**, usually held in April at the 33rd Street Armory at 33rd and Market streets.

**Blendo**
1002 Pine Street, tel: 351-9260. The place is packed to the rafters with a fun and funky collection of vintage furnishings, apparel, jewelry and housewares.

**Calderwood Gallery**, 1622 Spruce Street, tel: 546-5357. French Art Deco and modernist decorative arts.

**Eloquence Antiques and Decorative Arts**
1034 Pine Street, tel: 627-6606. Specialist in porcelain, silverware and jewelry.

**M. Finkel & Daughter**
936 Pine Street, tel: 627-7797. You will find two stories of 18th- and 19th-century furniture at this venerable shop, but the specialty of the business is antique samplers, needlework and embroidery.

**Happily Ever After**
1010 Pine Street, tel: 627-5790. A wide selection of antique toys.

**Lambertville Antique Flea Market**
River Road, Lambertville, NJ, tel: 609-397-0456. Old-stuff junkies will have a field day sifting through secondhand wares at 50 indoor shops and 250 outdoor stalls; only the truly devoted will find the jewels among the junk.

**Mixed Company**
60 N. 3rd Street, tel: 627-8688. Expect an eclectic mix of furniture, paintings, housewares and plain old kitsch, ranging from European antiques to pop art.

**Mode Moderne**
159 N. 3rd Street, tel: 627-0299. Furniture from the mid-20th century, plus contemporary versions of modern classics.

**G.B. Schaffer Antiques**
1014 Pine Street, tel: 923-2263. Period furnishings with an emphasis on the 19th century.

## Art Galleries

Many Old City galleries coordinate their openings for the **First Friday** of every month, when throngs of appreciative art lovers migrate from gallery to gallery. The event is followed by **First Saturday**, when artists, curators and gallery owners offer workshops, lectures and other informal get-togethers during the afternoon.

**Artists' House**, 57 N. 2nd Street, tel: 923-8440. Emerging artists, many from the Delaware Valley.

**Larry Becker**, 43 N. 2nd Street, tel: 925-5389. Contemporary abstract work with a minimalist flavor.

**Clay Studio**, 139 N. 2nd Street, tel: 925-3453. Exhibits of modern ceramic arts as well as classes and worshops.

**David David Gallery**, 260 S. 18th Street, tel: 735-2922. A wide range of major American and European work.

**Helen Drutt Gallery**, 1721 Walnut Street, tel: 735-1625. Contemporary ceramics and jewelry.

**F.A.N. Gallery**, 221 Arch Street, tel: 922-5155. Realist painting and sculpture from emerging and established artists, many from the Philadelphia region.

**Indigo**, 151 N. 3rd Street, tel: 922-4041. Art and artifacts from Asia, Africa and the Americas.

**Jaipaul Galleries**, 1610 Locust Street, tel: 735-7303. Ancient Indian art.

**Esther M. Klein Art Gallery**, University City Science Center, 3701 Market Street, tel: 966-6188. Exhibits feature a wide range of styles and media, with an emphasis on community outreach.

**Locks**, 600 Washington Square South, tel: 629-1000. The gallery shows major 20th-century figures as well as work by emerging and mid-career artists.

**Newman**, 1625 Walnut Street, tel: 563-1779. Traditional painting and sculpture, with a focus on 19th- and 20th-century American art and the Bucks County School of Impressionism.

**Nexus Foundation for Today's Art**, 137 N. 2nd Street, tel: 629-1103. Emerging and experimental local artists.

**Painted Bride Gallery**, 230 Vine Street, tel: 925-9914. Alternative and experimental art.

**Philadelphia Art Alliance**, 251 S. 18th Street, tel: 545-4302. A multidisciplinary gallery featuring visual, performance and literary work by regional artists.

**Rosenfeld Gallery**, 113 Arch Street. Tel: 922-1376. Emerging and established artists in all media and a variety of styles.

**Arthur Ross Gallery**, University of Pennsylvania, 220 S. 34th St. Tel: 898-4401. Housed in a Frank Furness building, the University's gallery shows work in a wide range of styles, media and periods.

**Sande Webster Gallery**, 2006 Walnut Street, tel: 636-9008. Contemporary work in a variety of media and styles.

**Schmidt/Dean**, 1710 Sansom Street, tel: 569-9433. Contemporary paintings, prints and sculpture by regional, national and international artits.

**Schwarz Gallery**, 1806 Chestnut Street, tel: 563-4887. Specializing in fine 19th and early 20th-century painting.

**Taller Puertorriqueño**, 2721 N. 5th Street, tel: 426-3311. Latin American and Caribbean artists.

**Temple Gallery, Tyler School of Art**, 45 N. 2nd Street, tel: 782-2776. Challenging contemporary work.

**Vox Populi**, 1315 Cherry Street, 4th Floor, tel: 568-5513. An art collective with experimental work.

## Bookstores

In addition to the shops listed below are numerous mall bookstores, including **Waldenbooks**, **B. Dalton** and **Borders Express**, which tend to be small and concentrate on bestsellers. The annual **Book and the Cook Fair** brings together cookbook authors, food critics and many of the city's finest chefs for a 10-day celebration of good eating and good reading.

**AIA Bookstore**
117 S. 17th Street, tel: 569-3186. The American Institute of Architecture's bookstore specializes in titles on architecture, art and modern design as well as stationery, toys and assorted gifts.

**Barnes & Noble**
Rittenhouse Square, 1805 Walnut Street, tel: 665-0716. A "super store," with tens of thousands of titles and a café.

**Bauman Rare Books**
1608 Walnut Street, 19th Floor, tel: 546-6466. Antique and rare volumes.

**Big Blue Marble**
551 Carpenter Lane, tel: 44-1870, www.bigbluemarblebooks.com. The kind of cozy neighborhood book shop we all wish we had around the corner.

**Big Jar Books**
55 N. Second Street, tel: 574-1650. Old City used book shop with a carefully chosen collection of art, literature, film, women's studies, kids' books and more.

**Book Corner**
311 N. 20th Street, tel: 567-0527. Sales at this used bookstore benefit Philadelphia libraries.

**Bookhaven**
2202 Fairmount Ave, tel: 235-3226. A refreshingly low-tech used book shop with an especially extensive history collection.

**Book Trader**
N. 2nd and Market streets, tel: 925-0517. The archetypal used bookstore – sprawling, cluttered and packed to the rafters.

**Borders**
1 S. Broad Street, tel: 568-7400; and 8701 Germantown Ave, tel: 248-1213. The other big chain of mega-stores.

**Chris' Corner**
1940 Pine Street, tel: 790-1727, www.pond.com/~chrisc. Books for young readers.

**Cookbook Stall**
Reading Terminal Market, 12th and Filbert streets, tel: 923-3170. Lovers of cookbooks will fall head over heels for this little shop in the city's lively food market.

**Famulus Books**
244 S. 22nd Street, tel: 732-9509. A wide selection of used books.

**Garland of Letters**
527 South Street, tel: 923-5946. New Age books and gifts.

**Giovanni's Room**
345 S. 12th Street, tel: 923-2960, www.giovannisroom.com. A highly regarded gay bookstore and hub of Philly's "gayborhood."

**Hakim's Bookstore**, 210 S. 52nd Street, tel: 474-9495. Specializing in African-American authors and themes.

**Head House Books**
619 S. 2nd Street, tel: 923-9525, www.headhousebooks.com. A community book shop with a busy schedule of author appearances, reading clubs, and children's events.

**Hibberd's Books**
1306 Walnut Street, tel: 546-8811. A used bookstore notable for art books and literature.

**Horizon Books**
The Gallery at Market East, 9th and Market streets, tel: 625-7955. A wide range of African-American titles.

**House of Our Own**
3920 Spruce Street, tel: 222-1576. University City bookseller with a brainy selection of new and used books emphasizing social activism, serious literature, history and world politics.

**Joseph Fox Bookshop**
1724 Sansom Street, tel: 563-4184, www.foxbookshop.com. Classy, old-time bookseller with carefully chosen collection of art, architecture, serious literature and children's books.

**Last Word Bookshop**
3925 Walnut Street, tel: 386-7750. Used books in University City.

**Miscellanea Libri**
Reading Terminal Market, 12th and Arch streets, tel: 238-9884. A small book stall in a busy marketplace packed with "pre-owned" treasures.

**Penn Book Center**
130 S. 34th Street, tel: 222-7600, www.pennbookcenter.com. University bookstore on the Penn campus.

**Philadelphia Museum of Art Store**
Benjamin Franklin Parkway, tel: 684-7960. An excellent selection of books on art and architecture, plus posters, prints, jewelry and other arty gifts.

**Portfolio at the Pennsylvania Academy**
118 N. Broad Street, tel: 972-2075. Museum shop of the Academy of the Fine Arts.

**Robin's Book Stores**
108 S. 13th Street, tel: 735-9600, www.robinsbookstore.com. Philadelphia's oldest independent bookstore has been hanging on despite competition from super stores and online retailers.

**Voices & Visions**
The Bourse, 111 S. Independence Mall, tel: 625-4740, www.vandvx3.com. This handsome shop aspires to be the "premier cultural nexus in Old City," with a strong arts collection and author/artist events.

**Wooden Shoe Books & Records**
508 S. Fifth Street, tel: 413-0999. A shop offering anarchist and radical literature run by a "non-hierarchical" collective.

**W. Graham Arader**
1308 Walnut Street, tel: 735-8811. Antiquarian book shop with antique prints, maps and atlases.

**Whodunit**
1931 Chestnut Street, tel: 567-1478. New and used mysteries and thrillers.

## Department Stores

Philly's great old department stores are a thing of the past. One by one, Lit Brothers, Wanamaker's, Gimbel's and Strawbrige & Clothier were done in by big-box stores, shopping malls and corporate consolidation. Most of the remaining department stores are found in shopping malls outside the city.

**Bloomingdale's**
The Court at King of Prussia, Route 202 at Mall Blvd, King of Prussia, PA 19406, tel: 610-337-6300; Willow Grove Park Mall, 2400 W. Moreland Road, Willow Grove, PA 19090, tel: 706-3300. Upscale fashion.

**JC Penney**
Cherry Hill Mall, 2000 Rt. 38, Cherry Hill, NJ 08002, tel: 856-488-0330. The workingman's and woman's department store.

**Lord & Taylor**
The Court at King of Prussia, Route 202 at Mall Blvd, King Of Prussia, PA 19406, tel: 610-992-0333; City Line & Belmont Ave, Bala Cynwyd, PA 19004, tel: 610-664-7050. Tasteful, conservative style.

**Macy's**
The Court at King of Prussia, Route 202 at Mall Blvd, King Of Prussia, PA 19406, tel: 610-337-9350; Willow Grove Park Mall, 2501 W. Moreland Road, Willow Grove, PA 19090, tel: 658-4700; Oxford Valley Mall, 2300 E. Lincoln Highway, Langhorne, PA 19047, tel: 752-1340; Cherry Hill Mall, 2000 Rt. 38, Cherry Hill, NJ 08002, tel: 856-665-5000. Mid-market retailer with a wide variety of quality clothing, housewares and accessories at reasonable prices.

**Neiman Marcus**
The Court at King of Prussia, Route 202 at Mall Blvd, King Of Prussia, PA 19406, tel: 610-354-0500. Elegant, high-end retailer,

with an abundance of designer fashions.

**Nordstrom**
The Court at King of Prussia, Route 202 at Mall Blvd, King Of Prussia, PA 19406, tel: 610-265-6111. Upmarket fashion, accessories, beauty products and furnishings

## Food

There are two spots in Philadelphia that gourmets should not miss: Reading Terminal Market and the Italian Market. Housed in a historic train shed, **Reading Terminal Market** (12th and Arch streets) has stall after stall of fresh fish, vegetables, meats and baked goods as well as counter service and restaurants offering everything from sushi to cheesesteaks to scrapple, Italian sausage and shoofly pie. The market is open 8am-6pm Monday-Saturday.

The **Italian Market** is a bit grungier but equally enticing. The offerings at this mostly outdoor market, stretching along 9th Street between Catharine and Wharton streets, are fresh and inexpensive. At least a dozen good Italian restaurants are within easy walking distance of the market, not to mention South Philly's longtime cheesesteak rivals, Pat's and Geno's at 9th and Passyunk.

**Bitar's**
947 Federal Street, tel: 755-1121, www.bitars.com. Customers at this small South Philly shop have a choice – order up falafels, shish-kabobs, gyros and other Middle Eastern specialties at a lunch counter or browse the grocery section for a variety of Mediterranean ingredients. There's a second location at 7152 Germantown Avenue in Mount Airy.

**Chef's Market**
231 South Street, tel: 925-8360, www.chefsmkt.com. Gourmet foods and prepared meals.

**Claudio**
924-26 S. 9th Street, tel: 627-

1873. An old-time cheese shop in the heart of the Italian Market with imported oil, meat, pasta, vinegar and much more, including a beautiful homemade mozzarella. About the closest thing to food heaven in South Philly.

**DiBruno Bros.**
930 S. 9th Street, tel: 922-2876; 1730 Chestnut Street, tel: 665-9220. The DiBruno family now has two stores specializing in exquisite Italian cheeses, olive oil, pasta and other gourmet goodies. The two-story Rittenhouse shop and café is much larger and hipper, but nothing beats the character, tradition and aroma of the original Italian Market location.

**Huong Vuong Supermarket**
1122-38 Washington Ave, tel: 336-2803. Primarily Vietnamese, but lots of products from around Asia.

## Jewelry

**Jewelers Row** – Sansom Street between 7th and 8th streets – is devoted exclusively to precious gems and metals. If you're looking for a gift, or thinking about getting hitched, the selection and prices can't be beat in Philadelphia. A few of the biggest shops are:

**Robbins 8th & Walnut**
801 Walnut Street, tel: 925-1877. A Jewelers Row institution with numerous branches in the Delaware Valley.

**Robinson Jewelers**
730 Chestnut Street, tel: 627-3066. A major diamond retailer with a broad selection and attractive prices.

**Safian & Rudolph**
7th and Sansom streets, tel: 627-1834. Engagement rings, wedding rings and custom-made jewelry of every variety.

**Sydney Rosen Company**
712-714 Sansom Street, tel: 888-859-5265. Large diamond showroom.

**Unclaimed Diamonds**
113 S. 8th Street, tel: 923-3210. Big discounts on jewelry that was put on layaway and never claimed.

Shop for jewelry elsewhere in center city at:
**Halloween**
1329 Pine Street, tel: 732-7711. Creative hand-crafted jewelry on Antique Row.
**Tiffany & Co.**
1414 Walnut Street, tel: 735-1919. Elegant and upper crusty, the Philadelphia home of the familiar blue box is the Shops at the Bellevue.
**Tselaine Jewelry Design**
132A Chestnut Street, tel: 923-1810. A small Old City shop and studio offering handcrafted pieces with gemstones and pearls.

## Men's Clothing

**Banana Republic**
1401 Walnut Street, tel: 751-0292. There are no surprises at this hugely successful chain store, just simple, slightly preppy khakis, jeans, shirts and sweaters.
**Boyds**
1818 Chestnut Street, tel: 564-9000. Every guy deserves at least one well-made, finely tailored suit, and this is the place to get it.
**Brooks Brothers**
1513 Walnut Street, tel: 564-4100. Classic, understated style. Pricey but worth it.
**I. Goldberg**
1300 Chestnut Street, tel: 925-9393, A Philly institution since 1919, this army surplus store is a great place to stock up on basics – jeans, cargo pants, T-shirts, sweatshirts and an assortment of durable outdoor wear. Don't forget the socks and skivvies.
**J. Crew**
1625 Chestnut Street, tel: 925-2739. Khaki pants, cable-knit and cashmere sweaters, polo shirts and other preppy staples are always in style at this Liberty Place outpost of the popular clothing catalog.
**Ubiq**
1509 Walnut Street, tel: 988-0194. Street-smart, casual fashion for men and women.

**Wayne Edwards**
1525 Locust Street, tel: 731-0120. A Rittenhouse Row shop with stylish, high-quality (and expensive) designer clothes from casual to formal.

## Women's Clothing

**Anthropologie**
5000 S. Broad Street, tel: 564-2313. Cool, mostly casual clothing for the young and fashionable.
**Guacamole**
422 South Street, tel: 923-6174. Sexy, skimpy, sometimes grungy clothes for the high school and college set.
**Joan Shepp Boutique**
1616 Walnut Street, tel: 735-2666. Upscale fashionista outpost on Rittenhouse Row specializing in pricey designer styles.
**Kimberly Boutique**
123 S. 16th Street, tel: 564-1066. Upscale boutique, edgy but feminine, on Rittenhouse Row.
**Me & Blue**
311 Market Street, 2nd floor, tel: 629-2347. Designer lines, vintage treasures and an original line of A-line skirts
**Molletta**
55 N. 3rd Street, tel: tel: 925-7733. High-end designer couture from lingerie, handbags and jewelry to complete ensembles, plus a selection of stylish housewares.
**Petulia's Folly**
1710 Sansom Street, tel: 569-1344. An elegant boutique with stylish, tasteful fashions.
**Public Image**
4390 Main Street, tel: 482-4008. Manayunk boutique known for hip, contemporary fashion.
**Vagabond**
37 N. 3rd Street, tel: 671-0737. A hip boutique with designer labels, a selection of vintage clothes and a few original items.
**Very Bad Horse**
606 N. 2nd Street, tel: 627-6989. Rock-star style in Northern Liberties, with lots of custom leather and jeans and edgy, over-the-top accessories.

## Music

**AKA Music**
27 N. 2nd Street, tel: 922-385. Plan to stay a while, because this well-stocked independent has a huge selection of new material as well as an alluring collection of used CDs and vinyl.
**Coconuts Music & Movies**
Columbus Crossings, 1851 S. Columbus Blvd, tel: 336-6095; and Roosevelt Mall, 2329 Cottman Ave, tel: 624-4423. Don't go looking for indie labels here; the selection is limited to mainstream music.
**FYE**
The Gallery at Market East, 937A Market Street, tel: 238-2140; 2437 S. 24th Street, tel: 468-2715; and Cheltenham Square, 2385 W. Cheltenham Ave, tel: 887-0702. A good place for pop hits, but you will find a reasonable inventory of non- mainstream material.
**Philadelphia Record Exchange**
618 S. 5th Street, tel: 925-7892. Remember the used record shop in *High Fidelity?* Well, this is about as close to it as you will ever come.
**Repo Records**
538 South Street, tel: 627-3775. Independent record shop with new and used CDs and vinyl. Treasure hunters will be richly rewarded in the discount bins and used record rack.
**Spaceboy Music**
407 South Street, tel: 925-3032. Music miners will revel in the apparent lack of organization. Dive into the racks of new and used CDs and records. You may not find what you are looking for, but you will probably discover half a dozen other items you never knew you wanted.

## Toys

**Character Development**
209 Haverford Ave, Narberth, PA 19072, tel: 610-668-1545. Ingenious toys and a thoughtful book selection at an inviting Main Line shop.

**Children's Boutique**
1702 Walnut Street, tel: 732-2661. Three floors of children's clothing and toys.

**Happily Ever After**
1010 Pine Street, tel: 627-5790. High-quality dolls and plush toys, many inspired by vintage television programs and fairy tales.

**O'Doodles**
8335 Germantown Ave, tel: 247-7405. Specialty toys and an extensive selection of illustrated children's books.

# TOURS

## Guided Tours

**'76 Carriage Company**
5th and Chestnut or 6th and Market streets, tel: 389-8687. Tour Independence National Historic Park, Society Hill and Old City in a horse-drawn carriage. Tours last 20, 30 or 60 minutes.

**Big Bus**
1119 N. Bodine Street, tel: 389-8687. Tour center city aboard a double-decker bus. Passengers can hop on and off at any of 20 stops. Departures from the corner of 5th and Market streets.

**Centipede Tours**
1315 Walnut Street, tel: 735-3123, www.centipedeinc.com. Customized tours for corporate clients, clubs and conference groups.

**Choo Choo Trolley**
4941 Longshore Ave, tel: 333-0320. Popular group tours on a trolley-bus.

**Fairmount Park Tours**
Philadelphia Museum of Art, 26th Street and Benjamin Franklin Parkway, tel: 763-8100. The Philadelphia Museum of Art offers tours of two historic houses in Fairmount Park as well as the "Schuylkill Stroll," a walking tour of Boathouse Row, architecture and outdoor sculpture.

**I Glide Tours**
1061 Kasmir Ave, Bensalem, PA 19020, tel: 735-1700, www.iglidetours.com. See the museum dis-trict on a Segway Human Transporter. Daily tours depart from Eakins Oval across from the Museum of Art.

**Mural Tours**
Philadelphia Mural Arts Program, 1729 Mount Vernon St, tel: 685-0754, www.muralarts.org/tours. Philly is gaining a reputation as a "City of Murals" thanks to the efforts of the Mural Arts Program. Tours depart from the Independence Visitor Center (6th and Market streets) Saturday and Wednesday mornings via trolley. Tickets are available by phone or at the Visitor Center.

**Philadelphia Bike and Moped Tours**
Tel: 514-3124, 334-0790 or 866-667-3395, www.philadelphiabiketour.com. Get around the city on a bike or motorized moped on these guided tours of such attractions as Independence Hall, Atwater Kent Museum, South Street and Eastern State Penitentiary.

**Philadelphia Carriage**
Chestnut Street between 5th and 6th streets, tel: 922-6840, www.philacarriage.com. Horse-drawn carriages clip-clop through Independence National Historic Park, Society Hill and Old City. Passengers have a choice of 20-, 30- or 60-minute tours

**Philadelphia Open House Tours**
The Friends of Independence National Historical Park, 143 S. 3rd Street, tel: 861-4971, www.ushistory.org. Guided tours focus on a variety of themes and neighborhoods. The schedule changes annually but usually includes Independence Park, Washington Square West, Chinatown, Queen Village, Society Hill, the Italian Market, University City, Manayunk, Fairmount Park and more.

**Philadelphia Trolley Works**
1119 N. Bodine Street, tel: 389-8687. Tours of the historic district and center city are available aboard a faux trolley.

**Ride The Ducks – Philadelphia**
6th and Chestnut streets, tel: 877-887-8225. Tour the historic district and waterfront aboard amphibious vehicles that motor around Old City and splash into the Delaware River at Penn's Landing. One caveat: customers are equipped with noisemakers that make a distinctive *quack*. Kids love them; adults should be prepared to exercise patience.

**Super Ducks**
5th and Chestnut streets, tel: 866-823-3825. 49-passenger amphibious vehicles tour the historic district and enter the Delaware River at Penn's Landing (though a legal challenge brought by rival Ride the Ducks may cause Super Ducks to alter its itinerary). Buy tickets at the boarding area at 5th and Chestnut streets near the Bourse.

## Walking Tours

**AudioWalk & Tour**
CD players and iPod downloads allow visitors to explore the historic district at their own pace. Rent CD players at Independence Visitor Center (6th and Market streets, last rental at 2pm, tel: 965-7676) or the Lights of Liberty shop (6th and Chestnut streets, 542-3789), or download an iPod tour at www.ushistory.org. Last CD rental at 2pm.

**Constitutional Walking Tour of Philadelphia**
Tel: 525-1776. Guided tours of the historic district begin at Independence Visitor Center at 6th & Market streets. The tours last about 75 minutes and cover slightly more than one mile. Buy tickets online (www.theconstitutional.com) or at the Visitor Center. Alternatively, a free self-guided walking tour and map can be downloaded as a pdf file from the website: www.theconstitutional.com.

**Foundation for Architecture**
One Penn Center, tel: 569-3187. A wide selection of walking tours focusing on the city's architectural history.

**Germantown Walking Tour**
Germantown Historical Society, 5501 Germantown Ave, tel: 844-0514. Walk in the footsteps of the "Germans, gener-

als and gentlemen" of historic Germantown, including the Deshler-Morris House and Grumblethorpe.

**Ghost Tour of Philadelphia**
Tel: 413-1997, www.ghosttour.com/Philadelphia.htm. A walking tour of the most haunted places in Old City and Society Hill, with tales about the lives – and afterlives – of the Founding Fathers and other notable (or notorious) figures. Purchase tickets by phone, online or in person at the Independence Visitor Center (6th and Market streets).

**Lights of Liberty**
Lights of Liberty Shop, 6th and Chestnut streets, tel: 877-462-1776, www.lightsofliberty.org. Customers use headsets to listen to narration by Walter Cronkite, Ossie Davis and Charlton Heston and a musical soundtrack performed by members of the Philadelphia Orchestra while images are projected on landmark buildings throughout the historic district. Book reservations online or by phone. A unique experience.

**Poor Richard's Walking Tour**
Tel: 206-1682, www.phillywalks.com. Comprehensive historic tours led by graduate students from the University of Pennsylvania.

**Quest for Freedom: Underground Railroad Walking Tour**
Independence Visitor Center, 6th and Market streets, tel: 965-7676 or 800-537-7676, www.independencevisitorcenter.com. A seasonal one-hour walking tour of sites associated with the Underground Railroad, a clandestine network of safe houses used before the US Civil War to smuggle fugitive slaves to freedom in the north.

**Taste of Philadelphia Food Tour**
Reading Terminal Market, 12th and Filbert streets, tel: 545-8007. Get the scoop on Philly food traditions like cheesesteaks, soft pretzels, water ice, hoagies, scrapple and shoo-fly pie at the famous indoor market. Tours start at the market's information desk.

## Cruises

**Riverboat Queen**
Penn's Landing, tel: 923-2628, www.riverboatqueenfleet.com. Delaware River cruises of varying lengths aboard replicas of vintage paddle wheelers. Boats depart in front of the Hyatt Regency at Penn's Landing.

**Schuylkill Banks Tours**
748-7445, www.schuylkillbanks.org. See Philly's "other" river on an afternoon, sunset or jazz cruise or on a guided kayak tour. Some tours include a visit to Bartram's Garden. Tours depart from the Walnut Street dock.

**Spirit of Philadelphia**
Pier 3, Columbus Blvd, tel: 923-4993, www.spiritcitycruises.com. Lunch, dinner and dance cruises on the Delaware River depart from Penn's Landing.

## SPORTS

### Spectator Sports

Philadelphia has professional teams in all the major American sports. Most play at the South Philadelphia sports complex, which encompasses Citizens Bank Park (Phillies), Lincoln Financial Field (Eagles), the Wachovia Center ('76ers and Flyers) and Wachovia Spectrum (soccer, lacrosse, tennis and assorted events). Tickets can be purchased from Ticketmaster (tel: 336-2000, www.ticketmaster.com), though seats for some pro teams (especially the Eagles) are often unavailable.

### Baseball
**Philadelphia Phillies**
Citizens Bank Park, Pattison Ave and Citizens Bank Way, tel: 463-1000, www.phillies.com.

### Basketball
**Philadelphia 76ers**
Wachovia Center, 3601 S. Broad Street, tel: 339-7676, www.sixers.com

### Football
**Philadelphia Eagles**
Lincoln Financial Field, 1020 Pattison Ave, tel: 463-2500, www.philadelphiaeagles.com.

**Philadelphia Soul**
Wachovia Center, 3601 S. Broad Street, tel: 636-0421, www.philadelphiasoul.com. Arena football.

### Ice Hockey
**Philadelphia Flyers**
Wachovia Center, 3601 S. Broad Street, tel: 218-7825, www.philadelphiaflyers.com

**Philadelphia Phantoms**
Wachovia Spectrum, 3601 S. Broad Street, tel: 465-4522, www.phantomshockey.com. Minor league hockey

### Lacrosse
**Philadelphia Wings**
Wachovia Center, 3601 S. Broad Street, www.wingslax.com. Indoor lacrosse.

**Philadelphia Barrage**
Tel: 610-355-8999. Outdoor lacrosse.

### Soccer
**Philadelphia Kixx**
Wachovia Spectrum, 3601 S. Broad Street, tel: 888-888-5499, www.kixxonline.com. Indoor soccer.

### Horse Racing
**Philadelphia Park**, 3001 Street Road, Bensalem, PA. Tel: 639-9000.

**Turf Club**, 7 Penn Center, 17th and Market Streets, tel: 246-1556. Restaurant with off-track betting.

### Boxing
**Legendary Blue Horizon**
1314 N. Broad Street, tel: 763-0500, www.legendarybluehorizon.com. A classic, old-time boxing arena.

### College Sports
The Big Five in Philadelphia area college sports are:
**University of Pennsylvania**
Weightman Hall, 235 S. 33rd Street, tel: 898-6151, www.pennathletics.com

**Temple**
www.owlsports.com
**Villanova**
Tel: 610-519-4100,
villanova.cstv.com
**LaSalle**
Tel: 951-1999, www.goexplorers.com
**St Joseph's**
Tel: 610-660-1712,
sjuhawks.cstv.com

## Annual Events

**Army-Navy Game**
Lincoln Financial Field, 1020 Pattison Ave, tel: 463-2500,
www.phillylovesarmynavy.com. For
most of its century-long history,
one of the country's great football rivalries has been played in
Philadelphia, usually in early
December.
**Dad Vail Regatta**
Tel: 542-1443, www.dadvail.org. More
than 100 schools compete in the
country's largest collegiate regattas, held on the Schuylkill River.
**Penn Relays**
Tel: 898-6151, www.pennrelays.com.
Usually held in late April or early
May, one of the country's largest
track meets has been convened
at the University of Pennsylvania
since 1893.
**Philadelphia International
Cycling Championship**
Tel: 610-676-0390, www.procycling
tour.com. A grueling 156-mile international bicycle race including
the punishing climb up the Manayunk Wall. The race begins and
ends in front of the Museum of
Art on the Benjamin Franklin
Parkway. One of the biggest pro
cycling events outside Europe.
**Philadelphia Marathon**
4301 Parkside Ave, tel: 685-
0054, www.philadelphiamarathon.com.
A full marathon (and 8K run) usually held in November.

## Participant Sports

### Bicycling

For information on bike tours and
other special outings, contact the
**Bicycle Club of Philadelphia**,
www.phillybikeclub.org. Bicycles can

be rented at the following shops:
**Bike Line**, 1028 Arch Street, tel:
923-1310, www.bikeline.com
**Drive Sports**, 2601 Pennsylvania
Ave, tel: 232-7900.
**Drive Sports 2**, 1 Boathouse
Row, tel: 232-7900. Call for
hours. This is an excellent place
to start a biking tour of Fairmount
Park.
**Trophy Bicycles**, 3131 Walnut
Street, tel: 222-2020,
www.trophybikes.com

Equipment and apparel are available at:
**Bike Addicts**, 5548 Ridge Ave,
tel: 487-3006, www.bikeaddicts.com
**Bike Line**, 1028 Arch Street, tel:
923-1310; and 4151 Main
Street, tel: 487-7433
**Breakaway Bikes**, 1923
Chestnut Street, tel: 568-6002,
breakawaybikes.com
**Bustleton Bikes**, 9261 Roosevelt Blvd, tel: 671-1910
**Cadence Performance Cycling**,
4323 Main Street, tel: 508-
4300, www.cadencecycling.com
**Jay's Pedal Power**, 512 E. Girard
Ave, tel: 425-5111
**Mike's Bikes**, 1901 S 13th
Street, tel: 334-9100
**Philadelphia Bike Shop**, 826 N.
Broad Street, tel: 765-9118
**Via Bicycle**, 606 S. 9th Street,
627-3370
**Wissahickon Cyclery**, 7837 Germantown Ave, www.wiss-cycles.com
**Wolff Cycle**, 4311 Lancaster
Ave, tel: 222-2171

### Canoeing and kayaking

**Philadelphia Canoe Club**, 4900
Ridge Ave, tel: 487-9674,
www.philacanoe.org. An excellent
source of information about training and organized trips throughout the Northeast.
**Schuylkill Banks Kayak Tours**,
tel: 610-983-9115, www.schuylkill
banks.org. Kayak instruction and
guided tour of the Schuylkill River
from the Walnut Street Bridge. Call
or check Web site for schedule.

### Fishing

With more than 30 mile of creeks

and rivers, Fairmount Park has
plenty of good places to wet a
line. Fishing licenses are available at city sporting goods stores
or can be purchased online at
www.fish.state.pa.us.

### Golf

**Golf Association of Philadelphia**,
700 Croton Road, Wayne, PA
19087, tel: 610-687-2340,
www.gapgolf.org, represents 132
clubs in the Delaware Valley and
will provide up-to-date information on special events and golf
course availability. The city owns
and manages five municipal
golf courses (tel: 877-1600,
www.golfphilly.com):
**John F. Byrnes Golf Course**,
9500 Leon Street, tel: 632-
8666. 18 holes.
**Cobbs Creek Golf Course**, 7200
Lansdowne Ave, tel: 877-8707.
Two 18-hole courses.
**Juniata Golf Course**, M and
Cayuga Streets, tel: 743-4060.
18 holes.
**Franklin D. Roosevelt Golf
Course**, 20th Street and Pattison
Ave, tel: 462-8997. 18 holes.
**Walnut Lane Golf Course**, 800
Walnut Lane, tel: 482-3370. 18
holes.

### Ice Skating

**RiverRink**
Columbus Blvd. and Market
Street, tel: 925-7565, www.river
rink.com. An Olympic-sized rink in a
heated pavilion at Penn's Landing.

### Skateboarding

**FDR Skate Park**
Pattison Ave. and S. Broad
Street, tel: 683-0205. The Skate
Park in South Philly offers skateboarders a concrete terrain park
designed by and for dedicated
skateboarders.

### Other sports

For information about public tennis courts, ball fields, basketball
courts, bocce alleys and walking,
jogging and horseback riding
trails, log on to the Fairmount
Park website, www.fairmountpark.com.

**A–Z**

# A HANDY SUMMARY OF PRACTICAL INFORMATION, ARRANGED ALPHABETICALLY

**A** Accidents 247
**B** Budgeting for a Visit 247
   Business Hours 247
**C** Car Rentals 247
   Clothing 248
   Consulates 248
**D** Discounts 248
**E** Electricity 248
   Emergency Numbers 248

   Entry Regulations 248
**G** Government 248
**H** Handicapped Access 248
   Health & Medical Care 248
**L** Liquor Laws 249
**M** Maps 249
   Media 249
**P** Parking 250
   Postal Services 250

**R** Religious Services 250
**S** Security & Crime 251
**T** Telephone Codes 252
   Time Zones 252
   Tourist Information 252
**W** Websites 252
   Weather 252

## **A** ccidents

In the case of an emergency or accident, dial **911**. Do not leave the scene of an auto accident until the police arrive.

## **B** udgeting for a Visit

Compared to New York or Boston, Philadelphia is refreshingly inexpensive, although perhaps not as cheap as it once was. If you need to economize, however, there are many options. Numerous websites offer discount lodging. Among them are www.travelocity.com, www.hotels.com, www.priceline.com, www.orbitz.com and www.hotwire.com. Hotel rates vary with season and day of the week. If your travel time is flexible, ask hotels about off-season rates and special

offers. Weekend specials can be especially attractive.

Mainstream restaurants can be expensive, but the city abounds in small, often family-run ethnic restaurants where the prices are modest and the food is excellent. Chinatown is usually a good bet for a cheap meal. Dining at BYOB (bring your own bottle) restaurants will help keep down liquor costs.

## Business Hours

Standard business hours are 9am–5pm. Many banks open a little earlier, usually 8–8.30am, and nearly all close by 5pm. Some have Saturday morning hours. Major department stores and malls are usually open 10am–7pm Mon–Sat, noon–5pm

Sun, with extended hours around the holidays. A few large supermarkets are open 24 hours.

At one time, the shops in downtown Philadelphia were famous for closing promptly at 5pm. That remains true in the business district, but the shops and restaurants around Rittenhouse Square, South Street and parts of Old City do business well into the night.

## **C** ar Rentals

Drivers must be at least 21 to rent a car; some renters specify 25. Rental agencies have offices throughout the city, but you will find the widest choices (and often the best rates) at the airport. A valid driver's license and credit card are required.

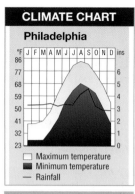

## CLIMATE CHART
### Philadelphia

- ☐ Maximum temperature
- ■ Minimum temperature
- — Rainfall

### Clothing

Philadelphia has four distinct seasons. Summer is hot and humid, with an occasional drenching cloudburst. Winter is bone-chilling. Though heavy snowfall isn't common, it isn't unusual to have two or three significant snowstorms per season. The best plan for spring and fall is to dress in layers so that you can put clothes on or take them off as the weather dictates. Although fancy restaurants and high-class hotels expect visitors to dress appropriately (some require jackets for men), Philadelphians are, by and large, an informal lot. Most casual shops don't mind if you wear neat shorts, a light shirt and tennis shoes during summer, although it's always prudent to call ahead. In the hip parts of town, especially on South Street, just about anything goes. One of the charms of center city is that you can walk just about anywhere, so be sure to wear comfortable shoes or sneakers.

### Consulates

**Canada**: 1500 John F. Kennedy Blvd, Ste 200, Two Penn Center, tel: 854-6380.
**Dominican Republic**: 437 Chestnut Street #216, tel: 923-3006.
**Israel**: 230 S. 15th Street, tel: 546-5556.
**Italy**: 1026 Public Ledger Building, 150 S. 6th Street, tel: 592-7329.

**Mexico**: 111 S. Independence Mall E, Ste 310, Bourse Building, tel: 922-3834.
**Sweden**, 1628 John F. Kennedy Blvd, # 2001, tel: 496-7200.

### D iscounts

**City Pass**, tel: 965-7676 or 800-537-7676. Purchase this pass by phone or in person at the Independence Visitor Center (6th and Market streets) for one-price admission to the National Constitution Center, Academy of Natural Sciences, Independence Seaport Museum, Philadelphia Zoo, Franklin Institute and Philadelphia Trolley Tours.
  **Philadelphia Pass**, tel: 965-7676 or 800-537-7676. The pass grants admission to about 30 attractions for a single flat fee. The attractions include the Franklin Institute, National Constitution Center, Philadelphia Zoo, Eastern State Penitentiary and Longwood Gardens. Passes can be purchased by phone or at the Independence Visitor Center (6th and Market streets).

### E lectricty

Standard American electric current is 110 volts. An adapter is necessary for European appliances, which run on 220–240 volts.

### Emergency Numbers

**Police, Ambulance, Fire**: 911
**Credit cards lost of stolen**:
**AmEx**: 800-528-2121
**Diners Club/Carte Blanche**: 800-234-6377
**MasterCard**: 800-307-7309
**Visa**: 800-336-8472

### Entry Regulations

### Visas & Passports

For a breakdown of up-to-date US entry regulations, visit http://travel.state.gov/visa/index.html. The Visa Office's mailbox for enquiries is usvisa@state.gov. Tel: 202-663-1225.

### Customs

Those over 21 may take into the US: 200 cigarettes, 50 cigars (plus an additional 100, not including Cuban-made, under a gift exemption), or 3 lbs of tobacco; 1 US quart of alcohol; duty-free gifts worth up to $100 (must remain in the US at least 72 hours). Do not bring in meat products, seeds, plants and fruits. For information: www.customs.ustreas.gov
  The US allows you to take out anything you wish, but consult the consulate or tourist authority of the country you are visiting next on its customs regulations for entrance.

### G overnment

Philadelphia is governed by a mayor, who is elected to a four-year term, and a city council of 17 members. Philadelphia voters are overwhelmingly Democrat. A Democrat has held the mayor's office for more than five decades.

### H andicapped Access

SEPTA has a good Web site (www.septa.org/service/accessible_septa.html) with information about accessibility for disabled travelers. SEPTA's Advisory Committee for Accessible Transportation can be reached at 610-353-6640. Or call Septa Customer Service at 580-7800.
  **Artreach** (tel: 568-2115, www.art-reach.org), a nonprofit organization dedicated to making cultural resources available to handicapped and underserved audiences, offers free or discounted tickets to select museums, institutions and events, and has an extensive online guide detailing accessibility of venues throughout the Delaware Valley.

### Health and Medical Care

In the event you need medical assistance, ask the reception staff at your hotel or consult the

Yellow Pages for the physician or pharmacist nearest you. Several hospitals also offer physician referral services for non-emergency visits:

**Children's Hospital of Philadelphia**, tel: 800-879-2467 or www.chop.edu

**Chestnut Hill Hospital**, tel: 753-2000 or www.chh.org

**Hahnemann University Hospital**, tel: 762-7000 or www.hahnemannhospital.com

**Temple University Hospital**, tel: 800-836-7536 or www.health.temple.edu/tuh

**Thomas Jefferson University Hospital**, tel: 800-533-3669 or www.jeffersonhospital.org

**University of Pennsylvania Medical Center**, tel: 800-635-7780 or www.pennhealth.com

If you need immediate attention, go directly to a hospital emergency room. Most emergency rooms are open 24 hours a day.

There is nothing cheap about being ill in the US, whether it involves a simple visit to the doctor or a spell in a hospital. The initial ER fee might be $250, and that's before the additional cost of X-rays, medicine and other special treatments has been added. It is essential to be armed with adequate medical insurance and to carry an identification card or policy number.

Pharmacies sell over-the-counter drugs without a doctor's prescription. For controlled drugs, including narcotics and most antibiotics, you must obtain a written doctor's prescription or, in some cases, you can ask the doctor to call the pharmacy directly.

For a medical emergency, call 911 for an ambulance or go to the nearest emergency room. There are more than 50 hospitals in the Philadelphia area. These hospitals are in or near center city:

**Children's Hospital of Philadelphia**, 34th Street and Civic Center Blvd, tel: 590-1000

**Hahnemann Hospital**, Broad and Vine streets, tel: 762-7000

**Hospital of the University of Pennsylvania**, 3400 Spruce Street, tel: 662-4000

**Thomas Jefferson University Hospital**, 111 S. 11th Street, tel: 955-6000

**Temple University Hospital**, 3401 N. Broad Street, tel: 707-2000

**Pennsylvania Hospital**, 800 Spruce Street, tel: 829-3000

**Graduate Hospital**, 1800 Lombard Street, tel: 893-2000

##  nternet Access

Most business hotels provide high-speed Internet access in the guest rooms; some also have business centers with computers, printers and other office equipment. Computers with Internet access are also available at no charge at Philadelphia public libraries and for a fee at Fedex Kinko's Office and Print Centers. In 2004, the mayor announced an ambitious plan to make low-cost wireless Internet access available throughout the city. Despite the objections of several commercial Internet service providers, the project is expected to be up and running in 2007.

## iquor laws

Thanks to the city's Quaker heritage, Philadelphia's liquor laws are arcane and restrictive. Hard liquor and a limited selection of wines (but not chilled wine) are sold at state liquor stores. Cold beer can be purchased at licensed convenience stores, delis, taverns or restaurants but tends to be expensive. For large quantities of beer at a decent price, you have to go to a beer distributor. Wine, beer and mixed drinks are available by the bottle or by the glass at restaurants with a liquor license. Restaurants that do not serve alcohol usually permit customers to bring their own. The legal drinking age is 21. You may be asked to show picture identification proving your age at bars, restaurants or liquor

stores. Alcohol may not be served at bars or restaurants after 2am, later at private clubs.

## aps

Insight Guides *Fleximap Philadelphia* is laminated for durability and easy folding, and contains travel information as well as exceptionally clear cartography.

## Media

### Print

**Philadelphia Inquirer** (www.philly.com/mld/inquirer) One of the country's best daily papers, with award-winning journalists and in-depth coverage of world, national and local news. Look for the Friday "Weekend" section for entertainment information.

**Daily News** (www.philly.com/mld/dailynews) The self-proclaimed "People Paper" is a daily tabloid, with good overviews of the news, a large sports section and popular special sections.

**Philadelphia Weekly** (www.philadelphiaweekly.com) A free, hip weekly available at street boxes, delis, laundromats and bookstores throughout center city, with reviews and listings of nightclubs, galleries, restaurants, shops and much more.

**Philadelphia City Paper** (www.citypaper.net) Free weekly focusing on arts, entertainment, local people and issues.

**Philadelphia Gay News** (www.epgn.com) A free weekly devoted to the latest news of interest to the gay and lesbian communities as well as information about local events and entertainment.

**Philadelphia Magazine** (www.phillymag.com) A glossy monthly magazine with feature articles covering culture, social life, politics and people in the Delaware Valley. The restaurant reviews are great for tips on the latest developments in the Philly food scene. The rundown of upcoming events, "Datebook," is very helpful.

## Radio Stations

There are more than 50 radio stations on the FM and AM dials in the Philadelphia area. These are some of the major ones:

KYW, 1060AM, News
WDAS, 105.3FM, Soul and R&B
WBEB, 101FM, Soft rock
WMMR, 93.3FM, New and classic rock
WUSL, 99FM, Hip-hop and R&B
WXTU, 92.5FM Country music
WOGL, 98.1FM, Oldies from the 1960s and 70s
WMGK, 102.9FM, Classic rock
WPPZ, 103.9FM, Gospel and Christian
WJJZ, 106.1FM, Smooth jazz
WPHT, 1210AM, Conservative talk
WPEN, 950AM, Sports
WHYY, 91FM, National Public Radio
WXPN, 88.5FM alternative contemporary music

## Television Stations

KYW Channel 3 (CBS)
WPVI Channel 6 (ABC)
WCAU Channel 10 (NBC)
WHYY Channel 12 (PBS)
WPHL Channel 17 (WB)
WPSG Channel 57 (UPN)
WTXF Channel 29 (Fox)

## **P** arking

Parking meters accept coins and Smart Cards, which can be purchased online (www.philapark.org/smartcards/purchase_smartcard.aspx) and shipped to you before your visit. Take note of the regulation signs. The red signs tell you when you can't park, the green signs will tell you when and how long you can park. There are garages and parking lots throughout center city, some operated by the Philadelphia Parking Authority (PPA), others by private owners. You will find PPA lots in center city at:

**Parking Plaza Garage,** 801 Filbert Street
**AutoPark at the Gallery Mall,** Market Street East
**AutoPark at JFK Plaza,** 1500 Arch Street
**AutoPark at City Center,** 15th and Arch Streets

**Philadelphia Gateway Parking Garage,** 1540 Vine Street
**AutoPark at Jefferson,** 10th and Ludlow Streets
**AutoPark at Olde City,** 2nd and Sansom Streets
**AutoPark at Independence Mall,** 5th and Market Streets
**Parkway Museums,** 19th and Callowhill Streets
**Rittenhouse Square,** 20th and Sansom Streets

## Postal services

You can count on post offices in Philadelphia to be open 9am–5pm Mon–Fri, 9am–noon Sat, although many locations, especially the larger ones, have extended hours. The Main Post Office (2970 Market St.) is open daily 6am–midnight. The William Penn Annex (900 Market Street) is open 8.30am–6pm Mon–Fri, 8.30am–4pm Sat.

For overnight delivery, try Express Mail. For expedited delivery, often within two days, ask for Priority Mail. Call 800-725-2161 or log on www.usps.com for information.

Post offices in center city:
**William Penn Annex,** 900 Market Street, 19107-9998
**Continental,** 615 Chestnut Street, 19106-9997
**Penn Center,** 1500 John F. Kennedy Blvd, 19102-9997
**John Wanamaker,** 1234 Market Street, 19107-9997
**B Free Franklin,** 316 Market Street, 19106-9996
**Land Title Bldg,** 100 S. Broad Street, 19110-9997
**Middle City,** 2037 Chestnut Street, 19103-9997
**Main Post Office,** 2970 Market Street, 19104-9741
**30th Street Station,** 2955 Market Street, 19104-9775
**Penns Landing,** 622 S. 4th Street, 19147-9997

## Courier Service

For overnight or expedited delivery of letters and packages, contact FedEx (800-463-3339 or www.fedex.com), DHL (800-225-

5345 or www.dhl-usa.com), or United Parcel Service (800-742-5877 or www.ups.com) for the office or drop box nearest you.

FedEx Kinko's shipping centers in center city:
**Philadelphia Marriott,** 1201 Market Street, tel: 923-2520
**121 S. Broad Street,** tel: 546-4710
**1500 Market Street,** tel: 563-6755
**216 S. 16th Street,** tel: 732-2033
**Commerce Building,** 2001 Market Street, tel: 561-5170

UPS locations in center city:
**1735 Market Street,** tel: 567-6006
**51 N. 3rd Street,** tel: 629-4990
**1500 Market Street,** tel: 800-742-5877
**Staples,** 1044 Market Street, tel: 923-0109
**Silver Star Shipping,** 122 N. 10th Street, tel: 829-4497
**Staples,** 1500 Chestnut Street, tel: 864-9520
**Can Do,** 1530 Locust Street, tel: 790-1100
**South Street Mail Box Plus,** 808 South Street, tel: 592-8000
**211 South Street,** tel: 733-9200

## **R** eligious services

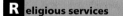

### Christian churches

**Arch Street United Methodist Church,** 55 N. Broad Street, tel: 568-6250
**Arch Street Friends Meeting House,** 320 Arch Street, tel: 627-2667
**Bethany Bethel Church of God,** 1123 Race Street, tel: 972-5560
**Chambers Wylie Memorial Presbyterian,** 315 S. Broad Street, tel: 735-4847
**Chinese Christian Church & Center,** 225 N. 10th Street, tel: 627-2360
**First Unitarian Church,** 2125 Chestnut Street, tel: 563-3980
**St. George Greek Orthodox Cathdral,** 56 S. 8th Street, tel: 627-4389

**Christ Church,** 20 N. American Street, tel: 922-1695
**Church of the Holy Trinity,** 1904 Walnut Street, tel: 567-1267
**Most Blessed Sacrament Church,** 610 Pine Street, tel: 610-845-2460
**Mother Bethel A.M.E. Church,** 419 Richard Allen Ave (6th and Lombard sts), tel: 925-0616.
**Old City Mission,** 162 N. 3rd Street, tel: 413-3040
**Old First Reformed United Church of Christ Church,** 153 N. 4th Street, tel: 922-9663
**Old Pine St Presbyterian Church,** 412 Pine Street, tel: 925-8051
**Old St. Joseph's Church,** 321 Willings Alley, tel: 923-1733
**Old St. Mary's Church,** 252 S. 4th Street, tel: 923-7930
**Queen of Peace Roman Catholic Church,** 314 Chestnut Street, tel: 570-226-4644
**Sheffield Ludlow Lutheran Parish,** 110 Church Street, tel: 814-968-3912
**St George's United Methodist Church,** 235 N. 4th Street, tel: 925-7788

**BELOW:** Avenue of the Arts.

**Cathedral of Sts Peter & Paul,** 1723 Race Street, tel: 561-1313
**First Presbyterian Church,** 201 S. 21st Street, tel: 567-0532
**Girard Avenue Welsh Presbyterian Church,** 1724 Arch Street, tel: 563-3763
**St. John the Evangelist Catholic Church,** 21 S. 13th Street, tel: 563-5432
**St. Mark's Parish,** 1625 Locust Street, tel: 545-9921
**St. Peter's Church,** 3rd and Pine Streets, tel: 925-5968
**Tenth Presbyterian Church,** 1701 Delancey Street, tel: 735-7688
**New Central Baptist Church,** 2139 Lombard Street, tel: 732-4267

## Synagogues
**Bnai Abraham,** 527 Lombard Street, tel: 238-2100
**Congregation B'nai Abraham,** 527 Lombard Street, tel: 627-3123
**Congregation Mikveh Israel,** 44 N. 4th Street, tel: 922-5446
**Israel Kesher Congregation,** 412 Lombard Street, tel: 922-7736
**Mishkan Shalom,** 4101 Freeland Avenue, tel: 508-0226
**Society Hill Synagogue,** 418 Spruce Street, tel: 922-6590
**Temple Beth Zion Beth Israel,** 300 S. 18th Street, tel: 735-5148
**United Synagogue of Judaism,** 1510 Chestnut Street, tel: 563-8809
**Vilna Congregation,** 509 Pine Street, tel: 592-9433

## Mosques
**United Muslim Masjid,** 810 S. 15th Street, tel: 546-6555

## Buddhist Temples
**Bo De Vietnamese Buddhist Temple,** 1114-20 S. 13th Street (at Washington Ave) 19147

## Hindu Temples
**Bharatiya Temple,** 1612 County-line Road, Montgomeryville, PA 18936, tel: 442-1499
**Samarpan Hindu Temple,** 6515, Bustleton Ave, Philadelphia, PA, 19149, tel: 537-9537

### Reservations

It is advisable to make reservations well in advance at all hotels, especially during the warm-weather tourist season. Reservations are essential at finer restaurants and always a good idea at more casual places. If a restaurant doesn't take reservations, you can call ahead and ask how long the wait will be, if any. Overbooking is not a big problem in Philadelphia. Most restaurants make a genuine effort to seat customers promptly.

### S ecurity & Crime

Like other big cities, crime is a concern in Philadelphia, but with a few common-sense precautions you shouldn't run into any trouble. For starters, don't carry large sums of cash or wear flashy or expensive jewelry. Hang on to your purse or shoulder bag and keep your wallet in your front pocket. Avoid traveling alone at night, and stay clear of deserted areas. Your best asset is knowing where you are and where you are going. With a little planning, you should be able to avoid dangerous areas.

If you take the subway at night, be sure to stand near other people or, if possible, a SEPTA police officer. Avoid riding in a car with just a few people in it. If you get on an empty bus, sit near the driver.

If you are mugged or run into some other trouble, call or go to the nearest police station and report the crime. The police may not be much help finding your assailant, but they can do the proper paperwork for insurance claims. There is no good response to a mugging. Your safest bet is to give the mugger your money and leave the area as quickly as possible. Report the crime immediately to the police.

For police, medical or fire emergencies, dial 911.

### Loss of Belongings

If any of your possessions are lost or stolen in Philadelphia,

TRANSPORTATION   ACCOMMODATIONS   ACTIVITIES   A – Z

report it to the police at once. It is unlikely that your property will be returned, but they will have you file reports necessary to make an insurance claim. Auto theft and break-ins are a problem in Philadelphia. Keep your car doors locked, and keep all belongings in the trunk. If you are traveling with anything particularly valuable, you may want to ask your concierge to lock it in the hotel safe.

### Lost Luggage

If your luggage is lost or delayed en route to Philadelphia by air, many airlines will deliver it to your hotel when, or if, it is found. If you don't already have insurance for lost or stolen luggage, ask your airline, travel agent or insurance company for a travel policy. Be sure each piece of luggage has an identification tag.

### Telephone Codes

The Philadelphia area code is 215. Area codes are necessary for long-distance calls – that is, calls outside the area code from which you are calling.

### Time Zones

Philadelphia is in the Eastern Time Zone. When it is noon in Philadelphia, it is 11am in Chicago, 9am in Los Angeles, 2am in Tokyo, 5pm in London and 8pm in Moscow. The clock is set one hour ahead on the first Sunday in April for daylight savings time and one hour back on the last Sunday in October to return to eastern standard time.

### Tipping

Service personnel in Philadelphia depend on tips for a large portion of their income. Gratuities are not automatically tallied into the bill. Some guidelines:
● Gratuities are not included in restaurant bills, unless you see a note on the menu or the bill to that effect. Waiters and bar-tenders are usually given 15 percent, somewhat more for exceptional service.
● The accepted rate for doormen, baggage handlers, skycaps and porters is about $1 per bag.
● Taxi drivers usually get 15 percent of the fare.
● Hairdressers, manicurists and masseurs usually receive 10–15 percent.
● It is not necessary – but always greatly appreciated – to tip chamber staff, especially if you stay at a hotel for several days.
● Parking valets should be tipped when they retrieve your car; $2 is usually adequate.

### Tourist Information

**Brandywine Visitor Welcome Center**, 1 Beaver Valley Road, Chadds Ford, PA 19317, tel: 610-565-3679 or 800-343-3983, www.brandywinecvb.com
**Bucks County Visitor Center**, 3207 Street Road, Bensalem, PA 19020, tel: 639-0300 or 800-836-2825, www.experience buckscounty.com
**Chester County Visitor Center**, Route 1, Kennett Square, PA 19348, tel: 800-228-9933, www.brandywinevalley.com.
**Independence Visitors Center**, 6th and Market Streets, tel: 800-537-7676, www.independencevisitor center.com. Information and tickets available for a wide range of attraction and tours throughout the city.
**Philadelphia Convention and Visitors Bureau**, 1700 Market Street, Suite 3000, tel: 636-3300, www.pcvb.org
**Valley Forge Convention and Visitors Bureau**, 600 W. Germantown Pike, Suite 130, Plymouth Meeting, PA 19462, tel: 610-834-1550, www.valleyforge.org

### Weather

Philadelphia's weather runs the gamut: hot and sticky in summer, biting cold in winter, pleasant but occasionally rainy in spring, cool and crisp in fall.

Summer brings sudden, intense rainstorms; winter has a few heavy snowfalls. Perhaps the most accurate thing one can say about Philadelphia weather is that it's unpredictable. Unseasonable cold or warm spells are not uncommon, Indian summer sometimes extends balmy weather well into October, and snow can fall as late as March.

### Websites

**Friends of Independence National Historic Park**, www.ushistory.org/independence
**Greater Philadelphia Tourism Marketing Corporation**, www.gophila.com
**Independence National Historic Park**, www.nps.gov/inde
**Independence Visitors Center**, www.independencevisitorcenter.com
**Pennsylvania Tourism**, www.visitpa.com
**Philadelphia Convention and Visitors Bureau**, gwww.pcvb.org
**Southeastern Pennsylvania Transportation Authority** (SEPTA), www.septa.org

### Weights and Measures

Despite efforts to convert to metric, the US still uses the Imperial system of weights and measures.

1 inch = 2.54 centimeters
1 foot = 30.48 centimeters
1 yard = 0.9144 meter
1 mile = 1.609 kilometers
1 pint = 0.473 liter
1 quart = 0.946 liter
1 ounce = 28.4 grams
1 pound = 0.453 kilogram
1 acre = 0.405 hectare
1 square mile = 259 hectares

1 centimeter = 0.394 inch
1 meter = 39.37 inches
1 kilometer = 0.621 mile
1 liter = 1.057 quarts
1 gram = 0.035 ounce
1 kilogram = 2.205 pounds
1 hectare = 2.471 acres
1 square kilometer = 0.386 square mile

# FURTHER READING

*The Autobiography and Other Writings* by Benjamin Franklin (Bantam, 1982).

*Benjamin Franklin: His Life As He Wrote It* by Esmond Wright, ed. (Harvard University Press, 1990).

*Burning Down The House: MOVE and the Tragedy of Philadelphia* by John Anderson and Hilary Hevenor (W.W. Norton & Company, 1987).

*By the Beautiful Sea: The Rise and High Times of That Great American Resort Atlantic City* by Charles Funnell (Knopf, 1975).

*Caught Dead in Philadelphia* by Gillian Roberts (Fawcett, 1988). The first entry in a popular mystery series featuring schoolteacher and part-time sleuth Amanda Pepper.

*The Cop Who Would Be King: Mayor Frank Rizzo* by Joseph R. Daughen and Peter Binzen (Little, Brown and Company, 1977).

*Decision in Philadelphia: The Constitutional Convention of 1787* by Christopher Collier (Ballantine 1987).

*Faces of Revolution: Personalities and Themes in the Struggle for American Independence* by Bernard Bailyn (Knopf, 1990).

*Franklin of Philadelphia* by Esmond Wright (Harvard University Press, 1986). A Franklin biography.

*Good in Bed* by Jennifer Weiner (Washington Square Press, 2002). "Chick lit" novels, including *Little Earthquakes* and *In Her Shoes*, which was made into a star-studded movie, are set mostly in Philadelphia.

*Have Your Cake and Kill Him Too* by Nancy Martin (NAL, 2006). A mystery series starring quirky Main Line heiresses the Blackbird Sisters.

*If Football's a Religion, Why Don't We Have a Prayer?*

*Philadelphia, Its Faithful, and the Eternal Quest for Sports Salvation* by Jere Longman (HarperCollins 2005).

*Kelroy* by Rebecca Rush (Oxford University Press, 1993). A novel of manners à la Jane Austen set in early 19th-century Philadelphia.

*"Let It Burn!" The Philadelphia Tragedy* by Michael Boyette (Contemporary Books, 1989).

*A Little Revenge: Benjamin Franklin and His Son* by Willard Randall (Little, Brown & Co, 1984).

*Men in Blue* by W. E. B. Griffin (Jove Books, 1991). The first in the gritty Badge of Honor crime series about the Philadelphia police.

*The Mercer Mile: The Story of Henry Chapman Mercer and His Three Concrete Buildings* by Helen Hartman Gemmill (Bucks County Historical Society, 1987).

*Miracle At Philadelphia: The Story of the Constitutional Convention May–September 1787* by Catherine Drinker Bowen (Back Bay Books, 1986).

*Oh! Dem Golden Slippers: The Story of the Philadelphia Mummers* by Charles E. Welch (Book Street Press, 1970).

*Pennsylvania: A Bicentennial History* by Thomas C. Cochran (W.W. Norton & Company, 1978).

*The Perennial Philadelphians* by Nathaniel Burt (Little, Brown and Co., 1963).

*Philadelphia: A 300-Year History* by Russell F. Weigley, ed. (W.W. Norton & Company, 1982).

*Philadelphia Architecture: A Guide to the City* by John Andrew Gallery, ed. (MIT Press, 1984).

*Philadelphia Fire* by John Edgar Wideman (Pan MacMillan, 1995). A writer returns to Philadelphia to write about the MOVE bombing.

*Philadelphia Gentlemen* by E.

Digby Baltzell (University of Pennsylvania Press, 1979).

*Philadelphia: Holy Experiment* by Struthers Burt (Doubleday, Doran & Company, 1945).

*Philadelphia: Portrait of an American City* by Edwin Wolf, ed. (Stackpole Books, 1975).

*The Philadelphia Reader* by Robert Huber and Benjamin Wallace, eds. (Temple University Press, 2006). Profiles of and by the most notable Philadelphians of the last 20 years, from the pages of *Philadelphia* magazine.

*The Price of a Child* by Lorene Cary (Vintage, 1996). Based on a true story of an escaped slave, this novel focuses on the Underground Railroad in Philadelphia.

*Rizzo* by Fred Hamilton (Viking Press, 1973).

*Still Philadelphia: A Photographic History, 1890–1940* by Fredric Miller et al (Temple University Press, 1983).

*Sunday Macaroni Club* by Steve Lopez (Plume, 1999). Former *Philadelphia Inquirer* columnist Lopez spins a yarn about South Philadelphia politics. His previous novel *Third and Indiana* is a darker tale about the gang infested "Badlands" of North Philadelphia.

*Tumbling* by Diane Mckinney-Whetstone (Touchstone, 1997). A moving family story set in an African-American neighborhood in South Philadelphia in the 1940s. Mckinney-Whetstone's other novels, including *Tempest Rising, Leaving Cecil Street* and *Blues Dancing,* are set against the backdrop of Philadelphia's black community of various periods.

*William Penn and the Founding of Pennsylvania, 1680-1684* by Jean R. Soderlund, ed. (University of Pennsylvania Press, 1983).

# ART & PHOTO CREDITS

All photographs by Bob Krist
except the following:

**Bridgeman Art Library** 20, 23
**Chester County Conference and
Visitors Bureau** 212B
**Cigna Museum & Art Collection** 17
**Independence National Historical
Park** 21, 30, 121
**Joyce Naltchayan/AFP** 28
**Library Company of Philadelphia**
18/19
**Library of Congress** 25
**Joseph Nettis** 149BL, 167
**Richard Nowitz** 36, 38, 182,
184, 194, 211, 214B, 215
**Pennsylvania Dutch Convention &
Visitors Bureau** 189, 190, 191,
192T, 193B, 195B, 196T
**Philadelphia Phillies** 49, 50
**Urban Archives, Temple
University** 26, 27
**G. Widman/Greater Philadelphia
Tourism Marketing Corporation**
179

**Pages 40/41**: *All photography:*
Bob Krist
**Pages 78/79**: *All photography:*
The Ronald Grant Archive except
*top center right:* British Film
Institute, *top right:* Topham
Picturepoint and *center left:* The
Kobal Collection.
**Pages 148/149**: *All photography:*
Bob Krist except 149BL: Joseph
Nettis
**Pages 198/199**: *All photography:*
Bob Krist

**Map Production:** Stephen Ramsay

©2007 Apa Publications GmbH & Co.
Verlag KG, Singapore Branch

# PHILADELPHIA STREET ATLAS

The key map shows the area of Philadelphia covered by the atlas section. An index of street names and places of interest shown on the maps can be found on the following pages. For each entry there is a page number and grid reference.

## Map Legend

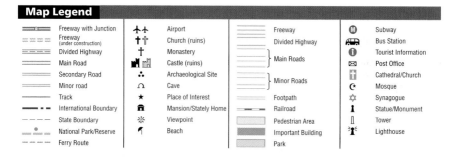

| | | | | | |
|---|---|---|---|---|---|
| Freeway with Junction | ✈ ✈ Airport | | Freeway | Ⓜ | Subway |
| Freeway (under construction) | † ✝ Church (ruins) | | Divided Highway | 🚌 | Bus Station |
| Divided Highway | † Monastery | | } Main Roads | ❶ | Tourist Information |
| Main Road | 🏰 🏚 Castle (ruins) | | | ✉ | Post Office |
| Secondary Road | ∴ Archaeological Site | | } Minor Roads | ✝ | Cathedral/Church |
| Minor road | ∩ Cave | | Footpath | ☾ | Mosque |
| Track | ★ Place of Interest | | Railroad | ✡ | Synagogue |
| International Boundary | ⌂ Mansion/Stately Home | | Pedestrian Area | ⚊ | Statue/Monument |
| State Boundary | ☼ Viewpoint | | Important Building | ⌷ | Tower |
| National Park/Reserve | ⚑ Beach | | Park | ⛴ | Lighthouse |
| Ferry Route | | | | | |

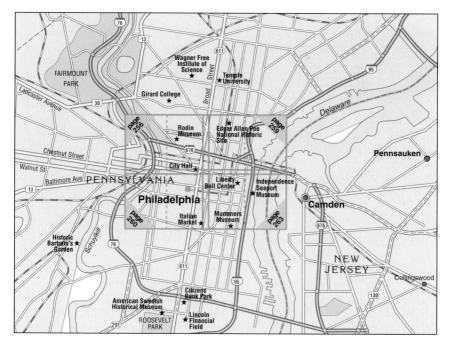

**A**

**B**

Boathouse Row

Kelly Drive

Pennsylvania Avenue

Aspen St

Meredith St

Perot St

26th Street

25th Street

Olive St

Fairmount Avenue

Walla

0          400 yards

0          400 m

Schuylkill

34th Street

76

FAIRMOUNT PARK

24th Street

Pennsylvania Avenue

1

Mantua Ave

34th Street

33rd Street

Melon St

Fairmount Water Works

Philadelphia Museum of Art

Wallace St

Mt Vernon St

Haverford Avenue

32nd St

31st St

Eakins Oval

Brandywine St

Spring Garden St

Napa St

24th St

Parktown Pla

2

33rd Street

34th St

Hamilton St

Baring St

Cornerstone

Pearl St

**MANTUA**

Powelton Avenue

Spangler St

Natrona St

Winter St

Summer St

MUSEUM DISTRICT

Race St

3

Lancaster St

34th Street

Cherry St

Arch St

32nd St

Race St

23rd St

Cherry

University City Science Center

33rd St

Cuthbert St

103rd Engineer's Armory

Arch Street

34th Street

M

3

Market Street

John F. Kennedy Blvd

30th St

Amtrak 30th Street Station

John F. Kennedy Boulevа

Ludlow St

30th Street

M

Market Street

Drexel University

Paul Peck Alumni Center

Schuylkill Ave W

Ludlow St

Penn Law School

Chestnut Street

Drexel Main Building

Ludlow St

Schuylkill

Mütter Museum

4

33rd St

Mandell Theater

32nd St

Chestnut Street

Chestnut St

22nd Street

23rd St

Walnut Street

31st St

30th St

Rittenhouse Laboratories

Class of 1923 Ice Rink

Walnut Street

Jones Way

Sansom St

University of Pennsylvania

**A**

**B**

A
B

Burns St
Carlisle St
Broad Street
Ogden St
Myrtle St
Park Ave
Parrish St
12th St
11th St
Ogden St
Poplar St
Darien St
Cambridge
6th St
Randolph St
5th Street

Brown St

**SPRING GARDEN**
N

Parrish St
10th St

1

Fairmount
M
13th St
Fairmount Avenue
Potts St
Melon St
Park Ave
Olive St
8th St
7th St
Percy St
Brown St
7th St
Marshall St
**Saint Nicholas** ✝
Parrish St
Reno St
Myrt

Watts St
Lemon St
Camac St
Wallace St
North St
Melon St
Fairmount Avenue
6th Street
5th Street
Olive

Broad St
**Congregation Rodeph Shalom** ✡
Lemon St
**POPLAR**
Mount Vernon St
Clay St
10th St
11th St
Wallace St
8th St
7th St
**LUDLOW**
Wallace

Green St
Brandywine St
Ridge Avenue
13th St
12th St
Brandywine St
Percy St
Perth St
Green St

2

M
**Spring Garden**
Spring Garden Street
Spring Garden Street
**Edgar Allan Poe National Historic Site**

Nectarine St
Buttonwood St
Nectarine St
Hamilton St
Noble St
13th St
12th St
11th St
10th St
Percy St
9th St
8th St
7th St
6th Street
5th Street

Callowhill Street
Carlton St
Wood St
Vine St
Willow St
**Callowhill Street**
Callowhill Stre

3

676
Summer St
Winter St
Spring St
Spring St
**CHINATOWN**
Franklin Street
**Franklin Square**
Wood St
Vine St
Lawrence St
New

Race Street
Chinatown M
Race Street
Florist St
**OLD CITY**

**Pennsylvania Convention Center**
Cherry St
Appletree St
**Chinese Friendship Gate**
**Chinese Cultural and Community Center**
9th St
**African-American Museum in Philadelphia**
Cherry St
Independence Mall West
**National Constitution Center**
Race Street
**US Mint**
Cherry St
Arch Stre

4

Arch Street
13th St
**Chinese Friendship Gate**
**Hilton Garden Inn**
Cuthbert St
8th St
Arch Street
7th St
**Free Quaker Meeting House**
**Arch Street Friends Meeting House**

Filbert St
Commerce St
**Reading Terminal Market**
12th St
11th St
10th St
**Greyhound Bus Terminal**
Filbert St
CHRIST CHURCH BURIAL GROUND ✝ ✝
**Congregation Mikveh Israel** ✡

M
**13th Street**
**Loews**
**11th Street**
**Market East Station**
**The Gallery**
Market Street
**Market Place East**
7th St
5th St
**Independence Visitor Center**

A
B

Rittenhouse
Laboratories

Palestra

Class of 1923
Ice Rink

Walnut Street

Jones Way

Sansom St

Walnut Street

34th Street

33rd Street

Franklin
Field

University
of Pennsylvania

30th Street

Locust St

28th St

22nd St

University of Pennsylvania
Museum of Archaeology
and Anthropology

UNIVERSITY
CITY

Manning St

24th St

Spruce St

Cyprus St

Convention Ave

South Street

76

Delancey St

Panama St

SCHUYLKILL
RIVER PARK

Fitler
Square

University
City Station

Center for
Advanced
Medicine

Pine St

Waverly St

Lombard St

25th St

24th St

Schuylkill

27th St

Taney St

26th St

Naudain St

21st Street

Tryon St

22nd Street

Rodman St

South Street

23rd St

Bainbridge St

Schuylkill Expressway

Kater St

Schuylkill Ave

Pemberton St

Fitzwater St

Catharine St

Academy Cir

Madison Sq.

Catharine St

Christian St

Grays Ferry Avenue

Kauffman St

Madison Sq.

Norfolk St

Christian St

Madison S

21st Street

Christian S

St Charles

Carpenter St

Montrose St

Peltz St

Kimball St

25th St

24th St

29th St

Ellsworth St

Washington Avenue

23rd St

League St

22nd Street

Kimball St

Grays Ferry Avenue

Ellsworth St

Alter St

Annin St

Federal St

Ellsworth St

Alter St

Oakford St

Ingram St

Manton St

Federal St

Latona St

Manton St

Titan St

Wharton St

Oakford St

29th St

Dover St

Newkirk St

28th St

Sears St

27th St

Earp St

26th St

Latona St

Titan St

Reed St

Bucknell St

Bonsall St

Wharton St

21st Street

20th St

Breeze Ave

0          400 yards

0          400 m

WARTON
SQUARE
PARK

25th St

Taylor St

Ringgold St

24th St

23rd St

22nd Street

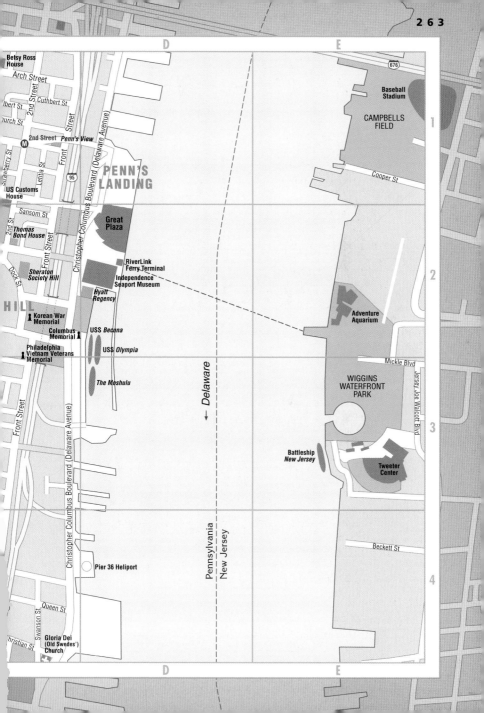

Betsy Ross
House
Arch Street
2nd Street
Cuthbert St
lbert St
urch St
Strawberry St
2nd Street
M 2nd Street   Penn's View
Letitia St
Front Street
Christopher Columbus Boulevard (Delaware Avenue)
95
US Customs
House
Sansom St
2nd St
Thomas
Bond House
Front Street
Dock St
Sheraton
Society Hill
HILL
Korean War
Memorial
Columbus
Memorial
Philadelphia
Vietnam Veterans
Memorial
Front Street
Christopher Columbus Boulevard (Delaware Avenue)
Queen St
Swanson St
Christian St
Gloria Dei
(Old Swedes')
Church

D

E

676

Baseball
Stadium
CAMPBELLS
FIELD
1

Cooper St

PENN'S
LANDING

Great
Plaza

RiverLink
Ferry Terminal
Independence
Seaport Museum
Hyatt
Regency

USS *Becona*

USS *Olympia*

The Moshulu

Adventure
Aquarium
2

Mickle Blvd

WIGGINS
WATERFRONT
PARK

Jersey Joe Walcott Blvd

3

← *Delaware*

Battleship
*New Jersey*

Tweeter
Center

Pennsylvania
New Jersey

Beckett St

Pier 36 Heliport

4

D

E

# STREET INDEX

2nd Street 259 C4–D1, 262
  C4–C3, 263 C2–C1
3rd Street 258 C4, 259
  C3–C1, 262 B4–C1
4th Street 258 C4–C3, 259
  C2–C1, 262 B4–C1
5th Street 258 B4–C1, 262
  B4–B1
6th Street 258 B3–C1, 262
  B4–B2
7th Street 258 B4–B1, 262
  A4–B1
8th Street 258 B4–B1, 262
  A4–B1
9th Street 258 B4–B3, 262
  A4–A1
10th Street 258 A4–B1, 261
  E4, 262 A4–A1
11th Street 258 A4–B1, 261
  E4–E2, 262 A4–A1
12th Street 257 E4, 258
  A4–A1, 261 E4–E1, 262
  A2–A1
13th Street 257 E4–E3, 258
  A4–A1, 261 E4–E1
15th Street 257 E4–E1, 261
  D4–D1
16th Street 257 D4–E1, 261
  D4–D1
17th Street 257 D4–E1, 261
  D4–D1
18th Street 257 D4–D1,
  261 D4–D1
19th Street 257 D4–D1,
  261 C4–D1
20th Street 257 C4–D1, 260
  C4, 261 C3–C1
21st Street 257 C4–D1, 260
  C4–C1, 261 C1
22nd Street 256 C4, 257
  C3–C1, 260 B4–C1
23rd Street 256 C4–C3, 257
  C1, 260 B4–C1
24th Street 256 C2–C1, 260
  B4–B1
25th Street 256 C1, 260
  B4–B2
26th Street 256 B1, 260
  A4, B2
27th Street 260 A4, B2
28th Street 260 A4
29th Street 260 A4–A3
30th Street 256 B4–B3,
  260 B1
31st Street 256 B4, A2
32nd Street 256 A4, A3–A2
33rd Street 256 A4–A1,
  260 A1
34th Street 256 A3–A2–A1,
  260 A1
103rd Engineer's Armory
  256 A3

**A**
Academy Circle 260 B3
Academy of Music 261 E2
Academy of Natural Sciences
  257 D3
Academy of Vocal Arts 261
  C2
Addison Street 261 C2, D2,
  262 A2
Adventure Aquarium 263 E2

African-American Museum in
  Philadelphia 258 B4
Alder Street 262 A3
Allen Street 259 D1–E1
Alter Street 260 B3–C4,
  261 C4, D4
American Street 259
  C3–D1, 262 C3
Amtrak 30th Street Station
  256 B3
Annin Street 260 A3,
  261 D4, E4
Anthropologie 261 D1
Antique Row 262 A2
Appletree Street 257 C3,
  D4, 258 A4
Arch Street 256 A3, B3,
  257 C4–E4, 258 A4–B4,
  259 C4, 263 C1
Arch Street Friends Meeting
  House 262 C1
Arch Street Presbyterian
  Church 257 D4
Arch Street United
  Methodist Church 257 E4
Aspen Street 256 C1
Athenaeum 262 B2

**B**
Back Place 261 E2
Bainbridge Street 260 B2,
  261 C2–E3, 262 A3–B3
Bank Street 262 C1
Baring Street 256 A2
Battleship New Jersey
  263 E3
Beach Street 259 D3
Beck Street 262 C4
Beckett Street 263 E4
Benjamin Franklin Bridge
  259 D4
Benjamin Franklin Parkway
  257 C2–D3
Betsy Ross House 259 C4
Boathouse Row 256 A1
Bodine Street 259 C4, D1,
  262 C1
Bonsall Street 260 B4
Bourse 262 C1
Bouver Street 261 C4
Bradford Street 262 A3
Brandywine Street 256 A2,
  257 C2–E2, 258 A2
Bread Street 259 C4
Breeze Avenue 260 C4
Broad Street 257 E4–E1,
  258 A2–A1, 261 D4–E1
Brown Street 257 D1, E1,
  258 A1–B1, 259 C2–D2
Bucknell Street 260 B4
Burns Street 257 E1,
  258 A1
Buttonwood Street 257 D2,
  E2, 258 A2

**C**
Callowhill Street 257
  D2–E3, 258 A3–C3
Camac Street 258 A2, 261
  E2
Cambridge Street 258 C1,
  259 C1
Cameron Street 257 D1

Campbell's Field 263 E1
Canal Street 259 D2
Capitol Street 257 D1
Carlisle Street 257 E1,
  258 A1
Carlton Street 257 D2, E3,
  258 A3
Carpenters Street 260 B3,
  261 C3–E4, 262 A4–B4
Cathedral of Saints Peter
  and Paul 257 D3
Catharine Street 260 A3,
  B3, 261 C3–E3, 262 A3,
  B4–C4
Chadwick Street 261 D4, D3
Chancellor Street 261 D1, E1
Center for Advanced
  Medicine 260 A1
Cherry Street 256 A3, C3,
  257 D3–E4, 258 A4–B4,
  C4
Chestnut Street 256 A4–C4,
  257 D4, 261 C1–E1, 262
  A1–C1
Chinese Cultural and
  Community Center 258 A4
Chinese Friendship Gate 258
  A4
Christ Church Burial
  Ground 262 C1
Christian Street 260 A3–C3,
  261 D3–E3, 262 A3–A4,
  B4, 263 C4
Christopher Columbus
  Boulevard (Delaware
  Avenue) 259 D4–D3, 263
  C4–D1
Church Street 263 C1
City Hall 257 E4
Civil War Library and
  Museum 261 D2
Class of 1923 Ice Rink
  256 A4
Clay Street 258 A2
Cleveland Street 261 C3
Clifton Street 261 E4, E3,
  262 A4, A3
Clinton Street 262 A2
Clover Street 261 E1,
  262 A1
Colombia Avenue 259 E1
Colorado Street 261 D4
Columbus Memorial 263 C2
Commerce Street 257 C4,
  D4, E4, 258 A4, 262 C1
Community College of
  Philadelphia 257 D2
Congregation Mikveh Israel
  262 C1
Congregation Rodeph
  Shalom 257 E2
Convention Avenue 260 A2
Cooper Street 263 E1
Corinthian Avenue 257 D1
Crease Street 259 E1
Crosskey Street 257 C1
Curtis Center 262 B1
Curtis Institute of Music
  261 D1
Cuthbert Street 256 A3,
  257 C4–D4, E4, 258 A4,
  263 C1
Cyprus Street 260 B1, 261
  E2, 262 A2, B2

**D**
Darien Street 258 B2, B1,
  262 A3, A2

Darien Way 262 A4
Day Street 259 E1
Delancey Place 261 C2
Delancey Street 261 B1,
  262 B2–C2
Delaware Avenue 259 E1
Delhi Street 262 A3
Dock Street 263 C2
Dorrance Street 261 C3
Dover Street 260 A4
Drexel Main Building
  256 A4
Drexel University 256 A4
Drury Street 261 E1
Dunton Street 259 D1

**E**
Eakins Oval 256 C2
Earp Street 260 A4
Eastern State Penitentiary
  257 C1
Edgar Allan Poe National
  Historic Site 258 B2
Edward Street 259 D1
Elfreth's Alley 259 C4
Ellen Street 259 D2
Ellsworth Street 260
  A3–B4, 261 C4–E4
Erin Street 257 D3

**F**
Fabric Row 262 B3
Fairmount Avenue 256 C1,
  257 D1–E1, 258 A1–B2,
  259 D2–C2
Fairmount Waterworks
  256 B1
Federal Street 260 A4–B4,
  261 C4–E4
Filbert Street 257 E4, 258
  A4–B4, 262 B1, 263 C1
Fireman's Hall Museum
  259 C4
First Bank of the United
  States 262 C2
First Unitarian Church 257
  C4
Fitler Square 260 B2
Fitzwater Street 260 C3,
  261 D3–E3, 262 A3–B3
Florist Street 258 C4
Folsom Street 257 D1
Forrest Theatre 261 E1
Francis Street 257 E1
Frankford Avenue 259 E1
Franklin Court 262 C1
Franklin Field 260 A1
Franklin Institute 257 C3
Franklin Square 258 B4
Franklin Street 258 B4
Franklintown Boulevard
  257 D3
Free Library of Philadelphia
  257 D3
Free Quaker Meeting House
  258 B4
Front Street 259 D3–D1,
  262 C4, 263 C3–C1
Fulton Street 262 B4–C4

**G**
Gallery, The 262 A1
Galloway Street 259 C1
Gaskill Street 262 B3
George Street 259 C1
Germantown Avenue
  259 D1
Girard Avenue 259 D1

Gloria Dei (Old Swedes')
  Church 263 C4
Graduate Hospital 261 D2
Grays Ferry Avenue 260
  A3–B3
Great Plaza 263 D2
Green Street 257 D1–E2,
  258 A2–B2, 259 C2
Greyhound Bus Terminal
  258 A4

**H**
Hall Street 262 A4, B4
Hamilton Street 256 A2,
  257 D2, E2, 258 A2
Hancock Street 259 D2–D1
Haverford Avenue 256 A2
Head House Market 262 C3
Head House Square 262 C3
Henry George School and
  Birthplace Musuem 262 A2
Hicks Street 261 D3, D2
Historical Society of
  Pennsylvania and Balch
  Institute 261 E2
Holy Trinity 261 C1
Hope Street 259 D2–D1
Howard Street 262 C4
Hutchinson Street 262 A3
Hyatt Regency Hotel
  263 D2

**I**
Iconic Street 262 B1
Immaculate Conception 259
  D1
Independence Hall 262 B1
Independence Mall West 262
  B1
Independence National
  Historical Park 262 B2
Independence Seaport
  Museum 263 D2
Independence Visitor Center
  262 B1
Ingram Street 260 A4

**J**
James Street 261 C1
Jersey Joe Walcott
  Boulevard 263 E3
Jessup Street 261 E3,
  262 A3
Jewelers Row 262 B1
John F. Kennedy Boulevard
  256 B4–C4, 257 D4
John F. Kennedy Plaza
  257 D4
Jones Way 256 B4, 260 B1
Juniper Street 257 E4,
  261 E3, E2

**K**
Kater Street 260 C2, 261
  D2, E3, 262 A3, B3
Kauffman Street 260 B3
Kelly Drive 256 B1
Kimball Street 260 B3, C3,
  261 E4, 262 A4, B4
Kimmel Center for the
  Performing Arts 261 E2

**L**
Lancaster Street 256 A3
Latimer Street 261 D1
Latona Street 260 A4, B4,
  261 D4
Laurel Street 259 D2–D1

Lawrence Court **262** B2
Lawrence Street **258** C4, **259** C1
League Street **260** B3, **261** C3, **262** A4, B4
Lee Street **259** D1
Leithgow Street **259** C1
Lemon Street **257** E2, **258** A2
Leopard Street **259** D1
Letitia Street **263** C1
Liberty Bell Center **262** B1
Liberty Place **261** D1
Locks Gallery **262** B2
Locust Street **260** B1, **261** C1, D1–E2, **262** A2–B2
Logan Square **257** D3
Lombard Street **260** B2, **261** C2–E2, **262** A3–C3
Ludlow Street **256** A4, B4, C4, **257** D4, **261** D1, **262** A1, B1

**M**

Macy's **261** E1
Madison Square **260** A3, B3, C3
Mandell Theater **256** A4
Manning Street **260** B1, **261** D1, **262** A2
Manton Street **260** A4–B4, **261** D4
Mantua Avenue **256** A1
Mario Lanza Museum **262** A4
Market East Station **262** A1
Market Place East **262** B1
Market Street **256** A4–C4, **257** D4, **258** A4, **261** E1, **262** A1–B1
Marlborough Street **259** E1
Marshall Court **262** B2
Marshall Street **258** C1
Marvine Street **261** E3, **262** A3
Masonic Temple **257** E4
Melon Street **256** A1, **257** E1, **258** A1
Melvale Street **259** E1
Meredith Street **256** B1
Merriam Theater **261** E2
Mickle Boulevard **263** E3
Mikveh Israel Cemetery **262** A2
Mildred Street **262** A3
Mole Street **261** D3
Monroe Street **262** B3
Monterey Street **257** D2
Montrose Street **260** B3, **261** C3–D3, E3–E4, **262** A4–B4
Moore College of Art **257** D3
Moravian Street **261** C1, D1
Moshulu, The **263** D3
Mother Bethel African Methodist Episcopal Church **262** B3
Mott Street **261** E4
Mount Vernon Street **256** A2, **258** A2
Municipal Court **257** D3
Municpal Services Musuem **257** E4
Mütter Museum **256** C4
Myrtle Street **258** A1, C1

**N**

Napa Street **256** A2
National Constitution Center **258** B4
National Museum of American Jewish History **262** C1
Natrona Street **256** A3
Naudain Street **260** B2, **261** C2, D2, **262** C4
Nectarine Street **257** D2, E2, **258** A2
New Market Street **259** D2
New Street **258** C4. **259** C4
Newkirk Street **260** A4
Noble Street **257** D2, E3, **258** A3
Norfolk Street **260** B3
North Street **257** D1–E1, **258** A1

**O**

Oakford Street **260** A4–B4
Ogden Street **258** A1, B1
Old Saint Joseph's Church **262** C2
Old Pine Street Presbyterian Church **262** B3
Olive Street **256** C1, **257** E1, **258** B1, C2
One Franklin Town **257** D2
Oriana Street **259** C2–C1

**P**

Plaza Paine, Thomas **257** E4
Palestra **260** A1
Panama Street **260** B1, **261** C2, **262** B2
Park Avenue **258** A1, **261** E3
Parktown Place **256** C2
Parrish Street **257** E1, **258** A1–C1
Passyunk Avenue **262** B4
Paul Peck Alumni Center **256** A4
Pearl Street **256** A2
Peltz Street **260** A3
Pemberton Street **260** B2, **261** C3, **262** A3
Penn Law School **256** A4
Penn Square **257** E4, **259** E2
Pennsylvania Academy of the Fine Arts **257** E4
Pennsylvania Avenue **256** B1–C1
Pennsylvania Hospital **262** A2
Pensylvania Convention Center **257** E4
Percy Street **258** B3, B4, B1, **262** A3
Perot Street **256** C1
Perth Street **258** B2
Philadelphia Art Alliance **261** D1
Philadelphia Museum of Art **256** B1
Philadelphia Stock Exchange **257** D4
Philadelphia Vietnam Veterans Memorial **263** C3
Physick House **262** B2
Pier 36 Heliport **263** D4
Pier Street **259** D3

Pine Street **260** B2, **261** C2–D2–E2, **262** A2–B2–C3
Plays and Players Theater **261** D2
Please Touch Museum **257** C3
Pollard Street **259** D1
Poplar Street **258** B1–C1, **259** D2
Portico Row **262** A2
Potts Street **257** E1, **258** A1
Powel House **262** C2
Powelton Avenue **256** A3
Prince Music Theater **261** E1
Print Center **261** D2

**Q**

Quaker Information Center **257** E3
Quarry Street **259** C4
Queen Street **262** B4–C4, **263** C4
Quince Street **261** E2, **262** A2

**R**

Race Street **256** A3, C3, **257** D3–E3, **258** A4–C4
Randolph Street **258** C1, **262** B4
Ranstead Street **257** C4, D4, **261** D1, **262** B1
Reading Terminal Market **258** A4
Reed Street **260** A4
Reno Street **257** E1, **258** C1
Richmond Street **259** D1–E1
Ridge Avenue **257** E1, **258** A2
Ringgold Street **260** B4
Rittenhouse Hotel **261** C1
Rittenhouse laboratories **260** A1
Rittenhouse Square **261** D1
RiverLink Ferry Terminal **263** D2
Rodin Museum **257** C2
Rodman Street **260** C4, **261** C2, **262** A3, B3
Rosenbach Museum and Library **261** C2
Rosewood Street **261** D3

**S**

St Charles **260** C3
St George's Greek Orthodox Church **262** A2
St John Newman Way **259** C1
St John the Erangelist **261** E1
St Luke & the Epiphany **261** E2
St Mark's **261** D1
St Nicholas **258** B1
St Peter's Episcopal Church **262** C3
St Philip Neri **262** C4
Samuel S. Fleisher Art Memorial **262** A3
Sansom Street **256** C4, **260** C1, **261** C1–E1, **262** A1–B1, C2
Sartan Street **261** E3, E2

Schell Street **262** A3
Schuylkill Avenue **260** A2
Schuylkill Avenue West **256** B4
Schuylkill Expressway **260** A2
Sears Street **260** A4
Second Bank of the United States **262** B1
Settlement Music School **262** B4
Shackamaxon Street **259** E1
Shamokin Street **257** D2
Shirley Street **257** D1
Smedley Street **261** D2
Soangler Street **256** A3
Society Hill Playhouse **262** A3
Society Hill Synagogue **262** B2
Sophia Street **259** D1
South Street **260** A1–B2, **261** C2–E3, **262** A3–C3
Sparks Shot Tower **262** C4
Spring Garden Street **256** A2, **257** C2–E2, **258** A2–B2, **259** C2
Spring Street **257** E3, **258** A3
Spruce Street **260** B1, **261** D2, **262** A2–C2
Stamper Street **262** C3
State Office Building **257** E2
Stock Exchange Place **261** D1
Strawberry Street **263** C1
Suburban Station **257** D4
Summer Street **256** A3, **257** C3, **258** A3
Swain Street **257** E1
Swann Memorial Fountain **257** D3
Swanson Street **263** C4
Sydenham Street **261** D1

**T**

Taney Street **260** B2
Taylor Street **260** B4
Temple Beth Zion-Beth Israel **261** D2
Thaddeus Kosciuszko National Memorial **262** C2
Theatre of the Living Arts **262** B3
Thomas Jefferson University and Medical Center **262** A1–A2
Titan Street **260** A4, B4, **261** C4
Tomb of the Unknown Soldier **262** B2
Tryon Street **260** C2
Tweeter Center **263** E2

**U**

Uber Street **257** D1
University City Science Center **256** A3
University City Station **260** A1
University of Pennsylvania Museum of Archaeology and Anthropology **260** A1
University of Pennsylvania **260** A1
University of the Arts **261** E2

US Customs House **263** C1
US Mint **258** C4
USS Becuna **263** D2
USS Olympia **263** D2

**V**

Van Horn Street **259** D1
Van Pelt Street **256** C4, **257** C3, **260** C1
Van Rensselaer Mansion **261** D1
Vernon Street **257** D1, E2
Vine Street **257** D3–E3, **258** A3, C3, **259** C4

**W**

Walden Street **257** C4
Wallace Street **256** A1, C1, **257** D1–E1, **258** A2, B2, C2
Walnut Street **256** A4–B4, **260** B1–C1, **261** D1–E1, **262** A1–B2
Walnut Street Theatre **262** A1
War Memorial **257** D3
Warnock Street **261** E3, **262** A3
Washington Avenue **260** B3, **261** D4–E4, **262** A4
Washington Square **262** B2
Water Street **259** D4
Watts Street **257** E3, E2, **258** A2, **261** E4
Waverly Place **261** E2
Waverly Street **260** B2, **261** C2, D2
Webster Street **261** D3, E3
West Rittenhouse Square **261** C1
West Way **257** C3
Wharton Street **260** A4–B4, **261** C4
Wilcox Street **257** C1, D2
Wildey Street **259** C1–E1
Willings Alley **262** C1
Willow Street **258** B3, **259** C3, D3
Winter Street **256** A3, **257** C3, **258** A3
Wood Street **257** D3, E3, **258** A3–C3, **259** C3
Wylie Street **257** D1

# INDEX

## A

Abercrombie House 82
Academy of Music 38,
115–16, 117
Academy of Natural
Sciences 140
Academy of Vocal Arts 39
accommodations 221–30
Adams, John 21, 81, 83
Adamstown 191
Adventure Aquarium 85–6
African-American Museum
120
Allen, Richard 84
American Civil War
Museum (Gettysburg)
194
American Philosophical
Society 66, 125, 156
American Swedish
Historical Museum 162
America's National Parks
Museum Shop 27
Amish 17, 189–96
Amish Experience 193
amusement parks 195,
196, 203
Andalusia 202–3
Antique Row 107
arboretums 171–2, 186,
213
Arch Street 119–20
Friends Meeting House 73
Presbyterian Church 141
architecture 35, 40–1
Arden Theatre 38, 74
Ardmore 184, 186
art galleries 36, 37, 74, 94,
103, 191
Arthur Ross Gallery 155
Artworks at Doneckers
(Ephrata) 191
Athenaeum 103
Atlantic City 198, 199
Atwater Kent Museum of
Philadelphia 103–4
Avenue of the Arts 29, 111,
115–16
Azalea Garden 142

## B

Bache, Benjamin Franklin
68
Bacon, Kevin 89, 96

Balch Institute 107
Baldwin, Matthias 23, 24,
26
ballet 37, 116, 117
Barclay, Alexander 82
Barclay Prime 127
Barnegat Light 199
Barnes Foundation 36–7,
186
art museum (Merion) 126,
186
Barry, John 80
Bartram's Garden 156
baseball 49, 50–1, 86,
161
basketball 49, 51, 153,
161
battles see Brandywine;
Germantown; Gettysburg
Battleship New Jersey 86
Beissel, Conrad 190–1
Bell Atlantic Tower 40, 141
Benjamin Franklin Bridge
85, 86
Benjamin Franklin
Memorial 75, 139–40,
148
Benjamin Franklin Parkway
29, 35, 40–1, 56,
137–41
Betsy Ross house 73–4
Bicentennial Celebration
28
bicycling 144, 172, 178,
198
Biddle, Nicholas 66, 202
Bingham Court 80–1
Bird-in-Hand 195
Bishop White House 70
Black Thursday 26
Blavatsky, Madame 154
Blue Horizon 50, 88
boat trips 86, 156, 208
Boathouse Row 51, 144
bookstores 94, 96, 108,
127, 129, 154, 178,
241
Bourse 71
Bowman's Tower 208
boxing 50, 176
Boy Scouts museum 185
Boyd Theatre 129
Brandywine, Battle of 168,
185, 212
Brandywine River Museum
37, 211–12

Brandywine Valley 38,
211–17
Brandywine Workshop 117
The Bridge: Cinema De Lux
155
British 18–19, 176
see also Revolutionary
War
Broad Street 111, 113,
115, 118
Bryn Athyn 183
Bryn Mawr 153, 184, 186
Buchanan, James 192
Buck, Pearl S. 205
Buckingham Valley
Vineyards 208
Bucks County 27, 201–9
Bull's Island 208
BYOB 44, 45–6

## C

Cairnwood 183
Calder family 35, 41, 84,
111, 112, 121, 138,
140
Camac Street 106–7
Cambodians 159
Camden Children's
Garden 85
Campbell's Field 86
Canal Day 172
Cape May 198, 199
Capone, Al 176
Carpenters' Hall 21, 70,
71
casinos 199
cathedrals
Philadelphia 155
Sts Peter and Paul 40,
118, 138–9
Catholics 24, 40, 80, 105,
118, 138–9, 186
Cedar Grove 146
Centennial Exhibition
(1876) 24, 41
Center City 36, 143, 167
Chadds Ford 37, 211
Chaddsford Winery 208,
212
Chamber Orchestra of
Philadelphia 116
Chanticleer 186
cheesesteaks 43, 95, 160,
163
Chef's Market 92

Chester County 27, 38,
211–17
Chestnut Hill 167, 171–2
Historical Society 171
Visitors Center 171
Chestnut Street 128, 133
Chinatown 36, 120
Chinese 120, 159
Chinese Cultural and
Community Center 120
Chinese Friendship Gate
120
Christ Church 40, 70, 72,
74
chronology 30–1
Church of the Brethren 170
Church of the Holy Trinity
127
Church House 80
Church of St Luke and the
Epiphany 107
Churchtown 190
cinema 38, 39, 88–9, 139,
155
Cira Centre 35
Citizens Bank Park 50–1,
161
City Hall 25, 35, 40, 41,
111–12
City Tavern 69–70
CityPass 64
Civil War 24–5, 141, 146,
169, 194
American Civil War
Museum (Gettysburg)
194
Library and Museum
132
Smith Civil War
Memorial 146
Soldiers and Sailors
Memorial 141
Class of 1923 Ice Rink
153
Clef Club 39, 117
Clinton Street 108
Cliveden 170
College Hall 155
Comcast SportsNet 161
Commerce Square 117
Concord Schoolhouse 169
Congregation Bnai
Abraham 84
Congregation Mikveh Israel
72
Congress Hall 23, 65–6

**C**

Constitutional Convention 22, 65, 67
Continental Congress 21, 65
Convention Hall 153
Cooper Memorial Organ 116
Cosby, Bill 89
covered bridges 208
Cret, Paul Phillippe 126, 137, 141, 186
crime 18, 24, 28, 29
Curtis Institute of Music 39, 128, 153

**D**

dance 37, 39, 117
Darby Creek 162
Davis-Lenox House 82
Decatur, Stephen 84
Delancey Place 131-2
Delancey Street 82-3
Delaware Art Museum (Wilmington) 215-16
Delaware Canal & Towpath 206
Delaware History Center (Wilmington) 216
Delaware Museum of Natural History (Wilmington) 214
Delaware River 29, 85-6, 138, 178, 206, 207
Delaware Toy & Miniature Museum (Hagley) 215
Delaware Valley 201-9
Deshler-Morris House 169
Devon Horse Show 184
Dexter, James 68-9
Dickinson, John 21
Dilworth, Richardson 27, 103
Dock Street 27, 69, 82
Doneckers (Ephrata) 191
Douglass, Frederick 84
Doylestown 203-5
Drexel University 151, 152-3
Drum Moir 171
Drury Lane 120
du Pont family 211, 213-16
Duane-Dulles House 130
Dutch 18-19, 119-20, 167, 211
Dutch Wonderland 195

**E**

Eakins, Thomas 41, 107, 114, 142
Eastern State Penitentiary 88, 175-6
Ebenezer Maxwell Mansion 170-1
Edgar Allan Poe National Historic Site 178
Electric Factory 39
Eleutherian Mills 215
Elfreth's Alley 40-1, 74
English Village 133
Ephrata 190-1
Erwin Stover House 208
Erwinna 208
Esherick, Wharton 185
Ethical Society 127
ethnic restaurants 47, 94, 119-20
ethnic studies 107
Eyre, Wilson 125

**F**

Fabric Row 92-3
Fabric Workshop and Museum 37
Faire Mount 41, 143
Fairmount 175
Fairmount Park 39, 142-3
Fairmount Water Works 143
Fallsington 202
Famous 4th Street Deli 97
farmers markets 172, 186
Fels Planetarium 139, 149
Festival Pier 86
festivals and fairs 39, 86, 130, 162, 172, 196, 202, 206
  arts and film 39, 126
  folk 39, 196
  sports 51, 172
Fields, W.C. 89
film 38, 39, 88-9, 138, 155
  see movie locations
Fine Arts Library 155
Fine, Larry 93
Finns 19
Fireman's Hall Museum 74
First Bank of the United States 23, 69
First Friday 36, 37, 74
First Person Arts Festival 39

First Saturday 74
First Unitarian Church 24, 133
Fishtown 178
Fitler Square 132
flag, first 73
*Flame of Liberty* 67
Fleisher Art Memorial 96-7
Fonthill 204
food and drink 43-7, 119-20, 128, 159-60, 163
  see also markets; restaurants
football 49-50, 153, 161
Forrest Theatre 104-5
Fort Christina (Wilmington) 216
Fort Mifflin 162
Frankford 178
Franklin, Benjamin 17, 19-20, 21, 22, 64, 66, 69, 75, 113, 131, 151
  burial place 72
  Franklin Court 67-8
  National Memorial 75, 139-40, 148
  statues 73, 75, 114, 153
Franklin Field 49, 50, 51, 153
Franklin Institute 139-40, 148-9
Franklin Square 73
Free Library of Philadelphia 139
Free Quaker Meeting House 72
Freedom Theater 38, 177
Furness, Frank 40, 113, 114, 117, 125, 133, 152, 155

**G**

Gallery (mall) 120
gardens 79-80, 85, 142, 156, 196, 213, 213-14, 215, 216
gay community 39, 107-8
General Lee's Headquarters (Gettysburg) 194
George, Henry 108
George III 20-1, 71, 156
Germans 19, 23, 105, 159, 190, 203
Germantown 22, 25, 167-70

Germantown, Battle of 168, 169, 185
Germantown Historical Society 168-9
Germantown Mennonite Historic Trust 169
Gettysburg 194
  Address 194
  Battle 25, 194
  National Cemetery 194
  National Military Park 194
Giovanni's Room 108
Girard College 176-7
Girard, Stephen 69, 176, 177
Girard Trust Building 40, 114
Gloria Dei (Old Swedes) Church 95-6
Goode, W. Wilson 28
Graff (Declaration) House 104
Great Plaza 85-6
Greater Wilmington Convention and Visitors Bureau 216
Greber, Jacques 137, 141
Green Dragon 191
Green Hills Farm (Perkasie) 205
Green Tree Company 80
Grumblethorpe 169

**H**

Hagley Museum 214-15
Hamilton, Alexander 22, 69
Hamilton Walk 156
Hancock, John 65
Hands-on House Children's Museum 28
Hard Rock Café 118
Haverford 153, 184
Haverford Arboretum 186
Haverford College 186
Haviland, John 116, 176
Head House Square 84-5, 93
Heinz National Wildlife Refuge 162
Henry George Museum 108
Herr House and Museum (Willow Street) 196
Hershey 196
hiking 162, 178
Hispanics 178

Historic Bartram's Garden 156
Historical Society of Pennsylvania 107
hockey 49, 51, 153, 161
Hog Island shipyard 26
Holy Trinity Roman Catholic Church 105-6
Hopewell Furnace Historic Site 190
Horticultural Center 146
hotels 29, 40, 114, 115, 118-19, 221-30
Houston, Henry 171

**I**

IMAX Theater 139
immigrants 23-4, 25, 47, 159, 172
Independence 21-2
Declaration of 21-2, 65, 67, 104
Independence Hall 23, 26, 27, 40, 64-5
Independence Living History Center 68-9
Independence Mall 29
Independence Park 27, 64, 66
Independence Seaport Museum 86
Independence Visitor Center 29, 61-3
Indiana, Robert, Philadelphia LOVE 117, 137
Indians 18, 19, 84, 121, 211, 212
influenza 26
Inns at Doneckers 191
Institute of Contemporary Art 37, 154
insurance 80, 126-7
Intercourse 195
internet access 249
Irish 19, 23, 24, 159, 172
Italian Market 47, 159-60, 161
Italians 25, 47, 88, 159-60, 172

**J**

Jackson, Andrew 66, 113
James A. Michener Museum (Doylestown) 205
jazz 39, 115, 116, 117

Jefferson, Thomas 21, 22, 61, 66, 69, 84, 104
Jewelers Row 103
Jewish Cemetery 106
Jewish community 25, 72, 83, 84, 106, 131, 159
John Chads House 212
John F. Kennedy Plaza (LOVE Park) 117, 137
John Heinz National Wildlife Refuge 162
Juniper Street 120

**K**

Kalmar Nyckel Shipyard (Wilmington) 216
Kelly, Grace 89
Kennett Square 212-13
Kensington 23, 24
Khyber 39
Kimmel Center for the Performing Arts 29, 31, 34, 38-9, 54-5, 116
Korean War Memorial 86
Kosciuszko, Thaddeus 84
Kutztown Folk Festival 196

**L**

Labor Day 39
Lafayette, Marquis de 64, 81, 113, 212
Lake Nockamixon 208
Lambertville 206, 207
Lancaster 192-3
Central Market 192-3
Cultural History Museum 193
Quilt & Textile Museum 193
Lancaster County 189-97
Historical Society 192
Land Title Building 115
Landis Valley Museum 192
Lanza, Mario 96
Latimer Street 130
Laurel Hill 145
Le Brun, Napoleon 73, 116, 138
Lee, Robert E. 25, 194
Lemon Hill 144
Leonard Pearlstein Gallery 155
Levy, Nathan 72, 106
Liberty Bell 20, 26, 29, 64, 65, 72, 106

Liberty Place 40, 112, 117, 129
libraries 66, 103, 107, 139, 155, 168, 202, 214
Library Company of Philadelphia 70, 107
Library Hall 66
Lights of Liberty Show 66
Lincoln, Abraham 24, 116, 194
Lincoln Financial Field 49-50, 161
Lititz 192
Lloyd Hall 144
Locks Gallery 103
Locust Street 129-30
Locust Walk 154-5
Loews Philadelphia Hotel 40, 118-19
Logan, James 20, 168
Logan Circle 41
Logan Square 138, 141
Long Beach Island 198, 199
Longwood Gardens 213
LOVE Park (JFK Plaza) 117, 137
Lumberville 208
Lutherans 170, 216

**M**

McArthur, John, Jr. 111, 131, 177
McGillin's Old Ale House 120
Macy's 118
Madison, James 64, 70
Magic Garden 94
Magnolia Garden 80
Main Line 25, 183-7
Main Line Art Center 186
Manayunk 23, 25, 28, 144, 167, 172
Mann Center for the Performing Arts 146
Margaret R. Grundy Memorial Library 202
Margate 198, 199
Mario Lanza Museum 96
Market Place East 120
Market Street 118, 119
markets 27, 46, 47, 82, 85, 92, 119-20, 126, 128, 191, 192-3, 206
Masonic Temple and Museum 113
Meade, George E. 25, 194
Mellon Bank Center 117

Memorial Hall 41, 145-6
Mennonite Information Center (Lancaster) 193
Mennonites 17, 19, 167, 169, 171, 192, 193, 196
Mercer, Henry Chapman 203-5
Mercer Museum 204-5
Merchants Exchange 40, 69
Merion 36-7, 126, 184
Merion Friends Meeting House 184
Merriam Theater 116
Mexicans 159
The Michener at New Hope 206
Mikveh Israel Cemetery 106
Montgomery County 27
Moore College of Art & Design 37, 140
Moore, Marianne 131
Moravian Pottery and Tile Works 204
Moravians 192
Morgantown 190
Morris Arboretum 171-2
Morris House 105
Morris, Robert 23
Moshulu 78, 86
Mother Bethel AME Church 84
Mount Airy 170
Mount Hope Estate and Winery 196
Mount Pleasant 145
MOVE 28
movie locations 38, 67, 88-9, 94, 153
Moyamensing Killers 24
Mummers Museum 161
Municipal Court 139
mural arts 35-6, 101-3, 106, 107
Museum of Archaeology and Anthropology 153
Museum of Art 36, 41, 88, 131, 142, 144
music 38-9, 105, 115-17, 128, 146
Mütter Museum 132, 133
Myrtilla (ship) 72, 106

**N**

Narberth 184
National Constitution Center 29, 63-4, 68

National Liberty Museum 67
National Museum of American Jewish History 72, 106
National Park Service 27, 61
National Parks Museum Shop 71
Nemours Mansion and Gardens 215
New Hall Military Museum 71
New Hope 206–7
New Hope Winery 208
*New Jersey* (battleship) 86
New Jersey coast 198–9
New Year's Day Parade 161
nightlife 86, 91–4, 108, 129
North Broad Street 175–7
North Star Bar 39
Northern Liberties 36, 39, 175, 177–8
Notman, John 125, 126, 129, 130, 139, 141

**O**

Ocean City 198–9
Ohio House 146
Old City 23–4, 26–9, 40–1, 61–77
Old City Art Association 74
Old City Hall 23, 66
Old First Reformed Church 72
Old Pine Street Presbyterian Church 83
Old St Joseph's Church 80
Old Swedes Church (Wilmington) 216
Once Upon a Nation 69
opera 38, 117, 193
Ormiston 145
Overbrook 184

**P**

Painted Bride Art Center 37, 74, 94
Palestra 153
Paradise 195
Park Hyatt at the Bellevue 115

parking 219, 250
parks 67, 82, 96, 126, 132, 142–3, 172, 178, 196, 207–8
see Independence Park; LOVE Park
Parry Mansion (New Hope) 207
Passyunk Avenue 160–1
Pastorius, Francis Daniel 19, 167
Peale, Charles Willson 65, 66, 84, 114, 142
Pearl S. Buck House (Perkasie) 205
Pearlstein Gallery 155
Peck Center Gallery 152–3
PECO Energy Liberty Center 66
Peddler's Village 205–6, 208
Pei, I.M. 80, 81, 117
Penn Center 27
Penn Mutual Building 103
Penn Relays 51, 153
Penn, William 17–20, 95, 121, 167, 177
Pennsbury Manor 201–2
statues 41, 108, 112, 121, 129
Welcome Park 70
Penn's Landing 39, 85–6
Pennsylvania Academy of the Fine Arts 37, 40, 113–14, 153
Pennsylvania Ballet 37, 116, 117
Pennsylvania Convention Center 29, 119
Pennsylvania Dutch Convention and Visitors Bureau 193
Pennsylvania Hospital 32–3, 108
Pennsylvania Railroad 25, 118, 183, 184, 195
Pennsylvania State House 21, 22, 64
Pennsylvania Supreme Court 65
Pennypack Park 142, 178

People's Light and Theater Company 38
People's Place (Intercourse) 195
Perelman Recital Hall 38, 116
Philadelphia 76ers 49, 51, 161
Philadelphia Art Alliance 37, 127–8
Philadelphia Cathedral 155
Philadelphia Clef Club 39, 117
Philadelphia County Court House 23, 66
Philadelphia Eagles 49–50, 161
Philadelphia Exchange 40, 69
Philadelphia Flyers 49, 51, 161
Philadelphia High School for Creative and Performing Arts 117
Philadelphia International Records 116
Philadelphia Kixx 161
*Philadelphia LOVE* 117, 137
Philadelphia Mummery 161
Philadelphia Museum of Art 36, 41, 88, 131, 142, 144
Philadelphia Orchestra 38, 116, 146
Philadelphia Phantoms 161
Philadelphia Sketch Club 107
Philadelphia Stock Exchange 118
*Philadelphia Story, The* 186
Philadelphia Theatre Company 117, 132
Philadelphia Trolleyworks 144
Philadelphia Vietnam Veterans Memorial 86
Philadelphia Water Works 29, 41, 143
Philadelphia Wings 161
Philadelphia Zoo 146
Philly Fringe 39

Philosophical Hall 66
Physick House 83
Pickett, George E. 194
Pietists 18, 19, 167, 190–1
Pine Street 107
Planetarium 139, 149
Plays and Players Theatre 117, 132
Please Touch Museum 41, 140–1, 145
Poe, Edgar Allan 69, 177, 178, 196
Poles 25, 84, 106, 172
Polish-American Cultural Center 70–1
population 23–4, 25, 27, 29
Portico Row 106
Portrait Gallery 66
Pottstown 190
Powel House 81
Powelton Village 156
Presbyterians 18, 19, 83, 84, 126–7, 168
Prince Music Theater 38, 115
Print Center 130
Printz, Johan 95, 162
PSFS Building 40, 118–19

**Q**

Quakers 17, 19, 96, 121, 167, 183, 213
homes 146, 169, 202, 212
meeting houses 72, 73, 184, 202
schools 153, 186
Welsh settlers 183–6
Queen Village 28, 94–7
Quince Street 106

**R**

Radnor Hunt Races 184
Radnor Meeting House 183
Railroad Museum of Pennsylvania (Strasburg) 195
railroads 119, 171, 206, 207
see Pennsylvania Railroad
Ralph Stover State Park 208

Reading Terminal Market 46, 47, 119–20
record stores 93–4
regattas 51
Rendell, Edward 28–9, 138
restaurants 43–7, 94, 97
see food and drink
Revolutionary War 21–2, 64, 71, 83, 101, 162, 185
see Brandywine; Germantown; Washington Crossing
Rice's Market 206
Richmond 178
Ringing Rocks Country Park 208
Rittenhouse, David 125
Rittenhouse Hotel 127
Rittenhouse Row 128
Rittenhouse Square 25, 36, 37, 79, 125–8
Rittenhouse Town 171
Ritz-Carlton Hotel 40, 114
RiverLink ferry 85
Rizzo, Frank 27, 28–9, 118
Roberts, Suzanne 97, 117
Rockland 145
Rockwell, Norman 103–4
Rockwood Museum and Gardens 216
Rocky 36, 38, 88, 89, 142, 159
Rodin Museum 36, 126, 141–2
Rose Garden 79–80
Rosenbach Museum and Library 130, 131–2
Ross, Arthur 155
Ross, Betsy 73–4, 96
rowing 51

**S**

St Augustine's Catholic Church 73
St Clement's Episcopal Church 141
St George's Greek Orthodox Church 105

St George's United Methodist Church 73
St John the Evangelist Catholic Church 118
St Mark's Church 129, 129–30
St Mary's Catholic Church 80
St Michael's Lutheran Church 170, 216
St Peter's Episcopal Church 83–4
St Philip de Neri Church 24
Salomon, Haym 72, 106
Samuel S. Fleisher Art Memorial 96–7
Sand Castle Winery 208
Sansom Common 154
Sansom Row 154
Sansom Street 129
Schuylkill Canal 172
Schuylkill River 25, 51, 143–4, 153, 156, 172
Trail 132, 144, 156, 172
Schuylkill River Park 132, 172
sculpture 35, 36, 67, 94, 114, 117, 138, 141
Seamen's Church Institute and Maritime Museum 67, 178
Second Bank of the United States 23, 30, 40, 66–7
Sendak, Maurice 130, 131–2, 141
Sesame Place (Langhorne) 203
Settlement Music School 96
Shackamaxon Creek 18
Shofuso 146
shopping 71, 91–4, 107, 111, 117, 118, 129, 196, 205–6
see also markets
Sight and Sound Millennium Theater (Strasburg) 195
skateboarding 117, 137
slavery and anti-slavery 21, 24, 84, 120, 169, 213
Smith Civil War Memorial 146
Smith, Robert 71, 83

Smucker's Harness Shop 190
Soap Lady 132, 133
Society Hill 27, 35, 40, 79–85
Society Hill Synagogue 83
Society Hill Towers 81
South Philly 159–65
South Street 52–3, 91–4
Sparks Shot Tower 96
Spectrum Sports Center 36
Spirit of Philadelphia 86
sports 29, 49–51, 153, 161
Spring Garden 175
Spruce Street 82, 105–6, 130
Stallone, Sylvester 88, 89, 142, 159
Starr, Stephen 44–5, 127, 128
statues 36, 56, 67, 84, 118, 131, 142, 177
see Franklin; Penn
Stein, Neil 45
Stenton Mansion 168
Stone Harbor 198
storytellers 69
Strasburg 195
Strawberry Mansion 145
Street, John E. 29
Strickland, William 40, 65, 66, 69, 83, 105, 117
Sturgis Pretzel House 192
Suburban Square 186
Supreme Court 23
Suzanne Roberts Theater 117
Swann Memorial Fountain 41, 138
Swarthmore 153
Swedes 19, 95–6, 162, 211, 216
Sweetbriar 146
Swiss 167, 196

**T**

30th Street Station 152
Taller Puertorriqueño 178
Temple Beth Zion-Beth Israel 131

Temple University 37, 153, 177
Thaddeus Kosciuszko National Memorial 84
Thaw, Harry K. 131
The Bridge: Cinema De Lux 155
The Gallery (mall) 120
theater 37–8, 39, 74, 93, 104–5, 115, 117
Theater of Living Arts 39, 93
Thomas Paine Plaza 118
Thompson-Neely House 208
Tiffany glass 115, 131, 155
Tinicum 162, 208
Todd House 70
Tohickon Valley Country Park 208
Tomb of the Unknown Soldier 101
Trinity houses 24, 82
Trocadero 39
trolley-buses 143, 144
Trump House 83
Tubman, Harriet 213
Tuttleman IMAX Theater 139
Twain, Mark 68
Tweeter Center 86
Two Liberty Place 40, 117
Tyler School of Art 37

**U**

Uhlerstown 208
Underground Museum 68
Underground Railroad 84, 169, 213
Union Fire Company 74
Union League 115
Unitarians 24
University of the Arts 37, 116–17
University of Pennsylvania 37, 106, 151, 153–6
US Customs Building 70
US flag, first 73
US Mint 23, 72
USS Becuna 86
USS Olympia 86

**V**

Valley Forge 22, 162, 168, 185
Van Rensselaer Mansion 126
Vansant House (New Hope) 207
Ventnor 198
Venturi, Robert 67, 70
Verizon Hall 38, 116
Vietnam Veterans Memorial 86
Vietnamese 120, 159
Villanova University 186
Viñoly, Rafael 116
von Steuben, Baron Friedrich 185

**W**

Wachovia Sports Complex 51, 161
Wagner Free Institute of Science 177
Walnut Street 129, 156
Walnut Street Theatre 37, 104

Walter, Thomas U. 83, 106, 111, 176, 202
Wanamaker, John 118, 119
Washington, George 21, 23, 56, 64, 68, 69, 113, 131, 169
in Revolutionary War 22, 167–8, 185, 207–8, 212
Washington Crossing State Park 207–8
Washington Square 101–8
waterfront 29, 85–6
Welcome Center 185
Welcome Park 70
Welsh 19, 183–6
West, Benjamin 114, 145
Westphal Picture Gallery 153
Wetherill Mansion 37, 127–8
Wharton Esherick Museum (Valley Forge) 185
Wharton House 82

Wharton School 155–6
Wheatland 192
White, Bishop William 70
White Dog Café 154
White, Stanford 114
Wi-Fi 29
Wilbanks' bell 65
Wilbur Chocolate Candy Factory Store 192
Wildflower Preserve (Washington Crossing) 208
Wildwood 198
Willow Street 196
Wills House (Gettysburg) 194
Wilma Theater 37–8, 116
Wilmington 211, 215, 216
wineries 196, 208
Winterthur Museum and Gardens 213–14
Wissahickon Creek 167
Wissahickon Valley 143
Wood double house 130

Wood Turning Center 24
Woodford 145
Woodlands Cemetery 156
Woodmere Art Museum 171
Woodward, Dr George 171
World of Scouting Museum (Valley Forge) 185
World Wars 25–6
Wyck 169
Wyeth family 37, 38, 107, 114, 211
Wynnewood 184

**Y**

yellow fever 70, 84, 146

**Z**

Zagar, Isaiah 94
Zinn's Diner 191
Zipperhead 93
Zoological Gardens 146

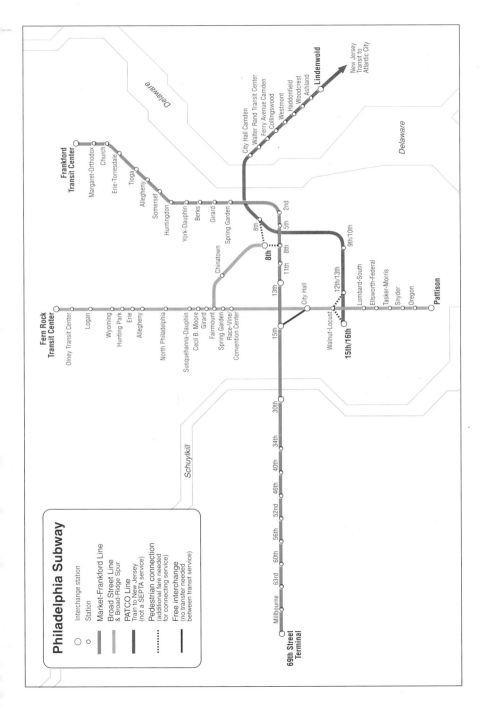